INDUSTRIAL
DEMOCRACY
IN EUROPE

INDUSTRIAL DEMOCRACY IN EUROPE

by
INDUSTRIAL DEMOCRACY IN EUROPE (IDE)
INTERNATIONAL RESEARCH GROUP

CLARENDON PRESS · OXFORD
1981

Oxford University Press, Walton Street, Oxford OX2 6DP

London Glasgow New York Toronto
Delhi Bombay Calcutta Madras Karachi
Kuala Lumpur Singapore Hong Kong Tokyo
Nairobi Dar Es Salaam Cape Town
Melbourne Wellington
and associate companies in
Beirut Berlin Ibadan Mexico City

Published in the United States by
Oxford University Press, New York

©Industrial Democracy in Europe (IDE)
International Research Group, 1981

British Library Cataloguing in Publication Data
Industrial Democracy in Europe (IDE)
International Research Group
Industrial democracy in Europe.
1. Employees' representation in management –
Europe
I. Title
331.89'14   HD5660.E9   80-41056
ISBN 0-19-827258-8

Typesetting by Hope Services, Abingdon
and printed in Great Britain by
Richard Clay (The Chaucer Press) Ltd.,
Bungay, Suffolk

PREFACE

The study of Industrial Democracy in Europe (IDE) is an international collaborative effort to assess the effects of national schemes for employee participation on a comparative basis. The first two publications of this study are interrelated This book presents the conceptual framework, methods, and findings of the IDE study. The second book *European Industrial Relations* provides a qualitative description of the various legal and socio-economic country contexts that were considered to be relevant to a study of industrial democracy. It describes the national background and 'local colour' while this volume provides the systematic international comparison. Together they should serve other researchers, practitioners of participation in industry, and the interested public.

Some twenty-five social scientists from about twenty major institutions of higher learning in the various countries collaborated in the conduct of this research. In many ways it became for all of us a significant experience in collective learning. Hence, the published products of the joint research have no individual authors. We decided to opt for collective authorship, which best reflects the style of collaboration of the group as a whole over the past years. The way we worked together made it impossible to attribute a specific idea or the origin of a concept to a given individual alone.

Various members of the international team took it upon themselves to write first and second drafts of various parts of this volume. The choice fell on them more because of their stated interest, expertise, and availability rather than because they were the only ones that could contribute to the drafts. Significant and detailed suggestions for improving drafts and general rewriting help was given by all national teams during a plenary draft review session and a special drafters' meeting. Although it is impossible to do justice to all individual contributions, some were very detailed and thorough and hence merit special mentioning, either because they carried the load of several drafts or contributed major parts to a given chapter: Chapter 2, Peter Abell; Chapter 3, Bernhard Wilpert; Chapter 4, Pieter Drenth; Chapter 5, Bengt Stymne; Chapter 6, Bernhard Wilpert; Chapter 7, Veljko Rus; Chapter 8, Erik Andriessen; Chapter 9, Frank Heller; Chapter 10, Peter Abell, Chapter 11, Thoralf Qvale.

Virtually all computer analysis was performed by Jörg Rayley in Berlin. The data organization scheme that facilitated comparisons owes much to the efforts of Wolfgang Potratz and Gabriele Freidank. The final manuscript was compiled by Bernhard Wilpert and many a version of it was typed by Ilona Köhler.

The deliberate attempt to decentralize the writing efforts and specific tasks for this publication was perfectly in line with the spirit of the whole collective-decentralized IDE research endeavour throughout (see Chapter 3). This way of organizing our research involved advantages and disadvantages. The advantages resulted from the fact that optimal use could be made of the specific competence and expertise available among members of the whole IDE team. The ensuing divergence of theoretical perspective and pluralism in style and language may be seen as a disadvantage. However, it is precisely this fruitful tension between idio-syncratic determination and striving towards collective consensus that marked the research.

We would like to thank Philippa Bevan for making a substantial contribution to the presentation of our materials in what we hope is the most useful structure for the reader.

The IDE International Research Group is indebted to many institutions that have supported its efforts. The International Institute of Management of the Science Centre Berlin carried the load of supporting the first planning seminars and lent crucial support to the international project by covering the costs of the international co-ordinating team (Bernhard Wilpert with the assistance of Wolfgang Potratz and Jörg Rayley at various phases of the research) and part of the associated overheads. Of particular importance to the whole project was the interest and unfailing support it enjoyed from Walter Goldberg, then director of the International Institute of Management.

A major grant from the Thyssen Foundation (Cologne) financed most of the IDE meetings and the necessary *ad hoc* assistance in the international co-ordina-tion efforts. A supplementary grant by the Ford Foundation (New York) made it possible to hire Gabriele Freidank as assistant for the co-ordination efforts.

Various national funding agencies have helped to cover part of the on-site expenditures at various plenary sessions. They have thus been of critical support at different stages of our research: *Maison des Sciences de l'Homme* (Paris), Nuffield Foundation (London), Boris Kidrić Foundation (Ljubljana), *Histadrut* (Israel).

For each of our meetings we gratefully acknowledge the hospitality of the hosting institution—usually the respective home institution of the national research team.

Belgium:	The Fonds voor Kollektief Fundamental Onderzoek and the Laboratorium voor Toegepaste Psychologie (Ghent University)
Denmark:	Handelshøskjolen in Copenhagen and Århus, Handelshøg-skoleafdelingen in Søderborg, Odense University Centre, Association for Young Businessmen's Education, Den Lett-stedska Fonden' (Sweden) and the Danish Social Science Research Council
Finland:	Finnish Academy, Foundation for Economic Education, Jenny and Antti Wihuri's Foundation, Helsinki School of Economics, Research Foundation of the Finnish Cooperative Banks
France:	CORDES and CRESST
Italy:	Consiglio Nazionale delle Ricerche (C.N.R.), Istituto di Statis-tica e Ricerca Sociale 'C. Gini'—Universita di Roma, Istituto per la Formazione et l'Addestramento Professionale—I.R.I. (I.F.A.P.)
Israel:	The Technion Research Foundation, Israeli Government—the Ministry of Labour, Israeli Institute for the Advancement of Labour Relations
Netherlands:	The Netherlands Organization for the Advancement of Pure

Research and the Free University (Amsterdam), State University at Leyden

Norway: The Department of Labour and Municipal Affairs and the Work Research Institutes

Sweden: The Bank of Sweden Tercentenary Foundation, Svenska Handelsbanken Foundation for Social Science Research, Swedish Institute of Management, Economic Research Institute, Stockholm School of Economics, Swedish Work Environment Fund, Swedish Social Science Research Council, and the companies participating in the research

UK: The Anglo-German Foundation for the Study of Industrial Society.

West Germany: The International Institute of Management of the Science Centre, Berlin

Yugoslavia: Raziskovalna Skupnost SR Slovenije

THE IDE INTERNATIONAL RESEARCH GROUP

Belgium: Pol Coetsier, Professor of Psychology, University of Ghent.

Denmark: Flemming Agersnap, Professor of Organization, Institute of Organization and Industrial Sociology, School of Economics and Social Science, Copenhagen

Finland: Oiva Laaksonen, Professor of Organization, Institute of Organization and Management, Helsinki School of Economics,

France: Dominique Martin, *Centre de Recherches en Sciences Sociales du Travail*, Sceaux

Italy: Francesco Consoli, *Universita Degli Studi di Roma, Istituto di Statistica*, Rome
Riccardo Peccei, London School of Economics

Israel: Eliezer Rosenstein, Associate Professor, Faculty of Industrial Engineering and Management, Israel Institute of Technology, Haifa

Netherlands: Erik Andriessen, Senior Staff, Free University, Amsterdam
Pieter J. D. Drenth, Professor of Psychology, Free University, Amsterdam
Cornelis J. Lammers, Professor of Sociology, State University at Leyden

Norway: Thoralf U. Qvale, Research Fellow, Work Research Institutes, Oslo

Sweden: Thomas Sandberg, Research Fellow, University of Uppsala.

UK: Peter Abell, Professor of Sociology, University of Surrey, Guildford, Surrey.
Frank Heller, Senior Staff, Tavistock Institute of Human Relations, London
Malcolm Warner, Professor and Research Co-ordinator, Joint Graduate Programme, Administrative Staff College, Henley-on-Thames, and Brunel University

West Germany: Bernhard Wilpert, Associate Research Fellow, International Institute of Management, Science Centre Berlin and Professor, Technische Universität Berlin
Jörg Rayley, International Institute of Management, Science Centre Berlin and Technische Universität Berlin
Yugoslavia: Veljko Rus, Professor of Sociology, University of Ljubljana.
Vesna Pusić, University of Zagreb, Zagreb
Corresponding Members:
   Professor Walter Goldberg, International Institute of Management, Germany; Professor Theo Pirker, Germany; Professor Jean-Daniel Reynaud, France; Professor Stanley E. Seashore, USA; Professor William H. Starbuck, USA.
Associate Researchers:
   Gabriele Freidank, international co-ordination; Janine Goetschy, France; Itzhak Gur-Lavie, Israel; Wolfgang Potratz, Germany. Titta Vadalà, Italy; Malcolm Wilders, Great Britain
International co-ordination:
   Bernhard Wilpert, Berlin

CONTENTS

PART I

THE RESEARCH AND ITS THEORETICAL FOUNDATIONS

1

THE RESEARCH PROJECT AND ITS MAJOR FINDINGS

THE AIMS OF THE RESEARCH PROGRAMME

The original momentum for this study came from the keen interest of some international public servants, who were interested in the conditions and real-life effects of industrial democracy in Europe. The nucleus of a viable international research effort was formed at the First International Sociological Conference on Participation and Self-Management in Dubrovnik, in 1972.

The project required the merging of a variety of interests in industrial democracy which included political and philosophical interests; interests relating to social science theory; methodological interests; interests arising out of ongoing or past research; and practical needs and interests (see Chapter 3). Very quickly, however, the main focus of the research was established—the differential distribution of power and influence in organizations subject to different types of national industrial democracy schemes. Recent developments in industrial democracy have been preoccupied with formal rule-making and the research was designed to establish if changes in positive law have, and can, bring about changes in structure and behaviour, and what conditions make for the success or failure of legislation to increase worker participation.

The twelve nations covered by the study exhibit a bewildering variety of participation schemes (see Chapter 2 and IDE, 1980) ranging from the fully-fledged self-management concept in Yugoslavia, through co-determination in West Germany, a variety of participation systems in Scandinavia, France, and Belgium, to the shop steward movement in the U.K. Most of these schemes have arisen in response to 'traditional' organization structures, where decision-making, particularly of 'important' decisions, is disproportionately centred towards the apex of the management hierarchy, and they all seek, in one way or another, to redress this balance in favour of those with more subordinate positions in the hierarchy. Our research was thus designed to answer the question as to whether the different national schemes are more or less successful in this respect.

Our empirical research revolved around four questions:

i. How do different forms and degrees of formalized rules and regulations for the involvement of employees in organizational decision-making account for the different distributions of actual employee involvement and influence?

ii. To what extent do situational and contextual factors moderate or co-determine the *de facto* fulfilment of participative norms?

iii. What are the social and psychological consequences of *de jure* and *de facto* participation?

iv. Do differences between national samples of respondents or organizations reflect underlying differences in socio-political structure and industrial organization?

It would be prudent at this point to mention the normative implications of the project. Though the participation schemes in operation in the twelve nations of the study are relatively unambiguous in regard to their intent concerning 'participation', they are by no means so clear when it comes to 'power' (see Chapter 2 for some discussion of these concepts and their relationship). Indeed, for some, the concept of participation carries no implications for the redistribution of 'power' at all—it is construed solely as a mechanism for increasing the effectiveness of communication. For others the whole point is to relocate power with groups who have traditionally been disadvantaged in this respect. For both, however, there should be interest in ascertaining whether or not the distribution of power is affected by the distribution of participation in decision-making.

THE THEORETICAL MODEL

For the purpose of this research the term 'industrial democracy' relates to the whole range of existing models inasmuch as they facilitate the (direct or indirect) participation of workers in their establishment's decision-making by some formalized system or institutionalized mechanism. To dispel possibly unwarranted expectations it should be pointed out right from the beginning that industrial democracy, in the sense of union or employee board-room representation, is only marginally treated in this study. The main reason is that only a few of the participating countries have introduced such representation to any significant degree —Yugoslavia being the important exception. And wherever such representation exists, it is restricted to large companies or industrial sectors not covered in the research, or union and employee representatives occupy a definite minority of available board-room seats. The emphasis is rather placed on the differential degree of participation of a variety of relevant groups in organizational decision-making. Since this centres on decision-making within establishments it excludes also such forms of employer-employee interaction as collective bargaining above the establishment level, and industrial relations features sometimes also referred to as industrial democracy.

The important concepts relating to our model are participation (direct and representative) and power. Participation which is legally or formally prescribed is *de jure* participation, while actual participation (*de facto*) is separated into two concepts—influence and involvement—the first attributable to groups, the second to individuals. These concepts are discussed in Chapter 2 in the context of three ways of conceptualizing and measuring power—the 'control of resources', 'reputational', and 'decision-making' approaches. The reasoning behind the selection of our participation concepts and their derivation from the socio-political ideas of industrial participation and democracy is also presented there.

The model presented in Figure 1.1 (which is discussed in greater detail in Chapter 2) postulates that the participative structure or *De Jure* Participation (PS) affects directly both *De Facto* Participation (PO)—Influence and Involvement—and a number of 'Outcomes' (O)—attitudes, aspirations, and actions which relate to participation. *De Jure* Participation may also affect O through its effect on *De Facto* Participation, while *De Facto* Participation may have an independent effect on Outcomes. A number of 'contextual' and 'contingent'

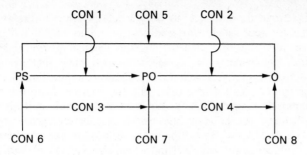

Figure 1.1 The IDE model

variables (CON 1–8), effective at country, organizational, and individual levels, affect the three variables and the relationships between them.

THE RESEARCH DESIGN

The variables in the model were measured using a variety of methods (see Chapter 4) including a large sample of respondents and key informants, examination of documents, and collection of other factual information. The study covered 134 comparable establishments in three different size categories and two sectors of the economy (banking or insurance and the 'metal industry') from twelve industrialized countries (eleven in Europe and Israel). There were 7,832 random sample respondents and 997 key informants drawn from the employees of the 134 establishments.

De Jure Participation (PS)

This is the formal, written-down, operative rules and regulations for involving various parties in decision-making. Two aspects of it were measured by analysing available relevant documents: Base and Mode. Formal participation may be based on national laws, collective bargaining contracts, or managerial policies, and an ordinal scale of the degree of formalization of participation[2] was used. The Mode (or amount) of participation was measured on a Guttman-type scale (with six points) ranging from 'no regulations' to 'group has final say'. The researchers completed the questionnaire for PS in consultation with a key informant from the establishment and an expert in company or labour law. The measurement was done on the basis of sixteen decisions (see Appendix A.1) and for seven groups related to the enterprise—workers (Group A); foremen (Group B); middle managers (Group C); top management (Group D); level above plant (Group E); representative bodies at establishment level (Group F); external bodies and institutions (Group G).

De Facto Participation (PO)

Influence (PO1) was measured in relation to the groups listed above and not to individuals. Expert respondents were asked to place each group on a five-point scale (ranging from 'no influence' to 'very much influence') in relation to each of the sixteen decisions listed in Appendix A.1.

Three measures, relating to individuals, were made in relation to Involvement (PO2): Actual Involvement (PO2a); Desired Involvement (PO2b); and Desired Influence of Representative Body (PO2c). PO2a was measured on a six-point scale ranging from 'I am not involved at all' to 'I decide on my own' and PO2b on a six-point scale ranging from 'I am not interested at all' to 'I want to decide on my own'. Respondents were asked to answer both questions in relation to each of the sixteen decisions mentioned above. Finally they were asked if they would like the main representative body to have a say in each of the sixteen decision areas (PO2c).

Outcomes (O)

These were defined as attitudes, aspirations, and actions relating to participation and were measured at the individual level. Five questionnaires were used: OPART (an assessment of direct and representative participation); OROC (rating of the Consequences of direct and representative Participation); OSAT (Satisfaction with Work, Company, and generally); CLIM (Climate, i.e. clarity of communication and Structure, and quality of management-employee Relations); and ORON (rating of Needs in the context of one's job). A number of indices were constructed from these questionnaires (for example OPART-E—the Evaluation of the Representative Body, OSAT-C—Satisfaction with the Company and a full list can be found in Appendix D.2.

CON variables

These contextual, contingent, and personal variables operate at the level of the individual, the company, and the country and were measured in a number of ways. The Personal Information Form (PIF) was administered to all respondents and key persons and produced information about job, size of work group, age, sex, years with the company, education, membership of representative bodies, and union membership. A company context questionnaire was answered by different experts in the organization and by a member of top management, and covered technology, organizational structure (e.g. professional differentiation, number of employees per level, functional specialization and formalization of the organization), personnel policy, economic data, and managerial philosophy. Data for the Country Context variables can be found in the Volume *European Industrial Relations* (IDE, 1980).

Samples

The company samples were not random—they were selected according to size, sector, and level of skill of employees. With each company a stratified sample of employees was randomly drawn using a formula which produces larger samples in the smaller companies and which accounts for differences in the number of employees at various hierarchical levels. The team used a variety of multi-variate techniques in the analysis of the data.

Before turning to the major empirical findings of the project to date, it is worth looking at the progress of the project, the publications attached to it, and problems arising from the international and inter-disciplinary nature of the project. The study started in 1972 and went through six phases: model-building; selection or creation of potential instruments; a pilot study; data collection; analysis and interpretation; and reporting. We are still in the final phase. From the study a number of publications have been, or are being, produced. Each firm was given a report, and preliminary country reports have been written. A number of international reports are planned of which this study is the first. The other describes industrial relations within each of the twelve countries studied, and more publications are planned. A number of articles, and monographs arising from the study have been, or will be published, as we shall see.

Collective international, inter-disciplinary research has specific organizational opportunities and constraints which affect the final research output to similar degrees as design, methods, and analytic strategies. The international team soon realized that it would be important to scrutinize the internal *modus operandi* and its group dynamical conditions and concomitants, and lay them open to readers, even though they may be trained to read and assess only the scientific content of a research project. Chapter 3 develops a micro-analytic approach taking into account those social processes that co-determined the kind of knowledge generated in the joint venture. Given that the research had to be both international and inter-disciplinary and, recognizing that the organizational structure of research has an impact on research output, a 'decentralized-collective' type of project was established. From the beginning the project was jointly conceived, developed, implemented, and evaluated by the collective of the international team.

One problem of analysis which was raised by the international nature of the research project concerns the comparability of our measure of *de jure* participation across countries. To the extent that formal participative structures are 'context-embedded' international comparability becomes a problem and this is further discussed in Chapter 6.

MAJOR FINDINGS AND CONCLUSIONS TO DATE

De Jure Participation

The major findings concerning *De Jure* Participation are discussed in Chapter 6. Some of the more important will be described here. The extent of codification in the field of industrial democracy varies by country. Yugoslavia has most formal rule-making in this area, followed by Italy, then Norway, Sweden, Denmark, West Germany, Belgium, Finland, France, Holland, the U.K., and Israel. For most countries (not, however, Israel, Finland, and Yugoslavia) law is the most important formal Base of participation, but, within countries, formal participative arrangements for different groups in the enterprise have different Bases. So far as the intensity of participation (Mode) is concerned patterns are rather complicated, but we were successful in identifying four types of country profile that are characteristic of the typical distribution of *de jure* participation found in our twelve countries. Other differences between countries related to differences in *de jure* participation are discussed below under 'cross-national perspectives'.

De Facto **Participation**

The major findings relating to Influence and Involvement are described in Chapter 7.

The distribution of Influence

The average amount of Influence per country was very similar, with the exception of Yugoslavia. In all countries except Yugoslavia workers had little Influence, while representative bodies had 'little to moderate' Influence. Most organizations in all countries except Yugoslavia can be considered as 'centralized', 'powerless', 'closed', and 'non-democratic' (see Chapter 7).

Hierarchy was the main determinant of the distribution of Influence. The Influence of most groups associated with the enterprise was positively correlated with the Influence of other groups, with the exception of top management, whose Influence was negatively related to the Influence of most of the other groups. This might be taken as a indication that influence (as measured by PO1) is distributed in a 'zero-sum' fashion between top management and subordinate groups.

Of the contextual variables only one had a considerable, and perhaps direct, effect on the internal distribution of influence—the mobilization of employees, although other variables had small effects (see Chapter 7). Workers' influence was most strongly predicted by institutional norms promoting participation in medium- and long-term decisions, and norms facilitating the participation of external bodies in short-term decisions (i.e. by aspects of *De Jure* Participation— PS).

Our findings suggest that industrial democracy is mainly conditioned by the socio-political environment and the institutional, normative set-up of the organization, rather than determined by technological, structural, or economic factors, and, therefore, possibilities for social change are greater than some people have thought.

The more strategic the decision, the more likely it is to generate conflict ('disagreement'). Our evidence suggests that increased influence of representative bodies brings conflict out into the open; strong 'traditional management' tends to reduce conflict; and increasing the direct involvement of workers has no discernible effect on levels of conflict.

The distribution of Involvement

Individual Involvement was distributed in a rather similar way to group Influence. Hierarchical level was the main determinant of levels of Involvement. The total amount of Involvement was relatively low, being particularly low for workers. Workers were most involved in short-term decisions and least involved in long-term decisions. Country was quite an important predictor of Actual Involvement. The twelve countries could be classified into four groups according to differences in employee involvement in different types of decision, suggesting that a number of different strategies for the democratization of industry are feasible.

The Involvement of workers was primarily predicted by:

i. institutional norms (*De Jure* Participation)—not mainly those which facilitate their personal participation, but those which regulate the participation of representative bodies and top management;

ii. leadership styles (for short-term decisions);

iii. the Influence of workers (for medium- and long-term decisions);

iv. sector.

This suggests that the distribution of influence and institutional norms are the most important determinants of individual involvement and that there can probably be no democratization of the organization if management practice is not democratized.

We also found that, within limits, the more involvement people have, the more they want, either personally, or through representation.

The relationship between Influence and Involvement

Three possible models of the relationships between *De Jure* Participation, Influence, and Involvement (the 'institutional', 'behavioural', and 'status' models) are discussed in the light of the evidence at the end of Chapter 7. It seems that each of the models is appropriate under certain conditions. Different models of industrial democracy seem to apply to different groups of employees, for different kinds of decision, in different sectors, and, primarily, in different countries. It seems likely that future research and theorizing in this area should start from a contingency-based typology of industrial democracy.

The Distribution of Outcomes

The findings relating to assessment and consequences of participation, satisfaction, organizational climate and the need for participation are described in Chapter 8. Only a few of these findings can be described here.

In most cases differences between country samples were significant. On average, employees were more positive about representative bodies in those countries where the formal regulations provide the bodies with relatively greater powers. Within countries attitudes were most positive in those companies where the actual influence of representative bodies was greatest. However, in most countries, while the majority of employees saw the representative bodies as contributing to the representation of workers' interests and wanted them to have more say in decision-making (particularly strategic decisions) a much smaller number of respondents considered that the work of these bodies had led to any reduction in inequalities of power, and both satisfaction with, and active interest in, the functioning of these bodies was quite low.

So far as attitudes relating to individual involvement were concerned the important differentiating variables were hierarchical level, union membership, and membership (past or present) of a representative body. Higher-level personnel while more willing to participate in representative bodies desired less influence for the bodies than workers did, preferring to exert personal influence over decision-making. Union members or those who had been or were members of representative bodies were more interested in participation than other employees and wanted more influence in company decision-making.

The relationship between Actual Involvement and Satisfaction which we found could be considered as an 'individual-level' phenomenon resulting from the fact that both depend on individual perceptions and a simple linear causal explanation—being more involved leads to greater satisfaction with work and company—is not suitable. Although individuals who see themselves as more involved in decision-making are usually more satisfied, the same does not hold for whole organizations: it is not true that overall satisfaction is higher in organizations where the influence of workers (either directly or through representatives) is higher.

Aspects of the *de jure* participation system, the actual distribution of influence, technology, and organizational structure were related to employees' attitudes relating to representative and direct participation, but not to satisfaction with the job and company in general.

For all attitude-indices differences between countries and between companies within each country were significant. While the perception people have of the effects of representative bodies seems to be determined by the actual functioning of these bodies, other attitudes (such as interest in representative participation, evaluation of direct participation, satisfaction with job and company) are often related to personal characteristics.

CROSS-NATIONAL PERSPECTIVES

It has been argued that countries can be 'clustered' on the basis of national, cultural, or geographical affinities. In Chapter 9 *a priori* groupings of countries were tested against our data on industrial democracy and the data were also searched for groupings without pre-setting country clusters. Neither method yielded very convincing results, although the first one produced some tentative support for the hypothesis of (very limited) differences between Latin and non-Latin countries.

Analysing the data by country a strong relationship between *de jure* and *de facto* participation was found at the level of the representative body. A similar relationship between *de jure* participation and inequality of influence was also found. However, it is often necessary to supplement more general explanations with country-specific explanations. Our analysis suggests that, in the field of industrial democracy, countries (as well as sectors and companies) have quite a wide range of choice of industrial democracy strategies which will lead to similar results.

These are some of the major findings of our research project which we are publishing in this volume. Another, published at the same time, contains country reports on industrial relations which provide the necessary background information on the relevant country contexts for this volume, as well as being interesting in their own right. We hope to publish further work in the near future containing supplementary analysis of the data, and covering topics such as the profiles of various sub-groups, structural (inter-level) effects on participation, dominant value patterns and participation, organizational forms and regimes in various countries, and alternative models of industrial democracy.

POLICY ISSUES

In Chapter 11 we try to draw conclusions for the practitioner using our research findings. By its nature this chapter brings the value premises of the research to the fore.

Further democratization of the enterprises covered by our study should aim at increasing the absolute and relative levels of involvement and influence of individuals and groups at the lowest organizational levels. The job hierarchy is the strongest determinant of inequality within the enterprise, and inequality is highest in the area of involvement and influence. Thus we expect that modifying the hierarchic characteristics of the work organization would be the most efficient single measure for democratization. However, such changes are beyond the range of arrangements for participation in the companies we studied. In principle, though, in order to succeed a strategy for democratization cannot concentrate on one single measure (like a separate scheme for participation in a decision-making body). It will have to include system changes along a number of dimensions. According to our results the most important, of these are:

i. increasing the scope and strength of the rules for participation so that these give a socially inter-linked (e.g. through the local union) *system* for formal representation covering all levels of the enterprise and all types of issue;

ii. democratization of the leadership style so that employees are better informed and, to a larger extent, can decide job issues on their own;

iii. further mobilization of employees (e.g. by involving them in representative functions) and extension of union activity.

There is clearly a need for more research on the dynamic inter-relationship between direct and indirect forms of participation. So far the national strategies aimed at democratizing industry have had a strong bias towards schemes for participation through representation. The current undemocratic state of industry is largely contingent on its bureaucratic and hierarchic organizational form which produces few opportunities for decision-making and learning on the job at lower levels, and a research and development strategy for systematic changes in both direct and indirect participation seems most fruitful.

NOTES

1 The 'metal industry' includes the production of mechanical, electrical, and electronics components, instruments, and tools, machine building and construction, metal processing, production of computers and machine tools.

2 The degree of formalization of participation (Base) should not be confused with the measure of Formalization in the organization (number of written rules, procedures, etc) used as a contingent variable in later chapters.

2

CONCEPTS AND THEORETICAL OUTLINE

THE VARIETY IN NATIONAL SCHEMES

The twelve nations covered by the study exhibit a bewildering variety of participation schemes, ranging from the fully-fledged Self-Management concept in Yugoslavia, through co-determination in West Germany, to a variety of participation schemes in Scandinavia, France, and Belgium, to the shop steward movement in the U.K. Most of these schemes have arisen in response to 'traditional' organizational structures where decision-making—particularly of 'important' decisions—is disproportionately centred towards the apex of a management hierarchy and they all seek, in one way or another, to redress this balance in favour of those with a more subordinate position in the hierarchy. Our research was, thus, designed to answer the question as to whether the different national schemes are more or less successful in this respect. In fact in one important respect it goes further than this; we sought not merely to describe the distribution of participation in decision-making but to ask the deeper question concerning the distribution of 'power' and involvement which arises as a consequence of participation in decision-making. Much of this chapter is concerned with the relationship between the concepts of 'participation' and 'power' and their respective definitions. However, in order that our more abstract deliberations may be placed in context in Table 2.1 we have given a synopsis of the various national schemes. We trust this will indicate their complexity and provide some impression of the institutional variety which has to be compared. For more detail the reader is referred to the copious literature and to 'European Industrial Relations'.

An informal study of the various national schemes of industrial participation prompts a number of observations:

i. As mentioned in the opening paragraph of the chapter, the institutional arrangements (formal and informal) associated with the idea of (industrial) participation are multifarious though cross-nationally there is repeated emphasis upon:

(*a*) participation in the overall governance of the enterprise (Boards of Directors, Supervisory Boards, etc.) and

(*b*) participation at a 'lower' level (plant, work group, department, etc.).

ii. The various institutional arrangements are almost invariably formulated in terms of the involvement of groups of individuals within (sometimes without) the enterprise in decision-making of differing types.

iii. The level of involvement in decision-making by a group or individual is conceived of as 'variable', usually in terms ranging from complete determination through co-determination and consultation to 'being informed' either before or after the decision is taken.

iv. The divergence between what is legally specified and sanctioned and what in

Table 2.1.
Variety of national industrial democracy schemes

Country	Political Context	In-company Arrangement
United Kingdom	Law on board level representation being discussed, but now vociferous employer opposition and unions only moderately interested. Traditionally law keeps out of industrial relations. Collective bargaining is not legally enforceable.	No statutory works' councils, but shop stewards' committees are prevalent. Growth in decentralized power (*de facto*) in recent years.
Belgium	Multi-party system not yet federalized. Communitarian problems and multi-unionism according to political, religious, and linguistic divisions. Bargaining on centralized and decentralized basis. High unionization with Christian, socialist, and liberal confederations.	No worker representatives on supervisory boards. Works' councils, safety and health committees, and union delegations. Former two have consultative role; last bargains. Christian and socialist unions disagree on forms of worker representation at company level.
Yugoslavia	Socialist country organized on decentralized community-based self-government. Capital communally owned.	Plant run by elected committee (workers' council). Each unit (basic association of organized labour) has its own representative committees.
Sweden	Strong union movement negotiating centrally with a likewise centralized employers' federation. Up to 1976 very little state interference in industrial relations.	Union 'clubs' that bargain with management mainly over wages. Safety committee with union majority. Works' council for information and consultation. Two workers' directors on the (only) board.
Holland	Parliamentary democracy with multi-party system. Moderate level of unionization organized according to political/religious lines. Bargaining takes place at central level in which government participates also, and at branch level worker participation regulated mainly through national laws.	No representation of workers on supervisory board. Most important representative organ is works' council. It has mainly advisory and consultative character. Recent development towards more authority for the works' council. Some activities of union representatives on the shop floor. Some developments towards institutionalization of consultation supervisor–work groups on day-to-day activities.
Germany (West)	Long standing tradition of introducing worker participation at company/plant level by way of statutory regulations (national laws). Collective bargaining (wages/working conditions) mainly above company level between well-organized, industry-based unions and employers' associations.	Works' council is central body for employee representation at plant/company level with information, consultation, or co-determination rights depending on issues. Generally, large companies have $\frac{1}{3}$ (500 employees) or $\frac{1}{2}$ (2,000 employees) of seats on supervisory boards for employee representatives. Two-tier company structure. *cont.*

Table 2.1 *cont.*

Country	Political Context	In-company Arrangement
France	Politicized arena of collective bargaining. Numerically weak union movement, divided by confederal allegiances, resists reformist solutions.	Works' council (*Conseil d'enterprise*) has consultative role. Few workers on board.
Finland	Centralized bargaining and high level of unionization. Degree of statutory participation behind pace of other Nordic countries.	Productivity committee for plants over 60 people, but are of low importance. Shop stewards and work protection delegates important.
Israel	Strong labour movement has institutionalized worker participation in its federation's own enterprises and public sector.	Works' committees in company and plant. Joint Productivity Councils in industrial plants and joint management in some Histadrut industrial plants only.
Italy	Politicized union movement, moderately well organized in manufacturing, but little state/legal interference *vis-à-vis* participation.	Factory councils, but not prescribed by legislation, depend on union strength.
Denmark	Strong labour movement co-operating with Labour Party and worker minority representatives on boards. High degree of unionization and centralized collective bargaining.	Co-operative committees in which workers' shop stewards take part (joint consultation) affect day-to-day situations. Shop stewards important.
Norway	Mixed economy. Strongly centralized and united labour movement with national unions bargaining 2-year collective agreements with equally centralized employers' confederation. Close co-operation between trade unions and dominant social-democratic labour party. High degree of unionization. Increasing state participation in national collective bargaining.	Local union representatives bargain with management with basis in collective agreement. Shop stewards take part in joint consultation/information bodies and safety committees. $\frac{1}{3}$ of board of directors and supervisory board members are elected by and among employees, after nomination by local unions.

practice occurs is often wide, and the informal arrangement may have an impact of equal importance as the formal arrangements.

These observations constituted the starting points of our research. Could the fine details of the various national systems be ignored by posing abstract questions in terms of the varying degrees or levels of participation implied by each national scheme, both in law (*de jure*) and in practice (*de facto*), whilst still producing results which were of practical comparative use?

SOME PROVISIONAL DEFINITIONS

Although it may be rather incautious, at the outset, to offer a definition of something as complex as 'industrial participation', we will, nevertheless, venture a provisional definition with a view to indicating, in a general way, the focus of our research. More precise definitions will be given later.

We will distinguish between two dimensions of participation—the amount (or extent or level) and the scope. Further, we distinguish between *de jure* and *de facto* participation. By the amount of *de jure* participation of the individual we mean the degree to which an individual has the legal right to be involved in the taking of a decision of a specified type. By amount of *de facto* participation of an individual we mean the degree to which an individual is, in practice, involved in the taking of a decision of a specified type. Clearly we should now be required to define 'involvement in the taking of decisions', but for the moment we leave this open, feeling that the spirit of the definitions is sufficiently clear.

Armed with these provisional definitions we can conceive of an individual's participation (*de jure* and *de facto*) as varying across a number of decision types —from 'all those decisions taken in the running of the enterprise' to very specific ones. Thus, we can define the second dimension of participation—the scope. The (*de jure* or *de facto*) scope of participation of an individual is the number of decision types in which he has some level of (*de jure* or *de facto*) involvement.

Furthermore, we can distinguish between the *direct* and *indirect* participation of an individual, the latter being through the agency of a representative (or delegate), the former implying personal involvement. This distinction is, however, nothing like as transparent as it might appear at first sight, but we will remain content with it for the moment (see Chapter 4). We, thus, use the word 'participation' indiscriminately to cover these various dimensions; it is our most general category (Dachler and Wilpert 1978). If participation is to be defined in terms of the involvement of individuals (or groups) in decision-making of various types, a further analytical distinction must be made. This concerns the intuitively obvious notion that decisions are of varying 'importance'. Quite evidently, by most standards, capital investment decisions carry greater 'importance' than, say, decisions concerning the allocation of a particular piece of capital equipment to a particular use. Though the idea of varying importance of decisions is easy to embrace intuitively, it is by no means easy to tie down analytically. Questions concerning importance 'for what' or 'for whom' immediately become pertinent. We may wish to try to distinguish between *objective* and *subjective* importance— the former being associated with the risks involved in the decision for the continuing and effective functioning of the enterprise and the latter being tied to a particular individual's assessment. We will not pursue these issues further here, but merely note that the involvement of an individual (or group) in decisions may well invite a 'weighting' in terms of importance—objective or subjective.

We will now turn to a general definition of industrial democracy since it is this phrase which enters our title and also the political debate surrounding participation. Then we will consider our theoretical models and, this accomplished, we return to the details of our conceptualization—in particular to the problem of abstracting workable concepts of 'power', involvement, and influence from the concept of participation.

Industrial democracy is difficult to define but a process of democratization is usually interpreted as a deliberate attempt to increase the participation of, or equalize the 'power' amongst, members of an industrial organization so that those traditionally deprived in these respects have more 'say'. However, the principles listed below may function as a guideline against which the process of democratization may be evaluated. Principle D.1. represents an extreme form of 'direct democracy' which is usually only applicable by itself in the smallest and simplest of organizations. In practice principles D.2. to D.4. have to constrain D.1. to enable industrial organizations to function. The problem of striking a balance between, on the one hand, D.1. and, on the other, D.2. to D.4. constitutes the central dilemma of industrial democracy (Dahl 1970, Abell 1979).

The principles are:

D.1. The principle of *political equality*
The principle whereby all members of the organization have the right to participate directly, on the basis of 'one person one vote', in all the decisions affecting the organization.

D.2. The principle of *representation*
The principle whereby individuals have the right to surrender all or part of their rights, as embodied in D.1., to chosen representatives or delegates.

D.3. The principle of *specific or special competence*
The principle whereby it is recognised that certain decisions call for specialized skills and thus become the proclivity of those with such skills.

D.4. The principle of *efficiency*
The principle whereby it is recognized that the concept of goal fullfilment is the *raison d'être* of the enterprise.

The question naturally arises as to how principles D.2. to D.4. should, in a democratic organization, constrain D.1. Democratic theory would seem to suggest a further principle which may in practice be difficult to apply, particularly over time with changing membership; namely that the decision to surrender decision-making autonomy through representation, perceived competence, or efficiency should be itself subordinated to principle D.1. so that *this* decision (meta-decision) is arrived at democratically. We thus add:

D.5. The principle whereby D.1. itself is used to determine how D.2. to D.4. may constrain D.1.

These principles are, of course, rather abstract and may best be interpreted as an extreme typification. In application they raise a series of problems. First, the set of decisions available to the organization may, in one way or another, be circumscribed by its socio-economic environment and one may consequently wish to enquire as to whether democratic principles apply in the wider society also. Second, and related to the first point, how should the members of an organization be defined; for instance it has been suggested that consumers should be represented in the decision-making process and, of course, in capitalist economic systems owners usually have decision-making rights. This is not the place to debate the details of who should or should not be included in the intra-organizational democratic process. We merely note that the problem raises fundamental issues concerning the franchise.

Third, we may wish to add to the principles mentioned above some statement guaranteeing the rights of minorities and also access to information to the point where an individual (or representative) can ' rationally' assess the options open to him. Furthermore, there are a series of problems surrounding the possible democratic autonomy of sub-systems (e.g. basic organizations of associated labour in Yugoslavia) which again raises the question to whom should 'members' refer in D.1.

We cannot, in the space available, debate these issues—let it suffice to say that in practice the principles we have outlined are not in their entirety embodied in theory or practice (with the possible exception of Yugoslavia) in any of the countries we have studied.

SENSITIZING HYPOTHESES AND MODEL 1

At the most general level we postulate a simple model as depicted in Figure 2.1.

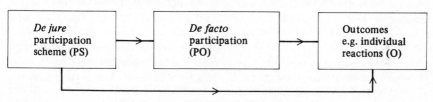

Figure 2.1 A simple sensitizing model

In other words we may state what we will term three major sensitizing hypotheses:[1]

S.H.1. *De jure* participation schemes have a systematic determinate effect upon the intra-organizational *de facto* participation distributions.

S.H.2. *De facto* intra-organizational participation distributions have a systematic determinate effect upon outcomes (e.g. organizational participants' attitudes, reactions, etc.)

S.H.3. *De jure* participation schemes have a systematic determinate effect upon outcomes *independently* of their impact upon the intra-organizational power distribution.[2]

Clearly these three 'hypotheses are expressed in such a vague manner as to preclude any precise testing, but they do give an overall perspective on the framework in which the research was set and from which, with suitable elaboration, we can derive more specific and testable hypotheses. It should be noted that for the moment we use the term 'participation' rather loosely to cover its various dimensions and also the implied 'power' distribution.

Before we continue, however, a few conjectures and reservations concerning the model in Figure 2.1 are perhaps called for; the first concerns the implicit 'causal' ordering. If we may be permitted to use the word 'cause' then we are postulating that the *de jure* participation schemes is *a* (not necessarily *the*[3]) cause of both the *de facto* participation distribution and the outcomes and moreover the *de facto* participation distribution is, in its turn, *a* cause of outcomes. Here there is a simple implication of temporal precedence: the *de jure* participation scheme (from now on—PS) is exogenously determined—presumably by national/regional/local[4] legislation; it is then enacted, at the level of the organization which in turn generates a *de facto* distribution (from now on—PO) and a series of outcomes (from now on generically—O). We also allow PS to 'cause' O independently. Now it takes little imagination to recognize that this puts a gloss upon a series of social processes which may well be extremely complicated. First of all we may wish to think of what technically would be feedback loops—specific O's could quite conceivably affect (causally) PO and even perhaps, in the long term, changes in PS. The analysis of such processes invites a longitudinal study embracing the inter-acting causes and effects of organizational practice and experience and various legal institutions. Unfortunately, except in the most qualitative way, such research would require an extremely costly design and was beyond our means. Hence, in the main, the simple 'causal' ordering mentioned above had to suffice.[5] There are reasons, however, to suppose that this is not too damaging to the research; one would suspect, for instance, that any 'feedback' from O to PS would be a relatively time-consuming process in relation to the impact of PS on PO and PO on O. Thus, one may reasonably assume that the short-term equilibrium between these 'variables' will be achieved in a time period which may be regarded as instantaneous with respect to the time period for O to affect PS. This is perhaps not true for the possible feed-back effects of O on PO; we will, however, in a further volume, attempt to test models which allow for these effects.

In general, however, since our research is based upon a cross-sectional design and thus, in effect, correlation measures are computed at one point in time, we have to assume that if the 'causal processes' embodied in our three central sensitizing hypotheses consume time (i.e. are not instantaneous) the organizations we study have experienced the impact of PS for a sufficient period of time for the equilibrium values of PO and O to ensue.[6]

FURTHER SENSITIZING HYPOTHESES AND MODEL 2

In practice the simple model presented in Figure 2.1, its vagueness apart, is still inadequate in a number of respects and was, as our research ideal, replaced by the more elaborate model already depicted inFigure 1.1 but shown here again (Figure 2.2) for convenience (IDE, 1976).

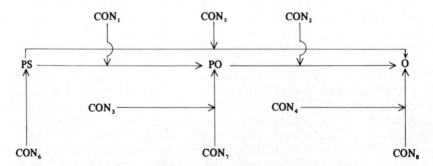

Figure 2.2 A more elaborate sensitizing model

In Figure 2.2:

CON_1 is any (contextual) variable which modifies the nature of the relationship between PS and PO (i.e. statistically speaking interacts with PS in affecting PO).[7]

CON_2 is any variable which modifies the nature of the relationship between PO and O (i.e. interacts).

CON_3 is any variable which modifies the nature of the relationship between CON_7 and PO (i.e. interacts).

CON_4 is any variable which modifies the nature of the relationship between CON_8 and O (i.e. interacts).

CON_5 is any variable which modifies the nature of the direct relationship between PS and O.

CON_6 is any variable which determines PS.

CON_7 is any variable which has a determining effect upon PO in addition[8] to PS.

CON_8 is any variable which has a determining effect upon O in addition to PO and PS.

It is to be further understood that:

i. The 'CON' variables may not be exclusive.

ii. Various feedbacks are possible.

As we mentioned earlier one may wish to think of O (overtime) feeding back to PS and PO (either as a modifier or additional cause) and PO feeding back to PS. The arrows have not been included in the diagram for the sake of clarity and in the light of our earlier remarks. Indeed, the reader may like to eschew the concept of causality altogether rather interpreting our models and results purely in terms of patterns of statistical association leaving open any interpretation in terms of the deeper-lying concepts of causal agency and direction.[9]

Informally, the most important way in which model 2.2 advances upon model 2.1 is by allowing factors characterizing the organization and perhaps the national culture to affect the relationships between PS, PO, and O. It may help the reader, at this stage, if we give an example. It has been argued, for instance, that the size of an enterprise may well modify the impact of PS upon PO, making PS either more or less effective in large organizations. Thus, 'size' would act as a (CON_1) variable; similarly 'size' may act as a (CON_5) variable mediating the impact of PS on say 'the level of satisfaction' (O variable) of individuals. On the other hand, the 'emphasis on democratic values in the wider society' may affect PO independently of PS, thus acting as a CON_7 variable. We would accordingly emphasize that the symbols in Figure 2.2 stand for classes of possible variables and in order to study their impact we would have to erect models enabling us to test for partial and interaction effects.

UNITS (LEVELS) OF ANALYSIS

It will have become apparent to the reader that the sensitizing models 1 and 2 are, as presently formulated, rather ambiguous in respect of the units of analysis involved. Nations, organizations, and individuals have all been rather casually referred to and the concepts of *de jure* and *de facto* participation distributions clearly invite the question—distribution across what? The detailed reasoning behind the selection of various units will be discussed in chapter 4, but we need here some general framework which will facilitate the derivation of reasonably precise ideas from our sensitizing models.

Our central variables PS, PO and O can generate measures at:

i. *the individual level.*

ii. *the group level*—groups A (workers), B (foremen), C (middle managers), D (top management), E (level above plant), F (representative bodies), and G (external groups)—the measure might be the mean of individual-level scores within each group.

iii *the organizational level*—a measure characterizing the distribution across groups A to G for each organization.

iv. *the organizational-set level* (e.g. an industrial sector)—measures aggregated from either the individual, group, or organizational level.

v. *the national level*—measures aggregated from either the individual, group, or organization levels.

vi. *the supra-national entity* (e.g. the Scandinavian countries)—measures aggregated from either the individual, group, organizational, or national levels.

It should be clear that we can, therefore, in principle specify a set of logically possible cross-level (structural) effects as depicted in Figure 2.3.

Independent variable characterizes:

		Indiv.	Group	Org.	Sub-nat.	Nat.	Supra-nat.
Dependent variable characterizes:	Individual	√	√	√	√	√	√
	Group		√	√	√	√	√
	Organization			√	√	√	√
	Sub-national entity				√	√	√
	Nation					√	√
	Supra-national entity						√

√ = possible cross-level effect

Figure 2.3 Logically Possible cross-level effects

It would be tedious to describe each logically possible type of analysis, but an indication of what is implied by the first row in Figure 2.3 should suffice to indicate the possibilities. For example, the variation in an individual-level variable like the 'satisfaction with participation' may be a function of (i) another individual-level variable—'personal power'; (ii) a group-level variable, e.g. the mean[10] power of the individual's group; (iii) an organizational level variable, e.g. the distribution of power in his organization and so on, up to the supra-national level.

There are two important things to note about this type of analysis; firstly, in practice, one would expect the 'higher order' cross-level effects to have diminishing explanatory power (i.e. explain less variance in the chosen dependent variable); secondly, in the context of testing for such effects the number of units of analysis diminishes as one progresses from the individual upwards. The theoretical significance of cross-level effects should become clear later in the chapter and the methodological problems will be discussed in chapter 4.

PARTICIPATION, POWER, AND COGNATE CONCEPTS

The concept of 'power' and its close relatives like participation, influence, control, and persuasion have, perhaps, generated more controversy than any other concepts in social science and despite the lengthy and sometimes acrimonious debates concerning the relative merits of one viewpoint rather than another, it is still not possible to find agreed definitions. It is, therefore, important for us to give a clear presentation of the theoretical conceptualization embodied in our research as both 'power' and 'participation' play such a central role; though in practice our operationalizations had, of necessity, to be less exacting than our theoretical deliberations would dictate.

In fact the definitions and operationalizations have been developed stepwise by the IDE group so that, despite initial disagreements which were never entirely resolved, we can now speak of IDE concepts and measures though terminological differences remained. The reasons for the initial disagreements were perhaps twofold: the first is connected with the nature of the concept of 'power' itself; if, as Kadishin (1968) and Nagel (1975) suggest, it is a 'disposition concept' and we also accept Carnap's (1939) analysis of such concepts in terms of reduction sentences, then 'power' is necessarily definitionally open. However, even if this is the case, we must assume that the partial definitions in terms of reduction sentences must be consistent one with another.

The second reason is more mundane and is attributable to the differing intellectual backgrounds of the researchers. Each professional group—and indeed each national team—brought a slightly different emphasis to the research. The psychologists amongst us, for instance, tended to favour a concept of 'power' based upon the idea of a personal ability or capacity (Lewin 1951, Cartwright 1959, French 1956) whereas the sociologists were more inclined to view it as both a group ability and to think in terms of the distribution of scarce organizational resources at the command of different groups (Janowitz 1975). In addition they were also concerned to emphasize the extent to which groups can control the 'structure of opportunities' and the role of 'rules' and 'values' underlying accepted institutional arrangements (Parsons 1966).

The research group had, therefore, to find some way of generating a reasonable consensus out of these very diverging orientations. We recognized at least three approaches to the conceptualization and measurement of power—namely (i) the control of resources approach; (ii) the reputational approach, and (iii) the decision-making approach (to include non-decisions (Bachrach and Baratz 1970). For reasons which will become apparent presently, a mixture of approaches (ii) and (iii) were adopted in the research.

The control of resources approach to power

The control of resources approach to power seeks to define and measure the power of an agent (individual or collective) in terms of the socially scarce resources he (it) controls. Thus, the greater the control an agent has of such resources, the greater is his power—and, in the context of his power *vis-à-vis* other agents, one is tempted to say that it is the difference[11] in their respective control of resources which is the important factor. This approach is closely allied with exchange theory (Blau 1964) which postulates that the power of an agent is proportional to the degree to which others are dependent upon him (for scarce social resources) and inversely proportional to the degree to which he is replaceable by others with alternative sources. Exchange theory has in one way or another been developed by Crozier and Thoenig (1976) and Hickson (1971). Each of these authors claims to show that when one agent copes with 'uncertainty' (the resource) for another agent, then the former is able to exert effective power over the latter. Thus, it is emphasized that it is not merely the control of resources that confers power, but resources that are wanted/needed by another agent. This formulation highlights the essentially relational character of the 'power' concept.

Exchange theory has, however, been rather heavily criticized but has, nevertheless, when used carefully, proved useful in organizational studies. The major difficulties, however, inherent in defining the power of an agent in terms of his control of resources are twofold. Firstly, since scarce 'social resources' are so diverse it is often difficult on an *a priori* basis, to instance them and, even if one can, their measurement properties are also often so intrinsically different that aggregation is extremely difficult. Secondly, an agent may in fact have potential control over resources, but fail for one reason or another, to realize this or make effective use of them and, thus, to define power in terms of controlled resources would make it difficult to draw a distinction between actual power exerted and potential power.[12] Though it may be possible, within this perspective, to differentiate between the possibility of using resources (potential power) and the actual use of resources.

Nevertheless it seems reasonable, to seek for a logically independent definition of 'power' (actual 'power') which could, in principle, be empirically related to the resources (potential power) an agent has at his disposal. In this context one would be interested in three types of variable; first the distribution of (scarce) resources amongst the contending parties. As mentioned these might be extremely diverse and (the use of force apart) are, in the final analysis, those resources for which there is a potentially effective demand from at least one party in the system under investigation. Furthermore, the resources might be renewable or depleting (March 1955), a point we will return to below. The second type of variable would describe the power actually exerted and the third would account for any observed disparity between the power exerted and political power (access to scarce resources). This third category would, in turn, comprise at least two further types of variable; the first emphasizing why the actor in question did (or did not) mobilize all the resources at his disposal and the second describing the variability in effective demand (Olson 1970).

Although it would have been gratifying to explore these complexities it seemed out of the question, given the research resources and the time available— a rather more robust approach was required, which nevertheless would not be conceptually at odds with the control of resources framework.[13] We, therefore, decided not to adopt the control of resources approach, but rather to seek a logically independent definition of power.

The reputational approach to power

The reputational approach, although the most commonly used of the three approaches in empirical research on organizations (Tannenbaum 1961) is, in fact conceptually rather unsoundly based (Abell 1977, Gundelach and Tetzsch- ner 1976). It lends itself to a number of interpretations, but the basic idea rests upon an assumption that individuals within the system under scrutiny can readily estimate either or both of their own or other agents' 'power'. Thus, merely by asking about the level or degree of power, it is assumed we can obtain valid and reliable measures of the concept. Although this technique has also been rather severely criticized, it does have the distinct advantage of being relatively easily and cheaply applied. Furthermore, in the hands of Tannenbaum and his colleagues it has proved extremely insightful, if not uncontroversial.[14]

It is evident that, in asking individuals about their own and others' amount of 'power' (or related concept), we must make some more or less explicit assump- tions; first, that the individuals concerned hold, if not identical, reasonably similar concepts of what it is for an agent to possess varying amounts of power; second, that it is meaningful to apply the concept to the agents in question; third, that the individuals are likely to make a reliable and objective estimate of the level of power of the agents, or at least, if we base the measure on the dis- tribution of responses of a sample or population of individuals, that any errors in the individual estimates randomize out. In this respect two possible types of bias can arise; cognitive bias which is attributable (even assuming the use of the same concept) to lack of knowledge of the objective situation and ideological bias attributable to distortion due to particular normative or evaluative orienta- tions and stereotyping (Lord 1977). Unfortunately the practitioners of the reputational technique have not always been over-assiduous in checking whether their respondents are using identical concepts, with the result that it is some- times rather difficult to interpret their findings, for it is not clear whether they refer to degrees of power or participation. In chapter 4 we will argue that this shortcoming can be, if not eliminated, at least minimized by the use of behavioural scales rather than patently judgemental ones.[15]

In view of the various shortcomings of the reputational approach we decided not to use it in its established form, though we were attracted to its operational simplicity and realized that, in one form or another, we would have to rely upon organizational participants' estimates.

The decision-making approach to power

If the weakness of the reputational approach to power is associated with the paucity of its conceptual underpinnings, then the strength of the decision-making approach lies with the relatively precise conceptual definitions it permits (March 1966, Simon 1953). However, this latter approach has, in its turn, been rather severely criticized (Bachrach and Baratz 1970), the burden of their criticism being that by centring attention upon decision-making one ignores those potential decisions which have, for one reason or another, been kept out of the decision-making arena. We will recommend, however, a slight emendation of the approach designed to overcome these criticisms (Nagel 1975).

From a decision-making perspective we may view an organization as a system comprising:

i. a set of *individuals* who may be categorized in a variety of ways (e.g. by 'level', department, and so on)

ii. a set (population) of *outcomes*: an outcome is any discriminable aspect of the organization (to include the action of individuals and categories of individuals)

iii. each individual has a *preferred outcome* (to include no preference) for each outcome.

It is then postulated that outcomes are a function of the preferences of the individuals and the extent to which any individual can get his preferences in the face of competing preferences embodied in outcomes is a measure of what we will term his power.[16]

We should note how this formulation relates to decision-making. If we restrict attention to explicit decision-making then (i) to (iii) are directly applicable assuming that preferences for decision outcomes of individuals and actual decision outcomes can be ascertained. But by not explicitly tying the formulation to overt decision-making we allow that certain outcomes are the product of non-decision-making or many interrelated decisions. It is perhaps, therefore, desirable to take this rather more expansive view of the decision-making approach. It has the advantage that it is not necessarily tied to face-to-face bargaining or decision-making processes. In modern organizations 'power' is often not exercised by direct involvement of participants within the framework of decision-making but indirectly through institutional arrangements and conditions. One of the dominant trends in large contemporary organizations is a decreasing reliance upon the amount of direct supervision of the work-flow, but at the same time trends exist toward an increasing use of control exercised through boundary regulations, control of the input of information, and through rules setting limits on the decision-making process (Blau and Schoenherr 1971). Despite these observations, however, our operational techniques centred upon decision-making because the 'political debate' surrounding the concept of participation is explicitly couched in terms of involvement in decision-making. However, given the scale of the research and the limited time and funds available, it was impracticable to study these processes *in situ*, rather we had to rely upon respondents' reports (see Chapter 4).

Nevertheless, given its close conceptual affinity with our research, it is worth exploring, in more detail, some of the assumptions and derivative concepts of the decision-making approach, for these will help us in the formulation of our more specific hypotheses in a later chapter. The decision-making approach to power can very reasonably be described as 'liberal' in spirit in taking revealed preference as the basis of computing an individual's power. Those of a Marxist persuasion, for instance, would wish to construe power in terms of the degree to which 'objective interests' rather than revealed preference can be embodied in outcomes (Lukes 1979). This is not the place to become embroiled in the issue of whether an agent's objective interests can in fact be ascertained if they do not coincide with his revealed preferences, but what should be noted is that, if they can, then the approach is, in principle, applicable. However, since our research was, in practice, not designed to examine these issues, we discuss them no further here, but merely point out that the extended decision-making approach to power still retains its appeal whatever position one takes in this thorny debate.

Queries of this nature do, however, raise the issue concerning the genesis of preferences. If one seeks to conceptualize and measure the power of an agent in terms of the weighting of his preferences in the outcome of decisions one is surely entitled to ask why he has the preferences he has in the first place. Clearly the processes, however complex, whereby one agent can 'shape' the preferences of others must be included in any concept of 'power' worthy of its name. A may be able to get his preferences embodied in decision outcomes by aligning B's preferences with his own and if B would otherwise have had alternative preferences then the process of alignment must count as part of A's 'power' over B. Models whereby one can chart how one agent changes (or establishes) the preferences of another have been discussed by Nagel (1975) and the distinction between, on the one hand, processes of influence, where such changes increase the bases for rational deliberation of an agent, and on the other, manipulation where they decrease them, has also been described (Abell 1977). This latter distinction points to the provision of information as the crucial issue and though in the present research we found it impracticable to research these issues in detail, we adopted a behavioural scale for the 'degree of participation' which explicitly asks the respondent the extent to which he is involved in making a number of decisions. The scale includes no involvement, the provision of information (involvement), and getting one's way in conflict situations (power).

There is a related issue concerning conflict; according to the above formulation, if all the organizational participants have identical preferences over all outcomes, then (i) the organization is completely consensual and (ii) there is no need for power as there is no conflict to be resolved. Thus, the concept of power is predicated upon the notion of competing preferences (i.e. conflict). This has led some researchers to reject the approach, feeling that concepts of power should not be predicated in this way. However, as we have seen above, if an organization is consensual or near consensual, then we can still search for processes of manipulation and influence to explain the consensuality; there do not appear, therefore, to be legitimate grounds for concern in this respect.

There are a number of problems associated with decision-making which make sole reliance upon this approach difficult. First, it is possible that organizational participants do not have clearly formulated preferences and thus power as a measure of the embodiment of preferences in outcomes cannot be measured. Second, it may be that participants change their preferences without any pressure' from others and although this can be allowed for in the mathematical formulation of the decision-making model, it renders the measures rather difficult to interpret. Furthermore, if one has to rely upon retrospective data an actor may well report preferences much nearer to the outcome than actually was the case at the time; he may, in other words, attempt to reduce the cognitive dissonance he experiences between his aspirations (preferences) and what he can effectively realize.

Bargaining power, involvement, and control costs

There is a further aspect of the concepts of participation and power which deserves attention. We have defined power in terms of the ability of an organizational actor to 'have his way' in conflict situations. However, we would clearly want to regard an actor who gets his way, but in so doing incurs high 'costs', as less powerful than one who has the same purchase on outcomes but incurs less costs (Harsanyi 1962). Thus, the concept of control costs must, of necessity, enter our deliberations. Of course these costs may be what are conventionally termed sanctions; A gets his way (e.g. B's compliance) by the expenditure of either positive or negative sanctions—though the conceptual problem of regarding negative sanctions as costs can be rather troublesome.[17] Be this as it may, it is important to distinguish between the amount of bargaining-power of an actor (i.e. his relative determination of outcomes) and the control costs (if any) accruing to him. We do not want to get embroiled in the various conceptual issues which surround the idea of costs, e.g. whether they are symmetrically perceived in inter-actor power situations, whether they are expendable, and whether they can be measured in terms of opportunity costs, as these issues fall outside the scope of our research. Nevertheless, a couple of points need making. Firstly, since the idea of control costs lies so close to the idea of 'power' (in the general sense of this term) it may be that in using reputational measures of 'power' individuals concentrate upon 'costs' rather than the 'amount' (as we have defined it) in giving their estimates. This is certainly possible with research instruments which allow respondents to rank actors in terms of 'much influence', 'little influence', etc. (Tannenbaum 1968). However, as we pointed out before, we have tried to obviate this problem by using in our research a scale with steps that each describe a discrete form of behaviour and which explicitly directs the respondent's attention to the provision of information (involvement) and getting one's way in conflict situations (power). Although we would not be so optimistic as to believe that all biases attributable to differing conceptions are thereby eliminated from our data, we do feel they are much reduced.

'Meta-Power' and 'Negative Power'

The term meta-power, to our knowledge, has been used in two rather distinct ways: first to refer to the process which determines by whom decisions are made; second, to refer to the practice whereby decisions are allocated (delegated) to an 'agent' but 'limiting parameters' are set upon the acceptable solutions to the decision—the area of discretion is, as it were, limited (Rus 1970). It should be noted, however, whichever interpretation we care to adopt, that these ideas are conceptually compatible with the decision-outcome model. In the first case the outcome in question is the allocation of the decision (type), in the second it is the determination of the limiting parameters. It is our opinion, therefore, that no additional conceptual apparatus is needed to study these phenomena, though specific questions would have to discover who determines the limiting parameters.

The concept of negative power has proved more difficult and the research group could not reach agreement on this matter.[18] A number of authors (Rus 1976, Etzioni 1969, Cartwright 1959) have emphasized the 'ability to resist change' as an important dimension of power relations. Some members of the IDE group felt that this ability (negative power) requires special treatment and found support for this position in Dahl (1957) who defines positive and negative power and its absence. Others in the group, however, felt that the concept of negative power can be handled perfectly adequately in the decision-outcome framework for resistance, they would argue, relates to a preference for preventing something from happening whilst another party has an active preference for it to happen. However, since agreement could not be reached, a series of optional instruments were included in our research, going under the label PO4 (see chapter 4).

The need for a synthesis of the three approaches

We have reviewed the merits and disadvantages of three approaches to the conceptualization and measurement of power, and since no one clearly recommended itself as the candidate for our research, we had the task of trying to find some sort of intellectual synthesis. First, for the reasons mentioned, we ruled out a definition of 'power' in terms of resources controlled, though we would, in principle, be open to the idea of empirically relating our measures to such 'resources'. Second, we also ruled out a sole reliance on decision-making; despite its relative conceptual rigour, the impracticalities and the difficulties mentioned above effectivly prevented us from adopting the approach, though, since the political debate concerning 'participation' is invariably couched in terms of involvement in decision-making, some reliance upon it seemed inevitable. Finally, though we were suspicious of its conceptual underpinnings, the reputational approach has the obvious merit of ease of application and, in the final analysis, it proved necessary to incorporate it in our research. However, in order that our respondents should have a clear and unambiguous idea of the underlying concept, we adopted a behavioural scale of 'involvement'.

In sum, then, the *desiderata* dictating our choice for the conceptualization and measurement of power were as follows:

i. The conceptualization should be, insofar as is possible, logically compatible with the control of resources and decision (outcome) approaches.

ii. The measurement techniques should be appropriate to comparative research across twelve nations and compatible with survey technique.[19] This effectively dictated some reliance on the reputational method.

iii. The conceptualization should, as far as is possible, be consonant with the 'political debate' concerning participation. This effectively dictated that it should derive from the degree of involvement of individuals/groups in decision-making.

Definitions of involvement, influence and power

We are now in a position to give reasonably precise definitions of our central concepts. In the spirit of our previous provisional definition of participation, the research concentrated firstly upon the personal involvement (PO2) of individuals (from groups A (workers) to G (external groups)) in sixteen decision-making areas. (These are listed in Appendix A and the rationale for their selection can be found in chapter 4). Second, the more general influence (PO1) over the same set of decisions was also measured for each group.

Operationally we allow the level or amount of personal involvement (Heller 1971) in a given decision to vary on an ordinal scale as follows:

i.   I am not involved at all
ii.   I am informed about the matter beforehand
iii. I can give my opinion
iv.   My opinion is taken into account
v.   I take part in the decision-making with equal weight
vi.   I decide on my own

So an individual's participation in decision-making provides him with more or less involvement on this scale in each of the sixteen decisions.

We further distinguish between *de jure* participation (PS) and thus involvement where the level of involvement is (i) written down and (ii) enforceable in law and de *facto* participation where the level of involvement is current practice whether or not it is written down or enforceable in law.[20]

The wider concept of influence was based upon a Tannenbaum-type scale running ordinally from 'no influence' to 'very much influence'. We did not attempt to codify this idea rigidly, as it was used to refer in a very general sense to the groups A to G. We thus asked experts to assess the degree of influence of each group on each decision and one of the central concerns in our research became the relationship between personal involvement (PO2) of individuals in groups A to G with the influence (PO1) of these groups. Thus, if we refer to Figure 2.1 once again we can imagine the 'box'—*de facto* participation (PO) being decomposed into two further boxes representing PO2 and PO1. A variety of models relating PS to PO1 and PO2 then becomes possible. For instance:

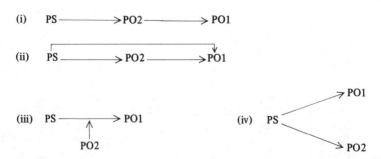

Some of these are explored in Chapter 7 and others in a future volume where 'O' variables are also incorporated.

The nature of the scale measuring PO2 should be emphasized; it draws the respondent's attention to specific 'objective' levels of involvement which, as we noted in the opening sections of this chapter, largely parallel the categories used in the political debate about participation. Furthermore, the final two categories clearly derive from the decision/outcome approach to the measurement of 'power'.

Although no use is made of the distinction in this volume it is possible, in the context of our previous deliberations, to distinguish between involvement in decisions which do and do not generate conflict (Figure 2.4).[21]

		Conflictual decisions	Non-conflictual decisions
Involvement category	1	$\tilde{C}$-Involvement	$\tilde{C}$-Involvement
	2		
	3		
	4		
	5	Power	
	6		

Figure 2.4 Involvement and Power

We thus define:

i. Power as the degree to which a group (or individual) can determine the outcome of decisions (of a specified scope) which generate conflict.

ii. C-Involvement as the amount of involvement a group (or individual) has in conflictual decision-making (of specified scope) which falls short of any determination of outcome.

iii. $\tilde{C}$-Involvement as the amount of involvement a group (or individual) has in non-conflictual decision (of a specified scope).

These concepts will be used in a future IDE publication.

FROM CONCEPTS TO DISTRIBUTION

Our research is concerned with the impact of the distributions of *de jure* or *de facto* participation (used to cover all the concepts from the last section); we therefore have to make some assumptions concerning the units of analysis to which we wish the concepts to apply. For reasons fully described in chapter 4, groups A to G were selected in the full recognition that alternative groups could equally well be defined. The research instruments were, thus, designed to measure the amount of participation (PO1 and PO2) of each group in a given oganization across a set of specified decision-types, though since the operational technique employed was reputational we also had at our disposal 'self' estimates of PO2. For the moment, however, we will concentrate upon the distribution of the amount of participation across the groups A to G.

We can conceptualize the participation (*de jure* or *de facto*) within an organization in terms of:

i. The amount of participation of a specified group over a) a specified decision-type, b) all decision-types, or c) a sub-set of decision-types (i.e. of varying scope).

ii. The distribution of participation across the groups A to G (or any sub-set of of groups) over a) a specified decision-type, b) all decision-types, or c) a sub-set of decision-types (i.e. of varying scope).

iii. The total amount of participation in an organization with respect to a) specified decision-types, b) all decision-types, or c) a sub-set of decision-types. The total amount of participation can clearly vary from organization to organization and also be variable-sum within organizations.[22]

iv. The degree of inequality in the distribution of the amount of participation in an organization with respect to a) a specified decision-type or b) all decision-types or c) a sub-set of decision-types.

Power: zero or variable sum?

We turn now to an important issue raised by our concepts of participation (that is involvement and influence)—are they zero- or variable-sum? A rather vigorous debate has surrounded this issue; on the one hand Lammers (1967), Parsons (1963), and Tannenbaum (1968) have argued strongly for a non-zero-zum conception of power, such that the increase in power of one agent need not necessarily be at the expense of another. On the other hand, others have either explicitly or implicitly argued that 'power' must, in principle, be zero-sum (Wright Mills, 1956). Undoubtedly some of the argument has been generated as a consequence of different definitions of the basic concept itself, but the question arises as to whether our concepts are zero- or variable-sum.

Let us first note that the scope of involvement and influence are clearly variable-sum. The participation of one group does not reduce the participation of another. Secondly, the first four categories of our 'involvement' scale for PS and PO2 (Figure 2.4) are also variable-sum—'being informed' etc., does not normally preclude other groups (or individuals) from being informed. The last two categories are, however, more controversial and thus our concept of power also. These both derive from the decision-outcome approach to power and if theoretically we define the amount of power of an individual (or group) as the extent to which his (its) preferences are embodied in outcomes (see footnote 16) then, over decisions (outcomes) of a specified scope, it appears that this measure is zero-sum (in the face of competing preferences). The degree of determination by one group/individual must be at the expense of others. However, having said this, since our involvement scale (including categories 5 and 6) is based upon respondents' estimates, it would clearly be possible to obtain results where a decision-type generates conflict and, at the same time, more than one party feels that it completely determines the outcome. Whether a 'finding' of this sort should be interpreted as a non-zero conception of power or as 'error' due to unclear conceptions (ideological or cognitive—see above) remains a point of disagreement amongst the IDE group. Since the influence scale (PO1) is not only based upon respondents' estimates but is purposely not closely tied to any precise conceptualization it remains an empirical question as to whether it exhibits the properties of a zero- or variable-sum concept (see Chapter 7).

A further and related point concerns the possibility of control costs being variable-sum. We will not consider these issues in detail because we have attempted to exclude this conceptualization of power from our research instruments. Clearly in the context of disputed decisions, if the costs incurred by A— say in gaining B's complaince—are received by B and they carry the same utility (Harsanyi 1962) for A and B then the situation is zero-sum with respect to costs. If, however, there is a disparity in their utilities, then the compliance can clearly be variable-sum. However, the conceptual interpretation of these costs will vary depending upon whether sanctions are expendable or not.

Before leaving this subject, we might note that involvement (as we have defined it) can also imply costs—the generation and provision of information is certainly not normally a costless business. Management, in traditionally structured organizations, is normally charged with the provision of information, and one might easily feel that the greater the costs accruing to a management team in generating and transmitting information to gain the non-conflictual involvement of its workforce, the less 'powerful' it is. But these considerations once again raise the issues of rational persuasion and manipulation which we alluded to above and unfortunately lie outside the scope of our research.

CONCLUSIONS

It has not been our intention in this chapter to deal with specific hypotheses deriving from our central theoretical model (Figure 2.2) but rather to point out some of the logical possibilities for analysis arising as a consequence of our concepts. The precise hypotheses and their relationship to other theoretical approaches will be found in subsequent chapters. Our research is concerned to study the impact of formally prescribed participation (PS) first on the actual level of participation (PO) and second either directly, or indirectly through PO, on specified outcomes (O). We have broken PO down into two subsidiary concepts; the degree or amount of personal involvement (PO2) and a more general but conceptually less rigorous concept of group influence (PO1). In each case (PS, PO1, and PO2) the concept is allowed to range over sixteen decision-types.

NOTES

1 We term them sensitizing hypotheses as they are not fully formulated and participation, as we have seen, is a complex concept.
2 That is to say any variable characterization of *de jure* participation will have an 'effect' upon outcomes holding *de facto* participation constant.
3 In model 2 below we allow for additional 'causes' of the *de facto* distribution.
4 See below.
5 Feedback models are introduced below and in a forthcoming sister volume.
6 We might note that our research is by no means unique in making this sort of assumption. Most 'causal' models in social science fail to account explicitly for the time dimension.
7 For instance, a model of the form:

$$PO = a + \beta \, PS.CON_1 + U$$

may be considered.

8 For instance, a model of the form:

$$PO = a + \beta_1 \, PS + \beta_2 D_2 + U$$

9 Furthermore, explicit inclusion of all these 'feedback' links can easily render any model unidentifiable.

10 A structural (cross-level) effect, for example, implies a model of the form:

$$O_i = a + \beta_1 Y_i + \beta_2 \overline{Y}_i + U_1$$

where O_i is an outcome characterising an individual i Y_i is a variable again characterizing the individual and Y_i is the mean of his group/organization etc. Y scores. See Blau (1964).

11 This makes rather heroic assumptions about the measurement of resources.

12 The distinction between actual power exerted and potential power pervades the literature. For example, Katz and Kahn (1966) treat 'power' as a potential act and 'influence' as an ability. Cox and Jacobson (1974) suggest that 'The influence (I) of an individual actor is the result of his power (C), as modified by his decision to attempt to convert his power into influence (a_a) and by the distribution of other influences within the organization on a particular issue. Then $I = X_a.C.D.$

13 This harks back to our previous point that an empirical relationship between 'resources' and an independent measure of power should be possible.

14 For this reason we actually included a Tannenbaum-type measure in our research in order that we might cross-validate it with our own measures.

15 Tannenbaum tends to use the concept of control at the theoretical level and a rating scale of 'influence' at the operational level. That is, he depends on individuals' judgements about 'levels of influence'.

16 A slightly more formal presentation may be of help here: let outcomes be given by O_j and the preferences of the n individuals by $X_1, X_2, ..., X_n$. Then:

$$O_j = f(X_{1j}, ..., X_{nj}; U_j), \tag{1}$$

where U_j is the usual stochastic term. If we specify (1) for example, in linear additive form we obtain:

$$O_j = P_1 X_{1j} + P_2 X_{2j} ... + P_j X_{ji} ... + P_n X_{nj} + U_n \tag{2}$$

where P_j is the bargaining power of individual j with respect to outcomes O_i. Thus, we are in a position to obtain a precise measure of bargaining power if we can obtain suitable measures in a population (or sample) of outcomes and preferences. For a fuller account see either March (1966), Nagel (1976), or Abell (1975).

17 There is a clear link between the concept of control cost and the control of resources approach.

18 Some members of the research group wished to emphasize the dialectical nature of power relations (i.e. their essential contradictory nature) and the processes of conflict resolution.

19 See chapter 4.

20 A slightly different coding was used for PS and PO2.

21 In practice (see chapter 4) we had to base the idea of conflictual decisions on questions about whether a specific decision-type did or did not generate conflict.

22 See below concerning the zero-variable-sum debate.

PART II

METHODOLOGY

3

PROBLEMS OF INTERNATIONAL AND INTER-DISCIPLINARY RESEARCH

AN IDEA DEVELOPS

The First International Sociological Conference on Participation and Self-management in Dubrovnik 1972 (Pusić 1972, 1973) provided an unique opportunity to review the state of the art in ongoing research on industrial democracy all over the world. First informal contacts were made with social scientists from several countries interested in pursuing a joint research project.

The lack of knowledge about the social and economic effects of comprehensive national schemes of participation and industrial democracy had long been of growing concern to the Commission of the European Community in its deliberations about the harmonization of corporate law in member countries (Pipkorn 1972, 1973, 1977) and its intention to promote collective European efforts towards improving employee involvement in the decision-making of companies (*Kommission der Europäischen Gemeinschaften* 1975, Wilpert 1976). The International Institute of Management, (Science Centre, Berlin), being already experienced in large international collaborative research ventures, (Heller and Wilpert 1977) saw fit to take up an earlier (spring 1972) suggestion of the EEC Commission to study 'the experience with different laws on industrial democracy'. From the beginning it was quite obvious that the scope of such research would surpass the intellectual and material resources of a single institute. Collaboration of scholars from various countries and an institutional pooling of support appeared to be highly advisable. Therefore, right after the Dubrovnik conference, the International Institute of Management invited colleagues from eight European countries, the USA and the EEC Commission to a workshop in Berlin (May 9–12, 1973)

'(1) to define some of the major practical problems posed by industrial democracy programs in the home countries of the participants;

(2) to review the major research efforts on issues of industrial democracy in these various countries;

(3) to attempt a joint definition of the main prevailing research needs (preferably in relation to the issues posed in the area of organization theory) and to develop the elements for an appropriate research strategy;

(4) to work towards the design of a concerted international research effort in that area'.

The individual motives of participants at that first workshop (which included an official from the EEC Commission) to do research in the field of industrial democracy were very widely spread. They included:

i. Political and philosophical interests which ranged from interest in problems of democracy at a macro-level and how to integrate man's work with the conventional notion of political democracy and in issues of freedom and self-government to the social issues of control and governance in and of organizations.

ii. Interests relating to social science theory. These covered theoretical perceptions of industrial relations as a set of instances of a general conflict and bargaining theory and as specific phenomena to be integrated in theories of social change at a macro-level.

iii. Methodological interests comprising interest in problems of measuring the participative potential of organizations, the measurement of organizational and individual characteristics in the context of participative situations, and methodological issues of international and inter-institutional comparison as well as problems relating to the development of dynamic models of organizational behaviour.

iv. Interests growing out of ongoing/past research. Such interests grew partly out of frustrations with generally prevailing legalistic comparativism or the perceived lack of rigour and comprehensiveness of comparative social science research in the area. Partly the interests stemmed from ongoing and past research on participation in which some members of the group were involved.

v. Practical needs and interests. These related to recent national as well as international developments (EEC) and the personal involvement of some of the participants in implementing change proposals for participatory systems and their implication for the governance of industrial organizations, as well as the interest in the general problems of social science research and its potential contribution to political institutions and policy making.

Given the diversity of interests it came as a surprise to all participants that the dynamics of discussion soon began to converge on the issue that proved to become the central challenge and joint focus for the whole IDE research group: *The differential distribution of power and influence in organizations subject to different types of national industrial democracy schemes.*

Two crucial decisions were made at this first IDE workshop. Firstly, that a joint research project should be developed collectively in relation to the central theme, and secondly that the research should not only cover the main EEC member countries but ought also to take into account the very important developments in industrial democracy in all Scandinavian countries, Israel, and Yugoslavia. Thus, the origin of the research, its particular topic, and the countries so far involved are genuinely European. However, right from the beginning the IDE team had its trans-Atlantic links by virtue of the collaboration with two outstanding American scholars: Stanley Seashore (Ann Arbor, Michigan) and William H. Starbuck (Milwaukee, Wisconsin), who both contributed significantly in the developmental stages of the project.

The series of international workshops that followed the first Berlin workshop already had participants from all eleven countries originally involved in the IDE research: Belgium, Denmark, France, Holland, Italy, Israel, Norway, Sweden, the U.K., West Germany, and Yugoslavia (with Finland joining in 1975/76). The diversity of the personal impetus of the new team members to be involved in a joint research on industrial democracy fitted well into the original spectrum mentioned above.

The first five workshops (Berlin, May, July, and October 1973; Paris, February 1974; Copenhagen, June 1974) saw the development of the theoretical framework, the research design, design of instruments, and their adaptation to the various vernaculars. The period from July 1974 to April 1975 was spent testing the validity of concepts, the instruments, and the feasibility of standardized procedures under fieldwork conditions in an extensive pilot study interrupted only by a pilot phase mid-term evaluation (Sixth IDE workshop, London, December 1974). The seventh plenary workshop in Bled, Yugoslavia (May 1975) marked the end of a two-year planning period. Its results were published by the IDE International Research Group (IDE 1976). The actual fieldwork of data collection began in summer and autumn 1975 and lasted in some countries until summer 1977.

A 'social contract' (see Appendix E) was developed in May 1975 and was accepted by the whole international team at the occasion of the Eighth plenary meeting (Paris, December 1976). It covers such aspects as collective ownership of the data, publication rights, and conventions on acknowledgements. In Bled (May 1975) it was also decided that all national teams would prepare a qualitative but standardized and comparable description of the national industrial relations contexts (Country-CON) which provide the materials for the second publication 'European Industrial Relations'. Similarly, first steps towards planning specific data analysis steps were taken in May 1975, i.e. prior to the actual field work. The Berlin-based team, which co-ordinated the international collaboration throughout the whole project, developed the necessary infrastructure for handling the data coding and data processing at the same time as individual country teams carried out their field work.

The 9th plenary meeting in Natanya (Israel) in October 1976 ratified the basic principles of a data analysis strategy developed meanwhile by the intensive work of a subcommittee. These principles were further elaborated and accepted by a special meeting of delegates from all participating countries in March 1977. The whole international IDE team met for its tenth plenary meeting at the occasion of the Second International Sociological Conference on Participation and Self-Management (Paris, September 1977). It dealt mainly with the mechanics of carrying through the data analysis and agreed upon the sequence in the elaboration of national and international reports.

The Analysis Committee proposed a draft outline of the international report which foresaw that individual chapters would be drafted by various team members, each in close co-operation and intensive interaction with a 'reference group' composed of a sub-set of all team members. First drafting efforts were done mainly during February and March 1978 in Berlin where access to computers and data base were most easily available. A second draft of the international report was completed after the 11th plenary IDE meeting in Rome (May 1978) which thoroughly discussed all chapters and developed guidelines for a second draft. Its progress was discussed at a meeting of drafters in Ghent/Belgium (November 1978). The twelfth plenary IDE meeting in Dubrovnik (March 1979) finalized the manuscript for this volume.

ORGANIZATION OF THE RESEARCH

It may have become clear from this historical account that the type of research we pursued required a particular mode of operation and co-operation. Organizational structures of research teams in general, and of international, inter-disciplinary teams in particular, have lamentably seldom been a topic of scientific discourse. And yet, as a wide range of organizational literature attests, structures impact outputs (Bavelas 1955). Why should it be different for research teams? Only a few references can be found in the literature.

Claessens (1962) discussed desirable research team compositions in terms of personality types and their optimal fit. Similarly, Fisch (1977) in his article, mainly reports studies of personal characteristics of team members and their effects on research outcomes. Joerges (1977) in his very perceptive discussion of conditions for scientific creativity reports little if any research on the microstructural aspects of research teams. An approach that is more focussed on organization-psychological issues is taken by Bilitza (1978), who considers the structure of research institutes, their leadership and group dynamic characteristics, and the relevant scientific community as their organizational environment. But little can be derived prescriptively for large project teams. Some of the few accounts of the forms and processes in international, inter-disciplinary research teams[1] are found in Szalai and Scheuch (1972), Mabry et al. (1966), and in Farah and Jennings (1977), whose experience is very much congruent with our own. Given that research teams can be considered as micro-organizations, and given that organizational forms are related to their eventual outcomes, it clearly matters which structure is chosen in international projects.

A comprehensive typology of approaches to 'gathering of information and the analysis of data across a number of distinct cultures, societies or political entities' has been developed by Rokkan (1969, p. 645). In this he distinguishes four major categories shown in Figure 3.1. He further differentiates the aspects of

	Sites/units of study	
	Within one nation	Within several nations
Research Organization In one nation only	I The typical single nation study	II Typically secondary analysis of data already available for several nations
In several nations	III Co-operative international research in one nation	IV The typical co-operative cross-national study

Figure 3.1 Typology of approaches to the gathering of data cross-nationally

design development, data collection, data analysis, and data interpretation which can either be done by one national team or internationally.

Fourcade and Wilpert (1975) have further refined Rokkan's category IV which is the only one relevant for our context. They distinguish between three types:

Type I: Centralized-hierarchical research project. It is the project that is conceived, developed, implemented, and controlled exclusively by one scholar or a group of researchers in one research centre. Data collection is done in various countries by the respective national team itself or with the help of collaborators ('correspondents'). Data evaluation, their interpretation, and funding is also provided centrally. As example might serve the study by Haire, Ghiselli, and Porter (1966). Centralized expenditure of funds and high control of conceptual tightness of such projects must be weighed against the costs of inadequate translation and 'enculturation' of instruments, procedures, lack of motivation on the side of correspondents, and the danger of ethno-centric data interpretation.

Type II: Semi-decentralized research project. Here a researcher or national team co-opts other national teams more or less on equal grounds into an already ongoing research effort in which the idea, theoretical framework, and methodology is already developed by the central group. The individual country study will typically be considered as a valid piece of research in its own right. Similarly, funds might totally or partially be provided nationally, giving national teams a relative high level of autonomy. Data interpretations might be carried out jointly or by the central team. The commitment of national teams to the international part of the research will depend on the salesmanship of the central group and its capability to build an international identification of national teams with the overall research.

Type III: Decentralized-collective research project. This is the type of research organization chosen by the IDE research group. From its very beginning the project was collectively conceived, developed, implemented, and evaluated by the international team. While funding and the implementation of national studies were fully the responsibility of national teams, the overall design, procedures, comparative analysis, and interpretation of collectively-owned data were decided and agreed by the whole international group. Only international overheads, such as data processing, standardization of procedures, and facilitation of international team meetings were funded centrally.

The consequences of such an organization of cross-national collaborative research can be identified on various levels. The requirement that all national teams obtain their funding from home country sources immediately implies a rather high level of personal risk and involvement on the part of the principal national investigators. Before a home country audience they take the responsibility for ensuring a high quality research endeavour. This makes it necessary that, from an overall project design perspective, national sub-studies be comprehensive enough to be considered as projects in their own right. Hence the IDE design characteristics of looking at variation within countries as well as between them. Furthermore, in the international team each national collaborator has high stakes in ensuring that the overall research 'fits' idiosyncrasies of their own home country. In consequence, each member becomes responsible for the national sub-study as well as for the international project as a whole—the project is 'owned' by each of the members.

TOWARDS A MICRO-ANALYSIS OF THE RESEARCH PROCESS IN INTERNATIONAL TEAMS

At present we observe a growing awareness of the need to expand cross-national research collaboration in the social sciences. This is particularly true for the field of organization-related research. The formation (in 1974) of an European Group for Organization Studies (EGOS) and the establishment of an Organizational Psychology Division within the International Association of Applied Psychology at the occasion of its 19th international congress (Munich 1978) give evidence of this trend as well as collaborative agreements between national science foundations (Kaase and Miller: undated). Concomitantly, comparative research is mushrooming (Roberts 1970). International collaborative research ventures seem to pose problems of a particular kind or at least magnify general problems encountered in any collaborative research project to new and qualitatively different dimensions. So it is not surprising to note that members of international comparative projects have become keenly interested in the internal and external factors that influence the functioning and results of the research process itself (Mabry et al. 1966, Szalai and Scheuch 1972, Farah and Jennings 1977).

We are here confronted with a fundamental, hitherto largely neglected, problem of the sociology of science. While in Karl Mannheim's tradition the sociology of knowledge has accumulated considerable knowledge about the socio-policial, historical, and economic conditions of the generation of knowledge, we are still missing a micro-analytical approach which focusses on the interactive processes among researchers working together in a team. From an *a priori* point of view it can be argued that outputs of research groups are similarly influenced and determined by power relations, processes of influence and manipulation, affective relationships, inter-personal perceptions and attitudes, situational constraints and opportunities as the output of factory workers in a production line. The main grounds for the plausibility of such an assumption lies in the fact that research groups are organizations working towards objectives. To accomplish those objectives they must make choices and implement decisions. Research production is a social process. If this is so, then it might be important—similar to the methodological controls we introduce in social science research—to identify those group-dynamical and situational parameters of the research process that co-condition the results rather than to look only at the final product (see Fourcade and Wilpert 1976, and Bell and Newby 1977 for first attempts at this).

In other words, we need to discover dimensions that are relevant for the evaluation of research processes themselves, because of their co-determining effects on research outputs. Conventional research ethics largely prevent this. We are trained and expected to legitimate problem focus, design, methods, instruments, and analysis in terms of stringency of scientific argumentation but not in terms of their contributory process background.

Early on the IDE team felt the need to look into the internal and external factors that affected the team's own research process. To acknowledge the need was one thing, to meet it another. The best that could be done was to use personal recollections and the thorough minutes of team meetings in order to distil a set of insights into those factors that retrospectively appear as important for any international team venturing into joint research.

Team composition

The whole IDE team was recruited from thirteen different countries and a large variety of disciplines (sociology and organizational sociology, industrial relations, organizational and industrial psychology, business administration, engineering, political science). Members further differed considerably in terms of age (from early twenties to late fifties), professional experience, scientific interest, and methodological orientation. Similarly, their social and language skills (the lingua franca of the project was English) varied drastically. So it was to be expected that jointly coming to terms with conceptual issues posed a major problem. Plenary meetings at times proved to be trying endurance exercises in collective socialization and in redressing the imbalance of communication and language skills. This may to some degree account for the comparatively long developmental period between 1973 and 1975 when a common project 'lingo' was developed that facilitated easy communication. And yet, often we discovered that a basic issue believed to have been thoroughly discussed and collectively resolved, emerged again as a major misunderstanding in subsequent meetings.

National and international funding agencies and research institutions are usually unfamiliar with such lengthy periods of project development which require seed money and a readiness of higher risk taking by funding bodies. Given the very desirable and fertile heterogeneity of the IDE team, the research itself would probably never have got off the ground without the initial generous support of the International Institute of Management (Science Centre, Berlin). Any research venture of this magnitude, composition, and approach is likely to encounter similar project development problems.

Infrastructure

Some twenty-five senior researchers from thirteen countries and some twenty research institutions collaborated in the IDE project over a period of more than five years. Some thirty additional research support institutions provided financial aid for national sub-studies or the international collaboration. The research thus implied the construction and maintenance of a major personal and institutional network that was to be operative over considerable space dimensions and time horizons. Differences in evaluation standards for project proposals, as well as ensuing differences in time-lags from proposal submission to approval often provided taxing problems to harmonize the timing of various research phases. It was to be expected that some country teams were faster in completing certain research steps than others simply due to better and faster resource access. In fact at the very end it became evident that the lack of funds in two countries prevented them from completing the field research in all of the various company types that were agreed upon internationally. Although considerable ambiguities of time-horizons must be considered as intrinsic aspects of any international research project, national funding agencies usually press for more precise time commitments. Any further extension of the time-plan for purposes of accommodating the two countries lagging behind would therefore have seriously jeopardized the overall time-limits posed on the other country teams. So it was decided to include them even on the basis of incomplete data sets.

Technical problems in multi-sited research like the IDE project quickly surpass the normal magnitude found in smaller ventures. Letters delayed due to postal slow-downs, coding instructions misunderstood by junior assistants who had not participated in plenary meetings, and data-tapes wrongly specified have further delaying effects. A case in point were our 'fool-proof' coding instructions. Since the data were to be read by an optical scanner in Berlin directly from coding sheets we simply had to instruct coders to code the values 'as you write' (i.e. for the majority of Western Europeans from left to right), since all necessary scale reversals would be done automatically by the scanner. No wonder we could make no sense out of the data our Berlin computing centre received from our colleagues in Israel!

In view of all the infrastructural uncertainties, the whole IDE research would probably have been doomed without the funding of an international overhead which facilitated about two plenary meetings every year and a modest international co-ordination budget to develop standardization, controls, and analysis procedures. Alas, to fund international overheads is uncommon for national fund granting agencies. In the case of our research we were finally successful, after substantial efforts, to obtain such a grant towards international overheads from two national agencies. This notorious reluctance of foundations is irrational if one considers the leverage effect which a small investment in international overheads receives through the multiplication effect of getting several nationally funded sub-studies simultaneously off the ground.

Dynamics

The choice of a specific model of project organization, team composition, and infra-structural parameters set the frame for the research process in an international team. We will try to illustrate this process by highlighting a few critical stages of the IDE research and by attempting to pin-point some of the crucial factors that retrospectively appear to have influenced its course. In the event it may become clearer how the process also conditioned results.

The biography of a research project—presumably like most biographies—can be described as a cumulative process of reducing options. In the phase of problem articulation the range of options appears to be widest. In the case of our study it was limited only by the institution that hosted the first project seminars and set the stage by inviting certain scholars to discuss the feasibility of joint research in the field of industrial democracy. Three factors seem to have been crucial in bringing the generally fluid atmosphere of the first seminars to a point where it started to 'jell': the personal fascination of each participant by the overall topic posed, the particular match of intellectual styles that stimulated each other, the general compatibility of personalities involved.

Design decisions immediately begin to limit the overall scope of a project for which at first appear to exist virtually infinite options. Those we discussed involved: focussing on macro-level factors such as political parameters of participation, comparing national policies, general values of country populations in connection with participation; focussing on institutional factors: trade union roles, multi-national companies, specific industrial sectors, specific companies and case studies versus cross-sectional approaches. Consensus, at this stage, is mandatory. Theoretical bases and conceptual orientations in the team have to be harmonized over lengthy and often stormy processes of consensus-seeking. Compromise solutions are often inevitable. They require compromise readiness among team members. On the benefit side of such consensus-building processes is the high level of commitment to the decisions taken. Costs, apart from the time requirement and frequency of necessary meetings, can accrue because compromise solutions may water down theoretical stringency. The unity of the collective effort becomes a value in itself for which it may be appropriate to give up niceties of theoretical purity. Here the tolerance of team members to live with somewhat ambiguous agreements is often tested to its limits. Age and the research experience of team members seemed to be important here, the younger members often having lower tolerance levels.

Decisions on choice of methods, procedures, and instruments further narrow the scope of a project because they determine effectively the data-base one is going to obtain in the end. At this stage we noticed hard bargaining among national teams. Everyone tried to bring in their 'pet ideas' in an apparent attempt to recapture what was possibly lost in the compromise decisions about overall design. Only at this stage was it decided—in a session that brought the whole team close to a breaking point—that a cross-sectional study was clearly to have preference over a longitudinal one. Pre-tests and pilot phase experiences helped to reduce maximal claims for the pursuit of certain research lines in favour of those that seemed feasible in terms of resource availability, time requirements, and access to data. Here the IDE team found it convenient to use the possibility of declaring a certain proposed feature of the research as 'optional' for teams interested (as 'mutualities') as opposed to those parts that were commonly obligatory ('communalities') or straight-forward national 'idiosyncracies'.

The actual fieldwork proved to be relatively problem-free apart from the usual problems inherent in any fieldwork of finding access to companies, respective delays, and standardization of procedures. A 'hand-book for field researchers', developed by the Berlin based co-ordination team, was quite useful for dispersing emerging uncertainties.

Planning the strategies and procedures for the final data analysis once more raised the internal level of conflict considerably. It quickly became evident that this crucial task was to have a major 'gate-keeping' effect on the final product by defining the options for possible data interpretation. Rather than developing the plans for analysis in plenary meetings, time constraints, limited funds, and required expertise suggested the appointment of an analysis committee which was to meet several times to develop specific guidelines for later data analysis. Appointing a limited number of team members to this committee proved to be a rather contentious decision-making process. Theoretical and methodological biases had to be balanced while keeping the committee to a size that would enable it to work efficiently. The mandate to the committee, that they should thoroughly discuss, and possibly implement recommendations that were submitted by non-members helped to alleviate tensions. Finally, it was in line with the collective spirit of the whole research that all country teams had to approve the analysis recommendations of the committee. The existence of a 'social contract' (see Appendix E) may also have contributed to the consensus because the collective ownership of data stipulated therein implied the opportunity for alternative data reanalysis.

Any purposive group, hence any research team, requires leadership. The leadership function in the IDE team was strongly affected by the group culture which was pre-conditioned by the collective-decentralized organizational model chosen for the research. Leadership was variable in the sense that different people or teams took on a leading role in shifting and moving decisions in certain directions, depending on the issues at stake, their respective interests, or expertise. If any national team felt strongly enough about a particular issue it could usually delay the decision-making or force it into its own preferred direction. Thus, no single locus of leadership existed. An institutional reflection of this situation in the IDE team was the particular mode of chosing a chairman for a given session. At some point on the agenda the chairman at his discretion, would turn to another colleague and ask him to take the chair and it was generally understood and agreed that the request could not be turned down. In fact it virtually never was.

The function of central administration and record-keeping with control checks (comparability of questionnaire translation, standardization of procedures for data collection and coding) is certainly necessary for any research. In the case of our study it was performed by the team at the International Institute of Management in Berlin. By virtue of preparing agendas and minutes of meetings this role implies a leadership role, too. It was further fostered by the decision that all data analysis was primarily to be performed in Berlin computing centres. Here quick decision-making on feasibility grounds becomes often unavoidable as anyone with experience in computer-based data analysis realizes. Basing the administration of international overhead funds in Berlin with the concomitant discretionary freedom of allocating priorities, strengthened opportunities for the Berlin team to influence certain decisions. This freedom, on the other hand, was limited by the earmarking of the grant items and the obligation to refer any major resource allocation to the international team as a whole.

Only the informal processes characteristic of any social system remain to be considered. Evidence is abundant that they existed in the IDE team as well. It would have been amusing, challenging, and revealing to unfold the meaning of stereotypes such as 'the Scandinavians think . . .' or 'the French want . . .' Similarly, the observable emergence of nicknames for individuals is also a feature that undoubtedly influenced the interactions and their results. Humorous after-dinner speeches with strikingly realistic caricatures of individual members or national teams could most likely be interpreted as tension-reducing and feedback devices as was an unforgettably successful charade evening at one meeting full of puns on individuals and IDE jargon. It was symptomatic of the team's mode of operation that informal preparations for a meeting or a session absorbed considerable time spent considering the 'group-dynamic' consequences of introducing a certain idea, plan, proposed line of action, and procedure. Such an awareness of group maintenance needs, shared by many members, may be necessary if decentralized-collective organization of research projects is to succeed. In consequence, it was the total configuration of structural, personal, and process elements in the IDE research that created an atmosphere of openness, mutual trust, commitment, lack of selfishness, and a general positive and supportive climate at meetings which made each of them a memorable event, even though discussions on substance and procedures may have been heated at times.

NOTE

1 For a more general review of the literature cf. Glaser (1977). Problems of inter-disciplinary research approaches are discussed in di Castri (1978).

DESIGN OF THE RESEARCH; METHODS AND INSTRUMENTS

GENERAL CONSIDERATIONS

In this chapter, emphasis will be put on operationalizations and analysis procedures with respect to the various variables and their interrelationships. In this large-scale project a wealth of information has become available, by means of a variety of data collection methods and analysis procedures. Of course not all of this can be reported and discussed in this chapter. A selection of problems and issues that are thought to be most relevant and necessary for a full understanding of the present study has been made.

The choice of the research design, and, consequently, the nature of the data that are collected, determine the possible insight into the phenomena under study. The type of research study chosen has led to a number of restrictions with respect to the conclusions that can be drawn from its results.

The present study can be characterized as an empirical field-study. The data have been collected *in situ* and neither an experimental control of irrelevant variables nor a planned manipulation of independent variables was possible. Of course, the data obtained in such a study are less artificial and the interpretations are more generalizable to real life situations than in a laboratory experiment or a simulation study, but, at the same time, conclusions, particularly pertaining to causal relationships, have to be more tentative.

It has been pointed out in Chapter 2 that the data that have been collected are, to quite some degree, reputational in nature. Not exclusively: as will be described in the next section objective measures of various organizational characteristics, personal antecedents, and participative structures of the companies have been made. In addition, some of the individual idiosyncrasies of reputational information have been avoided by averaging the scores over various key-informants. Also, attempts have been made to use data sources like minutes, documents, and other objective sources of information. But it cannot be denied that a large part of the information has a reputational character, which also calls for prudence in interpretation.

Most of the conclusions must be inferred from the given data, or from the interrelationships and patterns within the data. It was not possible to choose a design in which the phenomenon is studied by analyzing the effects of newly introduced measures of change in existing procedures either in a strictly experimental (random assignments of experimental and control group to the two treatments) or in a quasi-experimental design (Cook and Campbell, 1976). This again creates difficulties for conclusions and interpretations, especially with respect to causality.

On the other hand, in many cases extensive feedback procedures have been applied at the company and national level, so as to validate tentative conclusions and interpretations. In addition, attempts have been made to infer causality from the data, by applying principles of path analysis, cross-lagged panel analysis, multiple and moderated regression techniques and logical analysis.[1]

Another restriction in the design is related to the cross-sectional character of the study. Strictly speaking, if one wants to derive conclusions with respect to the impact of formal regulations on actual participative behaviour, this phenomenon should be studied in a transient situation in which a comparative analysis before and after the change is made. However, since it takes quite some time before such an important set of regulations is fully realized and implemented, such a longitudinal study would require quite a long time, even if such an occasion of major changes in the legalistic structure of participation in a country or in certain organizations did occur.[2]

On the other hand, in some countries significant changes in participatory structure have taken place during the study, and effects of changes could in fact be observed.

Within the limits of the chosen research design (a non-experimental cross-sectional field study using rather extensively reputational data) an attempt has been made to give optimal care to the usual methodological requirements. Instruments have been constructed and checked empirically before use, samples of firms and samples of respondents within them have been drawn according to strict regulations and are generally large, the information itself is as varied as possible within the given research objectives, and for the analysis at various levels of aggregation use has been made of a variety of multivariate procedures. Finally, the interpretation of the findings could be based on expertise from the different disciplines and theoretical orientations available within the international research team.

Phases of the study

It has taken over six years to plan, carry out and report this large scale study, which has developed through the following phases:

i. Model building

As has been described in chapter 2 quite some time has been devoted to the theoretical formulation of the main questions and research objectives, the definition of the different concepts, and the possible framework in which the variables and their relationships could be placed in a theoretically meaningful way. Various hypotheses and theoretical relationship patterns have been discussed and evaluated in the light of the existing literature and experience of the participants. Originally the model derived from these discussions could be typified as an heuristic model. It served as a source for the selection of concepts and their operationalization, and as a basis for the formulation of expectations and hypotheses. Gradually however, the ontological nature of the model received more attention, and part of the subsequent analysis will be devoted to the verification of the model itself, by testing the various interrelationship patterns, causal paths and feedback loops.

ii. Selection and/or creation of potential instruments

Once the theoretical framework and model had been adopted, the phase of the construction of questionnaires, scales and other indices started. In most instances no ready-made instruments were available and new scales and questionnaires had to be constructed. In this phase also the list of decisions, the basis of the study of the distribution of power and participation in organizations, was drawn up in its preliminary form. More specific attention to this decision-list will be given in the next section.

iii. Pilot study

An important part of the time prior to the actual data collection was devoted to attempts to test the model, the quality of the instruments and the research plan in general. In the first place the questionnaires and scales, which had been constructed in English had to be translated into the local languages. From cross-cultural research it is known that this is not merely a linguistic matter. In many ways the translation process can change subtle connotations of words and statements, and, particularly in the case of questionnaires to be used in a comparative study, careful attention has to be given to this translation. The translation was carried out very diligently, often with co-operation between linguists and social scientists. In a number of cases the so called 'translation–back–translation–method' (Brislin et al., 1973) was applied in order to reach maximum comparability with the English version, and hopefully with the other versions as well.

It should be pointed out that the very difficult problem of cross-cultural comparability of research instruments was not fully solved in the IDE research. Strictly speaking, conclusions on differences with respect to measured constructs (e.g. attitudes, satisfaction, involvement) are only permitted if a number of requirements with respect to the equivalence of the items or the scales have been met (Drenth and van der Flier, 1976). Not all of these have been given sufficient attention, although it is doubtful whether such an equivalence study for so many scales and questionnaires for twelve countries could ever be carried out. The researchers aimed at simple wording, identical formats and presentations, comprehensibility of the questions and problems for the respondents, and similarity of the various concepts and phenomena to be studied, so as to warrant comparability. Additionally, it should be pointed out that, during the three years of theoretical discussions, model building, scrutinization of the concepts, and their operationalizations, a common language and a common understanding of what should be looked for grew within the team as a whole. This, plus the fact that each national research team was well informed about the developments in the area under study within its own country, may be seen as another argument for the cross-national comparability of the findings.

In each country a pilot study was carried out in which preliminary tests of the conceptual framework were made and in which the feasibility of the approach and the quality of the instruments were investigated. In each country at least one firm, and in some countries two or three firms, were included in the pilot sample. The total sample of respondents per country varied from 30 to over 125. The results, which were reported in separate country reports, were discussed and, consequently, the definite instruments were composed. The reports contained the frequency tables, an evaluative discussion of the questionnaires and interview procedures, some scale analyses, and some preliminary interpretations of the results. In one case this led to an official publication (Dupuy and Martin, 1977).

The reports showed in the first place a number of shortcomings and insufficiencies in the design. It seemed necessary to add a number of open interviews with management. Also the need for more information on social and economic characteristics of the industry as well as the region seemed apparent. A number of questions, either to be used generally or by a particular country or group of countries were also suggested as a result of this pilot study.

Secondly, a number of important conditions and constraints became obvious. Anonymity turned out to be a problem in some countries. A logical and generally applicable scenario was felt to be important. Time-constraints (both in view of keeping respondents' attention, and in view of it being made available by management) had been a problem. The pilot study showed that the theoretical orientation of social scientists interested in workers' participation does not always meet easy understanding and acceptance by workers and other employees living in quite a different culture. Phrasing of sentences, use of terminology, and application of concepts did not always fit with the social reality and orientations of the worker. Thorough screening of questions and scales with respect to this basic communication problem seemed necessary. Also the need for more than just one method (questionnaires) in the study of participation was stressed. A number of decisions were made as to the optimal size of groups (in case of group interviews) and to the questionnaires that had to be administered individually. Considerable changes in the wording and phrasing of the sentences were proposed and accepted. In addition, definite choices were made as to the form of the questionnaires and scales.

Thirdly, a number of other problems were encountered and had to be solved. It turned out that problems pertaining to the particular nature of the industry were so crucial that it was suggested and accepted that the study be restricted to only one or two industries, if possible. Also, the sampling procedures created a number of difficulties: what to do with immigrants, foreign workers; how long does someone have to be working in the firm before he can be accepted in the sample. Questions like these were discussed and operational decisions made during this phase.

iv. Main phase; data collection

The sampling of the firms, the sampling of the respondents per firm, and the procedure of the actual data collection are described in detail below.

v. Analysis and interpretation

Part of the data of each country team was analysed in a preliminary way in order to write both the company reports and the country reports. At the same time all the data were coded and sent to the International Institute of Management, Berlin, for central analysis. In a second round most of the countries made some further analysis, especially in comparison with the general trends in the total sample, in order to write a second country report, in which the national results are compared with the international data.

vi. Reporting

Details of publications and reports which have resulted or will result from this study were given in Chapter 1, and are referred to later.

The decision list

In a number of studies of participative structures in organizations respondents are asked to rate the perceived amount of influence for different levels in the organization (see for instance the 'control graph' studies of Tannenbaum, 1968). In asking these general questions, of course, the assumption is made that an accurate picture of control can be obtained from the average of all members' general judgements. As discussed in Chapter 2, this procedure can be criticized on several grounds (Abell, 1975). One of the weak points in the procedure seems to be the general nature of the question asked. Respondents are left free to make their own choice as to the kinds of decisions or issues to which this perceived influence or power should refer. Even if respondents do refer to major and important decisions the question is not a standardized one, since the saliency of issues might change from one group, or level in the organization to another.

In the present study it was decided not to leave the question open to the respondent, but to control for unwanted variance. Not only has the question as to the perceived influence and involvement been specified in terms of particular decisions, but also a deliberate selection of decisions has been made in order to make possible an analysis over various types of decision. In addition, not only the general sample but also supposedly well-informed key respondents have been used for this rating process. The selection and formulation of the decisions (in the interview always called 'issue', 'matter' or 'subject') was done carefully and after long discussions and empirical pretesting.

A first list contained over fifty items with a large variety in content, importance for the organization, and time perspective. Items were derived from, and compared with, similar taxonomic systems and decision-lists in the literature (Chauvey 1970, Van Dongen 1970, Heller 1971, Naschold 1969, Negandi and Prasad 1971, and Steiner 1970). Each country carried out a preliminary check of the suitability, completeness, and overlap of this list in the pilot study. On the basis of the pilot results and to keep an equal list of decisions for each country it was decided to reduce the original list to sixteen decisions (while each country was left to supplement the list idiosyncratically). Considerations for the reduction and composition of the final list were: comprehensibility, clearness, relevance; applicability at different levels of the organization; minimum of overlap in terms of content; sufficient variance according to the content categories— social, personnel, economic; sufficient variance according to the scope and time perspective of the company. Since it was not possible to construct and formulate a completely uniform list for all groups of respondents, it was decided to compose two versions that would differ slightly: one for level A (workers) and one for non-A levels. The order of presentation of the decisions had to guarantee a sufficient mix with regard to content and saliency. For the lists of decisions and their exact wording, see Appendix A.

The choice of the decisions was not easy, particularly since no universe of decisions could be defined, and consequently no sampling procedure could be followed. This is also the reason why an unequivocal categorization of decisions was hard to make. On *a priori* grounds the decisions have been categorized as shown in Figure 4.1.

		Content of decisions		
		Work/social conditions	Personnel	Economic aspects
Time perspective	Short-term	Task assignment Personal equipment Working conditions Working hours Holidays	Training courses Transfers	
	Medium-term	Work study Wage levels	Dismissals Hiring procedures New department head Appointment own supervisor	Reorganization
	Long-term			Investment New product

Figure 4.1 Decision-set paradigm

Definition of groups/levels

The central question of this study is concerned with differences in participation, influence, and involvement between the different hierarchical levels in the organization, but also relevant groups or institutions within and outside the company have been included in this comparison.

For the definition of the groups[3] the following characterizations have been used:

A—Workers, white- and blue-collar, without supervisory functions.

B—First-line supervisors—foremen—(lowest level with supervisory functions).

C—Middle managers: according to establishment usage; all hierarchical levels above B and below D (including staff members at comparable levels).

D—Top management: according to establishment usage all persons considered to belong to the top management of the establishment.

E—Level above the plant: control or supervisory groups, managerial bodies (e.g. conglomerate management), shareholders, or owners.

F—Permanent representative bodies at the establishment level, no matter of what origin: works' councils, workers' councils, union representative bodies, and union representatives like shop stewards.

G—Bodies/institutions outside the company—external groups—(not necessarily outside the establishment): unions, banks, community councils, regional planning councils, etc.

The definition and selection of these groups were based on the consideration that primary attention should be paid to the bargaining groups taking a central place in the decision-making in organizations. A logical consequence was that hierarchical levels were selected. The choice of Group F (representative organs) resulted from interest in the question to what extent the 'power' of these organs was different from or identical to that of the workers in general (A).

VARIABLES AND INSTRUMENTS

For a systematic description of the various variables and instruments that have been used in this study the model, already described and discussed in chapter 2, may serve as a guideline. For the sake of illustration the model is presented again in Figure 4.2.

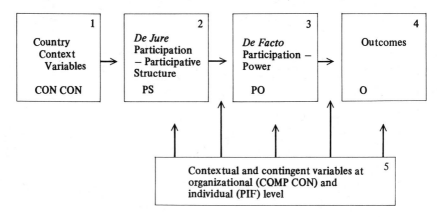

Figure 4.2 Hypothetical model of variable interactions

The following description of the various instruments and indices will follow the sequence of the variable boxes. The questionnaires are fully reproduced in Appendix A.

Country Context (CON CON: Box 1)

In a cross-national comparative study on the effects of different formal and/or legal systems of participation on the actual distribution of influence, power, and involvement in organizations, insight into the political, economic, and social backgrounds describing both the historical developments and the present situation in each respective country is of great importance. In the first place, the participation structures can only be fully understood if they are placed in a proper national perspective, and if they are seen as consequences of historical and social developments. Second, it is very likely that not only the participative and power structures themselves but also the relation between them has to be interpreted in the light of typical national socio-cultural and economic factors. In other words, the explanation of findings with respect to *de jure* and *de facto* participation and their interrelationships should be done in the light of the 'Country Context' information. Third, the analysis of the different national backgrounds can serve as a basis for generating interesting hypotheses. Cognizance of the rich historical and recent developments of industrial relations in the different countries may generate a number of questions that could be tested with the empirical material available in the study itself. Fourth, this information can serve as a basis for sub-grouping within the twelve countries. If some main groups of nations have to be distinguished within the realm of our study, a description of the socio-economic factors and industrial relations climate provides a fruitful basis for such distinctions.

Each country team has therefore produced a so-called Country Context Report and these are being published in a separate volume (IDE 1980). In order to guarantee maximum comparability and equivalence between the reports specific guidelines as to the content of the reports were formulated. The reports had to contain the following chapters:

i. Political power distribution;
ii. Economic situation of the country, and social stratification;
iii. Legal and factual aspects of the industrial relations system, the main bargaining structure, unions and public powers;
iv. Perspectives and prospective developments.

De Jure Participation Structure (PS: Box 2)

In the model the formal participation scheme in an organization (or in a country) is the core independent variable, and the researchers hoped for quite some variance in the PS box. The relationships between this and the other variables form a central section of the present research. The *de jure* participation structure describes the formal framework of participation in organizations. It may be based on national laws, bargaining contracts, or managerial policies. It should refer to formal, written-down, operative rules and regulations for the involvement of various parties in decision-making. Current practices are not covered by this index unless they are in some way enforceable. The level of formal participation was not investigated in a general way, but was specified with respect to the decisions or issues that have been selected.

Two questions have to be answered regarding *de jure* participation. In the first place, how can the amount of formal participation be measured and on what kind of scale does it have to be expressed? This scale should range from 'no access at all' to 'maximum say' in the decision-making process. It was decided to use the following six-point scale (called the Mode scale), to indicate the Mode of involvement of a particular group A to E:

1. No regulations.
2. Information (unspecified) must be given to the group.
3. Information *ex ante* must be given to the group (i.e. before the decision is made).

4. Consultation of the group is obligatory (i.e. group must always be consulted prior to the decisions taken).
5. Joint decision-making with the group (i.e. group has the power of veto and must give its approval).
6. Group itself has the final say.

The scale includes the well known trio 'information–consultation–co-determination' and has some similarity with Heller's Influence–Power Continuum (Heller 1976) and Vroom and Yetton's taxonomy of leadership methods (Vroom and Yetton 1973). The scale is a Guttman-type scale measuring the increasing degree to which a group participates in, and can determine the outcome of, the decision. Since the higher level includes all the previous ones, only one code nomination is theoretically possible.

Initially an extra level was included (see IDE 1976) between the present 3 and 4, namely 'Right of initiative (i.e. the group has the right to give an opinion about the issue on its own initiative'). This category has been dropped, since it has been found that it almost always collapsed with level 3. Apparently it was difficult to imagine a group having the right of being informed *ex ante* 3 and not having the right of initiative on that same issue. If this category is seen as a kind of general right to give advice, to present proposals etc. then this does not presuppose, for instance, the level 'information *ex ante* must be given', as a true Guttman-type scale should.

The second question is: What is the basis for the extent of participation indicating the kind of regulations, or laws that prescribe the participative involvement of the group or level in question? These Bases refer to normal situations, not to extreme conflictful cases. Basis categories such as constitution, laws, and bargaining contracts, have been included. For further details, see Chapter 6.

For the analysis of *De Jure* Participation and its relationships with other variables in the model the Mode scores have usually been used, while the Base scores will gain more attention in secondary analyses. Basically, the *De Jure* Participation information can be coded by organization as in the PS matrix described in Figure 4.3. A similar PS matrix per country can be constructed, which contains average mode scores over organizations in that particular country. In some

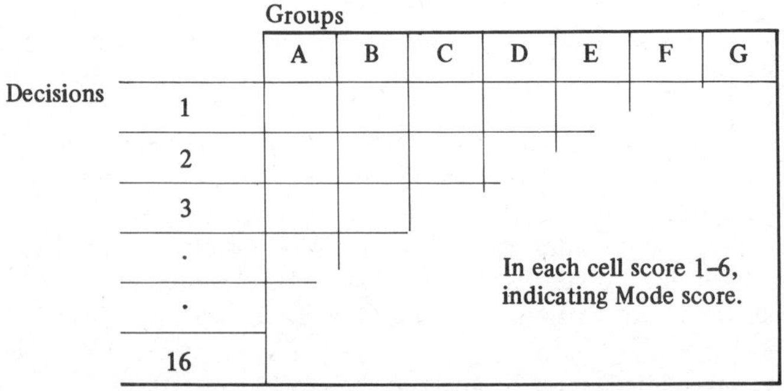

Figure 4.3 *De Jure* Participation (PS information matrix per organization or per country (average Mode scores over organizations)

countries there is very little variance between organizations since the *de jure* participation is mostly ·based upon national legislation or national bargaining contracts. In these cases the national PS matrix will hardly differ from the individual company PS matrices.

De Facto **Participation (PO: Box 3)**

De facto participation is the actual involvement, participation, and influence of the different groups. Several measures have been developed and used:

 i. Rating by experts (PO1).
 ii. Rating by the respondent (PO2).
iii. Other indices (PO 3).

In the following sections the different *de facto* participation indices will be described in more detail.

i. Rating of Influence by experts (PO 1)

Various types of questions were asked to the key respondents.

(*a*) Influence (PO1-a)

Key respondents were supposed to be experts with regard to knowledge of the distribution of power and influence within the company. They were asked to rate on a five-point scale, ranging from 'no influence' to 'very much influence', the amount of Influence which different groups have. Sometimes the expert could answer only part of the questionnaire, because of insufficient knowledge with respect to either part of the decision-list or some of the groups to be rated. Often the ratings of a number of key respondents were collected; in some extreme cases only one answer per cell per company could be obtained.

The key respondents were supposed to be experts but in the process of interviewing the researchers themselves could sometimes acquire a more accurate picture of the influence patterns than any single respondent. When the researchers felt that averaging experts' rating would provide a biased picture they substituted the researchers' ratings for that of the experts. In the majority of cases, however, differences between experts were treated as rating errors and the different ratings were averaged. In some countries sometimes substantial differences in key ratings were found, especially when key respondents belonged to different interest groups (management, unions). These differences will be the subject of secondary analysis.

The Influence matrix per organization has the form shown in Figure 4.4. It is also possible to construct a country Influence matrix; in that case the figures in the cells indicate the average PO1-a scores over organizations per country.

(*b*) Disagreement (PO1-b)

A second question answered by the key respondents was aimed at collecting information on whether or not the decision had usually involved disagreement,[4] to be indicated by answers: yes—no—no answer. Per organization a disagreement matrix can be composed as indicated in Figure 4.5. The extent of Conflict involved in a decision is indicated by the percentage of key persons that reported disagreement on that decision. These percentages can be averaged over decisions, indicating a total organizational 'disagreement' or 'Conflict' score.

Groups

		A	B	C	D	E	F	G
Decisions	1							
	2							
	3							
	.							
	.							
	16							

In each cell score 1–5, indicating average rating over key respondents

Figure 4.4 Influence (PO1-a) information matrix per organization

	Answer categories	·Yes	No	Don't know	No answer
Decisions	1				
	2				
	3				
	.				
	.				
	16				

Figure 4.5 Disagreement (PO1-b) information matrix per organization

(c) Final say (PO1-c)

In the third place the key respondents were asked to indicate which group (A through G) had the final say in case of a disagreement as reported in PO1-b. Because of the small numbers only simple frequency distributions were computed per country.

(d) Optional influence items (PO1 opt.)

In some countries a number of additional questions were asked on the power and participation structure. These concerned negative power (Questionnaire 4, 5, 6), metapower (7, 8), and effects and limitations with respect to the work of the works' council (9, 10, 11). There will be no further discussion of these questions here since this report will be restricted to the communalities in the questionnaires.

ii. Rating of Involvement by respondents (PO 2)

Three types of questions were asked to the general sample.

(a) Involvement (PO2-a)

Each respondent was asked to indicate the extent to which he perceived himself to be involved in the several decisions. The six options from the PS-scale were adapted for individual use:

1. I am not involved at all.
2. I am informed about the matter beforehand.

3. I can give my opinion.
4. My opinion is taken into account.
5. I take part in the decision-making with equal weight.
6. I decide on my own.
As will be clear the scale initially produces data at an individual level. Derived scores at the group and organizational level will be discussed below.

In a number of countries an experiment was carried out to identify the scaling positions of the different modes. In two countries rather large samples of judges completed the rating, whereas in three other countries smaller numbers of raters participated. Not all completed forms were useful; sometimes only one or two modes had been rated, or the rater had reversed the scale. The useful ratings were used to calculate average ratings per country and for the total sample. Table 4.1 presents the mean scale for the 4 modes between the given values of 0 for mode 1 and 10 for mode 6.

Table 4.1
Scale values for modes on a 10-point scale (1 = 0, 6 = 10)

Countries	Modes						N
	1	2	3	4	5	6	
Norway	0	1.65	3.46	5.70	7.48	10	62
Germany (West)	0	2.38	4.12	6.12	7.90	10	30
Holland	0	2.-	3.86	6.21	7.79	10	7
Belgium	0	0.9	2.1	4.7	6.8	10	5
U. K.	0	1.75	3.-	4.5	6.5	10	2
Total	0	1.84	3.60	5.78	7.57	10	106

The ratings based on the total sample show a remarkable interval character. With the exception of the 'jump' from mode 5 to 6, which is somewhat larger than the other differences, the average ratings produced a quite satisfactory equal-appearing interval scale. Admitted, this experiment had a small-scale character, and only five countries participated in the experiment. Moreover, there were some differences between countries (they may be interesting) and the variances were not negligable. Within the limits of this experiment, however, the results encouraged the researchers as to the usefulness of the scale.

(*b*) Desired Involvement (PO2-b)
A similar question was asked with respect to the amount of involvement that the respondents would desire. The same scale with identical scale positions was used for the measurement of Desired Involvement. This scale also provides individual scores in the first instance. The relation of this Desired Involvement score with the actual Involvement score (PO2-a) will be discussed below.

(*c*) Desired involvement of representative organ (PO2-c)
Finally the respondent was asked whether he would like the representative body (or, in companies where more than one representative organ existed, the most important body for participation for that issue) to have a say in the decisions in question (answers: yes–no–I don't know). This information has likewise been used at the individual level.

iii. Other indicators of influence and involvement (PO 3)

It was felt that a more in-depth study of a number of central decision-making processes would provide additional insight into the influence and power dynamics in the organization. A variety of techniques was to be employed, such as identifying bargaining systems, tracer techniques and the snowball technique.

Identifying bargaining systems is done by checking agendas and minutes of negotiations, works' council meetings, etc. On the basis of objective information and expanded by in-depth interviews with relevant partners in the bargaining process the initially preferred outcomes and ultimately preferred outcomes can be detected and the power employed in the solution of the problem can be estimated. In addition, coalition patterns and forces beyond control can be identified. Extensive use of this technique has been made in Abell's study in the U.K. coal-mines (Abell, 1975). Tracer techniques try to provide insight into historical developments of issues involving conflict by analysing phases in the historical process in this case looking particularly at the influence and initiatives of different parties or persons. The snowball technique is an interview technique which starts with an informant, who is relevant to a particular issue (involving conflict). On the basis of the first interview the next relevant informant is selected (often the opponent of the first interviewee). This may lead to the third person to be interviewed etc.

It will be clear that these methods are not mutually exclusive and that they may complement each other. A standard interview scheme for the PO3 methodology was developed. It was suggested that contentious issues derived from works' council minutes, and issues that were solved by influence processes and compromise should be studied. Secondly, it was advised that issues relevant for the shop floor as well as strategic decisions salient for management should be selected.

Unfortunately the PO3 exercise could not be carried out to the extent planned. Practical problems such as time, resources, and refusals on the part of management prevented a large-scale study along these lines. In a number of countries however some of these PO3 analyses were carried out and brought in interesting qualitative information.

A Conceptual Overview

At this point we can associate the different PS and PO measures to the theoretical definitions of participation, power and involvement, as developed in chapter 2. In Figure 4.6 the classification of the relevant terms and their operationalizations are indicated.

Firstly, the distinction between *de jure* and *de facto* participation, discussed in Chapter 2, is reflected in the PS scale on the one hand and the PO scales on the other. The PO1 scale and the PO2 scale reflect the concepts of Influence as rated by experts and Involvement as subjectively experienced by the sample respondents, respectively. Level two of the behavioural PO2 scale can be called 'informative involvement', levels 3 and 4 'consultative involvement' and levels 5 and 6 '(co) determination'.

Some authors like to refer to the '(co) determination' type of involvement as 'power'. In chapter 2 the concept of 'power', more specifically indicated as 'bargaining power', has been restricted to indicate (co) determination (PO2 level 5 and 6) in decisions which generate conflict. Although there is an index for the extent of conflict involved in (PO1-b question) a distinction between conflictual and non-conflictual decisions in relation to the involvement scores (PO2) could not be made, since the PO1-b question was answered by the experts and the PO2 question by the sample respondents. Therefore, the theoretical distinction between power, C-Involvement, and $\tilde{C}$-Involvement in Figure 2.4 could not be extended in the actual analysis and the concept of power in the strict sense, as developed in chapter 2, could not be analysed.

In Figure 4.6 a schematic classification of the concepts used and corresponding scales is presented.

	Participation	
	De Facto Participation	
De Jure Participation (PS-scale)	Influence (PO1 scale)	Involvement (PO2 scale)
1. No regulation 2. Information, general 3. Information ex ante 4. Consultation 5. Joint decision-making 6. Group final say	1. No influence 2. Little influence 3. Moderate influence 4. Much influence 5. Very much influence	*Informative* 1. Not involved 2. Information afterwards *Consultative* 3. Opinion given 4. Opinion into account *(Co) determination* 5. Equal weight in decision making 6. Own decision

Figure 4.6 Scheme with various scales and concepts

Outcomes (O: Box 4)

The term 'outcome' may suggest a variety of measures of various levels of aggregation, such as economic factors, inter-group relations, adaptability and growth of the organization. In this connection however, the term refers mainly to the respondents' evaluations of various aspects of participation, which have been measured with a series of questions and which have later on been aggregated in scale scores. The only objective indices of these attitudes, included in this study, were absenteeism and turnover. It should be pointed out that in a number of cases not only the aggregated scales scores, but also the individual items have been used.

This section will describe five major scales, only three of which can be considered more or less direct outcome scales, namely Satisfaction with Participation (OPART), Rating of Consequences (OROC), and Satisfaction (OSAT). The other two scales, Rating of Needs (ORON) and Climate (CLIM), turned out to have a more contingent or even conditional character with respect to the core variables, and have been applied accordingly in the course of the study. It is only for 'historic' reasons that both ORON and CLIM are presented in this section of outcome variables.

All five scales were tried out in the pilot phase in each country. For the decision as to the final format of the questionnaires the following criteria were applied:
  i. time required for administration;
 ii. international comparability of the data obtained;
iii. applicability for different levels and different systems;
 iv. avoidance of duplication;
  v. relation to other research results;
 vi. similar factor-analytic structure and homogeneity in different countries.

As has been said the objective was to use similar scales in all countries. For specific reasons a country team sometimes added new items or constructed new scales but each country also applied the standard set of scales. These will be discussed in this section. Homogeneity indices will be reported for the scales and sub-scales for each country separately. The tables with a-coefficients for each country are reproduced in Appendix B, 1-4. As the homogeneity-index Cronbach's alpha coefficient was used (Cronbach 1970: 161). The coefficients have been computed on the total sample.

i. Satisfaction with Participation (OPART)

The items in this scale have to do with the general evaluation of, and satisfaction with, participation. Most items have been written specifically for this study, with the exception of items 7-11,[5] which were taken from the study of Koopman and Werkman (1973) and which had the highest loadings on a participative leadership scale. The other items refer to the evaluation of indirect participation, especially through elected representatives (like shop stewards, works' councils, department councils, participatory committees).

On the basis of factor analyses three scales were constructed:
OPART-D, consisting of items 7-11, measuring attitudes to direct participation.
OPART-E, consisting of items 3, 5, 12 and 13, referring to the evaluation of the representative body (bodies)
OPART-I, consisting of items 1, 2, 4 and 6, indicating respondents' interest in the representative organ(s).

The highest homogeneities (App. Table 4.1, Appendix B) are found for the scale 'Attitudes to Direct Participation' (OPART-D), ranging from .74 to .87. This is apparently a reliable and homogeneous scale. The two other scales are less satisfactory. The a-coefficients for 'Evaluation of Representative Body' (OPART-E) range from .50 to .81, most coefficients being in the 60's and 70's. The 'Interest in Representative Body' (OPART-I) scale shows coefficients mostly in the .40's, the .50's, and the .60's and only three coefficients are .70 or higher. The interpretations with respect to the OPART-I scores should be made with some reservation. Item 15 in the 'Satisfaction with Participation' (OPART) scale has been treated separately. This item asks for a more general rating of the influence distribution with respect to the different groups in the company. This procedure is similar to the control graph method (Tannenbaum 1968). The data on item 15 have been treated in the following way: of the seven groups (A-G) average ratings of four groups (A, B, C, D) have been computed. Several derived scores (for example differences between groups (e.g. B-A, D-A), an overall average rating for a particular group, mean differences of a group with all other groups) can be based upon these OPART-15 scores. The pattern of scores for groups A, B, C, and D takes the form of a control graph.

As has been said, the 'Direct Participation' (OPART-D) scale has been used not only as a dependent variable in this study but also as a conditional or contingent variable. On theoretical grounds, it can be conceived that the evaluation of direct participation is influenced not only by the extent to which the subordinate is involved in decision-making and may determine this level of participation, but also by the extent to which formally prescribed rules for participation are fully realized.

ii. Rating of Consequences (OROC)

This scale is concerned with the perceived consequences of participation. Two separate but similar lists of questions were made up, one for indirect participation through elected representatives (OROC-R) and one for direct participation (i.e. decision-making in one's own job (OROC-D). Both scales consist of five questions (information, acceptability of decisions, quality of decisions, promotion of interests, increase of influence) plus a number of optional items (6–9). On the longer scale two factors were hypothesized: one concerned with efficiency (items 1, 2, 3, 6, 7) and one with power equalization (4, 5, 9). This expectation was not substantiated by factor analysis. This is the reason why just one (shorter) scale (1–5) has been used. The homogeneities for the two scales in the different countries are given (App. Table 4.2) in Appendix B. We see that in general the alpha coefficients for the two sub-scales are satisfactory and the interpretations of these scales can be assumed to be based on sufficiently reliable scale information.

iii. Rating of Needs (ORON)

This scale is aimed at discovering the importance which is given to the needs 'to have influence in one's own job' (3) and 'to have effective representatives in the representative body' (7) among some seven other needs to be fulfilled in the job. Respondents had to pick the three most and the three least important items from the list of nine, producing a score of 0, 1, or 2 per individual for each need. As indicated in the introduction to this section, the 'Rating of Needs' was treated as a contingent variable, and more specifically as a personal background variable.

iv. Satisfaction (OSAT)

The items in this scale reflect the general satisfaction which respondents have with respect to their work, working conditions, colleagues, supervisors, etc. Most of the questions were derived from a Belgian scale used by Vervinckt (1975). In the first place a total score based upon all items was used (OSAT). In addition, two extra scales were constructed, the first, (OSAT-W), concerned primarily with the job and the work (items 1, 5, 10, 12), and the second, (OSAT-C), concerned with management, working conditions, and the company in general (items 3, 6, 9, 13). For the a-coefficients see Appendix B, App. Table 4.3. The reliabilities of the different satisfaction scales are quite satisfactory, especially those of the total scale (OSAT) and 'Satisfaction with Work' (OSAT-W).

The coefficients for 'Satisfaction with Company' (OSAT-C) are slightly lower, but in general not below standard.

v. Climate (CLIM)

This form consists of thirteen items and is aimed at measuring the 'climate' of the organization. Items are based on publications by Litwin and Stringer (1967), and Payne and Pheysey (1971). Within the total scale two sub-scales could be distinguished. The first scale (CLIM-S meaning 'Structure') based on the first 10 items is designed to measure the clarity of authority relationships and communication, and the visibility of the structure of the organization. The second (CLIM-R meaning 'Relations') based on items 11–13, is concerned with management–employee relations. The alpha coefficients for these two sub-scales for the different countries are presented in Appendix B. App. Table 4.4. It can be seen that the first sub-scale is very satisfactory. With one exception the homogeneities differ very little between the countries and are of a high magnitude. The second scale raises more difficulties. In a number of countries (Sweden and Denmark) the homogeneity is satisfactory, in others it is low (U.K. and Yugoslavia) and in the rest it is moderate. One has to realize, of course, that the scale is very short (only 3 items).

The scores on the 'Climate' scales can be analysed at an individual level but seem only to make sense at a higher level of aggregation (department, company). Here again it should be pointed out that this variable has been treated as a contingent or context (at organizational level) variable and not as an outcome variable.

A number of closing remarks and a discussion of an overall factor analysis on the total sample and per country will conclude this section. For Climate, Satisfaction with Participation, and Satisfaction 5-point Likert-type scales were used in the original questionnaire. For each scale an average score has been calculated for each respondent. This score has been multiplied by 10, resulting in minimum and maximum scores of 10 and 50. A similar procedure for the Consequences scale (4-point scale) resulted in a range from 10–40.

Principal component analysis was carried out on all scales for the total sample and for each country separately. The relevant (App.) Tables 4.5 through 4.8 are presented in Appendix B. In App. Table 4.5 the inter-correlation matrix for the total sample (N=7857) is given. The following variables have been included: CLIM-S, CLIM-R, OROC-I, OROC-D, OPART-D, OPART-E, OPART-I, OSAT-W, OSAT-C. Based on this inter-correlation matrix a principal component analysis has been carried out. In App. Table 4.6 the eigenvalues and explained variances after each factor extraction are listed. One sees a sharp decline in eigenvalue until a level below 1.00 after the second factor. The first two components, explaining 57.7 percentage of the total variance, can probably be seen as the two main reliable factors responsible for most of the common variance in the scales.

A varimax rotation with Kaiser normalization (Kaiser 1958) has been applied on this two-factor solution. The results are presented in Table 4.2. The two factors can be interpreted without much difficulty. The first factor represents the scales that refer to the general company and work climate. The second factor

Table 4.2
*Factor loadings on two factors after varimax rotation
with Kaiser normalization (general sample, N=7857)*

	Factors	
	I	II
Variables		
CLIM-S	.57	.23
CLIM-R	.67	.16
OROC-I	.14	.76
OROC-D	.26	.57
OPART-D	.55	.27
OPART-E	.32	.67
OPART-I	.06	.61
OSAT-W	.57	.11
OSAT-C	.83	.12

is composed of all scales that are concerned with participative procedures and traditions in the organization. It is remarkable that OPART-D, which is a scale evaluating the consequences of direct participation, does not load on factor II, but on the first factor. Apparently the impact of the direct supervisor-subordinate relationship and consequences of participative leadership are seen rather as an aspect of the total work and organizational climate than as part of the participative structure of the organization.

This same factor extraction and rotation has been applied to the data at the national level. In App. Table 4.8 (Appendix B) the country results are presented. In most countries a picture similar to the general one described in Table 4.2, was found. The only striking difference in this comparison concerns the position that the scale OROC-D takes in the two-factor structure. In a number of countries the rating of Consequences of Direct Participation is seen within the reference system of the general organizational and work climate in the company (France, U.K., Holland) and in the others as part of the general (primarily representative) participative framework. This may be an indication of the extent to which, in the different nations, direct and indirect participation are seen as being intrinsically related.

Contextual and Contingent Variables (Box 5)

Questions to be discussed in this section reflect either organizational variables measured by a separate and quite elaborate questionnaire (COMP CON),[6] or personal background variables recorded in a personal questionnaire (PIF). Both groups of variables have in common that not only the direct straight runs are interesting as a description of organizations and individuals participating in the study (see chapter 5), but that they have been used extensively as moderating or contingent factors in the study of various interrelationships between the core variables.

i. Personal Information Form (PIF)

In this form, which the respondent had to fill in personally, various background data are obtained concerning function, job level, and department; sex, age, education, and nationality; and whether the respondent had been or was a member of a representative body. Information on the job level provided the opportunity to classify respondents as belonging to one of the four levels, workers, foremen, middle managers, or top management. The question on membership of representative body referred to possible classification within level F. Age was coded according to the significant phases in working life (see Miller and Form 1951, and Laaksonen 1972) as follows: less than 21, 21–30, 31–45, 45–60, more than 60. The PIF questionnaire was administered to all respondents and key persons.

ii. Company Context (COMP CON)

The Company Context questionnaire is an instrument with some 200 questions to be answered by different experts in the organization, and, so far as the top management interview is concerned, by a member of top management. Many of these questions have been based upon previous studies, particularly the Aston studies (Pugh et al. 1968, Pugh et al. 1969, Pugh and Hickson 1976).

The following categories of information are covered by the COMP CON list:

(a) Technology, including: product complexity; skill-level of workers; production flow interdependence; and complexity of equipment.

(b) Organizational structure, including: size; differentiation; vertical stratification; and formalization.

(c) Personnel structure, including: inequality; stability of employment; absolute level of reward to workers; labour dissatisfaction; and union strength.

(d) Financial and economic variables, including: establishment's independence; market position; environmental stability; growth; productivity; and capital intensity.

In the top management interview a number of open questions were asked on the economic strategy of the company, the managerial ideology relating to personnel, the role of managers, unions, the economic situation, etc., and a subjective rating of the profitability, efficiency, growth, morale, and adaptability of the company (in comparison with other organizations in the field) was obtained.

Overview of questionnaires

In summary the IDE instruments can be listed as in Figure 4.7.

SAMPLES AND METHODS OF DATA COLLECTION

Sample of Organizations

Although the present study has a cross-sectional character, the information collected for each firm was so elaborate and extensive that it seemed impossible to draw a very large and representative sample of organizations in each country. It was felt rather that a careful stratification should be made so as to provide sufficient relevant variance. Three variables were chosen as a basis for such stratification: size, industrial sector, and level of education (or skill requirements)

Source	Form[a]	Information on
Representative sample	Form 1.1	Personal Information Form (PIF)
	Form 1.3	Involvement (PO2-a)
	Form 1.3	Desired Involvement (PO2-b)
	Form 1.3	Desired Involvement of Representative Body (PO2-c)
	Form 1.4	Satisfaction with Participation (OPART)
	Form 1.5	Rating of Consequences (OROC)
	Form 1.7	Rating of Needs (ORON)
	Form 1.6	Satisfaction (OSAT)
	Form 1.2	Climate (CLIM)
Key persons	Form 2.1	Rating of Influence (PO1)
	Form 2.1.1	Influence extension (PO1 ext.)
	Form 2.1.2	Influence optional (PO1-opt.)
	Form 1.1	Personal Information Form (PIF)
Specialists, in or outside the company	Form 3.1	Company Context (COMP CON) and interview with top manager
	Form 3.2	De Jure Participation (PS)
Researcher himself (with specialists)		Country Context (CON CON)
		Other indicators of Influence and Involvement (PO3).

[a] The term 'Form' refers to the questionnaire, see Appendix A-2.

Figure 4.7 Overview of IDE instruments

of employees.

So far as size is concerned, three classes were adopted:

i. small (less than 100 employees, preference about 80);
ii. medium (100–500 employees, preference about 300);
iii. large (500–1500 employees, preference about 750).

It was decided that companies with more than 1500 employees should not be included.

With respect to industrial sector, two categories of industry were selected: manufacturing and service. Within the manufacturing sector metal engineering industries were chosen; within the service industry either banking or insurance companies.

The third differentiation—between 'high' and 'low' skilled—was only used within the manufacturing organizations, where it was considered to be more relevant than in the service industry. It is assumed that firms in the 'low skilled' category would be producing all types of components (mechanical, electrical, electronics), machine building, and construction, and metal processing. Firms in the 'high skilled' category would produce all types of instruments and tools (mechanical, electrical, electronics), computers, and machine tools. Where there was a combination of high and low skill requirements in one establishment the researcher had to decide which was the dominant one. Where there was a discrepancy between technology and skill requirements (they do not always correlate) the latter condition was considered prevalent.

The three principles of classification produce the matrix shown in Figure 4.8.

Sector

| | | Service | Manufacturing | |
			High-skilled	Low-skilled
Size	< 100			
	200–500			
	501–1000			

Figure 4.8 Sample matrix of organizations

The minimum strategy was to find at least one organization per cell. Participating countries were encouraged to expand their firm sample, however, beyond the internationally agreed number of 9, and at the same time—for idiosyncratic reasons—to add other sectors. Table 4.2 contains the actual number of firms per country that were included in the final sample, on which the comparative analyses have been carried out. The definition of establishment created some discussion. The question was whether an establishment should be legally independent and could not be part of a larger corporation. It was decided to accept the latter possibility as long as there existed *de facto* independence in major decision-making and a separate representative body (e.g. a works' council). It can be seen that only two countries were not able to include the minimum number of firms in the study, for financial or practical reasons. Others were able to include a good deal more than the minimum of 9 firms.

In specific country reports and with respect to within-country analyses the varying number of firms is not problematic. On the contrary, the more firms included the more reliable the results will be. However, for comparisons and for general conclusions based upon the total sample data differences in the number of organizations and, consequently, differences in the number of respondents per country could raise difficulties. There can be two types of deviation from the required minimum of 9 companies. In the first place, the absolute number of companies may vary, and secondly, the extra companies (above 9) may not be evenly distributed over the 9 cells. In fact, this is what has happened in a number of cases (see Table 4.3). It was nevertheless decided to include all organizations in the analysis. Only in rare cases the differences in numbers per country are not taken into account automatically in the analyses of variance or multiple regressions. The only instances in which the problem might be relevant are those in which organizations per cell over countries are being pooled, or in which organizations within countries are pooled. In these cases average scores per cell per country rather than absolute scores had to be used.

Table 4.3
Number of organizations in total sample

| Country | Service | | | Manufacturing | | | | | | Total |
| | | | | High-skill | | | Low-skill | | | |
	Small	Medium	Large	Small	Medium	Large	Small	Medium	Large	
Norway	1	1	1	1	1	1	1	2	1	10
Sweden	5	1	1	2	3	2	4	2	2	22
Denmark	1	1	1	1	1	1	1	1	1	9
Finland	2	1	1	2	1	1	2	1	1	12
U. K.	2	2	1	2	1	1	1	1	3	14
Germany (West)	1	1	1	1	2	1	1	1	1	10
Holland	2	1	1	1	2	1	4	3	1	16
Belgium	1	1	1	1	2	2	1	1	1	11
France	1	1	1	1	1	1	1	1	1	9
Italy	1	—	1	1	1	—	1	1	1	7
Yugoslavia	1	1	1	1	1	1	1	1	1	9
Israel[a]	—	—	—	—	1	1	1	1	1	5
Total	18	11	11	14	17	13	19	16	15	134

[a] All are Histadrut establishments

General sample of respondents

A preliminary remark should be made about the use of the word 'sample'. Strictly speaking this term may be incorrect, since it suggests that national *representative* samples have been selected and used in the study. As will become clear in the next section this is not the case. The sample of respondents has been drawn from the organizations participating in the study. It can, therefore, not be representative for the national work-force as a whole, and probably not even for the work-force in the selected industries. In this book the term 'sample' has been used, nevertheless, and the reader should be aware of its restricted meaning. It will be clear that unequal percentages of respondents per organization had to be selected; equal percentages would result in a heavy over-representation of the larger companies. Sample respondents per firm have therefore been selected with a formula used previously by Coetsier (1966) which produces larger samples in the smaller companies. (For details of calculation, see Appendix A-4.)

Foreign workers were included, provided they had at least six months experience in the company and had no major language problems. Key persons could also fall within the total sample but overlap was avoided as much as possible. Representatives of top management were interviewed with the total questionnaire, but not all forms were appropriate at this level. It was decided to replace refusals as if they were missing persons. Therefore, a safety factor of 10 per cent was added to each sample in order to have the opportunity for replacements. The actual sizes of the samples in the different countries are given in Table 4.4. The distribution per country per level is given in App. Table 4.9 in Appendix B.

Sample of key persons

Key persons were selected from the following groups: top management, works' council members, members of joint productivity councils, union representatives in the company (including shop stewards), the personnel department, middle management, direct supervisors, and other activists. In Table 4.5 the total numbers of key persons have been listed by country and by type of organization. It can be seen that the numbers of key persons vary substantially over countries. This need not be a problem, since average scores are being used for key persons' ratings.

Methods and procedures of data collection

The method of selecting the organizations differed somewhat from country to country. Of course, one condition was whether the firm would fit in the matrix (Figure 4.8). Another important condition was whether the company would allow the study to take place and would be willing to co-operate. In some countries possible candidates were approached sequentially. In others larger groups of possible acceptable firms were approached at the same time and afterwards a choice was made from those that had expressed interest.

In a number of meetings and discussions with management representatives

Table 4.4
Number of respondents (general sample) per type of organization

| Country | Service | | | Manufacturing | | | | | | Total |
| | Small | Medium | Large | High-skill | | | Low-skill | | | |
				Small	Medium	Large	Small	Medium	Large	
Norway	42	57	85	21	73	59	33	104	137	611
Sweden	122	77	106	118	201	256	171	136	245	1432
Denmark	38	39	77	36	45	66	35	48	84	468
Finland	208	78	76	114	48	58	90	56	62	790
U. K.	70	99	85	59	39	63	50	50	186	701
Germany (West)	34	49	62	30	98	89	35	64	85	546
Holland	74	60	121	31	72	117	79	102	75	731
Belgium	39	43	58	32	75	179	29	27	106	588
France	65	114	89	40	52	132	34	70	67	663
Italy	38	–	110	36	60	–	34	57	82	417
Yugoslavia	35	43	88	40	52	89	35	61	100	543
Israel	–	–	–	–	53	137	43	42	67	342
Total	765	659	957	557	868	1245	668	817	1296	7832

Table 4.5
Number of key respondents per type of organization

Country	Type of organization			Manufacturing						Total
	Service			High-skill			Low-skill			
	Small	Medium	Large	Small	Medium	Large	Small	Medium	Large	
Norway	2	4	15	3	9	5	3	6	12	59
Sweden	31	8	6	16	33	19	24	13	12	162
Denmark	18	11	14	2	14	32	12	17	29	149
Finland	6	3	3	6	3	5	7	6	7	46
U. K.	8	12	6	7	3	4	5	4	14	63
Germany (West)	4	2	11	2	4	3	3	6	5	45
Holland	13	12	16	7	26	27	34	24	13	172
Belgium	3	4	13	1	23	36	6	17	21	124
France	4	5	3	2	5	5	1	3	7	35
Italy	4	–	10	77	8	–	3	12	10	54
Yugoslavia	9	9	9	10	10	8	10	10	5	80
Israel	–	–	–	–	2	1	1	3	1	8
Total	102	70	106	63	145	145	109	121	146	997

and a local co-ordinator the selection of respondents (general sample), key respondents, and other contacts took place and the interviewing procedures were planned. Rooms were reserved and times and dates fixed. As often as possible information on the content and objectives of the research study was given to the sample and key respondents beforehand.

The actual data collection was carried out through:

i. Group interviews: respondents were interviewed in groups of about 5 people. Each respondent had to fill in the precoded questionnaires. The sequence of forms is similar to the one reproduced in Appendix A2. The interviewer went through the form, explaining the questions one by one and checking as much as possible whether the tasks and the questions were understood properly. These group sessions took from 1½ to 2½ hours. After the formal phase of filling in the questionnaires very often some free discussions were held with the groups in order to get some subjective feeling of people's reactions to the study, the questions, and the subject of investigation. This very often provided rich material to be used for illustrative, descriptive, or case study purposes in the different country reports.

ii. Individual interviews (key figures): these interviews were less standardized, although here also a standard set of questionnaires had to be filled in. In addition, however, most of the time a long and open in-depth interview followed.

iii. Other research activities: these included the top management interview, interviews with the expert informers on the Company Context information and the study of minutes of works' council meetings, yearly reports, announcements on notice-boards etc. (For more details see the Field Handbook, reproduced in the Appendix A.4). After the collection of the data, these were coded according to instructions in a detailed code-book which was constructed centrally, and used by all country teams. One set of computer cards was produced for use in each country, and another, or a set of optical reading sheets, was sent to the International Institute of Management in Berlin, where the central data-processing and analysis were carried out.

AGGREGATED AND DERIVED SCORES

In this section a short description will be given of the various aggregated and derived participation scores, which have been used in the study, and which were based on the primary information discussed above. In view of the technical character of the information this discussion will be brief most of the substance being presented in Appendix C. Three types of aggregated or derived scores can be mentioned:

i. In the first place there was the question whether the information on the sixteen decisions should be kept separate or aggregated to cluster scores, and whether any weights should be attributed to the separate decisions or to the clusters of decisions in calculating 'total' scores (over the sixteen decisions—see below). Logical and empirical analysis suggested that three clusters of decisions could be used in the analysis in addition to the sixteen decisions separately: short-term decisions (1, 4, 5, 10, 12, and 16), medium-term decisions (2, 3, 8, 9, 11, 13, 14) and long-term decisions (6, 7). No arguments could be found for applying different weights for these clusters in the calculation of the total score.

ii. For the *De Jure* Participation (PS) scores, and the Influence (PO1) scores the basic data matrices have been given in Figures 4.3 and 4.4. For each of the seven groups (A through G) and each of the sixteen decisions a score ranging from 1–6 for the PS and from 1–5 for the PO1 is available. In both cases this matrix has first been expanded with three rows for the three clusters described above and with one row for the total set of decisions. Second, a column for the sum of the (PS and PO1) scores over the groups A, B, C, D, and F has been added. This latter score indicates the *De Jure* Participation/Influence score in the whole organization with respect to the particular decision, decision cluster or total set of decisions. Moreover, a number of specific score patterns have been identified and used, both for the PS and PO1 scores, such as:

(*a*) A variance score, based on the standard deviation of the total scores over the hierarchical groups A through E.

(*b*) A number of difference scores, based on the difference in cluster or total score for various groups (e.g. management (D) and workers (A), or participative body (F) and workers (A)).

(*c*) A number of inequality scores for various groups, based on the mean difference in total or cluster score between that particular group and the other hierarchical groups in the organization.

iii. In the third place a number of derived Involvement (PO2) scores have been used. Basically, the PO2 scores are individual scores, ranging from 1–6. Aggregation over individuals per group produces involvement scores at the organizational level. As with *De Jure* Participation and Influence here also a score for the three decision-clusters and the total set of decisions have been calculated. Finally, the sum of these total scores over the three levels A, B, and C indicate the total involvement in the whole organization. What has been described in this paragraph applied both for Actual Involvement (PO2 a) scores and Desired Involvement (PO2 b) scores.

In addition, the use of a difference score between Desired and Actual Involvement as an indication of the level of 'deprivation' was considered. However, on the basis of a number of methodological and metrical considerations and supported by the results of some empirical analyses, the researchers decided not to use these difference scores.

In Appendix D (D.1) all variables which have been mentioned in this chapter are listed systematically, including a verbal description, the measurement and the name of the concept. In the Overview of Variables and Scores (D.3) an indication is given at which level of aggregation the scores are available or can be obtained.

ISSUES OF ANALYSIS

In Figure 4.2 the research model has been presented in its simplest form: a hypothetical causal flow from the *de jure* participation structure to *de facto* influence and involvement and to outcomes and other dependent variables. It will be clear that in reality the pattern of interrelations between the listed and other potential variables is much more complicated. The analysis procedures should therefore leave sufficient room for the disclosure of these more complex patterns. It seems that the more elaborate sensitizing model presented in Figure 2.2 is more realistic and a better guideline for the analysis. A number of considerations should be kept in mind and are illustrated in that figure:

i. Several other factors will probably (co)determine the PS, PO, and O variables as well, either directly or indirectly (in Figure 2.2 indicated by $CON_{1,2,...,7,8}$). Some of these variables have been measured and are available for analysis, others have not been identified in the present study. Accordingly, multiple regression seems to be the appropriate approach to adopt.

ii. On theoretical grounds it can be expected that the causal chain of relations, if existing, will not be exclusively one-directional. This is why several feedback loops have been drawn in the figure, indicating the possible reciprocity of the relations. It can be conceived, for instance, that certain actual participation behaviour patterns will eventually influence the formal participation structure (PS). Likewise, certain reactions and evaluations can shape both the formal and the *de facto* participation and influence patterns. This means that easy conclusions on the causal nature of relations on the basis of correlations between variables should be avoided. Causal interpretations should either be based upon strong theoretical grounds, or on more sophisticated models of analysis that do allow for such interpretations.

iii. Not only may a number of extra variables co-determine the core variables in this study, but also a large number of such variables might be expected to have a moderating or intervening effect with respect to the interrelationships between the core variables. In the figure these variables are indicated with CON (contingent variables). Furthermore, this role of moderator can also be played by some of the outcome variables. For instance, satisfaction with participation (OPART-D) may function this way. This complex pattern of relationships requires the application of multivariate approaches in addition to simple covariance techniques.

iv. As has been mentioned already in Chapter 2, one of the most difficult and complicated problems in this type of research is the choice of the proper unit of analysis each time. At least seven different levels of analysis can be distinguished, six of which are illustrated in Figure 4.9. They can be described in the following somewhat more compact way:

(*a*) Level of country, or groups of countries. The primary rationale of the international comparative character of this study is not merely to enlarge the number of observations and to increase the variance within the data, but to study the effects of the different formal systems of participation on the actual influence and involvement patterns in organizations. The European scene has been taken as a sort of natural laboratory and the existing different PS systems as the given independent variable. It will be clear, therefore, that one of the central objectives of this study is to identify different patterns between the participating countries. Analysis at the country level will therefore be an essential and significant part of the research. Certain countries may be grouped together, having similar patterns of relationships. Such a grouping could either be the result of an empirical taxonomical analysis of the available data, or be

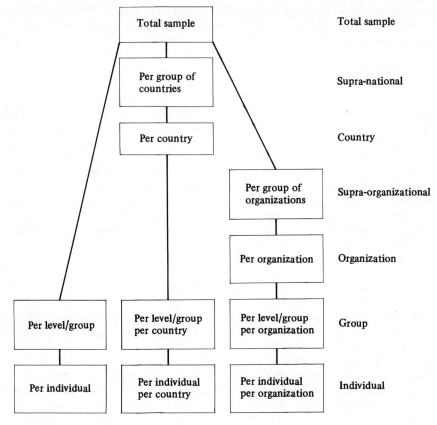

Figure 4.9 Overview of different types of sub-groupings for analyses at different levels

made on *a priori* grounds (for example types of culture, history, industrial relations system) and be used as an independent factor (see Chapter 9).

(*b*) Level of organizations, or groups of organizations. Differences between organizations may be substantial, especially with respect to questions that pertain to organizational issues, such as the influence of company policy, tradition, and climate with respect to participation. Sometimes, the analysis between organizations has to be done separately for each country, although the number of observations will often be small (9 or even less). More often, especially if the variance within countries is larger than the variance between countries, the organizational analysis can be done across countries. With respect to the grouping of organizations three obvious bases for classification are present: size, type of industry, and educational level of workers. Also other bases for classification of the organizations may be used, chosen on *a priori* grounds or empirically generated.

(*c*) Level of group in the organization. Distinctions between hierarchical levels or groups is another important central issue in this research, since issues of influence and power in organizations pre-eminently refer to the differences between these levels and groups. In particular level A (workers) and F (works' council or other representative organ) received much attention, in relation to levels C and D (management).

(d) Level of individuals, or groups of individuals. As can be seen in Appendix D3 a considerable number of variables were measured at an individual level, although, of course, many of them can easily be aggregated at a group, organizational, or country level. At the item and scale level all primary analyses for the composition of scales and the determination of their psychometric qualities were carried out at the individual level; sometimes per country, sometimes for the total sample. Furthermore, depending on the question itself, and on the ratio of variances further analyses have been carried out over all individuals in the total sample, over all individuals within national samples, over all individuals (across countries) per level, over all individuals per level per country, over all individuals per level per organization, or over various categories or groups within these total samples of individuals. In addition to the formally distinct levels and groups (A–G) other categories of individuals have been distinguished as well. The PIF questionnaire contains a number of variables that have served this purpose.

Three problems should be indicated at this point. In the first place the number of observations at different levels is important. As we reach a higher level of aggregation the number of units of analysis become smaller. This certainly applies at the national level. 'Only' twelve countries were involved and there is not much to be expected in terms of significant differences or similarities at the level of country comparisons (see for instance Chapter 9). The same difficulty applies when one tries to explain phenomena at a lower level (e.g. organization or group) by possible determinants at a higher (e.g. national) level. In an analysis of variance at the individual level with 7832 subjects and country as the independent variable the degrees of freedom between groups = 11, and within groups = 7820!

Second, the problem of cross-level testing *per se* causes problems. The explanatory power of the higher level variable (e.g. nation) for variables at a lower level (e.g. organization) depends on the difference between the organizational variance between nations and that within nations. The smaller this difference the lower the explanatory power. Particularly if the levels are remote (e.g. the individual level as compared with the national level) the assumption of large differences in variance is not likely to be realistic. In fact, such differences will primarily occur if the national variable is merely a 'summarized' individual variable, such as educational level, unionization, and the like. It is however questionable whether the latter can be called true 'national' variables.

Moreover, there is the classical difficulty of 'ecological' correlations (Robinson 1950). It can be argued that it may not be justified to make inferences about relationships between variables at an individual level on the basis of correlational data based upon groups as units. As an example, it may be incorrect to conclude that there is a relationship between union membership and works' council membership for *individuals*, if a correlation between degree of union membership and degree of works' council membership has been found at an organizational or national level. It may be true that union members do not tend to be members of works' council but that in organizations with high unionization unorganized workers are more likely to be active on works' councils. On the other hand a correlation at an individual level may disappear at a higher level of analysis since the individual variables may be cancelled out being similarly distributed in all organizations or nations; the Durkheimian type of fallacy (Blalock 1961). Essentially, the problem is that in shifting units we may be affecting the degree to which other unknown or unmeasured variables are influencing the picture, and it may be difficult to assume that all such potentially confounding influences have been brought under control.

A third problem relates to the fact that in this study representative national samples have not been used. The firms were chosen in a select way and within the firms representative samples of individuals were selected. This means first, that when differences between groups, organizations, or nations are to be explained in terms of individual characteristics possible sample biases should in fact be controlled for especially with respect to Personal Information Form (PIF) variables. This applies particularly for Chapter 8, where many analyses are made at an individual level. In a number of instances this has been tested and the findings have been corrected for PIF variance. It should be said, however, that the results did not show a great need for a systematic application of such corrections, since the differences were only small. In addition, one should avoid explaining away true indications of cultural and social differences between countries. Educational level, size of female work-force, and the like could be true determinants of national differences.

Second, it means that correlations computed at the individual level per country may be due to firm averages. In other words we would in fact have an organizational variable but would treat it as an individual variable. Empirical investigation on a small sub-sample did not suggest this problem to be too serious, however. Likewise, correlations at the organizational level across countries may be due to country differences. Empirical investigations showed this problem to be somewhat more serious. Consequently, interpretations at the organizational level across countries should be made with the necessary reservations.

Types of analysis

As was demonstrated in the previous section, a varied series of analyses has proved necessary to explore the richness of the available data, and to get a fuller insight into the complex interrelationship patterns.[7] In this section these analyses will be discussed somewhat more systematically.

i. Uni-variate analysis. The simplest level of analysis is the uni-variate level, at which frequency counts for different groups and total samples are produced. Technically this level of analysis does not create many problems, which is not to say that interpretation is always easy. Problems of response sets, social desirability, rating errors, and biases prevent straightforward interpretation of the data and acceptability of the answers at face value. Moreover, one has to take into account the reliability of the various instruments and scales. Reliabilities of the latter are not always of a satisfactory magnitude.

ii. Bi-variate analysis. Analyses at this level are still rather simple and straight-forward. Scores, means, or variances are compared between groups, co-variances between two variables are established or one-way analyses of variance are applied. Especially at the level of individuals the number of observations is very large. It would therefore be unrealistic to apply as a matter of routine the classic significance levels as criteria for the acceptability of a correlation coefficient or other relationship indices, since this would lead to a large number of significant, but often irrelevant correlations. Which particular covariance index has been used and which criteria have been applied in each case will be indicated in the next chapters where the respective relationships will be discussed and interpreted.

iii. Multivariate analysis. With the complexity of information given in this study multivariate analysis procedures are often appropriate. One may think of non-linearity, three (or more)-way analysis of variance, the effects of moderator and contingent variables, taxonomic analysis, and the like. It will be clear that the choice should be guided by theoretical expectations and considerations, and that mechanistic analysis procedures should not be applied.

So far as the central variable sets in the model are concerned two sets of inter-relations are of particular interest, and will receive special attention in this section. These are the relation between *De Jure* Participation (PS) and *De Facto* Participation (PO) and the relation between *De Facto* Participation and Outcome (or dependent) variables.

(*a*) *De Jure* Participation–*De Facto* Participation (PS-PO). The decision whether to use Influence (PO1) or Involvement (PO2) is a theoretical issue, depending on the scientific meaning to be attributed to the two measures. The problem does however have a technical aspect since Involvement and *De Jure* Participation have been expressed on the same scale (a six-point scale), whereas for Influence a different scale has been used. Within Influence and Involvement a large number of specific measures have been developed. Not all of them are equally useful at all levels of aggregation, as the scheme in Appendix D.2 shows. In most cases more than one, and sometimes quite a variety of PO variables have been used in the analysis. *De Jure* Participation is an organizational variable; consequently the *De Facto* Participation measures have to be used at the organizational level also. Since in a number of countries the PS scores do not show any variance, an analysis within countries would not make sense. The comparative analysis therefore has been carried out over organizations across countries, and over countries.

One of the more exciting questions in this study is which variables have an influence on the relationship between *De Jure* and *De Facto* Participation (PS-PO) and what is the nature of this influence. A number of conditional (CON) and personal (PIF) variables as well as some dependent (O/D) variables could be relevant in this respect. In the interaction between PS, PO, and CON we could distinguish theoretically six possibilities for such an effect:

i. CON as an intervening variable:

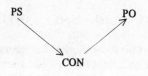

No direct relationship exists between PS and PO, but, because PS influences CON, and CON in its turn determines (partly) PO, a relationship PS-PO is to be found. Or CON can increase a direct correlation between PS and PO.
ii. CON as a moderator variable:

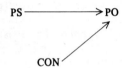

The relationship PS-PO is modified by CON, which means a statistically significant interaction effect of PSxCON on PO. Within different sub-groups to be distinguished on the basis of CON, different predictions of PO by PS will be found. This is a multiplicative model.
iii. CON as a determinant of the difference between two variables:

$$CON \longrightarrow (PO-PS)$$

CON is the independent variable and correlates with the difference score PO minus PS.
iv. CON as a (co)determinant of the dependent variable

The predictability of PO is increased if CON variables are added in the regression formula. This is a linear additive model.
v. CON as an antecedent variable:

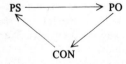

CON determines both PS and PO and therefore creates a spurious correlation between PS and PO. CON can also spuriously increase an existing correlation PS-PO.
vi. CON as element in a circular chain:

PS ─────────→ PO
  ↖   ↙
     CON

PS determines (partly) PO, PO determines (partly) CON, and CON determines (partly) PS again.

Some evaluative remarks on these models can be made. Within the framework, and with the kind of data in this study, models 1 and 5 cannot be distinguished properly. In both cases the same test has to be applied namely, does the relationship PS-PO decrease significantly if CON is kept constant. Moreover, on theoretical grounds both models are difficult to accept. It is hardly likely that CON variables (Company Context variables or Personal variables like Satisfaction or Needs) determine the formal, legal participative system in a country or in a company or that the formal system determines CON variables. Therefore, both models 1 and 5 were left out of the analysis.

For a test of model 6 one needs longitudinal data. This model cannot be tested by data available in this study. In addition, here again the unlikely assumption has to be made that CON variables can be expected to (co)determine PS.

Model 3 also produces a number of difficulties. In the first place in a number of countries PS is constant over organizations. At the country level the model therefore should be reduced to CON→PO, which is essentially the same as part of model 4. Secondly, a number of the statistical problems with respect to difference scores as discussed in Appendix C are also relevant in this case.

For the international analysis primary attention has been given to models 2 and 4. The linear additive and the multiplicative models can both be tested by the same regression formula:

$$PO = \beta_1 PS + \beta_2 CON + \beta_3 PS \times CON + \mu$$

in which: β_1 indicates the extent to which PO is determined by PS, independently of CON;

β_2 indicates the extent to which PO is determined by CON, independently of PO;

β_3 indicates an interaction effect, demonstrating that CON is a moderator in the relation PS-PO

A variety of CON variables were included, and several multiple regression analyses were carried out in order to optimize the prediction of PO by PS and CON.

(b) *De Facto* Participation–Outcome/dependent variables (PO-O/D). What has been said in the foregoing about the different aspects of *De Facto* Participation and the nature of the different PO indices applies here as well. Since the dependent variables have been measured both at the individual and organizational levels, which is also true for *De Facto* Participation (Influence at the organizational level, Involvement at the individual level—which can be aggregated at the organizational level) the relationship between PO and O/D could be studied both at an individual level and an organizational level, by using individual scores or organizational scores. Using the individual scores the relationship has been studied per level across countries, and per level per country. Using the organizational scores the relationship has also been studied per level across countries, and per level per country. Which PO scores and which O/D scores have been selected for the respective explorations and analyses has depended on the particular hypotheses, and will be discussed fully in Chapter 8.

The influence of external factors on the PO-O/D relationships are interesting. A number of PIF variables, CON variables, and O/D variables other than the one under study can be considered. With the exception of model 3 (it does not seem meaningful to consider the difference between O/D and PO) all six models are also applicable in this case: CON as an intervening variable (1), CON as a moderator variable (2), CON as a (co)determinant of O/D (4), CON as an antecedent variable (5), and CON as an element in a circular chain (6). However the nature of the study and the kind of data do not permit any conclusions on model 6. This model cannot be tested in the present study.

Also in this case models 1 and 5 cannot be distinguished properly. Again the same test has to be applied for both models: does the relationship between PO and O/D decrease significantly if CON is kept constant and no discriminant conclusion as to the two models can be made. Nevertheless, partial correlations have been computed for quite a number of variables.

Model 2 is a very appropriate model here. The model is tested by calculating the β coefficient for the interaction term PO×O/D in the regression formula.

Model 4 is also applicable in many cases, and requires a multiple regression equation with PO and CON as predictors and O/D as dependent variables. The β weights for PO and CON indicate their independent contribution to the prediction of O/D. Models 2 and 4 can be tested at the same time by applying the regression formula:

$$O/D = \beta_1 PO + \beta_2 CON + \beta_3 \dot{C}ON \times PO + \mu$$

A final comment should be made on the taxonomical analysis, which has been applied in the attempt to identify 'types' of country with respect to participation structures or the interrelationships between selected variables. Basically two types of taxonomical analysis have been applied. In the first place a taxonomy based upon the principles of profile analysis. Clusters of countries have been identified with more or less similar profile patterns with respect to a number of relevant variables (selected from the PS, PO and O/D sets). A second type of taxonomy is based upon similarities or differences in patterns of interrelationships between relevant variables. These interrelationships could range from a simple level (intercorrelations between two variables) to highly complex interrelation patterns involving more than two variables with higher-order interactions. The variables which have been selected, and the procedures of profile and taxonomic analysis which have been applied are more fully described in Chapter 9.

To sum up, an attempt has been made here to give a complete account of the procedures and the design of the study, the selection and testing of the instruments, and the way the data have been collected and analysed. The discussion had to have a somewhat technical character, occasionally, but it was felt necessary to give the reader who is interested in the methods and procedures, as full as possible an insight into the methodological basis of the IDE study. Only a comprehensive description of the methodology can provide an opportunity for verification and replication.

NOTES

1 Not all of these will be published in this volume. The more complicated analyses will be reported in later publications.

2 In the meantime a more longitudinal study of the effects of changes in the participative system has been started in Sweden and Finland.

3 In the rest of the book, the terms 'group' and 'level' are used interchangeably.

4 Although this question aims at possible conflicts, care has been taken not to

use the word conflict, but rather disagreement, so as to avoid too serious connotations.

5 The item numbers refer to the numbers in the questionnaire (see Appendix
A.2).

6 The complete Comp Con list is available, upon request, from the International Institute of Management, 1000 Berlin 42.

7 Not all results of these analyses will be reported in this volume. Particularly
the more complex and sophisticated analyses will be treated in later publications.

PART III

MAJOR FINDINGS

5

THE RESPONDENTS AND THEIR ORGANIZATIONS

AIM AND OUTLINE

The major hypothesis of this study is that the higher the amount of participation in decision-making which is formally prescribed for a certain group, the more of a factual say the members of that group will have. However, it is conceivable that there are factors other than formal prescriptions that are related to the influence of a certain person or group. The impact of such other factors could completely overshadow the possible effect of formal prescriptions, they could weaken or alternatively amplify them. Such contextual or contingent variables include characteristics of the individual like degree of education and characteristics of the organization he or she is working in. The main task of this chapter is to describe the respondents and the companies included in the study to give a general idea of how the sample is composed and of the variation in the contextual variables.

In addition we will discuss the kinds of effect that could be expected to be produced by characteristics of the sample other than the degree of *de jure* participation. Two types of effect have to be discussed: effects on influence and involvement and on outcomes. The outcomes used in the study are mostly attitudinal measures of satisfaction with various aspects of the organization. Therefore we will for the rest of this chapter use terms like attitudes, opinions, and satisfaction interchangeably with outcomes.

Since the amount of *de jure* participation is a factor that varies mainly between nations, special consideration will be given to the possible effects stemming from other types of difference between national samples. Therefore tables and figures will be presented that make it possible to compare national averages on the different contextual variables. Such presentations might help in suggesting which contextual factors could have influenced national differences in influence, involvement, and outcome variables.

It is also of great interest to ask the question if differences between national samples also reflect some underlying difference in social structure and industrial organization between the countries of the study. However, a more detailed description of the industrial relations system of the different countries takes so much space that it has been placed in a volume of its own (IDE 1980). In this chapter comparisons between sample differences and real national differences will therefore be very limited. It should also be pointed out that the sample was never intended to be representative of the whole industrial relations system in the countries investigated. By concentrating on firms of the same size from the same industrial sectors it was rather hoped that the differences between countries in the context factors would be minimized.

Figure 2.2 in Chapter 2 shows how contextual factors might enter the main model (see also IDE 1976). We will first concentrate on the background characteristics of the almost 8,000 respondents included in the general sample.

The backgrounds of individuals may be aggregated and seen as also reflecting aspects of the social structure of the organizations studied. In turn the social structure of the organization is related to social structure in the local and national context.

After the discussion of the variables which have been measured at an individual level we turn to a presentation of the variables measured only at an organizational level. The discussion of organizational variables starts with organizational success and, while it is possible that participation may have an impact on organizational performance, in this book organizational success is treated mainly as a context variable upon which participation and outcomes are contingent. The discussion then covers size, environmental factors, structure, and technology. In this discussion we will pay some attention to the interrelations between context variables. Most intercorrelations between variables that are discussed are shown in App. Table 5.1 in Appendix F.

Significance tests of correlational strength are not usually shown in this chapter. However, a correlation of ± .19 can be regarded as significantly different from 0 on the 5 per cent level when the number of observations is around 100, provided the observations were drawn in a random way.

At the end of the chapter we return to a special aspect of the social structure of organizations. This aspect deals with organizational climate and leadership style.

As pointed out in Chapters 2 and 4 the context variables could affect the main variables and the relationships between them in many ways. In this chapter we will not attempt to specify exactly what kind of relationships the context variables may have with other variables. Rather we will provide a few examples of relationships suggested by earlier research. Mostly, these examples treat the contextual variables as possible determinants (CON 1, 2, 7, 8 in Figure 2.2, Chapter 2) of *de facto* participation and outcomes in addition to or in lieu of the formal prescriptions.

HIERARCHICAL LEVEL

As discussed in Chapter 4 (for exact figures see Appendix B App. Table 4.9) the respondents of the general sample were stratified according to hierarchical level. In the following chapters different hierarchical levels will always be treated as separate units of analysis. One reason for this is related to the operationalization of the concept of industrial democracy. In Chapter 2, a process of democratization was said to involve more influence for lower levels and fewer differences between higher and lower levels. Another reason for keeping hierarchical levels separate in all analyses is that level can be expected to have strong relationships with influence and satisfaction (Tannenbaum et al. 1974, Korman 1971). If level is not controlled for it would be impossible to say if differences in influence between the work-forces of different organizations could be ascribed to differences in rules about participation or to the fact that some organizations (research-orientated for example) have more high-level employees than others.

Even if the answers given by respondents from different organizational levels are not averaged into an unweighted organizational or national mean, differences in hierarchical stratification may anyway influence the outcome variables. For example, if an organization has an unusually high proportion of lowest-level employees, each one of these may feel himself or herself as belonging to a rather industrialized environment and as being a member of a relatively isolated group of workers. There are suggestions in the literature that workers in such circumstances are likely to show signs of dissatisfaction (Katzell, Barett, and Parker 1961, Kerr and Siegel 1954).

The relative number of workers could also have an impact on influence. If a participative system approaches the democratic 'one man one vote' system, a higher proportion of workers should mean more influence for the workers. A high proportion of workers also means that there are fewer managers around to control the workers and we know from the research of Maurice et al. (1977) that the size of the management hierarchy varies considerably between similar organizations in different countries.

Table 5.1 shows the relative number of employees at the lowest hierarchical level in the sampled organizations. This proportion is fairly stable in all countries but there are slightly higher proportions of workers in the Yugoslavian and

Table 5.1

Percentage of the total number of employees in the investigated organizations belonging to a certain organizational level

Country	Workers (A)	Foremen (B)	Managers (C+D)
Norway	73	19	8
Sweden	88	6	6
Denmark	83	8	9
Finland	81	12	7
U. K.	83	10	7
Germany (West)	(78)[a]	(14)	(8)
Holland	81	11	8
Belgium	83	10	7
France	83	9	8
Italy	(76)	(17)	(7)
Yugoslavia	90	6	4
Israel	85	13	2
Mean of national samples	82	11	7
n =	12	12	12

[a]( ) = many observations missing

Swedish samples of organizations (90 and 88 per cent). The low proportion of workers in the Norwegian sample is due to one firm with an exceptionally high proportion of supervisors. Table 5.1 shows also that there are, on average, 10 per cent supervisors and 7 per cent higher managers in our organizations. The middle management group also includes different types of staff expert. In some of the analyses of the questionnaire-data supervisors and middle managers have been collapsed into one category. In most national samples this group consists of two-thirds supervisors and one-third managers. In the Danish and Yugoslavian firms this collapsed category is only one-third supervisors. In the Dutch sample the collapsed group consists of 83 per cent supervisors. The top management level which never consisted of more than 2 per cent of the employees and often under 1 per cent has mostly been left out of the analyses.

JOB CONTENT AND OCCUPATIONAL CATEGORY

There is a good deal of evidence indicating that even when the effects of hierarchy have been taken into account, the type of job a worker holds will affect both his influence and the satisfaction he derives from work.

Starting with the broad dividing line between white- and blue-collar jobs we can observe with Crozier (1971): 'In the general progress of human organizations toward complexity, differentiation, and intellectualization, white collar employees are, despite certain appearances, definitely ahead of manual workers. The norms they submit to are often less constraining, but they are more numerous, more complex, and involve the individual more. The white collar employees are more socialized, and at the same time there is more need for participation. In general they necessarily find themselves pushed to take an interest in the activities of their company' (p. 158). However, Crozier points out that there are also some tendencies which limit the chances for white-collar participation especially in banks and insurance companies. One is the apathy created by the formalism and complexity of the bureaucratic chain. Another is the promotional ladder and the stratification of workers into various specialities which lead to a rejection of certain individuals and certain groups. There is also some evidence that white-collar workers hold more positive attitudes towards their jobs and their company than production workers (Locke and Whiting 1974, Kahn 1974). There are also reports of less clear differences between white- and blue-collar workers (Sheppard and Herrick 1972).

In the blue-collar category different types of job permit the worker varying degree of control over his situation (Blauner 1964). The assembly-line worker could be looked upon as an artisan stripped of almost all influence over his job. The socio-technical approach to industrial democracy builds on the assumption that if work is reorganized in a way that gives workers more control over their immediate work situation this will eventually pave the way for a desire and capability to participate also in broader issues (Thorsrud and Emery 1969). Some findings point to the fact that skilled workers and especially maintenance workers have a work situation that does not just give them more freedom but also control over other groups who are dependent on them (Crozier 1964).

The findings concerning job content and satisfaction follow the same pattern as the relationships between content and influence. More qualified workers experience more work satisfaction, less monotony, and have fewer health problems (Gardell 1976, Kornhauser 1965). Hofstede (1976) found a relatively high degree of satisfaction among unskilled, auxiliary plant workers. Such workers like maintenance workers are not bound by the production flow. Rubenowitz

(1977) found a strong relationship between freedom from technological restraint and satisfaction with work.

Table 5.2 gives a crude division of the types of job held by our lowest-level respondents. It can be seen that the percentage of blue-collar workers in the metal manufacturing firms is remarkably even and, with one exception, within the range of 79–80 per cent. The workers who say they belong to the technical function are usually maintenance or other 'indirect' workers who, according to the reasoning above, should exhibit more autonomy and satisfaction. This group is proportionately large in Germany, the U.K., and Italy and small in Holland, France, and Norway. These differences may wholly or partly be due to the fact that in some countries maintenance work is not looked upon as a specialized function but is integrated into the production function.

The total worker group on which most figures relating to workers in this report is based contains usually between 35 and 50 per cent white-collar workers. The percentage of white-collar workers is slightly higher in France and Finland due to relatively more respondents than in other countries from the service sector. The low proportion of white-collar workers in Israel is due to the fact that no banks or insurance companies were included in that sample.

DEMOGRAPHIC CHARACTERISTICS

Sex

In most cultures men dominate both political offices and positions in the management hierarchy. Even in organizations where the rank and file are mostly women, the leadership positions are often occupied by men. On average, men value achievement and self-expression more while women value social relationships (Herzberg 1957, Centers and Bugental 1966). Linking these findings together one would expect that more dominating and aggressive behaviour is a prerequisite to becoming influential and that a work-force dominated by women would have difficulties in making use of legal provisions for participation. However, it could also be argued that female values are more consonant with a creed of participation based on equality than are traditional masculine and managerial values (Hofstede 1978). We have not been able to find any reports on relationships between the sexual composition of the work-force and influence though Hofstede (1978) reports less of a stress on masculine values in countries where the number of women in professional or managerial positions is high.

Katzell, Barret, and Porter (1961) found that satisfaction was lower in companies dominated by men. Gardell (1976) found that women experienced repetitive engineering jobs as less monotonous than men but that there was not any difference between men and women in more qualified jobs. Korman (1971) draws the conclusion that there is no firm evidence to support the hypothesis that women experience higher work satisfaction than men.

The proportion of female employees in our sample is 27 per cent. As can be seen from Table 5.3 there are many more women in the service sector than in metal manufacturing. Many more women than men are to be found among non-promoted employees. A special index was constructed to show the degree

Table 5.2
Distribution of lowest-level blue- and white collar respondents (per cent)

| Country | Manufacturing | | | | Both Sectors (Manufacturing and Service) | |
| | Blue-collar[a] | | Production and Technical | White-collar[b] | Blue-collar | White-collar |
	Production	Technical				
Norway	79	6	85	15	59	41
Sweden	70	13	83	17	66	34
Denmark	79	11	90	10	61	39
Finland	64	15	79	21	42	58
U.K.	65	20	85	16	54	46
Germany (West)	41	30	71	29	52	48
Holland	83	3	86	15	57	43
Belgium	71	13	84	16	64	36
France	74	5	79	20	47	53
Italy	66	19	85	15	55	45
Yugoslavia	74	12	86	13	59	41
Israel	75	12	87	12	87	12
Mean of national samples	70	13	83	17	59	41
n	12	12	12	12	12	12

[a]Blue-collar = level A respondents in the manufacturing companies who have said that they belong to production and technical departments.

[b]White-collar = all level A respondents from service companies and manufacturing level A respndents from administration, sales, accounting.

Table 5.3
Percentage of women in the sample

	Sector		
Level	Metal	Service	Total
Middle managers	7,5	20,1	12,5
Foremen	5,6	30,3	14,0
Workers	24,1	60,8	34,6
Total sample	18,0	47,7	27,2

of Male Domination in the sampled organizations. A company was assigned a high score if it had more men at the worker and managerial levels than the average company. The Israeli and Dutch companies are clearly more dominated by men than companies from the other countries. The British and Finnish companies are less dominated by men than the others. Actually, the majority of the Finnish respondents are women, an observation that is consistent with the fact that the percentage of all women who work in Finland is higher than for other countries.

Age and Tenure

On the whole there is a positive relationship between age and level of satisfaction (Saleh and Otis 1964). This may be due to a tendency for dissatisfied people to leave the company (Vroom 1964), for older employees to move on to better jobs and for a process of adaption and dissonance reduction to take place. Positions of prestige and power in organizations are usually not held by their youngest members (Tannenbaum 1974). If such findings could be generalized to hold within hierarchical strata as well, a more mature work-force could be expected to have more influence than a younger one.

Both age and tenure increase with the hierarchical level of our respondents. Workers are on average 35 years old and have worked 10 years in the company. Top managers are, on average, 10 years older and have worked for their present company 5 years longer. Workers from the service industry are, on average, 33 years old compared with 36 in the metal firms. Each firm was assigned a score on an index called Stability of Workforce based on age and tenure for both workers and managers. Of course tenure and age is correlated ($r = .56$, $n = 7340$) and the stability measure is an indicator of the degree to which an establishment has a work-force consisting of older employees with relatively long tenure. The averages for the national samples of firms vary considerably. Firms in the samples from Norway, Sweden, Denmark, Israel, and West Germany are high on stability. The work-force is especially low on stability in the Yugoslav, Belgian, and Finnish firms. The three last samples happen also to be the ones with the highest proportions of women in their work-force (the correlation between stability and male domination is $r = .25$, $n = 134$).

The stability measure is related to personnel turnover ($r = -.22$, $n = 111$). Stability is not just brought about by a low quitting rate but also by stagnation and little recruitment of new workers. The correlation between the stability of the work-force and organizational growth, measured in terms of the increase in the total work-force between 1974 and 1976 is r = −.24 (n = 106).

Education

A person's educational background could be expected to affect his possible influence in different ways. Other people may be more willing to listen to a person who has expertise in a certain area and sometimes formal education is interpreted as an indicator of such expertise. More education could also mean a better ability to understand, and thereby to manipulate, one's own situation. It could also make a person less dependent on his present employer by giving him easier access to alternative employment. Tannenbaum et al. (1974) report a considerable flattening out of hierarchical power differences when the educational level of lower echelons is relatively high. Korman (1971) summarizes research on the effects of education on satisfaction by saying that if the hierarchical level of a person is kept constant, then one finds consistently a negative relationship between education and satisfaction.

In this study a scale consisting of the categories (i) primary education (ii) secondary education (iii) higher education and (iv) university training was used to measure Educational Level. On average, the group with the lowest educational level is workers in metal manufacturing. Workers in the service industry and the whole supervisory group are on a clearly higher educational level than workers from the manufacturing firms. The middle management group is somewhat better educated. According to our measure the average education levels of workers are especially high in the Italian, Belgian, and U.K. samples of firms and especially low in France.

Although vocational training of various length was included as category three of the scale in some countries, our measure of education reflects, on the whole, an academic bias. It is not a true reflection of a person's skill-level or his understanding of production and organizational processes. Therefore an attempt to construct a better measure of the skill-level of the work-force is presented below.

Foreign Workers

Because of language problems and cultural handicaps, foreign workers can be expected to have less influence than native ones. As is indicated by Hofstede and Kranenburg (1974) the attitudes of foreign workers are influenced by the values of their home culture, their adaptation to the new country's values and the kind of jobs they hold. Hypotheses suggesting that foreigners attach more importance to earnings and less to the content of jobs were not confirmed in that study. On the whole foreigners and natives reported comparable levels of satisfaction even if their opinions on different aspects of their situation varied.

The number of companies in our sample with a substantial proportion of foreign workers is rather small as can be seen from Table 5.4. The number of foreign respondents in the national samples is 10 per cent in Sweden, where one factory dominated by Finnish workers was included, between 1 and 4 per cent in France, West Germany, Belgium, and Norway and under 1 per cent in all

Table 5.4
Percentage of foreign workers in the sampled companies

Percentage of foreign workers	Number of companies
0	57
1–10	37
11–20	8
21–50	10
50–100	1
unknown	21
	134

other national samples. Due to the relative unimportance of the foreign work-force in most of the national samples, no further analyses of that variable are reported in this volume.

EMPLOYEE MOBILIZATION AND RESOURCES FOR PARTICIPATION

One aspect of the social structure of an organization which could be expected to influence the effect of laws and agreements covering participation is the extent to which the work-force is organized as a collectivity which can be mobilized in order to make use of the *de jure* provisions for participation. Unionization is one way to accomplish such a mobilization of the workers. On the whole, a high degree of unionization should strengthen the capacity of the employees to influence (Flanders 1976).

Observations of a relationship between unionization and discontent have led authors of American personnel management textbooks to conclude that the cause of unions is discontent and that they should therefore be taken as an indicator of bad management (French 1978). This is hardly the view of most European industrial relations scholars. As Clegg (1976) points out the trade union is the industry's opposition without which the industry would become a dangerous autocracy. Unionization is a means to legitimize discontent and to provide a channel for articulating and discussing discontent. The degree to which the company is unionized is therefore one of the factors that have to be kept in mind when the relationships between influence and attitudes are discussed.

The role of Yugoslav unions is different from that of the unions in the other countries. In general terms the Yugoslav unions have a responsibility to check that the self-management system does not end up in liberalism or anarchy (Rus 1977). In particular they are not supposed to act as advocates for employee interests but to mediate in strikes or other conflict situations (Rus 1977, Blumberg 1968).

Table 5.5 shows that there is fair correspondence between the degree of unionization in our sample and the degree of unionization in the different countries (Spearman's Rho = .85 p = < .01). A perfect correspondence between our sample and the national averages cannot be expected since the national averages are based on the whole working population while our figures are strongly influenced by the metal sector where unionization is generally stronger than in

Table 5.5

Unionization in the national sample of organizations and national averages

Country	Unionization (% of work-force)			
	Sample		National average	
Norway	85	(5[a])	60[b]	(6)
Sweden	93	(3)	90	(2)
Denmark	97	(1)	70	(5)
Finland	72	(7)	81	(4)
U.K.	60	(9)	55	(7)
Germany (West)	44	(10)	36	(10)
Holland	36	(11)	35	(11)
Belgium	61	(8)	48	(8)
France	27	(12)	20	(12)
Italy	72	(6)	45	(9)
Yugoslavia	86	(4)	90	(2)
Israel	94	(2)	90	(2)
Mean	68		60	
n	133		12	
S.D.	28.5			
F (one way analysis of variance)	21.0 ($p < 0.0001$)			

[a]Rank order in brackets
[b]The national averages are estimated from various published reports.

other sectors. The figure for Italy is also affected by the fact that the companies sampled were in the north where unionization is higher than in the south.

In this study we pay special attention to formal provisions for participation that specify that employees should be represented on advisory and decision-making bodies. If a sizeable proportion of the employees are members of such bodies this would increase the opportunities for employee participation. Therefore the proportion of lower-level employees who are representatives can be expected to affect the relationship between *de jure* participation and influence. In investigations of voting behaviour the feeling of being able to influence (subjective political competence or efficacy) has been found to be positively related to the individual's tendency to participate (Almond and Verba 1961). However, if the participative bodies are seen more as a management tool to get consent (Fox 1974), a sizeable proportion of employees on these bodies may well contribute to more widespread feelings of powerlessness and also, as suggested by Mulder (1971), less ability to influence.

If these bodies function as a device to integrate lower level employers into the culture of the company and the surrounding society high participation could be expected to lead to high satisfaction with the company. If being a representative gives the feeling of being a hostage or having been cheated of promised influence high participation might lead to high dissatisfaction.

Figure 5.1 shows the average degree of unionization and the average percentage of workers in the sampled companies from different countries who have been members of some representative body. Former (rather than current)

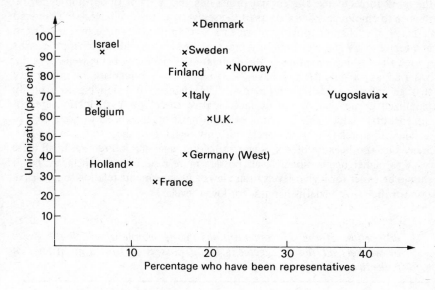

Figure 5.1 Average percentage of the lowest-level employees in organizations from different countries who are members of a union and who have served as representatives on a participative body

representatives were chosen because a number of the current representatives were picked out for special interviews making this group slightly under-represented in the sample. The figure does not show, however, the considerable variation that exists between companies within each country. The national samples fall into five clusters. One consists of the Nordic countries where unionization is about 90 per cent and about every fifth worker has served as a member of a representative body. The proportion of workers with experience as representatives is almost as high in the second group consisting of the samples from France, West Germany, and Holland, but in the sampled organizations from these countries only a minority of the workers is unionized. Unionization in the Italian and U.K. companies falls in between the first two groups while the numbers of former representatives remain about the same.

The companies from Israel and Belgium are relatively high on unionization but the workers have functioned as representatives only to a very limited extent. In both Israel and Belgium the representative system is concentrated in one body with relatively few members. Yugoslavia stands out with 40 per cent of the workers having served on some self-management body. The number of workers that report themselves as union members is also quite high. It should be kept in mind, though, that a Yugoslavian worker automatically becomes a member of the union if he does not specifically state that he does not want to be.

Both a high degree of unionization and a high proportion of employees belonging to representative bodies could be seen as conditions for mobilizing the work-force to use the formal provisions that provide opportunities for influence to employees. The aspects of the social structure that have been described earlier in this chapter could be regarded as individual assets or resources that can be mobilized by the members of a group in order to wield influence. It can be argued that having a job high in the occupational hierarchy, being well-educated, being a man, being older, and having long tenure in a job increase the probability that an individual will be influential. The chances of belonging to a highly mobilized group and possessing individual resources for participation are not spread out evenly. Table 5.6 shows that in most organizations workers are disadvantaged in relation to managers not only because of their status in the hierarchy but also because of sex, lower education, age, and job tenure. In all these respects higher occupational levels possess more resources, which mean that it should be easier for higher levels to use laws and agreements relating to participation for their own benefit than it is for lower levels.

Table 5.6

Proportion of the 134 organizations in the sample of which the group of workers ad the management group possess at least a given level of collective resources

Group characteristic (possession of resources)	Workers (A)	Managers (B+C)	Managers÷Workers[a]
Average age of 40 years or more	19%	53%	2.79
Average tenure of 10 years or more	34%	85%	2.50
More than 50% men	72%	96%	1.33
On average, more than a secondary education	28%	71%	2.54
More than 20% of the group have served as representatives	35%	58%	1.66
More than 75% unionized	50%	42%	0.84

[a]The last column is constructed by dividing the two proportions and shows the relative advantage of the management group over workers.

This tendency is reinforced by the fact that a much higher proportion of managers (26 per cent of all middle managers) than of the rank and file (12 per cent of all workers) are members of a representative body. There are two reasons for this. Many managers sit on representative bodies as part of their official duties. In addition to this, they have the right to be represented as a group on representative bodies and since managers are relatively few in numbers, a relatively large proportion of them has to serve as representatives. Not even unionizaton diminishes the disadvantages of rank and file very much in relation to managers. The average unionization for work-level employees in the whole international sample is 71 per cent while for middle managers it is 60 per cent.

Each organization in our sample was assigned a score on a measure called Employee Mobilization, based on the degree to which both workers and managers are unionized and members of a representative body. This measure does not correlate strongly with any other of the measures based on the individual's background. Only two somewhat significant correlations were found between the other background variables. The Skill-level of the workers is negatively correlated with the Stability of the Work-force ($r = -0.23$, $n = 131$, sector partialed out). There is also a positive correlation between Male Domination and the Stability of The Work-force ($r = 0.21$, $n = 131$, sector partialled out). Since some of the indicators of resources are uncorrelated or even negatively correlated no consistent pattern could be expected showing some countries having relatively skilled and experienced workers while the workers in others lack equivalent resources. However, the group of workers in the French and the Belgian sampled companies rank consistently low on all the indicators discussed here. Sweden ranks consistently relatively high (c.f. IDE 1980, ch. 3).

ORGANIZATIONAL SUCCESS

We will now turn to the data that exists only at the organizational level for the 134 investigated organizations. These data have been gathered through interviews with one or a few top managers in each organization. Often the questions concerned personnel statistics and other quantitative and qualitative descriptors of the firm. Due to the fact that different people with different backgrounds were involved in gathering company data in the different countries, there are problems of comparability and problems of communicating from the companies to data-file in Berlin. These problems have tended to make the data somewhat unreliable thereby depriving these organizational measures of some of their explanatory potential. On the basis of theoretical considerations and factor analyses we have tried to construct a smaller number of indicators with an acceptable level of reliability.

One group of such context variables could be labelled Organizational Success. There might be a relationship between participation and organizational success. A high degree of participation could, for example, mean that employees become more motivated to work (Blumberg 1968, Vroom 1964), more pressure is exerted on the individual to conform to production norms (Coch and French 1948), there is less of a need for the employees to use their energy in beating or sabotaging the system and therefore less need for management to create a costly system for control and close supervision (Fox 1974). There are a number of studies that have attempted to evaluate the relationship between different forms of participation, including workers' ownership, and productivity. Many of them show a positive relationship and 'nothing in the literature suggests that participation significantly harms productivity' (Stokes 1978).

All these consequences of participation would mean increased organizational success. In the public debate arguments pointing to possible negative effects of participation are not hard to find. Employees may use their influence to block the hiring of more people even if that would be profitable and may be less inclined to make risky decisions. The protection of jobs at the individual plant may be given priority over maintaining the satisfactory performance of the whole firm. Participation could also mean that a lot of the organization's resources are spent on unproductive meetings, that expert opinions and other advantages of specialization are overlooked, or that effective decision-making is deadlocked in a continuous conflict between management and representatives of the workers.

However, this study does not deal with possible economic and other outcomes of participation at the level of the organization (though FitzRoy and Hiller (1978) outline some ways to use IDE data for these purposes). Organizational success is rather looked upon in this report as a factor that may affect the relationship between *de jure* participation and *de facto* participation and outcomes. Success could be expected to have a strong positive relationship with *de facto* participation—successful firms could afford to grant their employees more freedom (Farris. 1975). On the other hand, success may provide owners, top management, and bankers with an increased ability to resist any demands for power-sharing. So long as the economy seemingly performs well, the traditional economic ideology of the free entrepreneur is reinforced.

There are two theoretical schools on which the definition of the concept of success can be based. One is the system-orientated school (Katz and Kahn 1966, Seashore and Yuchtman 1967) which holds that success is that which contributes to the organization's ability to survive and mobilize resources. Common indicators for success in this line of thought are growth (in resources controlled by the organization) and favourable attitudes toward the organization by groups who have power to help or destroy it (Thompson 1967). In this study the only growth data we have at the organizational level is the increase of number of personnel between 1974 and 1976. Attitudinal data on success were gathered in each company by asking the top executive how he evaluated the company's profitability, efficiency, growth, morale, market adaptability, technological adaptability, and the adaptability of the personnel policy. However, it is hardly the attitudes of the top executive which determine the survival of a company. Survival is rather determined by the attitudes of bankers, government, owners, customers, and employees (March and Simon 1958). The top executive may, on the contrary, have a personal interest in subscribing to positive attitudes in order to reduce deep anxieties about the real success of the company. Therefore management appraisal is a dubious measure of organizational success. Quitting rates and absenteeism are possible indicators of how successful the organization is from the point of view of the employees. There are no clear differences between the national averages of either organizational growth or management evaluation of success. Neither are these two indicators of success correlated. The top managers' evaluation of success correlates weakly with how other managers and workers evaluate the organizational climate in terms of clarity of communication and structure ($r = 0.18$–0.22, $n = 100$–118). It lacks relationships with the rest of the contextual variables.

The second theoretical school regarding organizational success builds on the theory of the firm and theory of finance. A successful firm is according to these views one that manages to use its resources—capital and manpower—in an effective way. Common measures to evaluate this are return on invested capital and return on owners' capital (Weston 1961). However, using these measures a firm that chooses to pay its workers higher salaries, will be deemed less effective than an identical firm with lower salaries. Therefore, instead of looking at return (profit before accounting adjustments) one could look at 'value-added' (sales minus costs paid to suppliers) and measure effectiveness as value-added per dollar invested or per man-hour worked. There is also the theoretical possibility of constructing a mathematical formula called a production-function which shows what value-added can ordinarily be expected from a firm that puts X man-hours and Y dollars capital into its operation. If this expected value-added is compared to the reported value-added one gets a residual value which could be interpreted as an indicator of effectiveness. This residual factor is the contribution of disembodied technical progress, which represents learning how to use capital better and how to co-operate better within the firms (Faxén 1978). Faxén shows that 'disembodied progress' was responsible for 42 per cent of the total technical progress in Swedish manufacturing industry between 1947 and 1964.

The theory of labour-managed economies suggests that organizational success in highly participative firms will mean something else than in the truly capitalistic firm. The worker-managed firm will be less eager to grow than capitalist firms. The capitalist will continue to hire workers so long as they bring him some profit but the worker-managers will stop expanding operations if a new worker means decreasing the average profit per worker (Vanek 1970, Ward 1958).

The attempts made in the study to assemble financial data from our 134 organizations encountered many problems. Often, disaggregated data for the investigated establishments were not available or they were refused us as too sensitive. Attempts will, however, be made in another study to analyse the partial set of financial data available (FitzRoy and Hiller 1978). Also an enlarged project is being planned to make a more intensive study of the relationships between measures of participation and measures of success like financial performance and productivity.

The literature survey in this section has indicated that different types of relationship between organizational success and participation exist. We have also pointed at types of measure of success that could be constructed from the contextual data that were gathered in the investigated companies. Since financial data were obtained from only a small number of companies they have not been reported in this volume. A measure of success based on the top managers' evaluation seems to be more a reflection of organizational climate than other types of performance. This leaves us with organizational growth and possibly absenteeism and quitting rates as potentially usable indicators of success to be used in the analyses.

SIZE

In the system-orientated type of organization theory, size is regarded as an outcome of success and an indicator that the organization can attract resources (Katz and Kahn 1966). In our data there seems to be no association between organizational size and growth in number of employees during the period 1974–76. This observation could be explained by assuming that growth is very uneven and may shift from period to period. A large firm may not necessarily have achieved its size by a long and steady growth but may have done it through one intensive expansion period, whereupon it stagnated. Moreover, the firms in our sample have not achieved any growth during the measured period 1974–76.

In this study our interest lies not mainly in the origin of size but more in the consequences of size or the phenomena related to size. Most studies show a negative relationship between the size of the work group and attitudes of members (Porter and Lawler 1965). It is not clear if this relationship holds for the whole organization as well. It could be argued that almost all of the organizations in this study are well beyond the size of the small integrated group where everybody could participate in all aspects of organizational life. Even if size does not affect participation directly it could be expected to be associated with other company characteristics which in turn are related to participation. The size of the company could, for example, be expected to be related to hierarchy (Williamson 1975). The number of hierarchical levels could in turn be expected to influence the possibilities for participation for lower levels. Such possible correlates of size will be discussed in the following sections on structure and technology. The size distribution of companies in our organizational sample is given in Figure 5.2.

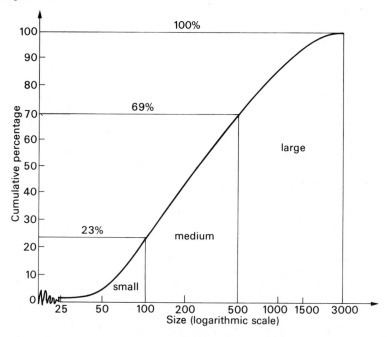

Figure 5.2. Distribution of the sampled establishments according to size. The horizontal lines show the proportion of companies belonging to each size category. (Mean = 270, Median = 251, n = 127.)

ORGANIZATIONAL ENVIRONMENT

Classical economic theory and systems theory see the relationship between the organization and the environment as a crucial one. Stinchcombe (1965) states, for example, that an organization tends to import the kind of social structure that is prevalent in society at the time when the technology, on which the organization builds, reaches its full maturity. The social structure tends to change very slowly after that time. Stymne (1970) shows how a Swedish employer's association established an institutionalized pattern of relationships with the trade unions and the government and built up a supporting internal structure which was very difficult to change when the needs of members changed. Chandler (1962) demonstrates how organizational choice of strategy, which means decisions to produce for certain markets, will lead to a certain organizational structure. The literature on strategic choice that uses concepts from Chandler, Ansoff (1965), and capital budgeting stresses the relationship between the market strength of a business and its capital structure, on the one hand and its independence on the other (Boston Consulting Group 1968).

The competitive position of a firm is strong if the firm is in an expanding market, if it has a large market share relative to its competitors, if the competitors are weak, if there are many buyers, and if the quality of the products is better than the competitors. Moreover success (measured as return on invested capital and cash flow) is high if the capital/sales ratio is low and the value added per work-hour is high (Schoeffler et al. 1974, Buzzel et al. 1975).

These strategic theories are definitely not developed in order to explain participation. They state, among other things, that being in a benign environment increases the probability of financial success. And as was suggested in the last section, successful firms may afford participation. But, as the strategic theories hint, a good market situation is not always a gift of Providence. It may well be the result of a skilful financial policy where production units are, with a terminology borrowed from the Boston Consulting Group, looked upon as milk-cows, dogs or stars and are accordingly milked, kicked, or pampered. If an active disinvestment policy (selling out or closing unpromising units) is a prerequisite for the good market position, then one may well find a negative correlation between market position and participation. The reverse of that proposition seems often to hold as well: when an organization has ended up in an impossible environmental situation then there is a sudden surge in the level of participation among the workers and their representatives.

Among the questions in the questionnaire used in this study the respondents were asked about what was most important for them in their jobs. Most of them answered: 'security of employment'. A good market position would probably be instrumental in fulfilling such a need. On the other hand, there are studies indicating that employees of firms in rich communities are more dissatisfied than workers in poor communities (Sexton and Yu-Chi-Chang, 1976/77). Satisfaction is based on comparisons with what seems to be possible for others in the en-environment.

An index of marketing position called Strength of Competitive Position was constructed by combining the following aspects of the firm's business environment: degree of competition, market share, share of production exported, company position in the market, and the state of the economy (according to a top manager's evaluation of the business cycle). The West German firms are, on average, high on this measure of Strength of Competitive Position while Israeli firms are low. The marketing position is generally deemed stronger for the metal than the service organizations.

The organizational environment is not just economic, it is also political. Rhenman (1973) and Selznick (1957) have, for example, pointed out the importance of a leadership function that specifies the mission of the organization and sees to it that the services of the organization become indispensable to the environment. This type of institutionalized organization is a far cry from the enterprise in a free and competitive economy. The firm under pure competition has absolutely no freedom (Simon 1969) but in spite of its well-defined place in society, Selznick's organization has a good deal of freedom—its survival being in a way, guaranteed by the organizational set (Evan 1976) or organizational network (Metcalfe 1975). Selznick's reasoning about leadership implies that the institutionalized organization is based on participation because legitimization presupposes broad support for the values on which the organization is built. The sense of sharing the firm's 'distinctive competence' would also imply that a certain pride is reflected in the attitudes of the work-force.

Table 5.7

Status of the sampled establishments in relation to company of which they are a part

Type of establishment	Relative Frequency (%)
Branch	20.1
Head branch	10.4
Subsidiary	26.9
Principal unit	23.9
Data missing	18.7
Total	100
n	134

A basic measure of independence is whether a unit is just a branch of a larger company or if it has a more autonomous status. As can be seen from Table 5.7 about a quarter of our units can be regarded as independent companies. About a fifth of the establishments are only branches in a larger company. A more complex index of the Formal Independence of a unit was constructed on the basis of a number of variables which, together with the reasoning behind the construction of the index are described below.

i. Number of years since the organization's foundation. Older organizations have had time to create a distinctive competence and to be fitted into an institutionalized network.

ii. Directors are not founders. If the founders are still active, the chances are that they will use the organization for their purposes rather than being interested in its role in society.

iii. Weak external financial interest. No outside power group can dictate policy.

iv. Public accountability. An indication that the organization has a broader responsibility than just to one owner, family, or a larger firm.

v. More than branch status. The organization is not the tool of a corporate management.

vi. Organization engages in stock production rather than in order production. Sign that it is the organization that defines its competence, not the customer.
vii. Largest customer is a minor outlet. The organization is not locked into a monopsony situation.

There are just a few inter-correlations stronger than r = 0.20 among the items of this index. Since the index correlates significantly with five out of the other contextual indices it could be deemed to have some reliability in spite of the low level of inter-correlations between items. Although there is a good deal of variation in the degree of independence within countries, the firms in the Danish sample are, on average, the most independent ones, while the Belgian and Dutch sampled firms are the least independent ones. On the whole the service firms are more independent than the metal manufacturing firms.

These notions of organizational independence have clear parallels with the concept of a well-integrated personality in dynamic psychology (Selznick 1952). Against the background of such notions it can be argued that an organization that is not dependent on either the whims of unpredictable markets nor the power of one outside actor is freer than other organizations to engage in participative practices.

Emery and Trist (1969) have used ideas similar to Selznick's in analysing how organizations in oligopolistic markets with union power and political interference tend to end up in a situation where they lose control (turbulence). The remedy is to form matrices of organizations where actors are linked together by a common value-system. Following Emery and Trist's argument it can be expected that a high rate of change in the environment will decrease the possibility that the organization can control its own fate and therefore the possibility that workers can influence what is happening. On the other hand, the motivation to participate may increase in a highly unstable situation. The unions can, for example, attempt to persuade the government to step in and impose some order in a situation that is fast deteriorating. Turbulence can also be expected to make individual employees anxious thereby reducing the degree of satisfaction.

A measure of the instability of the political environment was constructed by adding together the scores for answers which the interviewed top executive gave to questions about the frequency of changes in government control over the industry, in public attitudes, and the relationships with unions. There are quite strong differences between how executives from different countries have judged the changeability of their company's political environment. The political environment has been judged as especially unstable in the U.K., Norway, and Finland and as especially stable in Yugoslavia, Sweden, Holland, and West Germany. The political involvement of banking and insurance is reflected in the fact that the political instability of their environments is generally judged to be greater than that of the metal firms.

If we look upon the correlational pattern of the environmental variables we can observe that they are all related to Sector. The managers of service firms find themselves in a politically more changeable environment, they have less competitive strength, and they are formally more independent than the metal firms. Even if Sector is partialled out there is some tendency for managers of formally more independent units to perceive their environment as more variable than managers of more dependent units ($r = 0.17$, $n = 123$). Size is positively related to both Formal Independence ($r = .19$, $n = 123$) and Competitive Position ($r = .27$, $n = 125$) even when Sector is partialled out. There is also a small correlation between Independence and Employee Mobilization ($r = .19$, $n = 127$, sector partialled out).

TECHNOLOGY

The technology of an organization may influence possibilities for participation and satisfaction either directly or indirectly by affecting organizational structure. 'Technology is a technique or complex of techniques employed to alter "materials" (human or non-human, mental or physical) in an anticipated manner . . . technology rests upon the knowledge of the raw material' (Perrow 1965, p. 915). This knowledge can be carried by the people who work on the material, it can be built into the design of the product, the design of the whole production process, or the equipment. One starting point for the conceptualization of technology is therefore to find ways to describe the distribution and organization of knowledge among the different carriers.

One aspect of technology is how much knowledge is required by the individual, lowest-level employee. One extreme is represented by a job where the worker carries out one or a few simple machine-paced operations on a mass-fabricated type of product. Marx said that a capitalist society is driven to an incessant accumulation of capital which transforms technology in ways which induce an ever-increasing division of labour (Braverman 1974). Labour becomes alienated and a mere appendage of the capitalist mode of production (Blauner 1964). Durkheim (1974) suggested that the division of labour might lead to *anomie* and related problems for social integration. Also Weber saw the growth of rationality as a thought-system and as represented by the bureaucracy as an ideal-type organizational form having possible repercussions for individual freedom. Since these early writers there is ample evidence that with jobs that are highly specific, repetitive, and machine-paced, and where control over work is minimized and the use of personal skills restricted, a high level of dissatisfaction and psychosomatic disorder emerges (Walker and Guest 1952, Chinoy 1955, Woodward 1958, Gardell 1971). Also, alienation with loss of interest in the situation, in one's self and in the collectivity seems to result (Blauner 1964).

As was also pointed out above findings about the effects of individual jobs could lead us to expect that holders of routinized and machine-paced jobs would be especially dissatisfied and have little opportunity and motivation to participate. In this study we have not been able to construct a measure of the degree to which individual jobs are subdivided and stripped of content. As a proxy, an index of Skill-level has been constructed based on the relative number of skilled and unskilled workers in the company, the average education of workers, and how a specialist from the management team has evaluated the ability of workers to deal with unexpected situations. The samples from the different countries are not significantly different on this measure. The correlations between Skill-level and two of the other indicators of a more advanced technology used in this study are small. The third correlation, with Product Complexity, is positive (r = .24, n = 129, sector partialled out). These correlations do not lend support to the assumption that more advanced technologies increase the proportion of dull jobs among workers as long as skill-level is accepted as an indicator of content of jobs. The design of jobs may well vary considerably even if some of the over-all technological parameters are given. The Volvo Kalmar assembly plant shows that job enlargement and meaningful group work may be possible even in a situation of a completely pre-planned production flow and highly automated equipment (Agurén et al. 1976).

The type of product produced is an important aspect of technology. In our sample there are two main types of product: financial services and manufactured metal products. The two sectors differ strongly in three respects: the workers in the service firms are on a higher skill-level; there are many more women among them; and they are exclusively white-collar employees. Thompson (1967) classifies service organizations like insurance companies as having mediating technologies. In a mediating technology the problem is often to make a quick response to a customer who demands a certain service, usually by retrieving and processing some information related to the needs of the customer. The employees that work in direct contact with customers will therefore have a good deal of autonomy in relation to management. In principle, every customer could be treated differently but, to ensure a good economy, operations have to be governed by standardized rules. This standardization may become even more pronounced with more advanced degrees of computerization.

Dubin (1958) has argued that many workers look upon the job in an instrumental way and that they are not likely to respond positively to enlarged and challenging jobs. The quality of inter-personal relationships seems to be more important to workers than challenging work (Hofstede 1977). Many jobs in banks and insurance companies are much closer to the customer than jobs in manufacturing. This may give service workers a greater chance of fulfilling their social needs than workers in manufacturing industry and help produce more positive attitudes among service workers. Although the relative number of employees that has contacts with customers may increase with computerization, this development sometimes make customer contacts more impersonal and is a hindrance to contacts between peers.

In addition to skill-level and type of product, three indices were constructed to measure the degree to which equipment in the organization was automated, the extent to which the production flow was inter-linked (e.g. how long it takes before a breakdown at one point stops the whole process), and the complexity of the product(s). These measures are related to Woodward's (1965) concept of technological complexity. Hickson et al. (1969) found that measures of this type could be added up to form an index of the integration of work-flow. They concluded that their index only measures the technology of production operations. It does not say much about the technology of organizational sub-systems other than production. Since Hickson et al. show that the number of work-flow employees decreases with increasing work-flow integration, it is likely that the attitudes and experiences of the whole work-force will be less affected by operations technology the more integrated (or complex) this technology is.

They also indicate that the number of indirect workers increases with higher work-flow integration. This finding indicates that the room for individual freedom and for satisfying jobs may well increase even for the production workers in a more complex technology.

Our discussion has provided several arguments why we should not expect any strong negative relationship between the level of production technology and the participation opportunities and satisfaction levels of the work-force. It is still conceivable though, that Braverman's thesis is valid if we look only at production workers and if we hold their type of job and skill-level constant. It could be argued that the very meaning of a process of increasing technological complexity is that a good deal of control over work is moved away from the shop-floor to technical specialists, planners, designers, and suppliers. The lack of control may make the individual feel lost. Because of the capital that the technology represents human values may tend to become neglected in comparison with economic and technical values. The handling of expensive equipment and products may also be a source of stress and anxiety.

Even such a restricted and conditioned hypothesis could be countered by pointing at a number of factors that contribute to influence and satisfaction even if job-type is held constant. One such factor that contributes to influence is that automation often provides the worker with a more perfect tool. Another is that when the production flow gets very complex it may become extremely dependent on continuous observation and care by workers, which will make them influential. The threat-potential of strikes increases in a capital-intensive technology. There are also factors associated with increased technical complexity which could contribute to more positive attitudes even if the number of unqualified jobs is kept constant. Working with advanced equipment and being responsible for valuable machinery and equipment may add to a sense of pride. Working on a sophisticated product may be an important source of satisfaction even if it does not provide more influence for the individual. One could also argue that technical progress is one of the basic values in the societies studied. Therefore, being associated with a highly complex technical system might induce a sense of participation in a valuable collective effort and a sense of collective pride and satisfaction.

There are small differences in average Skill-level of workers and Automation-levels between the national samples. West German and Finnish sampled firms are somewhat higher than the other national samples on Technological Interdependence while the Dutch and Danish sampled firms are lower. There are considerable differences in the average Product-complexity between the sampled organizations from different countries. The Norwegian, Finnish, West German, French, and Yugoslavian samples are high on this measure while the samples from Sweden, Denmark, and Belgium are low.

There are economic measures that could be used as indicators of technical complexity, like the average value of the capital equipment per employee. A proxy for this, at the national level, is the gross domestic product per inhabitant, which, on the whole, is a sign of the capital-intensity of an economy. The correlations of the national samples rankings on Skill-level, Automation-level, Technological Interdependence, and Product-complexity with GDP are all small, although consistently negative. This may be an indication that, in the more advanced economies, questions of handling technical complexity are resolved at the level of the (often multi-national) industrial group or corporation. In principle, development and design are carried out at these levels and the individual establishments are only allocated specified tasks.

Table 5.8 shows that Skill-level and Automation-level in the service firms are higher than in the metal firms. When Sector is partialled out, Skill-level seems unrelated to Automation-level but positively related to Product-complexity ($r = .24$, $n = 129$). Automation-level is positively related to both Product-complexity

Table 5.8
Correlations between Sector and the other technological variables

	Sector[a] (Service = high)	Partial correlations/sector constant			
Skill-level of workers	.41	—			
Automation-level	.21	$-.05$[b]	—		
Technological Inter-dependence	$-.17$	.10	.25	—	
Product-complexity	$-.15$	.24	.30	.16	—

[a]Dummy variable Manufacturing = 1, Service = 2.
[b]Intercorrelations between the variables of technological complexity when Sector is partialed out.

($r = .30$, $n = 127$) and Technological Interdependence ($r = .25$, $n = 127$). There is a slight tendency for Product-complexity to be central in this network of correlations indicating that complex products could be achieved either by an automated and interdependent technology or by a highly skilled work-force.

Size is related to only one of the technological variables, namely Automation-level ($r = .34$, $n = 122$). Sector is, as has been pointed out before, correlated with all the three indicators of organizational environment. The service companies are generally higher than the metal firms on Formal Independence and Political Instability but lower on Competitive Position. There is also a correlation between Competitive Position and Automation-level (0.31, $n = 124$, sector partialed out).

ADMINISTRATIVE STRUCTURE

The measures of administrative structure used in this study are, to a large extent, based on the measures discussed in Pugh et al. (1968). Their research can be placed in the tradition that tries to build on Weber's conceptualization of what a bureaucracy is. They suggest that Weber's ideal-type is replaced with a more elaborate taxonomy based on factors extracted out of empirical research. Weber's (1947) definition of a bureaucracy defines an administrative structure as a system of role expectations and norms which are intentionally related to the organization's goal. In the work of Pugh et al., as in our own, the rationality aspect of the administrative structure does not play a very prominent role. More attention is paid to how many different types of role there are, the relative proportion of different roles, the extent to which rules are formalized, etc.

Five indices of administrative structure were constructed from the interviews with specialists in the organization and from examination of charts and records. The first measure is Functional Differentiation which is defined as the number of specialities represented by at least one full-time employee. This measure is based on a list suggested by Pugh et al. (1968). A second item is the average Span of control of the Top Managers. This measure could also be taken as a sign of differentiation, since the larger the span of control, the more specialities there are. A third measure is Formalization, which is constructed by counting the number of rules, procedures, instructions, and communications which are written down in a number of specified areas. The analysis of Pugh et al. suggests that 'formalization and standardization are closely related and can both be taken as indicators of the degree to which organizational activities are structured. The fourth measure, Vertical Span, is defined as the largest number of levels that can be found between the top executive and a lowest-level employee. Pugh et al. found this measure was also an indicator of the structuring of activities. Their results show that vertical span is also an indicator of the absence of a sizeable supportive component. Our fifth measure is based on three interrelated variables and is called Intensity of Control. An organization that is high on Intensity of Control has only a few workers supervised by each supervisor, it has a high proportion of administrative workers in relation to the number of work-flow employees, and it does not employ an incentive payment system. Intensity of control very much resembles factor III 'Line control of work-flow' used by Pugh et al. Subordinate ratio and recording of role performance have negative loadings on this factor and the number of clerks has a positive loading. It could be seen as an indicator of the degree to which more personal rather than impersonal forms of control are used within the organization. A deeper treatment of the control part of the administrative system would require data about the planning and scheduling system and about the kind of reporting and information systems used.

A high degree of differentiation and specialization could mean that influence is spread out in the organization and that the legitimacy of differences in goals and affective and cognitive orientations are recognized (Lawrence and Lorsch 1967). The uniqueness of each person may be more easily accepted in a more specialized system. Lammers (1977) cites a number of studies which indicate that organizations with quite an elaborate hierarchical form are less authoritarian than organizations with relatively simple forms. This is also in line with Pugh et al. (1968) who report a strong, negative correlation between specialization and centralization of decision-making. Such a result could be interpreted to mean that opportunities for participation would be greater in more differentiated organizations. But there is also a danger that the specialities of a highly differentiated organization also serve as justifications to keep the non-specialized workers out of all interesting tasks like design, planning, co-ordination, and customer contacts and to confine him to a job the content of which is determined by the specialists (Thorsrud and Emery 1969). An example of this is that the specialized language and technical knowledge of computer systems specialists makes it extremely difficult for other employees to influence the systems design process even if deliberate attempts are made to get them involved (Docherty et al. 1977). In spite of the fact that more differentiated organizations seem to create more jobs for highly trained specialists, it is not inconceivable that they make the jobs for a minority of employees ever more sub-divided and meaningless. These are at the same time jobs that easily can be eliminated by means of continued automation.

Specialization may operate in a similar way in relation to attitudes as in relation to opportunities to influence. Specialization could mean challenging and socially valuable roles for many, but a rather unrewarding situation for an unspecialized minority.

Formalization is shown to be strongly related to specialization in the study by Pugh et al. (1968) though conceptually, it can be seen as different from specialization. It could be interpreted as an attempt to increase the predictability and to regulate behaviour according to explicit rules. In this respect it could be linked to Burns and Stalker's (1961) concept of a mechanistic structure. A mechanistic structure is difficult to change. It is designed not to change in order to be able to run as undisturbed and effectively as possible. Formalization may therefore mean less possibilities to influence. However, since *de jure* participation, by definition, is a kind of formalization, it may be more easily transformed into action in a culture which is already accustomed to formal rules. When a person moves from a mechanistic structure to a more organic one he can be expected to be relieved of a number of constraints which he may have perceived as annoying. On the other hand, the increased ambiguity in the organic structure may induce feelings of insecurity and stress (Kahn et al 1964). Satisfaction and formalization may therefore have a curvilinear relationship so that extremely high degrees of formalization as well as a total lack of formalization both induce dissatisfaction.

A high value on the measure of Intensity of Control could mean that most workers are closely supervised and that they therefore have very little freedom. The presence of supervisors and other human agents and the absence of impersonal incentive payment systems may, on the other hand, be interpreted as providing access to people that potentially can be bargained with or otherwise influenced. Whether a high Intensity of Control increases or decreases the ability of lower-level employees to influence may be determined by value considerations and by the role conceptions of the supervisors and experts. Do they see their duties as issuing orders or do they see themselves as teachers and consultants in relation to the workers (Stymne 1977)?

The average rating and rank orders of the sampled companies from different countries on the adminstrative indices are shown in Table 5.9. The largest differences are found in Vertical Span. On average more than 5 hierarchical levels in between the top executive and the workers are reported in Holland and the U.K. The Swedish and Belgian units investigated are reported to have an average of less than 3 layers between top and bottom. The differences between countries are also rather large for Functional Differentiation. The Yugoslav firms stand out as highly differentiated while the Danish, French, and Swedish firms have considerably lower degrees of Functional Differentiation.

Table 5.9
Administrative structure

	Functional differentiation (16 = high)	Vertical Span (max = 6)	Formalization (max = 16)	Span of Top Managers	Intensity of Control 3 = high
Norway	9.5[a] (4)[b]	4.7 (4)	7.5 (8)	6.1 (2)	1.7 (11)
Sweden	6.5 (9)	2.7 (11)	10.9 (2)	9.9 (1)	1.8 (8)
Denmark	6.0 (12)	3.5 (7)	8.8 (6)	4.7 (4)	1.5 (12)
Finland	8.6 (6)	3.3 (8)	9.8 (4)	3.4 (7)	2.2 (5)
U.K.	6.5 (10)	5.3 (2)	10.4 (3)	3.4 (6)	2.3 (4)
Germany (West)	9.9 (2)	3.1 (9)	7.9 (7)	2.6 (10)	2.5 (1)
Holland	7.6 (8)	5.3 (1)	7.3 (9)	5.3 (3)	2.3 (2)
Belgium	9.5 (5)	2.8 (10)	9.6 (5)	3.0 (8)	1.8 (9)
France	6.2 (11)	3.7 (6)	7.1 (10)	3.8 (5)	2.3 (3)
Italy	9.8 (3)	?[c]	5.6 (12)	2.5 (11)	2.1 (6)
Yugoslavia	12.4 (1)	4.9 (3)	12.1 (1)	3.0 (9)	1.8 (10)
Israel	8.2 (7)	4.2 (5)	7.0 (11)	?	1.9 (7)
Mean	8.1	3.8	8.9	4.9	2.0
S.D.	3.9	1.5	3.8	5.6	0.65
n	129	98	132	107	127
F (one way analysis of variance)	2.8 (p=0.003)	6.76 (p<0.001)	2.43 (p=0.01)	1.7 (p=0.08)	2.06 (p=0.03)

[a] Averages for national samples
[b] Rank order in brackets
[c] (?) = Many observations missing.

When our measures of administrative structure are inter-correlated a simple pattern emerges. The degree of Functional Differentiation correlates with all other measures, but the other measures do not have any significant inter-correlations. This means that the administrative structure of our firms can roughly be described as ranging from much to little differentiated. The correlations between differentiation and the other measures are shown in Table 5.10.

Table 5.10
*Correlations between Functional Differentiation and the
other measures of administrative structure*

	Functional Differentiation	n	p
Vertical Span	.35	94	< .001
Formalization	.31	128	< .001
Span of Top Managers	.34	104	< .001
Intensity of Control	−.22	124	.01

Woodward (1965) drew the conclusion from her findings that technology is more important as a determinant of organizational structure than size. Hickson et al. (1969) lean the other way and say that size is more important. They suggest that Woodward was not able to detect this since her size range was so restricted. Our data seem to support the Aston group's hypothesis. The correlation between Size and Functional Differentiation is $r = 0.68$ ($n = 123$). Functional Differentiation correlates also with two of the indicators of technology, namely Automation-level ($r = 0.25$, $n = 126$) and Product-complexity ($r = 0.27$, $n = 128$). Differentiation is also related to environment and correlates $r = 0.21$ ($n = 127$) with Formal Independence and $r = 0.25$ ($n = 125$) with Competitive Position. However, the correlations between differentiation on one hand and technology and environment on the other disappear or are reduced when Size is kept constant. Also, the other indicators of administrative structure are related to Size. In addition to this there is a negative correlation between Vertical Span and Employee Mobilization ($r = -.20$, $n = 97$) and a positive correlation between Vertical Span and organizational Growth ($r = .26$, $n = 79$). There is also a positive correlation between Intensity of Control and Sector ($r = .27$, $n = 127$), that is control seems to be more personal in the service industry.

The analysis of relationships between our measures of administrative structure and other variables leaves us with Size as the most powerful predictor of structure. We have not been able to find support for a technological imperative that dictates the shape of the structure or for the hypothesis that the structure is a mapping of the environment. The strong correlation between Size and Functional Differentiation could possibly be interpreted as a necessity for organizations to become more differentiated as they grow larger. The attractiveness of growing larger is indicated by the positive correlations between Formal Independence and Competitive Position on the one hand and Size on the other. Of the indices describing administrative structure only Functional Differentiation correlates strongly with Size. This suggests that other aspects of administrative structure like the number of hierarchical levels and the character of the control system can vary according to an act of organizational choice (Trist et al. 1963, Rice 1963). If our findings and also the findings of others who generally report weak relationship between technology and structure (Gerwin 1977) are interpreted in this way it follows that it is not necessary to ask what kind of administrative arrangements for participation are technically feasible. We would rather expect that, independently of the technology used, there is a choice between adminstrative arrangements to be made, for example, in terms of forms of employee participation. The value orientations of those involved will probably influence the outcome of that choice.

ORGANIZATIONAL CLIMATE AND RATING OF DIRECT PARTICIPATION

Organizational climate and leadership styles are aspects of the social structure of an organization which are probably influenced by the structure and value patterns in the surrounding society (see Chapter 9). Generally we would expect that groups that perceive the organizational climate as good are also likely to judge other aspects of the organization favourably. Also, the way the leadership style of one's supervisor is seen could be expected to be related to one's attitudes concerning other matters.

The concept of leadership style has been elaborated by Rensis Likert. He suggests a typology of four different types of organizational regime ranging from authoritarian to participative. In the participative form the behaviour of the supervisor is described as developing 'his group into a unit which, with his participation, makes better decisions than he can make alone. He helps the group develop efficient communication and influence processes which provide it with better information, more technical knowledge, more facts, and more experience for decision-making purposes than the leader alone can marshal.' (Likert 1961: 170). Also, variables describing the organizational climate are included in Likert's model. Organizational climate has been defined as 'a relatively enduring quality of the internal environment of an organization that is (a) experienced by its members, (b) influences their behaviour and (c) can be described in terms of the values of a particular set of characteristics of the organization' (Tagiuri and Litwin 1968). Likert (1967) sees organizational climate as a variable determining the boundaries for the behaviour of lower-level supervisors and through them having an effect upon the opinions and attitudes of workers towards work and other attributes of their employer organization.

Likert claims that his participative system four, which includes both a democratic leadership style and a supportive climate, will result in positive outcomes in terms of productivity and satisfied personnel (Likert 1967). Since one of the main characteristics of system four is a flat influence structure, a participative leadership style should go hand in hand with a high degree of influence for the members of groups or organizations with participative supervision. Actually, Likert's writings may be interpreted as showing that real power-sharing can be established if, and only if, his system four is established. If that theory holds leadership style and climate should be able to explain differences in *de facto* participation and *de jure* participation should be quite irrelevant.

Likert's model has been criticized for being based on an assumption that consensus is always good for the functioning of an organization. More recent research has suggested that leadership style and situational requirements interact so that different styles of leadership apply in different situations (Vroom and Yetton 1973). According to this line of thinking Heller (1971) indicates that there are types of leadership behaviour other than obtaining consensus that may be even more conducive to participation. Such styles of leadership could be delegation or autonomy. Exactly how employees will respond to their superiors' behaviour is, according to these theories, dependent on other situational characteristics.

An index called Rating of Direct Participation was constructed by adding the following items together: (i) superior consults you before taking decision; (ii) boss gives you reason for changes; (iii) boss gives you opportunity to decide on your own; (iv) you can tell your boss if you had a different opinion. The average rating of the workers in any organization can be taken as an indicator of the degree of participative leadership. Organizational climate was divided up into one structural dimension, which concerns clarity of authority relationships, communication, and procedures, (Climate-Structure) and one relational dimension reflecting the quality of relationships between management and other employees (Climate-Relations).

The ratings of organizational climate by supervisors is usually more positive than that of workers. The supervisors' ratings are correlated ($r = 0.60$, n = 123) with the ratings of workers. The ratings of middle managers are a bit higher still than the ratings of supervisors. The middle managers' ratings are correlated, though not so strongly, with the ratings of both workers and supervisors ($r = .37-.49$, n = 134). There is a strong correlation between how workers rate the relational aspect of the climate and how they rate direct participation ($r = .64$, n = 131). If countries are rank-ordered according to their positions on these two indices, an interesting shift in Yugoslavia's position can be observed. While Yugoslavia is among the lowest on quality of management–employee relations, it is second on workers' rating of direct participation.

From Table 5.11 it can be seen that rating of direct participation is also more favourable at higher hierarchical levels. This means that workers experience a less benign climate and less of a participative leadership style than management. If Likert's theory about the importance of style of leadership and climate holds, a further cause why the level of influence of workers is so depressed and why they are unsatisfied has been added. Earlier, relative lack of resources for participation was suggested as another explanation.

Table 5.11 also shows that, although workers in all countries rate direct participation lower than managers, the rank-orders of the countries are, on the whole, the same for workers and the two management groups. In three instances there are, however, considerable shifts in a country's position when workers and managers are compared. The managers in the Finnish and French sampled firms rate direct participation much more highly than the workers. The case in Yugoslavia is the opposite. While workers' rating of direct participation is among the highest, managers' ratings rank among the lower.

Some relationships can be found between the climate and direct participation

Table 5.11

Rating of direct participation in the national samples

Country	Workers .		Foremen		Middle managers	
Norway	32.4[a]	(5)[b]	39.1	(4)	41.8	(4)
Sweden	31.1	(7)	38.3	(5)	40.9	(5)
Denmark	37.9	(1)	45.2	(1)	45.8	(1)
Finland	29.6	(10)	37.7	(7)	43.9	(2)
U.K.	31.5	(6)	37.2	(9)	39.3	(7)
Germany (West)	33.0	(4)	39.2	(3)	–	
Holland	33.3	(3)	39.5	(2)	40.9	(6)
Belgium	30.1	(8)	36.8	(10)	36.7	(9)
France	29.6	(9)	37.7	(6)	42.4	(3)
Italy	28.7	(12)	36.6	(11)	35.3	(10)
Yugoslavia	34.2	(2)	37.6	(8)	39.1	(8)
Israel	29.4	(11)	31.2	(12)	32.1	(11)
Mean	31.8		38.2		40.7	
S.D.	3.66		4.37		5.59	
n	131		124		94	
F (one way analysis variance)	6.88	(.001)	4.22	(.001)	4.35	(.001)

[a]The measure based on the average rating of these hierarchical groups in each organization.
[b]Rank orders in brackets.

and other contextual variables. In organizations where Absenteeism is high workers, supervisors, and middle managers rate direct participation in more negative terms ($r = -.23-(-.34)$, n = 67-68). Supervisors also rate the quality of management-employee relationships as high in organizations with a stable work-force ($r = .28$, n = 128). This gives an indication that there is some relationship between the behaviour of workers and the way different groups evaluate direct participation.

There are no relationships between Size and the climate and leadership measures. However, in firms that have avoided contraction middle managers rate clarity of communication higher than their colleagues from contracting firms ($r = -.28$, n = 93). For both workers and managers the quality of management-employee relations is judged more positively in older firms and in firms which have no founders among their directors ($r = .20-.34$, n = 101-112). Workers and middle managers in service firms rate the relational aspect of climate and direct participation higher than their counterparts in metal manufacturing ($r = .19-.31$, n = 94-134). Workers rate these aspects low in firms with a highly interdependent work-flow ($r = -.20-(-.28)$, n = 129-132). At the same time their supervisors give higher ratings to the structural part of organizational climate when the work-flow is interdependent ($r = .22$, n = 126). Workers rate relations lower in organizations with complex products ($r = -.25$, n = 132). Workers give higher ratings to clarity of communication and structure in organizations which are high on Functional Differentiation and where the top level has a wide span of control ($r = .23-.25$, n = 98-128). Formalization is negatively related to workers' rating of the quality of management–employee relationships ($r = -.20$, $n = 134$).

There are strong differences between employees from different organizations in how they rate organizational climate and direct participation. This may make these contingency variables potential powerful co-predictors of *de facto* participation and attitudinal outcomes. However, the disagreement that exists in the literature about the meaning of both climate and leadership style complicates the interpretation. The sizeable differences between countries in these variables suggests that some extra-organizational factor, like value orientations in society, plays an important role when evaluations of climate and direct participation are made.

CONCLUSIONS

To sum up, we now have presented background data on our almost 8,000 respondents and the 134 organizations they come from in order to see if there are some characteristics that—on the basis of received theorizing and research—may be assumed to influence the aspects of participation and attitudes that are analysed in later chapters.

One conclusion drawn is that the kind of job a person holds is important for participation and attitudes. However, job category is not included in the analyses but it can indirectly be analysed since 100 per cent of the service industry respondents are white-collar workers against less than 20 per cent in the metal sector.

Since jobs at higher hierarchical levels can be expected to have more power and status attached to them in relation to lower levels, level is always analysed separately. In this chapter we have also demonstrated that levels are different in several respects that may increase the disadvantages of lower levels. People on lower levels are, for example, younger, have less tenure, have less education, consist of a lower percentage of men, have fewer members who have served as representatives, work in a less favourable organizational climate, and are subjected to less participative supervision.

The degree to which employees have an opportunity to participate in decision-making can be seen as an aspect of how the administrative structure of an organization is arranged. Our analysis of the data describing the investigated establishments show that there are no strong relationships between administrative structure on the one hand and production technology and organizational environment on the other. This points to the conclusion that aspects of the administrative structure are a matter of choice rather than being predetermined by a technological imperative or environmental pressures. However, there seems to be quite a strong pressure to change the structure in the direction of increased differentiation when the organization becomes larger.

It has also been shown that the sampled organizations vary in the way and extent to which employees are mobilized in order to influence according to country. The Yugoslav system mobilizes a large proportion of employees as representatives. The Nordic countries have a system where unions are the main way for workers to influence and where unions organize almost everybody. The

Continental countries have systems where unions usually mobilize just a minority. The bodies with elected employees that exist at the establishment level in these countries have, however, produced a fair number of people who have served as representatives. The way in which, and the extent to which, employees are mobilized in some kind of system that will represent their interests will probably affect both their degree of actual participation and their attitudes towards the system. This is especially important since the respondents were not asked to evaluate the ways unions handle the interests of employees but only how the representative bodies handle these matters (c.f., IDE 1980).

6

FORMAL NORMS AND PARTICIPATION

INTRODUCTION

The central theme of this research is about measuring the impact of formal rules and regulations for participation on the actual involvement of employees in organizational decision-making. This presupposes the independent measurement of such rules and regulations—*de jure* participation (PS) which then must be related to behavioural data—*de facto* participation (PO). In this chapter we will present our findings of how countries and companies differ with respect to *de jure* participation. Before reviewing the methods employed and presenting the data itself we shall briefly discuss the general theoretical and methodological problems of comparing legal (formal) systems cross-nationally.

The Nature and Functions of Formal Forms

The meaning of laws or any other kind of formal rules or norms in society has challenged some of the greatest minds concerned with social theory and societal analysis. Montesquieu, Durkheim, and Weber are but a few of those who may be mentioned. While this is not the place to trace their lines of thinking about law, some conceptual perspectives relevant for this research must be described.

The sociology of law has distinguished three types of norm relating to behaviour and behavioural expectations: folkways, mores, and legal norms (König 1971).[1] Folkways are considered as relatively stable patterns of behaviour, deriving their legitimacy merely from the implicit consensus of those using them (usages—Sumner 1940). In most cases, it is not possible to identify the specific rational roots of such habits and customs, and only minor sanctions are to be expected in case of non-compliance.

Mores can, in turn, be distinguished from folkways, although they too are in use as a result of habitual practice. They are considered as consciously and verbally formulated rules, intrinsically related to significant events in the human life-cycle such as birth, marriage, and death. Behavioural deviance from mores will be more strictly sanctioned by the group which adheres to these norms, than is the case for deviance from mere folkways.

Legal norms have further characteristics differentiating them from folkways and mores. They exist as verbally formulated distinguishable formal rules—written down or enacted—which tend to be defined and integrated into a logically consistent system of normative regulations, in effect a code. In this sense, a collective bargaining agreement—although not strictly being a law—would also have the logical status of a 'legal' norm. Conformity to legal norms is often accomplished with the help of special institutions and groups charged with law enforcing responsibilities—judges, police, governmental or joint control agencies. As such, legal norms—unlike folkways and mores—have not 'always been there' but were, at some point in time, explicitly promulgated and stated by authorized groups or institutions. To what end?

A perceptive observer, Borucka-Arctowa (1977: 156), contends that 'by including in legal regulation some defined patterns of behaviour which were until now regulated by customary moral and organizational norms one may intend:

a) to stimulate and complete certain changes occurring in the sphere of behaviour and previously coming under the influence of normative systems other than legal;

b) to control the changes occurring in other normative systems;

c) to preserve and establish a status quo desirable from the view point of legal policy;

d) to remove the customary, moral and other norms considered to be undesirable for the life of society.'

This statement of normative intentions covers two fundamental aspects of legal norms. They can be used as instruments of directed social change, thus giving legitimacy to events and behaviour which will occur in the future—'anticipatory legitimacy'. However, they can also be used as instruments to preserve or 'freeze-in' a status quo perceived to be desirable by dominant interest groups—'ex post legitimacy'.

The question whether legislation—or for that matter any kind of formal rule-making by authorities or contracting parties—can bring about any social change whatsoever, is not only far from being trivial but is, in fact, of great interest to all kinds of policy-makers. The issue relates to two of the main trends in the traditional sociology of law, one which regards law as an independent variable in a cause-and-effect chain; and the other which regards social change as the major force promoting legislative innovation in a stimulus-response pattern. In line with this argument, Sumner (1940) insisted that legally induced 'changes which are opposed to the mores require long and patient effort, if they are possible at all', but that 'changes which run with the mores are easily brought about' (94-95). A somewhat integrative view is taken by Nagel (1970) who views the relationship of law and change as being reciprocal. In this light, the process of legalization is seen as resulting from continuous socio-political interaction and the degree to which law promotes social change or to which it only 'rides the waves of change' is dependent on a variety of contingent conditions of an economic, social, political, and cultural nature. Some of the practical implications of these positions will be taken up again in Chapter 11 when we discuss the policy aspects that emerge from our findings.

Norms for Participation

Virtually all West European countries, and a good many Third World countries, presently are deliberating upon or already are trying to establish new legal norms to regulate the involvement and participation of employees in company decision-making. The issue of promoting 'industrial democracy' through statutory rules has, in fact, become one of the central items on the agenda of social policy formulation in modern societies. This is true not only for countries with somewhat weak or divided trade union movements but also in countries where unions and the labour movement play a key role in the economic and political system like in Scandinavia and the U.K. Various authors have reviewed the trends and cross-currents of the ongoing lively discussions in European countries (Batstone and Davies 1976, von Beyme 1976, Business International 1974. Hondrich 1970, King and van de Vall 1978, Lecher and Sieling-Wendeling 1977). Underlying these debates is the belief that positive law will indeed bring about changes in formal structure and behaviour in work organizations. It is precisely this 'voluntaristic' notion[2] that can be put to the test by this research.

It seems a feature of these national developments that they receive attention with a relatively developed awareness of what is going on in other countries. Reasons for this are manifold. Mass media, international business activities, travel, and internationalization of professional contacts have led to a 'shrinking world' that makes it mandatory to discuss one's home country issues with reference to what is happening abroad. An additional thrust towards an international dimension originates from the Commission of the European Community which has decided to explore possibilities of and needs for harmonizing national schemes for industrial democracy within its member countries (Pipkorn 1978). The motives for the Commission's attempt to develop a unified legislative policy in this area are partly due to legal requirements: the Treaty of Rome calls for the creation of an internal market among all member countries and differences in industrial democracy schemes are considered as barriers to that end. Partly it is due to social policy requirements: the intention to create a true community for all workers in member countries. Finally, it is partly due to practical considerations: to alleviate obstacles for internationally active companies which would have to adjust to various different management-labour regulations (cf. Wilpert 1977). Efforts to develop a statute of the European Company—*Societas Europea*—(Nagels and Sorge 1977) and the harmonization efforts through the 'Greenbook' (Kommission 1975) provide testimony to the Commission's efforts.

However, one critical weakness in all these national and international considerations is the lack of persuasive evidence from social science research, as to how these various schemes function in reality. Thus, the debates are carried on mostly on the basis of political axioms and opinion about the nature of the real world rather than established facts. If participation is seen as 'the most vital organizational problem of our time' (Mulder 1971: 31) then this is a most lamentable state of affairs. This situation reflects the general shortcomings of international comparative organization research, a field that is not yet well developed (Roberts 1970). The problem is further aggravated when hotly-debated, value-laden issues form the focus of research, as in the case of the IDE study: *de facto* participation and power distribution related to formal rules and regulations (*de jure* participation). The study takes place in a context where some unionists and industrial sociologists (e.g. Fox 1974) have warned that formalized participation schemes may actually curtail the freedom of unions to promote the interests of their members. Similarly, reactions to the suggestions of the Bullock Report in the U.K. to put worker directors on the boards of companies show that the pressure towards participation schemes cannot be taken for granted everywhere. Comparative research evidence, which attempts to be both hard and unbiased, is thus urgently needed.

The IDE Research Problem

The international comparison of normative systems has generally been marked by descriptive approaches with little, if any, attempt to quantify and to measure differences systematically. First comprehensive proposals for a global approach to study legal systems cross-nationally were made by Evan (1965, 1968); however, the necessary development of indicators remained rather preliminary. Theoretical advances that might improve the comparison of legal systems have only recently been made (Black 1976, Evan 1978). The same holds for international comparisons of industrial relations systems and national systems of employee participation: descriptive legal comparativism predominates (see the various publications of the Geneva-based International Institute of Labour Studies, Dunlop 1958). Yet, the self-restriction of comparative jurisprudence to describing idiographically various national normative systems, and hence the lack of rigorous measurement tools for systematic legal comparisons is only one aspect of a two-sided problem. The other is, as described above, our lack of knowledge regarding the *de facto* behavioural consequences of different norms and legal systems of participation.

An international, comparative study offers the unique chance to investigate the conditions under which legislation concerning the structure and functioning of work organizations, or indeed any formal structure, may be effective. By using the existing differences of national participative systems as quasi-experimental treatments, we can thus try to remove, to some extent, one obstacle to designing more effective schemes of participation. This could occur if we broaden the fund of knowledge about the conditions which make for the success or failure of legislation to increase worker participation. The research paradigm involved is clearly of the type of classical impact studies. After verifying the existence of some kind of formal rule or norm one confronts its intention with its *de facto* effectiveness, that is either the degree to which it achieves compliance in social interactions (Hirsch 1971) or leads to other non-intended consequences (Blankenburg 1977).

PROBLEMS OF CROSS-NATIONAL COMPARABILITY

The 'Context-embeddedness' of Legal Norms

Formal rules, norms, and regulations are not isolated phenomena but must be seen as contextually-defined categories: different contexts may specify the precise significance of identically phrased norms quite differently. This poses substantial problems for any attempt to identify the 'true' meaning of given norms, that is to establish their comparability. At least five major inter-related characteristics in the encompassing societal (national) system seem to be relevant for the purpose of our study: dominant values, legal traditions, characteristics of the surrounding institutional area, differences in intra-organizational differentiation, and politico-economic climate. Countries differ qualitatively in these characteristics; and such differences may confound comparability.[3]

i. Dominant Values

One of the fundamental ways in which social values demonstrate their impact is by forming cognitive maps in the minds of people. If Germans in general feel that, in spite of occasionally vociferous articulation of divergent interests, employees and unions on the one hand and employers on the other are basically 'in the same boat', they will—in the long run—favour co-operative problem solution. If the French, on the other hand, think that, in the long run, there 'really' exists a fundamental cleavage between management and labour, then they will tend to perceive industrial relations, normally oppositional. It is from such core beliefs about the intrinsic nature of society that norms about 'proper' interactions are derived. These core beliefs might be seen as differing from one extreme (both parties have practically no common, and only conflicting, interests and, hence, participation through elected representatives in management decision-making can only be viewed as a managerial strategy, to corrupt workers' true interests) to the other (both parties have much more in common than conflicting interests and hence, works' councils and the like provide opportunities for an effective articulation and pursuit of workers' interests). One might hypothesize from this that specific legal norms for participation take on quite a different meaning and dignity, depending on their respective value-embeddedness. Thus, it could be that legislative efforts to promote employee participation are most important in the middle ranges of this polar dimension, while in a basically consensual setting, they are deemed unimportant, and in a basically conflictual setting they are perceived as illegitimate.

ii. Legal Tradition

Countries not only differ in their dominant value orientations but also in their legal traditions, which in fact might be a reflection of the dominant consensus as to the main functions and objectives of legislative means. In the field of industrial relations Germany is characterized by a long-standing tradition of structuring 'social partner relations' through legal, statutory provisions. Such provisions frequently are phrased as assertive or prohibitive 'command' norms (Feeley 1976) with a deliberate attempt to formulate them in a logically consistent manner. This characteristic might flow from a basic belief that social change can best be promoted through legislation. Quite different is the Italian preference for 'guaranteeing' legislation in industrial relations which tends to codify ('freeze-in') a given power relationship reached at a certain point in time by way of industrial conflict. Feeley describes such norms as status or 'right-conferring' norms. Still another legal tradition can be described in the case of British labour law which, until recently, was predominantly 'negative' in the sense that it consisted of regulations which by means of 'facilitating norms' created the necessary freedom for collective bargaining and carved out an enclave of judiciary non-interference for industrial relations (Clegg 1976, MacDonald 1976, Streeck 1978). Somewhere in between specific command norms and facilitating norms might come norms that stipulate minimum requirements (e.g. a certain number of employee representatives on supervisory boards) with the implicit or explicit recommendation that these minimum standards should be surpassed with the aid of freely negotiated arrangements between bargaining parties, possibly up to a stipulated maximum level. It can easily be seen that different legal traditions might favour different types of legal norm with differential comprehensiveness and applicability (Dachler and Wilpert 1978) and thus confound their comparability.

Such differences may be highlighted by norms which have a different social scope, as for instance a national law prescribing the involvement of employee representatives in organizational decision-making of all companies compared with a company-specific collective bargaining agreement prescribing the very same behaviour for only one company. Apart from the difference in the social range or applicability of norms, the example illustrates also differences in the origin (source) or base of a particular norm which, taken in itself, may be phrased in identical terms. Given the fact that countries do differ along both dimensions (scope and base of their participative norms), how then is one to take account of these differences and unravel the underlying dynamics systematically? In the case of the national law one is led to consider political bargaining processes leading to a particular bargaining outcome (the legal norm) of the respective power distribution at a national level. In the case of a company-specific collective bargaining agreement one would have to interpret the result as an outcome of the idiosyncratic history of, and power relations in, a particular firm.

iii. Characteristics of the Institutional Environment

This realm refers to the set of 'relevant other organizations' for enterprises. By and large this is the set of organizations that have some kind of regulatory function vis-à-vis the structure and processes of intra-organizational participation: unions, employers' associations, the state or community powers. As Blankenburg (1977) points out the effectiveness of legal norms is influenced at three levels—the level of norm promulgation (e.g. parliament, government), the level of target groups of the law, and the level of institutions that enforce compliance to the norm. Since, in each country, unions, employers, and state authorities (including labour courts) are all likely sometimes to have diverging interpretations of given regulations and their objectives (or their legitimacy) it may once more be extremely difficult to obtain an 'objective' picture of legalization pertaining to participation. This situation is bound to increase the difficulties for systematic cross-national comparisons. Common belief-systems among the parties involved cannot be assumed to operate within a country or even across countries.

iv. Differences in intra-organizational differentiation

Further methodological problems emerge in the context of dissimilar national traditions regarding internal company structures. They may occur at at least three levels. At the level of national corporate law which differs between countries by prescribing a monistic company board structure (one-tier boards), or a dualistic structure (with distinct executive and supervisory boards: two-tiers), or by allowing companies to choose either. At yet another level, we are confronted with considerable national differences in the degree of differentiation regarding the number, form, and functions of institutions for intra-organizational employee representation. As can be seen in the description of national industrial relations systems (cf. see the volume 'European Industrial Relations'), we find rather unified employee representation structures (as in the case of German or Dutch works' councils which are the central, if not exclusive, unit of employee interest representation) as well as rather diversified representational bodies with quite distinct tasks and functions (as for instance in Norway, Sweden, or the U.K.).

Similarly, at the level of intra-firm union structure a relatively heterogeneous picture emerges in cross-national perspective. Predominantly single union patterns with little or no intra-firm bargaining rights (e.g. Germany) exist next to multiple union structures with comprehensive intra-firm bargaining traditions (e.g. the U.K.). Levels of unionization vary from high (Israel) to low (France, West Germany, Holland—see Chapter 5). Furthermore, different unions within the same company may vary drastically in their attitudes toward employee involvement in company decision-making.

Given this international variety in internal structural and functional differentiation in companies, any attempt to compare given norms relating to organizational units in one country to similar norms in another country relating to dissimilar structural units can be criticized for attempting to compare the incomparable.

v. Social, political, and economic climate

Finally, the 'true meaning' of norms of participation may vary from country to country as a consequence of the prevailing 'Zeitgeist' and its reinforcing socio-economic and political conditions. The extent of social inequality, levels of education and information, the rate of economic growth and extent of prosperity, the political culture, social stability, recent major political events (e.g. a government linked to the labour movement comes to power) are all factors that can be assumed to influence the degree to which existing rules and regulations for participation are likely to be taken seriously in a country. Since some of these factors are unlikely to be identical in different countries, and since economic cyclical movements occur over time also within one country, one is forced to develop a keen awareness of the limits of a straight-forward comparison of legal norms.

Inter-disciplinary problems

The difficulty of establishing what legal norms for participation mean as a consequence of differential embeddedness in national contexts requires conceptual tools that are fit to bridge various systems levels. Ideally, they should cover cultural value-orientations, national legal traditions and socio-economic features, the institutional environment, and intra-organizational characteristics. Methodologically, this multi-level or 'open systems' approach demands inter-disciplinary operationalizations and data analysis strategies. But it is a lamentable fact that, in spite of the omnipresent lip service paid to the idea of multi-disciplinary research, its conceptual and methodological requirements have not gone beyond the developmental state of early childhood (Wold 1977).

In the context of our study it soon became clear that one of the crucial problems would be to operationalize legal terms in such a fashion that they could be related systematically both to aspects of the 'macro' environment such as were described above in connection with national historical economic, and socio-political conditions and to some 'micro' characteristics of organizational behaviour, such as employee involvement in decision-making and its social (power distribution), psychological (attitudes towards participation, work satisfaction), and economic consequences. However, the theoretical and methodological equipment to do this still needs to be further developed.

Conclusion

From all that has been said so far it should be clear that research of this kind faces rather complex problems. As we saw, there is an intrinsic weakness in any attempt to operationalize legal constructs for comparative purposes. The problems emanate from the very nature of legal norms, their vagueness, their diversity, and contextually created shifting qualities. However, the attempt to bring the problems at least one step nearer to their solution had to be made. Emery's observation in connection with the need to study organizations in an open systems perspective holds true for our situation: 'The fact that it faces us with the task of analysing forbiddingly complex environmental interactions gives us no more of an excuse to isolate organizations conceptually than the proverbial drunk had when searching for his lost watch under the street lamp because there was plenty of light when he knew he had lost it in the dark alley' (1969: 8).

THE IDE SOLUTION: MEASURING PARTICIPATIVE STRUCTURE (PS)

Chapter 4 contained a detailed account of the methods employed to obtain a measure of legal norms pertaining to participation. What follows is a brief recapitulation to save the reader additional cross-checking when we report the findings. The totality of 'all formal (i.e. written down) operative rules and regulations that prescribe a certain involvement of various groups in intra-organizational decision making' (IDE 1976: 181) was named 'participative structure' (PS) or *De Jure* participation. The definition of PS thus relates, in the first place, to organizational settings. It is also important to emphasize here that this definition covers *all formal* norms and not just *legal* norms prescribing participation (c.f. IDE 1980 for respective country-contexts).

The seven groups which were assumed to be of relevance in organizational decision-making are described in Chapter 4: A—workers/employees without supervisory functions; B—first line supervisors, foremen; C—middle managers; D—top management; E—level above establishment (e.g. supervisory boards or conglomerate management); F—permanent employee representative body; G—bodies/institutions outside the company.

National differences in company structure and forms of employee representation immediately become important here. Group E, the level above establishment, could either be a supervisory board (in a two-tier system), occasionally with employee representation, or a superordinate board of directors (as in the

case of an establishment that belongs to a larger multi-sited company or a conglomerate). In any case, the 'level above establishment' was intended to refer to
the establishment's policy-making and review unit. Some of our countries have
employee representation for certain company sizes on this top-level board (see
IDE 1980). Such schemes present some problems for the exact measurement
of *de jure* participation. On the one hand, every board member has the same
de jure potential to participate in the establishment's policy making, irrespective
of being elected by shareholders or by employees. On the other hand, employee
representation is (except for Yugoslav enterprises) always a minority representation for the companies included in this research. Instead of weighting the particular formal rights of participation with the limiting minority status we have
chosen not to differentiate such instances in our subsequent measures of *de jure*
participation.

Group F, the employee representative body within the establishment, may, in
some cases, (e.g. in West Germany or Holland) be only one body, namely the
works' council, or the employee representative functions (depending on the
issues at stake) may be split among several representative bodies, as is the case
for most countries (see Table 6.1). In the Scandinavian countries and the U.K.
it is almost exclusively the status or functions of unions or even of a single
union representative that is reflected in what we henceforth always call 'representative bodies' (group F). In these countries unions are the main spokesmen
for the employees in a company and the representative bodies that exist are
mainly forums for union–management consultation and sometimes decision-
making. Furthermore, in countries which have no homogeneous national system
prescribing particular representative structures, we may find different forms of
employee representation in different establishments within a single country.

Finally, group G also varies considerably between countries and within countries: regional union headquarters, banks, employment offices, state safety
officers, local community administration, employers' associations, and the like
may constitute bodies external to a given establishment which hold some *de
jure* participation stake in the decision-making processes of the establishment.

After the identification of various groups it was the decision-set (cf. chapter
4) which served as a further methodological step towards the standardization of
data collection. It consists of 16 decisions that can be broken down into decisions with short-, medium- and long-term effects (decision-clusters) as well as into
decisions with work, social, personnel, and economic content (Appendix A.1).

The source, or in our terminology, the Base of a given norm prescribing the
involvement of any of our seven groups in decision-making was assumed to stem
from ten possibilities (cf. chapter 4). These can be aggregated into

 i. laws (constitution, national and regional laws);
 ii. collective bargaining contracts (national, regional, sectoral, company, estab-
    lishment);
iii. managerial policies;
iv. other (e.g. generally valid and enforceable management prerogatives).

The guiding question was: what are the existing participative structures (formal
rules and regulations) *in a given establishment* (i.e. we are dealing with an
organization-specific measure) prescribing the involvement of one or more

Table 6.1
Representative Bodies in IDE research

Country	Types of representative body
Belgium:	works council/safety committee/union delegation[*] (depending on issue at stake)
Denmark:	shop stewards[*]/works council
France:	safety committee/works council/delegation of personnel[*]
Finland:	works council/shop steward[*]/labour protection committee
Germany (West):	works council[*]
Italy:	works council (*consiglio di fabbrica*)[*]
Israel:	safety committee/workers committee/ joint productivity councils/joint management
Holland:	works council
Norway:	local union[*]/works council/departmental council/safety and work/environment committee/personnel committee
Sweden:	works council/health and safety committee/local union[*]/ shop safety representatives[*]
U.K.	works consultative council/shop steward committee[*]
Yugoslavia:	workers council

[*]Composed only of employee representatives. Others, not asterisked, are joint committees with varying ratios of employee–employer representation.

of the seven groups in decision-making? The type or intensity of involvement that was prescribed was named the Mode of participation. It was measured along a continuum from 'no prescribed involvement' (because no specific regulation existed for a group) to 'final say by the group'. Thus, each of the six steps of the continuum consisted of a discrete type of behaviour reflecting the degree of a group's *de jure* participation in and (towards the upper end) command over decision-outcomes. The data were collected by asking both management and employee representatives in an establishment whether there existed formal participative rules for any of the 16 decisions.[4] If disagreements over the existence of such rules or their specific stipulations emerged, the divergence of opinion was solved with the help of an outside expert in labour or corporate law. Although the attempt was made to make the 16 decisions as specific as possible, their applicability sometimes appeared doubtful or they still seemed ambiguous. In such cases we had to rely on the judgement of the research team which had to settle the difference. This raises the important issue of the internal validity of our PS measures as opposed to what might be called the general conceptual or logical validity of legal systems comparisons discussed above. Measurement errors may stem from the inadequacy of instruments or from the way they are used.

Our PS measures, like any research instrument that attempts to capture the richness of real life in the form of scientific data, necessarily imply simplifications. With our instrument we are likely to capture only command-type norms while 'facilitating' norms, which may be extremely powerful in shaping behaviour, are largely unregistered. We can pin-point their existence (see IDE 1980) but we have no way as yet of capturing them systematically. Further, we limit ourselves to 16 decisions and it is a heroic assumption to believe that they are fully representative of all the issues involved in participation (see chapter 4 for a more detailed discussion of this issue). This limitation, apart from the deliberate neglect of some issues due to shortcomings in theory (ignorance of the universe of organizational decisions) and resources (limited funds and time), may have a distorting effect in countries which possibly have different formal rules applying to different decision issues. Also, we limit ourselves to seven potential bargaining groups instead of differentiating heterogeneous groups further. While we do have data at a national level on the *de facto* composition of, let us say, group G (external bodies) it seemed advisable for a first international comparison to lump them together in one group category. Finally, the possible intensity of *de jure* participation is put into six possible categories of the 'Mode of participation' although, in some instances, national participation systems foresee additional sub-categories. This reduction seemed appropriate in view of the fact that for most countries the six behaviourally-defined steps of the Mode scale were adequate and those countries with more detailed norms could easily be fitted into the Mode scale.

Of a different nature is the possible scoring error due to differences in the application of the PS measures. So it may be that different national teams—due to the intrinsic ambiguity of many formal norms—coded similar norms differently and hence produced a high error variance. The only empirical test of validity would have been to exchange national teams by letting different teams collect PS data in the same country. This procedure was not feasible due to the high costs involved. The mandatory operating procedure to cross-check any PS information with management, unions, and a legal expert on the basis of written-down materials provided the main quality control. In one country we had a situation where PS data collection was conducted in a way that came close to an inter-rater agreement procedure: two sub-sets of the national team collected PS data independently. Although there were slight differences in the two data sets suggesting procedural differences, the overall results were rather stable, thus giving sufficient confidence in the validity of the data obtained.

In spite of all the theoretical and methodological caveats the IDE team believed that it was extremely important to attempt a first approximation of an independent (i.e. non-reputational) measurement of formal norms for participation that permits a good deal of comparability between different industrial organizations and national systems.

FINDINGS: THE PATTERNS OF PARTICIPATION STRUCTURE

Extent of formalization

It was not known in advance how the twelve countries in our study would differ regarding the degree of overall formalization or legalization of participation as measured by our methodology. Hence, the first task is to identify characteristic patterns in the formal norm systems—in patterns of *de jure* participation.

As a first step we can map out the average frequencies of decisions (out of our 16) for which some kind of formal rule prescribes involvement on the part of the respective group. The sum total of the average number of decisions with a PS Base might be considered a rough and global index of the degree of formalization relating to participation in a country. Of course, it says nothing about the quality or intensity of the intended participation. Also, no differentiation is so far made with regard to the nature of existing Bases (laws, bargaining agreements, etc.). It rather reflects a country's relative preoccupation with formal, statutory rule-making (codification) in the field of industrial democracy (see Table 6.2).

Yugoslavia, Italy, Norway, Sweden, Denmark and West Germany take the first places of the rank order, followed by Belgium, and Finland. Among our countries, the U.K. and Israel reflect the lowest concern with formal participation, rules and regulations. Operations in British and Israeli companies seem strongly grounded in custom and practice as opposed to those countries favouring higher levels of codification. The low score for Holland (third lowest) seems to be due to the fact that virtually no special PS provisions seem to exist for first-line supervisors and middle management as tapped by our decision-set.

Looking further at the degree of overall legalization as it relates to our seven groups, we note a group of countries with a peak for the top management level (D)—Belgium, Finland, West Germany, Italy, Israel, Holland, Sweden—and a group of countries with a peak for the level above the establishment's top management (E)—U.K., France, Norway—while Denmark has a peak in both and Yugoslavia has its peak at the worker level (A). The characteristics of a nation's corporate law and the differential functions of top management or supervisory bodies as well as dominant beliefs as to the need to protect the rights of different groups might be a basis for explaining these differences.

Finally, it may be of interest to note that Yugoslavia, Norway, and Italy are the countries with relatively high scores for group G—groups and institutions outside the establishment. For Norway these outside groups are mainly union headquarters, state inspectors, or banking associations, for Yugoslavia they are mainly community councils or banks. As pointed out above, this category G (depending on the institutional setting) potentially covers a wide range of different categories and the results must be interpreted with caution. It is for future research and analysis to decide whether high scores for a country reflect the view that individual companies should be closely linked to their general institutional environment whereas countries with fewer rules and regulations pertaining to outside groups might consider companies as relatively self-contained entities.

Plotting the relative frequencies of existing PS norms (Figure 6.1) for an establishment's top management (group D) against PS norms for its internal employee representative bodies (group F), we obtain a rather clear-cut pattern of four country groupings: two groupings with a balance of formal rules and two with a relative imbalance. The U.K. has few regulations for both top

Table 6.2
Degree of Formalization for Participation (Bases)

Group	Norway	Sweden	Denmark	Finland	U.K.	Germany (West)	Holland	Belgium	France	Italy	Yugoslavia	Israel
Workers (A)	9.0[a]	8.2	5.9	10.7	3.7	10.0	5.0	6.4	4.7	11.6	15.3	0
Foremen (B)	7.6	10.1	6.9	10.7	3.7	9.0	0	9.8	4.6	9.4	12.6	0
Middle managers (C)	7.5	10.1	8.8	10.7	3.3	9.0	0	10.8	4.4	10.7	14.6	0
Top management (D)	15.9	13.6	14.8	16.0	4.0	16.0	16.0	11.8	6.9	14.3	14.1	10.6
Level above plant (E)	16.0	12.4	14.8	0	4.1	2.0	7.0	5.9	12.6	7.9	7.2	2.0
Representative bodies (F)	6.4	12.7	9.3	4.9	4.0	14.0	13.0	10.8	11.0	12.6	13.8	10.2
External groups (G)	8.9	1.7	2.2	1.7	1.3	1.3	3.0	4.5	3.0	7.0	8.4	0
Total	71.3	68.8	62.7	54.7	23.8	61.3	44.0	60.0	47.2	73.5	85.6	22.8
Country Rank	3	4	5	8	11	6	10	7	9	2	1	12

[a] Average frequency of decisions (out of 16) with a PS Base

management and employee representatives while the majority of countries (Belgium, Denmark, West Germany, Italy, Israel, Holland, Sweden, and Yugoslavia) have a high degree of formalized participation for both management and employee representatives. The other two groupings are marked by a relative imbalance of formal participative norms. France has a relatively high degree of formalization for representative bodies, while Finland and Norway have an imbalance in favour of top management. Finland, West Germany, Holland, and Norway are characterized by very high formalization scores for top management which has a *de jure* participation claim to virtually every decision. What may be operating here is a Nordic-Germanic concern with formalizing managerial rights and responsibilities, either through detailed and explicit rule-making or the general recognition of managerial prerogatives which are enforceable through judicial action on the basis of constitutional ownership or company law rights.

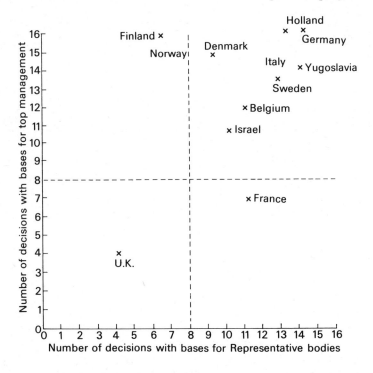

Figure 6.1 *De Jure* Participation for top management and representative bodies

The overall pattern, however, does not quite coincide with traditionally established clusters such as Germanic, Nordic, Latin, and Anglo-Saxon countries (Haire et al. 1966).

Bases of participation

Another way of looking at PS Bases is to investigate the degree to which various

countries make use of different types of Base in their rule-making for participation. One way of doing this is to plot frequencies of different Base-types. As pointed out above, we can break down the various Base categories into:
  i. laws;
 ii. collective bargaining contracts;
iii. managerial policies;
iv. other.

The graphic representation of their respective frequencies (category (iv) can be neglected here) shows the extent to which different countries use different legal bases for participation (Figure 6.2).[5] The Yugoslav findings, which show management policy as very important, deserve special explanation. 'Management policy' here stands for 'self-management policy' arrived at after a process

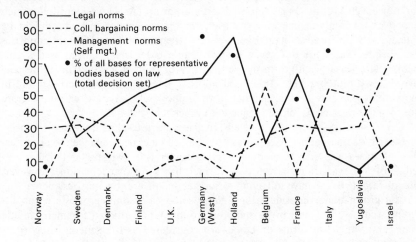

Figure 6.2 Differences in the relative frequency of various types of norm (Base types) used for *de jure* participation (as a percentage of all norms identified in the organizations of a country).

of negotiation among the employees in an establishment. So it differs from a one-sided written-down rule promulgated by top management as one may find it in Western countries and could be considered more like a bargaining outcome. Furthermore, it is interesting to note that the U.K., which is among the countries with the lowest degree of overall legalization pertaining to participation (see Table 6.2), is among those countries which, when it comes to making a rule for participation, employs legislative means in more than 60 per cent of cases.

For the majority of our countries, law is the major road to formalizing participation. However, at least for Israel and Finland, collective bargaining is of highest significance. Since the rules and regulations based on self-management agreements in Yugoslavia can, mutatis mutandis, be considered as outcomes of varying forms of bargaining, Yugoslavia might be counted with the countries leaning toward rule-making through collective bargaining even though this process might not always be labelled thus. But it is also quite evident from our data that in different countries the law is used differentially to assign participative rights to representative bodies (Figure 6.2). It appears that 86 per cent of Bases for the participation of German works' councils (group F) are derived from law, as compared, for instance, to the case of Norway where only 7 per cent of all PS Bases for group F are of the legal type. Since the formal frameworks providing legitimacy for the actions of representative bodies vary considerably, their relative effectiveness can be measured. The question is do systematic differences in effectiveness exist or are different formal arrangements functionally equivalent (i.e. produce the same distribution of influence and power)?

Before turning to the Modes of participation we will briefly look at the differences among countries in preferring different Bases for formal participation for our seven groups. For each decision and group (A–G) we identified which Base was used in the majority of cases, that is we singled out what might be called a group's 'predcminant Base'. We can then show how different countries use specific Bases for our seven groups (Table 6.3). If a country used a particular Base for a given group in the majority of cases it was put in the respective cell without brackets. If it used another Base for the respective group in more than one case (but altogether in the minority of cases) it was once more put into the respective cell, this time with brackets.

The first thing to note is that all ten Bases were used at least in a minority of cases by some country. This was not at all to be expected since the classification of Bases was arrived at by *a priori* considerations without detailed knowledge of the variation in existing formal bases for participation. However, the different Bases have different priorities in different countries, depending on the group under consideration and in some cases some groups are not differentiated at all. This can be said for groups A–C (workers, foremen, middle managers) which—in terms of Bases—are considered as the general category of 'employees' by virtually all countries. Base 'constitution' and Bases 3 'regional law' and 5 'regional collective bargaining contract' appear least often in a predominant role. The constitution is used only in West Germany and Norway for top management or the level above (presumably owners) while national law is most frequently the basis of participation for all groups.

Of some interest are the distinct country groupings that emerge when we consider the ways in which countries tend to secure legal participative rights for representative bodies (group F): France, Finland, West Germany, and Holland by national law; Denmark, Sweden, Norway, Italy, the U.K., and Israel by some kind of collective bargaining contract; Belgium through management policies; and Yugoslavia through rules and regulations derived from self-management.

Modes of participation

Knowing the nature of specific legal Bases for participation does not render any information about the quality and intensity of prescribed employee involvement in decision-making. We hope to gain that insight with the help of our six-step continuum of Modes which measures the second dimension of *De Jure* Participation:

the extent of prescribed involvement in the making of each of the sixteen decisions for each of our seven groups (A–G). Thus, in each establishment, through an analysis of the texts of existing Acts and formal, written-down rules, regulations, or collective agreements, we obtained for each group 16 Mode scores reflecting the extent to which a group should, formally, be involved in the making of each decision. The average Mode score of a group in a firm over all 16 decisions would thus describe its overall participative potential, the total *De Jure* Participation in the firm. Similarly, national averages of the Mode scores for each group could be looked upon as an index of the *De Jure* Participation or participative potential granted to that group in a country on a formal basis. Table 6.4 gives the scores for total *De Jure* Participation over all 16 decisions per country and group.

On the basis of the average Mode score profiles (total decision-set) we can roughly distinguish four patterns which are characteristic for the twelve countries in our study: the Low Profile Pattern, the Hierarchical One-Peak Pattern, the Hierarchical Two-peak Pattern, and the Representative Peak Pattern.

The Low Profile Pattern is marked by relatively low Mode scores for all groups with only minor peaks for top management (D) and representative bodies (F). It is characteristic of Belgium and the U.K. (Figure 6.3). The general implication of such a pattern is that no one of our groups, chosen on the basis of their presumed relevance for organizational decision-making, is very much favoured by formal rules and regulations in their legal participative potential relative to the other groups.

The Hierarchical One-Peak Pattern is typical of France, Norway, and Sweden in the sense that their Mode profiles characteristically peak in group E, the level above the establishment's top management, the top management itself having relatively high Mode scores. This pattern may, in part, be explained by corporate law in these countries which apparently gives high prerogatives to supervisory levels (boards of directors) relative to executive management even in the day-to-day operations which are reflected in our decision-set. This is of considerable methodological importance, because studies of the distribution of organizational power and influence have tended to confine themselves strictly to internal hierarchical levels and not to consider outside power sources (e.g. Tannenbaum et al. 1974). It is important to note, however, that the representative bodies (group F) in France and Sweden—in comparison with those in the other ten countries—still have relatively high Mode scores, and for France alone, the Mode score for representative bodies (F) is even higher than the score for top management (D).

The Hierarchical Two-Peak Pattern appears to be typical of the majority of our twelve countries: Denmark, Finland, West Germany, Italy, Holland, and Israel. Its characteristic feature is a dramatic absolute peak of Mode values for top management (group D) with a slump for the level above the establishment (group E) and another (smaller) peak for representative bodies (group F). Formal rules and regulations in these countries appear to favour clearly the role of top management in intra-organizational decision-making. The formal participative potential of representative organs may vary from relatively high (West Germany) to relatively low (Finland).

Table 6.3
Predominant Bases for various groups in various countries

Groups	Bases									
	Constitution	National law	Regional law	National collective bargaining	Regional collective bargaining	Sectoral collective bargaining	Company collective bargaining	Establishment collective bargaining	Management policy	Other legal Bases
Workers (A) Foremen (B) Middle managers (C)		(S)ª (SF) (DK) N (I) D NL (DK) (DK		(I) (B) SFll		DK (B) N	(S) (Yu)	GB N	B S I Yu	(DK) (Yu) DK DK
Top management (D)	N	F D (I) (GB) NL N SF DK Is		(B) Is	F	B	(Yu) (Is)	GB (Is)	B D I GB S Yu DK	D
Level above plant above plant (E)	D N	(B) F I (D) UK NL N S DK		(B)		(B) (S) (I)	(Yu) Is	GB	B D (Yu) DK	(Yu)
Representative bodies (F)		(B) F (I) D (GB) (S) NL SF		(SF) (I) (N) S DK Is	(F)	(D) (NL) (I) N (S) DK	(S) Yu I	GB (Is) (I)	B (S) I Yu (Is)	
External groups (G)		F D I GB NL S SF DK	Yu	(N)		N DK	(Yu)		B (Yu)	

ªCountries in brackets: in minority of decisions the respective Base category was also found

Note: S = Sweden; SF = Finland; DK = Denmark; N = Norway; I = Italy; NL = Holland; F = France; D = Germany; GB = U.K.; Is = Israel; B = Belgium; Yu = Yugoslavia.

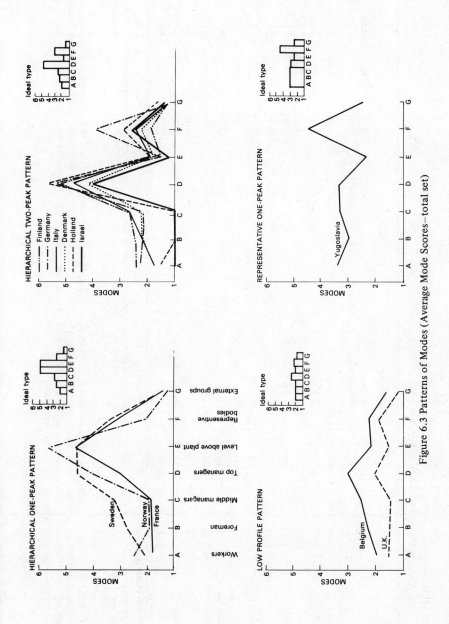

Figure 6.3 Patterns of Modes (Average Mode Scores—total set)

Table 6.4
Total De Jure Participation of all groups in the whole organization

Country	Groups						
	Workers (A)	Foremen (B)	Middle managers (C)	Top management (D)	Level above plants (E)	Representative bodies (F)	External groups (G)
Norway	2.44[a]	1.88	1.87	4.09	5.71	1.86	1.18
Sweden	2.07	2.71	3.17	4.52	4.53	3.29	1.32
Denmark	1.74	2.22	2.65	4.75	1.93	2.55	1.32
Finland	2.43	2.49	2.68	5.39	1.57	1.92	1.41
U.K.	1.51	1.49	1.46	2.08	1.55	1.82	1.20
Germany (West)	2.25	2.16	2.13	5.43	1.63	3.95	1.18
Holland	1.62	1.00	1.00	5.60	2.00	2.97	1.75
Belgium	1.96	2.26	2.55	3.06	2.21	2.58	1.68
France	1.79	1.80	1.83	2.90	4.63	3.10	1.38
Italy	1.82	2.17	2.81	4.25	1.90	2.31	1.30
Yugoslavia	3.40	3.02	3.35	3.36	2.38	4.53	2.50
Israel	1.00	1.00	1.00	4.16	1.55	2.59	1.00

[a] Average Mode of participation scores for groups and countries (Total set) Scale from 1-6 (1 = no prescribed involvement, 6 = the group has final say over decision).

Note: Correlations of average Mode of participation scores of the total set of sixteen decisions for groups A-G with the respective scores of the clusters for short-term and medium-term decisions are in the ranges of .81 to .97 (only exception: short-term decision scores of group G correlate with total set only .75). Correlations with scores for long-term decisions are somewhat lower (.55 to .78) which may be due to the fact that only two decisions (investment and new product) enter this cluster.

The Representative Peak Pattern applies to Yugoslavia alone. It is marked by an absolute peak of Mode values for representative organs while the difference in Mode scores between the other groups is distinctly small. Hence, one might even speak of an 'inverted hierarchical *de jure* participation potential' where the centre of formal decision-making power is at the level of employee representative organs.

It is important to note that we have so far only considered the average Mode score of groups A–G of all companies in a given country. It might be, however, that these scores vary from one company to another. Therefore, the variance of all the Mode scores for workers in a country will tell us whether workers (or any other of our seven groups) in different companies in a country can rely on more or less the same level of *de jure* participation. Table 6.5 provides us with that information for three of our seven groups, namely workers (A), top management (D) or the level above the plant (E)—which ever has a higher Mode score—and representative bodies (F).

Table 6.5
Uniformity and Diversity in De Jure Participation

Country	Variance of Mode scores		
	Workers (A)	Top management (D) Level above plant (E)	Representative bodies (F)
Norway	.045[a] (8)[b]	.142 (8)	.244 (6)
Sweden	.540 (1)	1.566 (2)	.417 (3)
Denmark	.054 (7)	.362 (5)	.164 (7)
Finland	.035 (9)	.781 (3)	.591 (2)
U.K.	.070 (6)	.110 (10)	.264 (4)
Germany (West)	00 (11)	00 (12)	.001 (12)
Holland	.009 (10)	.001 (11)	.016 (11)
Belgium	.177 (3)	.320 (6)	.077 (9)
France	.096 (4)	2.066* (1)	.067 (10)
Italy	.369 (2)	.759 (4)	.663 (1)
Yugoslavia	.071 (5)	.251 (7)	.256 (5)
Israel	00 (11)	.230 (8)	.146 (8)

[a]Variance of Mode scores for selected groups per country (total set)
[b]Country ranks according to diversity in brackets.

In the case of our West German and Dutch companies we can see that virtually all companies have practically identical levels of *de jure* participation for workers. The same is true for each of the two other groups. The variance of Mode scores tends towards zero. Both countries are among those that rely most heavily on statutory legal means of introducing participation (see Figure 6.2) and whatever is added in rules based on collective bargaining or management policy appears to be identical for our Dutch and West German companies. Both countries would have to be placed at the 'uniformity' end of a continuum that ranges from extreme uniformity to diversity in *de jure* participation schemes. The process of standardizing participation rules is here at its most advanced.

At the other end of this continuum we find Sweden and Italy where collective bargaining agreements (Sweden) and management policy regulations (Italy and Sweden) seem to be used as means of experimentation and diversification on a standardized legal base. Both countries are among those four in our study that least use law to establish participation (see Figure 6.2). We can further observe that in most countries the variance of Mode scores for top management levels (group D or E) tends to be higher than the variance for workers or representative bodies, which most likely reflects higher discretionary freedom to set the 'rules of the game'.

Another way of looking at the relative difference in *de jure* participaton between various hierarchical levels is to consider the score difference between the PS Modes of the worker level (group A) and internal top management (group D). For this purpose we consider now our four different sub-sets of decisions, i.e. the total of all 16 decisions, short-term, medium-term, and long-term decisions (Table 6.6). Once more we note considerable differences between the various countries. Inçreases in differences from one set of decisions to the next indicate a relative reduction in *de jure* participation for the group of workers in relation to top management.

The difference in scores does not necessarily increase as we go from short- to medium- to long-term decisions. While it remains relatively stable in the case of Holland, we observe steady increases for Italy, Belgium, and the U.K. In the case of France, Finland, West Germany, and Sweden we note an increase in score differences from short-term to medium-term decisions and a decrease from medium- to long-term decisions. This decrease is likely to be the effect of a loss of relative power by top management *vis-à-vis* the level above the establishment when it comes to important economic decisions such as large investments. In the case of Denmark, Norway, Israel, and Yugoslavia we find a decrease in score differences moving from short- to medium-term decisions and an increase moving to long-term decisions.

Our difference measure of Mode scores might, in some sense, be considered as a type of refined formal, legal control graph (Tannenbaum 1968) in as much as it depicts the existing potential for formally legitimate involvement of various organizational groups with regard to different decision-types. While research in the control graph tradition has been based on respondents' estimates of the perceived general influence of various hierarchical levels irrespective of decision-types, our Modal difference score describes the legitimating normative system for the influence of hierarchical groups on specific decisions.

Looking at the Modal difference scores between the lowest and highest hierarchical levels in an establishment gave us an estimate of the relative prescribed involvement of these two groups. Informative as it may be, the measure nevertheless implies a serious loss of information, since it fails to discriminate between different possible configurations of prescribed formal influence and control by ignoring the position of intermediate hierarchical levels. One could argue that in order to assess the precise nature of prescribed organizational control it is important to look at the described influence of one level relative to all others. A way of doing this is to calculate the rate of prescribed influence of, let us say, group A relative to the respective influence of groups B, C, and

Table 6.6

Top management–worker differences in De Jure Participation

Country	Short-term Decisions		Medium-term Decisions		Long-term Decisions		Total set Decisions	
Norway	1.92[a]	(6)[b]	1.50	(9)	1.55	(8)	1.65	(8)
Sweden	1.88	(2)	2.96	(5)	2.48	(5)	2.45	(6)
Denmark	3.52	(3)	2.91	(6)	3.39	(4)	3.01	(4)
Finland	2.31	(5)	3.71	(3)	3.58	(3)	2.96	(5)
U.K.	.54	(10)	.50	(11)	1.36	(10)	.56	(11)
Germany (West)	2.50	(4)	4.27	(1)	2.00	(7)	3.18	(2)
Holland	4.00	(2)	4.14	(2)	4.00	(2)	3.98	(1)
Belgium	.12	(11)	1.73	(8)	1.91	(8)	1.11	(9)
France	1.26	(8)	1.30	(10)	-.06	(12)	1.11	(9)
Italy	1.26	(8)	3.0	(4)	4.14	(1)	2.43	(7)
Yugoslavia	0.0	(12)	-.48	(12)	1.11	(11)	-0.04	(12)
Israel	4.17	(1)	2.26	(7)	2.40	(6)	3.16	(3)

[a]Difference of mean Mode of participation scores top management and workers.
[b]Country ranks in brackets

D. Thus we obtain a measure of the inequality of total *de jure* participation of workers (group A) relative to all other hierarchical levels:

$$\text{EQPS to (A)} = \frac{(\text{PS mode A} - \text{B}) + (\text{A} - \text{C}) + (\text{A} - \text{D})}{3}$$

Table 6.7 gives the results for all countries over the total set of 16 decisions.

Denmark, Italy, Sweden, and Finland have relatively low rates of prescribed 'influence-equalization' for the lowest hierarchical level, while, France, the U.K., and Norway approach the point of balance between the levels. This point is surpassed by Yugoslavia as a consequence of the inverted hierarchical legal potential described in Figure 6.3. Belgium, West Germany, and Holland appear somewhere in between the countries with low and countries with high prescribed influence equalization for workers relative to higher hierarchical strata.

The same type of analysis can be made for the prescribed influence of representative bodies (see Table 6.7 column 2). Comparing columns 1 and 2 we see that, in general, representative bodies have higher relative *de jure* participation (formal influence potential) than workers. The only exceptions occur in Norway and Finland where the relative weight of representative organs in terms of formal rights appears to be even lower than that of workers. But this apparent lack of *de jure* participation potential may, in some cases, be largely counter-balanced by relatively high *de jure* participation levels of employees via their representatives on supervisory boards (as for instance in Norway). These countries seem to favour a policy of not giving straightforward representative bodies increased involvement opportunities, whereas France, West Germany, Holland, Sweden, Israel, and Yugoslavia prescribe considerably higher levels of formal involvement potential for representative organs (relative to hierarchical

Table 6.7

Inequality of De Jure Participation for workers and representative bodies in relation to other hierarchical levels (PS modes, total set)

Country	Inequality for workers (A) in relation to foremen, middle and top managers		Inequality for representative bodies in relation to foremen, middle and top managers	
Norway	−.17[a]	(3)[b]	−.75	(10)
Sweden	−1.40	(11)	−.18	(8)
Denmark	−1.46	(12)	−.66	(9)
Finland	−1.09	(9)	−1.60	(12)
U.K.	−.16	(2)	.14	(6)
Germany (West)	−.99	(6)	.71	(3)
Holland	−.99	(6)	.44	(5)
Belgium	−.67	(5)	−.04	(7)
France	−.38	(4)	.92	(2)
Italy	−1.26	(10)	−.77	(11)
Yugoslavia	.15	(1)	1.29	(1)
Israel	−1.05	(8)	.54	(4)

[a]A negative score indicates that workers are worse off than the other groups. The lower the figure the lower the group's relative *De Jure* Participation. A score of zero would indicate equality.

[b]Country ranks in brackets.

levels above worker level) than for workers. The same is true, although to a lesser degree, for Belgium and Denmark. Given the marginally higher formal involvement potential given to representative bodies (compared with workers) by the U.K. and Italy one might be led to the conclusion that these two countries pursue a policy of keeping the formal influence potential for workers and their representatives in some balance and, if at all, increase the weight for both at the same time.

However, the picture is not quite so straightforward as it appears. Assuming that what counts in organizational decision-making is the relative power and influence potential of top management (group D) or the level above (group E) and the representative bodies of employees (group F) irrespective of further internal hierarchical *de jure* participation differentiation, we can consider the difference of Mode scores of these two groups which can be derived from Table 6.4. Countries vary with regard to the differential weight that representative bodies can muster *vis-à-vis* top management or the level above the plant. This picture becomes more complex when we look at different decision-types. Some countries provide less formal participation to representative bodies when it comes to important decisions (long-term) as compared to short- and medium-term decisions (Belgium, Denmark, the U.K., Italy, Finland, and Israel). Some increase the relative weight of representative bodies with the importance of decisions (France, Germany, Holland, Norway, and Sweden). A *de jure* power balance between representative bodies and top management regarding important decisions exists in the case of Yugoslavia.

These last considerations lead us into an analysis of the locus of legal decision-making power with reference to different decisions. One way of pursuing this line of analysis further is to examine the degree of centralization of decision-making within organizations, i.e. to look at differences between countries in the formal arrangements for making different kinds of decision. For purposes of this discussion we operationally define:

i. **centralized** *de jure* decision-making: all decisions per country with an average Mode score of at least 5 for top management or the hierarchical level above top management, i.e. these highest hierarchical levels hold either a veto power or can make the decisions in their own right. The reader is reminded that we are here dealing with national averages of all company scores, that is there could be a high variance of Mode scores between establishments: we do not consider cases that are above or below the mean. This holds also for the operationalizations below.

ii. **decentralized** *De jure* decision-making: all decisions per country with an average Mode score for supervisors and middle management higher than the average Mode score for either top management or the level above.

iii. **democratic** *De jure* decision-making: all decisions per country with an average Mode score of 4 or more for the representative bodies in establishments, i.e. at least the prior consultation of the representative bodies is obligatory before the decision is made. Sometimes the representative bodies may even have—on average in the countries—a veto power (i.e. a Mode score of 5 or more).

Looking at the synopsis of the findings (Table 6.8), we note that West Germany, Holland and Norway are characterized by the existence of formal rules and regulations of some kind that give higher management levels at least the power of veto for all sixteen decisions of our decision set. In Finland higher management has at least the power of veto for fourteen of the decisions. In Belgium, the U.K., and Yugoslavia such formal centralization of decision-making is virtually absent. In the case of the British companies this can be seen as a consequence of the generally low level of formalized rule-making for participation. Yugoslav companies, on the other hand, have a high level of formalization (cf Table 6.2) and this fact can only be explained as a deliberate attempt not to endow traditionally powerful upper hierarchical levels with additional *de jure* influence.The reverse holds for Israeli Histadrut firms where the little formalization that exists is heavily concentrated on upper hierarchical levels.

Relatively little use is made of the possibility of formally decentralizing decision-making by giving more rights to intermediate than to upper hierarchical levels. Wherever this is the case (in Swedish, Belgian, and Yugoslav establishments) it is almost exclusively restricted to work-related decisions: general work conditions, transfer of workers, tools, and task assignment.

Rules for sharing formal decision-making power democratically between top management levels and representative bodies in the case of at least 8 of our 16 decisions exist in Yugoslav (12 decisions) West German (12), Dutch (8), and French (8) companies. Representatives must at least be consulted and in some cases they have a veto power. They do so in Yugoslav companies in the case of

Table 6.8
Locus of de jure decision-making power for sixteen decisions: centralized, decentralized, democratized

Country	Decisions[a]															
	1	2	3	4	5	6	7	8	9	10	11	12	13	14	15	16
Norway	+[b]	+	·+	+	+	+	+	+	+	+	+	+	+	+	+	+
Sweden	+	+	+	v	v	+	+	+	o+	+v		v	o+v		+	o
Denmark	o+[c]	+	o+		+	+	+		+	+	+	v		v		+
Finland	o+	+	+	+	+	+	+	+	o+	+	+	+	+	o+		+
U.K.	+												+			
Germany (West)	o+	+	o+	o+	o+	o+	o+	+	o+	+	o+	+	o+	o+	o+	o+
Holland	o+	+	o+	+	+	o+	o+	+	o+	+	o+	+	+	o+	+	o+
Belgium	ov[d]									v			v			
France	o+	+		+v		o+	o+		o+	o	o	+	o+		o	o
Italy			+	+		+v		o	o	ov	o	v	+		o+	o
Yugoslavia	ov	o	o	ov	ov	o			o			v	o		v	ov
Israel	o+	+	+	+	+	+	+					+	o+	o	+	o+

[a] A list of the decisions can be found in Appendix A.1.

[b] + Mode score $\geq$ 5 for top management/level above (centralization).

[c] v Mode score of supervisory or middle management level > than mode score for top management/level above (decentralization).

[d] o Mode score $\geq$ 4 for representative bodies (democratization).

Note. Average Mode of participation scores of all companies in a country were considered.

decisions about the appointment of new department heads, hiring rules, participation in training courses, major investments, appointments of superiors, pay levels and dismissals. Works' councils in West Germany have the legal right to veto in relation to decisions—those on hiring rules, participation in training courses, permanent transfer of workers, pay level of employee groups, use of work study techniques, holiday plans, and working hours. Representative bodies in Holland have veto powers in relation to decisions regarding working conditions and working hours while the legal framework in Israel enables representative organs to veto only decisions on the application of work study techniques.

It is of further interest to note that, in some countries, the strategies of centralization, decentralization, and democratization are used side by side, as for instance in Denmark, Sweden, Finland, Germany, Holland, France, and Israel while only Yugoslav (and in one instance Swedish) establishments combine rules for decentralized and democratized decision-making. We probably have here a historical effect. Corporate law in Western countries has traditionally supported the power of managerial levels. This is now complemented by greater formal participation by employee representatives on the basis of collective bargaining or new laws. In Yugoslavia, in contrast, the situation after World War II enabled drastic and radical changes in legal and formal frameworks to be made.

CONCLUSIONS AND PROSPECTS

Explorations into new areas, bold as they may be, should be made carefully. We have described, at some length, the theoretical and methodological problems connected with the new venture to measure formal participatory systems systematically for comparative purposes. In spite of our caveats, we are convinced of the usefulness of our measures for describing and depicting differences and similarities in participative systems in different countries. In this chapter we were not able to go into any details in discussing how some of the characteristic formal participative features we discovered in nationally-grouped companies relate and correspond to more qualitative descriptions of national industrial relations systems or other cultural, social, political, and legal peculiarities. In some cases we are able to hint at the contextual fabric of dominant values or world images and their concomitant legal traditions that have an impact on formal systems pertaining to participation in industry. Thus they shape both the formal normative and the institutional frameworks of participation, the emergent differentiation of structural forms and functions as well as the goal orientation of what has been called the 'meta-powers' (Baumgartner et al. 1976): those regulatory forces that are able to structure the interactions and relationships of actors—in our case of the seven bargaining groups (A–G) considered relevant in organizational decision-making.

This limited analysis, carried out with new instruments which are still to be improved and further tested, shows that the data obtained do not contradict what we otherwise know about industrial relations systems in various countries. The reader is once more referred to this volume's accompanying publication on industrial relations. The patterns of formal rule-making for participation which we identified do not fit easily into ready-made categories or country 'clusters' as they do in some other cross-national comparative studies on attitudes (Haire et al. 1968, Hofstede 1978). However, this chapter deals not with attitudes or sentiments but with formal, codified norms for participation that can be identified by relatively objective procedures. While it is quite conceivable that espoused attitudes or values of people from different countries cluster along the lines of some assumed cultural affinity among the countries in question, data from other social spheres may not. This has, in fact, been established already for legal systems: litigation rates of civil cases in countries belonging to the same legal culture (e.g. the Romano–Germanic or the common law family) may be drastically different (Ehrmann 1976). Such evidence, like the evidence presented in this chapter, could force us to abandon popular, and apparently self-evident, classification schemes lumping countries into geographic or cultural groupings irrespective of the social phenomena under study. Rather, we ought to search for empirically-derived taxonomies which can vary with the issues under investigation.

The examination of other national legal (formal) systems in terms of their legitimating bases and prescriptive norms (our Modes) might open up possibilities for corroborating our findings in the field of industrial relations and participation with data from other social domains. After all, it may be that legal systems 'behave' (Black 1976) in predictable fashion, that, for instance, overall indices of legalization remain constant from one social area to another in a given country, or that they vary in a systematic fashion.

However we are not chiefly concerned with the behaviour of normative systems as such. The main interest is in how they shape the behaviour of people and institutions. We have talked about *de jure* participation. Now we turn to *de facto* participation and its corollaries. It is in the following three chapters that the crucial test is applied—can our measures of formal norms for participation be successfully linked to data from other social sciences relating to *de facto* behaviour in and of organizations.

NOTES

1 Part of the following is based on Wilpert and Freidank (1977).

2 Voluntarism is here understood in terms of purposive, directed social change efforts, rather than in terms of the Anglo-Saxon understanding of voluntarism in industrial relations as freely negotiated agreements between unions and employers.

3 For a detailed description of the specific national circumstances and the industrial relations systems of the participating countries the reader is referred to the accompanying IDE publication 'European Industrial Relations'. (1980).

4 Our concept of Mode, therefore, has nothing in common with the 'mode' in statistical distributions as the most frequently occurring value. We denote Mode to be the manner in which formal (legal) texts prescribe the participation of our groups A to G in organizational decision-making.

5 Instead of showing bar-graphs we connect points for the sake of better comprehension.

7

DE FACTO PARTICIPATION: INFLUENCE AND INVOLVEMENT[1]

The quality of *de facto* participation can best be analysed through considering the relation between influence and involvement. Involvement which does not produce greater influence for participants is frequently characterized as pseudo-participation (Pateman 1970) or as manipulative participation which contributes to the greater integration of participants into the existing order but does not improve their chances of promoting their own interests. Bolweg, for instance, defines participation precisely as 'the presence of workers or their representatives during the decision-making process without substantially influencing the decision-outcomes' (Bolweg 1976: 91). Accordingly, the term 'industrial democracy' is reserved for situations in which workers' involvement increases their influence and power.

This chapter should give some further insight into the relation between influence and involvement. However, it should be said that there are some quite substantial limitations deriving from the research design which we cannot avoid in our analysis of relations between influence and involvement. The first limitation is a theoretical one: due to differences of opinion within the IDE team we were not able to pose an unambiguous hypothesis about the relationship between influence and involvement. We can neither postulate that greater involvement causes greater influence, nor that greater involvement is a consequence of greater influence. Since there is some evidence for both hypotheses (Rus 1979b), we would like to keep these questions open until the end of the chapter where we will try to answer them on the basis of the previous analysis.

There are also operational difficulties in referring to the relationship between influence and involvement. As is clear from Chapter 4, we are measuring the distribution of influence by asking experts from management circles and union representatives how much influence is exercised by different levels in the organization. For involvement, we have asked a sample of employees about their predominant mode of involvement in 16 specified decision-making processes. As one can see, the population and the instruments are different and therefore there are reasons to suppose that these two sets of instruments are measuring different dimensions of reality. It is perhaps especially important that the scales on which we are measuring influence and involvement are also different. Influence is measured on a Likert-type ordinal scale while involvement is measured on a Guttman-type scale of different behavioural modes of participation. Also, in the first case we are measuring *group influence* and in the second case *individual involvement*. These differences taken together allowed us to suppose that we were measuring two theoretically independent variables. Any correlations between them should be ascribed to a real relationship between influence and involvement in organizations, rather than to measuring instruments which overlap.

PATTERNS OF INFLUENCE DISTRIBUTION

The distribution of influence

Data about patterns of influence distribution have been collected by the reputational method. This method was used since we accepted a phenomenological definition of 'influence'. According to this influence is not *'ding an sich'* but *'ding für uns'*. It is not something independent of our perception, but exactly that which we perceive: we react to our perceptions of influence and not to something behind them.

Further problems connected with the reputational method are not theoretical but methodological. Criticism of the reputational method usually derives from the fact that information is collected from respondents who are not sufficiently involved in the matters they are evaluating. In such cases 'culturally-based stereotypes' can substantially modify the perceptions of respondents (Lord 1977). We have attempted to avoid this bias by only asking experts who have been selected from managers and union representatives about the influence of different organizational groups. From this point of view, our data are probably more valid than data collected by the control graph method (Tannenbaum 1968) in which the reputational method is used on a sample of employees.

Another problem of validity arises from the discrepancy between the very complex and ambiguous notion of 'influence' and our quite narrow uni-dimensional operationalization of it. Validity problems relating to the instruments used in this research resemble those of Tannenbaum. A multi-dimensional theoretical definition of influence and power is related to a uni-dimensional, operational definition by which the word 'influence' is used without further explanation in our questionnaires. It is possible that some respondents understood the word 'influence' positively, some negatively, and others in both ways (Rus 1979). It is also possible that some respondents understood the word to mean only behaviourally exercised influence attempts and that others understood it as a more latent relationship based on control over resources. Needless to say, these 'unclear' relations between the nominal definition and the operationalization of influence (Gundelach and Tetzschner 1976) raise some questions about the instrumental validity of our instruments. In an attempt to analyse this internal validity, and perhaps increase it, we are also using Tannenbaum's control graph, which will be compared with our instruments.

By limiting the use of our reputational influence measure to expert respondents and by narrowing our questions to sixteen specific decisions and not only to hierarchical levels or whole organizations, we also hope to increase the face validity of our instrument.

Finally, problems of validity also include problems of interpretation. Because of the difficulties mentioned above our interpretation of influence remains very broad and open. In this chapter we shall limit ourselves to a negative definition of influence which is more complex and also more ambiguous than a positive definition. We shall interpret influence as something which does not coincide either with meta-power or with involvement, or with non-decision-making activity. The relationship between influence and power will also remain undefined since our instruments are not sufficiently refined to discriminate between these two phenomena. Furthermore, we believe that our data reflect different kinds of influence: that which is defined as a dependence relationship; that defined as a resource-based relationship; and that based on the involvement of employees. We shall not interpret the data contained in this chapter exclusively as behaviourally conditioned influence, or as resource-based power, or as legitimate power based on rules and regulations.

By stressing these negative definitions of influence we are trying to interpret our data as broadly as is possible. At the end of this chapter we will attempt to develop a more specific interpretation of our data by reviewing some of our theoretical concepts and reassessing their possible interpretations in the light of the empirical evidence.[2]

The data presented here have been aggregated and analysed at the organizational level. In the preceding chapter analysis mostly took place at national level and in the following chapter the analysis will focus mainly on the individual level. The reason for analyzing our data on influence at the organizational level lies in the supposition that we are dealing with basically structural dimensions of organizations. Data aggregated at this level primarily reflect a patterned distribution of influence which is, to some extent, independent of individual or group behaviour. We are not in favour of identifying these patterns with behavioural patterns of groups within organization as was done by Katz and Kahn (1966). We assume that the distribution of influence is conditioned not only by collective group behaviour but also by existing rules and regulations, the allocation of resources in organizations and external power coalitions.

At the same time, we do not identify patterns of influence distribution with organizational structure. According to our hypothesis these patterns are the outcome of personal or group behaviour and of organizational constraints or conditions. Our conceptualization of the relationship between influence and organizational structure is analogous to that developed by Ouchi (1977) for the relationship between control and structure. He does not identify control with organizational structure, although he stresses the close relationship between them.

Another reason for interpreting our data about patterns of influence distribution at the organizational level is based on our preliminary computations which showed position in the organizational hierarchy to be the main determinant of patterns of influence. According to these preliminary results, hierarchy is a better predictor of influence distribution than country differences, size of organization, and sector.

Patterns of Influence Distribution Across Levels and Decisions

The following analysis covers all levels or groups identified in our research, from workers to external societal groups. In our discussion, however, we shall pay particular attention to the three levels most relevant for the analysis of industrial democracy: level A (workers), level D (top managers), and level F (representative bodies). The amount of influence exercised by these levels and the power inequalities which exist between them are, in fact, decisive for the promotion of the interests of employees within contemporary organizations.

Table 7.1 shows overall patterns of the distribution of Influence (PO 1a)

Table 7.1
The distribution of Influence across levels and decisions[a]

Decisions	Influence (PO1a)							
	Workers (A)	Foremen (B)	Middle managers (C)	Top management (D)	Level above plant (E)	Representative bodies (F)	External groups (G)	Total
Working conditions	2.7[b]	3.1	3.5	4.1	2.5	3.4	2.1	3.1
New department head	1.2	1.6	2.5	4.5	2.8	1.9	1.2	2.2
Hiring procedures	1.4	2.5	3.3	4.0	2.2	2.3	1.4	2.5
Training courses	2.2	2.7	3.5	3.9	1.8	2.3	1.3	2.5
Transfers	2.5	3.1	3.7	3.7	1.6	2.5	1.2	2.6
Investment	1.3	1.8	2.7	4.3	4.4	2.0	1.8	2.7
New product	1.3	1.7	2.8	4.3	3.8	1.9	2.0	2.5
Appointment own superior	1.3	1.5	2.0	3.6	2.8	2.0	1.3	2.7
Pay levels	2.0	2.4	3.1	4.2	2.7	2.9	1.7	2.7
Personal equipment	2.8	3.5	3.6	3.2	1.7	2.0	1.2	2.6
Reorganization	1.7	2.4	3.4	4.4	2.8	2.4	1.8	2.6
Task assignment	2.2	3.9	3.6	2.7	1.4	1.7	1.2	2.4
Dismissals	1.7	2.9	3.4	4.1	2.0	3.2	1.8	2.7
Work study	2.0	2.8	3.5	3.9	2.1	2.7	1.4	2.6
Holidays	3.2	2.9	3.1	3.1	1.6	2.2	1.2	2.4
Working hours	2.8	2.4	2.7	3.8	2.0	3.2	1.5	2.5
Short-term decisions	2.5	3.2	3.5	3.6	1.8	2.5	1.4	2.6
Medium-term decisions	1.6	2.2	3.0	4.1	2.5	2.4	1.4	2.5
Long-term decisions	1.3	1.8	2.7	4.3	4.2	1.9	1.9	2.6
Total	2.0	2.6	3.2	3.8	2.4	2.4	1.4	2.5

[a]PO1a—experts' judgments

[b]1 = no influence
2 = little influence
3 = moderate influence.
4 = much influence.
5 = very much influence

across organizational levels and across each of the sixteen selected decisions for all 134 organizations sampled in the twelve countries. The mean scores for short-, medium- and long-term clusters of decisions are also included. At the bottom of this table the mean scores for the total sample of 134 organizations are presented; of course, suppressing all differences at country or company level and giving a picture only of the dominant trends for the sample as a whole.

The data presented in this table can be described in two basic ways:
i. by looking at the distribution of influence across organizational levels. Such *vertical* patterns refer to the amount of influence of particular levels in relation to other levels and to relative differences (or inequalities) amongst them;
ii. by looking at the distribution of influence across decisions and clusters of decisions. Such *horizontal* patterns refer to differences in the amount of influence exercised by particular levels over different types of decision or over different clusters of decisions.

As can be seen from the bottom row of Table 7.1, the vertical distribution of influence within organizations shows what may be called a perfect hierarchical pattern with workers possessing the least influence and top management the most. In addition, the distribution of influence is such that the gap between adjacent levels is the same throughout the organizational hierarchy. This hierarchical pattern in the distribution of influence does not apply in the case of extra-organizational levels. Bodies at the corporate level and external societal groups such as outside unions, local communities, banks, etc. have substantially less influence than top and middle management, even though they might be legally superordinate to them. One possible explanation for this finding is that these extra-organizational groups tend to exercise their power in a less visible and direct fashion through institutional means and through control over resources rather than through direct involvement in the decision-making process. Another possible explanation for this finding relates to the nature of our decision-set. Our 16 decisions refer mainly to intra-organizational problems and extra-organizational groups may not be particularly interested in influencing such 'local' issues.

If we now turn our attention to the absolute amount of influence of particular levels, we can see that workers and representative bodies have 'little influence' on the 16 selected decisions and that top management has 'much influence'. If we interpret these absolute values from the point of view of industrial democracy, we must conclude that influence tends to be distributed hierarchically in work organizations and that, on the whole, industrial democracy remains in an embryonic state of development.

However, what is true of all organizations across all decisions taken together is not necessarily true for particular decisions and clusters of decisions. The results presented in Table 7.1 show that a hierarchical distribution of influence also exists within each particular cluster; top management has the most influence and workers the least in short-, medium- and long-term decisions alike (Clusters 2, 3, and 4 respectively). There is, nevertheless, considerable variation in the degree of inequality between levels from one cluster of decisions to another: inequality is least in the case of short-term decisions and greatest in the case of long-term decisions. The more strategic the decisions, therefore, the greater the concentration of influence in the hands of top management.

Workers, supervisors, middle management, and representative bodies exhibit similar horizontal patterns of influence across the various clusters of decisions. These levels have the most influence on short-term decisions, and the least on long-term decisions. The patterns for top management, for corporate bodies, and for external societal groups, however, are just the opposite. These levels have less influence on short-term and medium-term decisions than on long-term decisions. It seems that Gundelach and Tetzschner (1976) were correct in supposing that not only the quantity of influence but also its quality varies across levels.

If we take into account both vertical and horizontal patterns of the distribution of influence, a relatively new picture emerges from our data. This picture contains at least three implications:

i. If we attribute greater weight or power to long-term decisions than to medium- and short-term decisions, then the quantitatively even distance between levels within organizations (see last line of Table 7.1) disappears, and the degree of inequality in the distribution of influence becomes more marked. The distance between middle management and top management is, in reality, greater than that between middle management and lower levels since middle management has an opposite pattern of horizontal distribution from top management. In other words, if one takes into account not only the amount but also the quality of influence, middle management turns out to be far less powerful than previously suggested. The same could be said for representative bodies and corporate bodies: both levels have the same amount of perceived influence, but they have opposite patterns of horizontal distribution; corporate bodies have a relatively greater amount of influence on long-term decision-making and little influence on short-term decisions, while representative bodies have moderate influence on short-term decisions and little influence on long-term decisions. In other words the amount of influence is quite similar but its quality substantially different.

ii. Although the decentralization of influence is quite obvious, such decentralization is limited mainly to short-term decisions. Influence upon medium-term decisions can be found to a greater extent only at the middle management level, while influence upon long-term decisions is concentrated in the hands of higher management. In these 134 organizations in twelve European countries, decentralization does not imply the sharing of strategic power with lower organizational levels on the part of top management. It mainly means the decentralization of influence on short-term routine types of decision. As such, decentralization implies a kind of 'programme participation' (Burns 1967) which is predominantly oriented toward the execution and not toward the formulation of goals.

Consequently, one cannot expect that this type of decentralization will enable lower levels in the hierarchy to increase their control over organizations. It is more probable that this type of decentralization frees higher levels from routine decision-making and enables them to spend more time on crucial issues. As such, this kind of participation tends to increase the dependence of lower levels without at the same time increasing their influence.

iii. Very distinct horizontal patterns of influence distribution could increase the degree of segmentation within organizations and thus increase the costs of integration. In hierarchical organizations, however, the costs of such segmentation may be more acceptable than the costs deriving from the possible conflicts which would result from the establishment of greater power-sharing among different levels.

A more detailed analysis of horizontal patterns could be attempted by looking at the vertical distribution of influence for particular types of decision. Since such an analysis can be done directly by the reader, we will concentrate on those decisions over which workers and representative bodies have the greatest influence. In such a case we can talk about the democratization of decision-making processes. Among our 16 decisions there are only three which can be seen as relatively democratically controlled:

   i. decisions which refer to the work environment (1)
  ii. decisions which deal with the dismissal of employees (13)
 iii. decisions about holidays (16).

Workers and their representatives seem to have the greatest influence on those issues which, in most European countries, tend to be strongly regulated by legislative norms. External legal regulations seem to constitute important supports to the internal democratization of decision-making.

Decisions which are controlled more by lower and middle management rather than by workers' representative bodies could be qualified as decentralized but not as democratized decisions. Decisions which may be described as decentralized occur in the areas of:

   i. permanent transfer of employees (5)
  ii. replacement of personal equipment (10)
 iii. assignment of tasks to employees (12).

These three types of decision regulate some of the conditions of the work-flow and do not have the same strategic value as do issues relating to dismissals. But, given that these types of decision are not usually regulated either by legislation or by internal rules, they could well constitute important sources of discretionary power for supervisors and middle management.

Decisions controlled mainly by top management and by bodies at the higher corporate level could be treated as centralized decisions. There are at least four areas of decision which should be described as strongly centralized:

   i. appointment of a new department head (2)
  ii. major capital investments (6)
 iii. introduction of new products (7)
  iv. appointment of immediate superior (8).

These four issues relate to economic questions and to personnel policy indicating that top management retains strong control over these areas of decision-making. While a high degree of centralization with respect to economic questions was expected, such strong top management control over personnel policy was not.

Top management's tight control over personnel policy is not usually mentioned in the management science literature. However our data demonstrate that this is exactly the area over which top management exercises the greatest control. According to the data presented in Table 7.1 control over the nomination of managers is perceived to be the most distinctive and most exclusive right of top management. The greatest concentration of influence occurs in relation to those types of decision which, according to Dahrendorf, should be the most democratized if one wishes to introduce into work organizations the criteria that apply in the case of political democracy (Dahrendorf 1965).

Even though economic and personnel policy questions are amongst the most centralized issues, they are by no means the only types of decision over which top management exercises more control than other levels. In fact, top management has the greatest influence on fourteen out of the sixteen decisions studied in our research. This means that not only the amount, but also the scope, of top management's influence is very high. This, in turn, reduces the likelihood of power-sharing within organizations, inhibits the step-wise creation of intra-organizational pluralism, and ensures top management's continued control over organizational decision-making. From this point of view managerial control differs substantially from the control of professionals which is intensive, but at the same time quite limited or narrow, in its scope.

Finally, some attention should be paid to the last column of Table 7.1: the total or average amount of influence of all levels varies considerably from one decision to the next. The total amount of influence is highest for those decisions where there is the highest degree of power-sharing (decisions about the work environment, wages, the dismissal of employees, etc.), and lowest in those cases where power-sharing is also lowest (as in decisions about the appointment of a new department head or a new superior). The greater the concentration of influence at a particular organizational level, therefore, the lower the total amount of influence is likely to be and the more likely it is that zero-sum type of conflicts might arise within the organization.

Patterns of Influence Distribution Across Countries

On the basis of some of our preliminary computations it would appear that, after hierarchical level, country is the second strongest predictor of the distribution of influence. Table 7.2 presents patterns of the distribution of influence across these two dimensions. As can be seen, there is considerably greater variation across levels than across countries. The 'total', or average, amount of influence per country varies between 2.4 and 2.6, with the exception of Yugoslavia where the average is 3.0 (see bottom row). The unequal distribution of influence across organizational levels, on the other hand, is far more pronounced. This suggests that hierarchical ordering within organizations is a much stronger determinant of the distribution of influence than any other factor or differences which are implicitly operative within any particular country.

The very low average scores reported in the bottom row of Table 7.2 suggest that most of the organizations studied might be characterized as 'powerless' systems. However, even though such powerless systems might seem to be anarchic, in reality they are not, in this case because of the highly centralized decision-making which is controlled by top management. We suppose that this centralization of influence is one of the main reasons for the relatively low total amount of control exhibited by these organizations.[3]

A third important point about the data reported in Table 7.2 concerns the fairly low levels of influence that external societal bodies appear to have over organizational decision-making. As we have mentioned before, it is possible that the indirect influence of external groups is actually greater than it is perceived

Table 7.2
The distribution of Influence by country[a]

Level	Belgium	Denmark	Finland	France	Germany (West)	U.K.	Italy	Israel	Holland	Norway	Sweden	Yugoslavia
					Influence (PO1a)							
Workers (A)	1.6[b]	2.0	2.0	2.1	1.9	2.0	2.1	1.6	2.1	2.3	2.0	2.7
Foremen (B)	2.2	3.0	2.6	2.9	2.3	2.4	2.7	2.8	2.7	2.7	2.5	2.8
Middle management (C)	3.1	3.2	3.5	3.0	3.0	3.2	3.2	3.1	2.9	3.3	3.1	3.1
Top management (D)	4.2	3.6	4.0	4.7	4.4	3.9	4.1	4.3	3.7	3.7	3.5	3.6
Level above plant (E)	2.9	1.9	2.3	3.0	1.6	2.8	2.0	2.1	2.0	2.0	2.7	2.9
Representative bodies (F)	2.4	1.9	1.5	2.1	2.6	2.2	2.5	2.4	2.1	2.1	2.8	3.9
External bodies (G)	–	1.4	1.3	1.5	1.2	1.5	1.6	1.2	1.2	1.3	1.3	2.2
All levels	–	2.4	2.4	2.6	2.4	2.6	2.5	2.4	2.4	2.5	2.5	3.0

[a] PO1a—experts' judgments.
[b] 1 = no influence.
   2 = little influence.
   3 = moderate influence.
   4 = much influence.
   5 = very much influence.

to be. Even taking this possibility into account, however, the difference in the amount of influence exercised by top management and by external groups is such that one is probably justified in concluding from our data that, on the whole, work organizations in our 12 countries are still relatively autonomous and closed in relation to their social environment.[4]

The amount of influence of workers and representative bodies does not vary substantially across countries. If we exclude Yugoslav enterprises, workers in all countries have 'little' influence over the set of 16 decisions and representative bodies have between a 'little' and a 'moderate' amount. In all countries, therefore, the degree of democratization of decision-making processes within work organizations appears to be fairly low.

The particular picture within each country does not vary very much from the general pattern discussed above. Most organizations in all countries are centralized, powerless, closed, and non-democratic. Yugoslav enterprises appear to be the only exception to this general pattern. According to the data in Table 7.2 Yugoslav enterprises are not as powerless as enterprises in the other countries and they are more pluralistic, more democratic, and more open to environmental influences.

In this context, it is also worth noting that, in most countries, the amount of influence of workers and of representative bodies decreases from short-term to long-term decisions, while the influence of top management increases. Here again Yugoslavia and, with minor modifications, the Scandinavian countries are exceptions. In Yugoslav organizations the influence of both the Workers' Councils and top management grows as one moves from less important to more important decisions, although this trend is less pronounnced in the case of top management than in the case of Workers' Councils. It appears that the influence of Workers' Councils grows to some extent at the expense of that of top management. But even if this is true, it is obvious from the Yugoslav case that, under certain conditions, an increase in the amount of control exercised by representative bodies does not necessarily constrain the power of top management. It seems therefore that, in such a case, a zero-sum game no longer applies. As is obvious from Table 7.2, in such systems the total amount of influence also tends to be higher. One can suggest, therefore, that one of the outcomes of this type of variable-sum game might be a greater degree of organizational density and the establishment of more pluralistic patterns of power distribution.

Finally, if we use the criteria for the 'centralized', 'decentralized' and 'democratized' distributions of influence as they have been used above, it becomes evident that across countries decentralization and democratization do not coincide (see Table 7.3). In fact the relationship between decentralized and democratic patterns of influence distribution tends to be negative. It is possible that countries with more developed decentralization of influence are not pressed to develop high democratization as well. Decentralization might transfer tensions toward the lower levels of the hierarchy and, in this way, offers chances for conflict resolution at the local level. In this way, decentralization functions, perhaps, as a compensatory mechanism for democratic patterns of influence distribution.[5]

Table 7.3
Patterns of Influence distribution

	Pattern of distribution of Influence (PO1a)		
Amount of Influence	Centralized[a]	Decentralized[b]	Democratic[c]
High	Belgium, France	Denmark, Norway, Finland	Yugoslavia, Sweden
Low	Denmark, Holland, Denmark, Norway	Germany (West), Belgium	Denmark, Finland

[a]Amount of Influence of top management and external groups.
[b]Amount of Influence of foremen and middle managers.
[c]Amount of Influence of workers and representative bodies.

Inequality and the Amount of Influence

In looking at the distribution of influence within organizations we have found that, in almost all countries, workers tend to have only a very limited amount of influence over the set of 16 decisions. This lack of control on the part of workers, however, could well have different effects depending on the amount of influence exercised by other groups and on the overall degree of inequality in the distribution of influence. Thus, for example, as a number of writers have pointed out, the relative position of different groups is a critical element in power relations. The power of a given group often depends more on the powerlessness of other groups than on the 'absolute amount of power' that the dominant group is able to exercise (Emerson 1962).

The importance of looking at power inequalities is also brought out by Mulder's work, even though his experiments focus only on the expert power of participants and are developed at the level of group dynamics (Mulder 1971). In particular, when used as an analogy and translated into the context of the present research, what his findings suggest is that a more even distribution of influence should be seen as a basic precondition for effective workers' involvement rather than being viewed simply as a possible outcome of greater participation. This, incidentally, is also one of the main points stressed by Zupanov (1973), who, on the basis of his analysis of the Yugoslav experience, concludes that power equalization is not only an outcome but primarily a necessary condition for the authentic involvement of workers in systems of self-management.

Our research design does not enable us to establish the direction of the causal relation between the total amount of influence and the extent of inequality in the distribution of influence across hierarchical levels, but the results of bivariate analyses carried out on our data clearly demonstrate that such relations exist over all countries and organizations (see Table 7.4).[6] We have already discussed one example—Yugoslavia is characterized by both a greater average amount of influence and a more even distribution of influence across organizational levels than the other countries (see IDE 1980, ch. 12).

Table 7.4
The relationship between amount and inequality of Influence

Inequality indices	Amount of Influence (PO1a) Levels							Clusters of Decisions			Total
	Workers (A)	Foremen (B)	Middle managers (C)	Top management (D)	Level above plant (E)	Representative bodies (F)	External groups (G)	Short-term	Medium-term	Long-term	
Difference between levels (D–A)	–.77	–.25	–.08	.85	–.16	–.24	–.30	–.06	–.13	–.20	–.15
Variance of Influence between all hierarchical groups	–.45	–.25	–.07	.55	–.33	–.27	–.26	–.12	–.24	–.22	–.23

Note: $p \leqslant .05$ if $r > .15$.

The greater the overall degree of inequality within organizations, measured in terms of the difference in the amount of influence of workers and top management, the lower the amount of influence of workers, supervisors, representative bodies, corporate bodies, and external groups. The only positive correlation is that between the degree of inequality and the amount of influence exercised by top management. Table 7.4 also shows that the more uneven the distribution of influence, the lower the total amount of influence that the different levels tend to exercise over the set of 16 decisions as a whole and over medium and long-term decisions taken separately. Similar results are obtained if we measure inequality in terms of the variance of influence between all hierarchical groups: all correlations between this measure of inequality and total influence scores are negative, again, with the exception of top management.

Clearly, the question remains whether the generally low levels of control exercised by workers over decision-making are a function of the generalized inequality which exists within organizations or whether this inequality is itself a historical consequence of the traditionally powerless status of workers within hierarchically ordered organizations. It is also unclear whether there is a direct causal relationship between these two phenomena since we cannot exclude the possibility that their interdependence is based on some third factor such as the presence or absence of conflicts. In spite of these unanswered questions, the results of the present analysis are highly relevant since they suggest that the overall powerlessness of organizations and especially the powerlessness of workers is closely related to the uneven distribution of influence within these systems.

Power-Influence Relations between Hierarchical Levels

Having looked at the degree of centralization and inequality in the distribution of influence, we can now turn to a correlational analysis of the interrelationships between the influence scores of different hierarchical levels. More specifically, we wish to argue that positive correlations between the amounts of influence exercised by different groups are indicative of the prevalence of variable-sum games among the groups concerned. Broadly speaking, these are instances in which increments in the amount of influence exercised by one group coincide with increments in the amount of control of other levels. In contrast, when increments in the influence of one group are associated with decrements in the amount of control exercised by other levels a zero-sum game may be said to exist.

Most organizational theories suggest the existence and prevalence of variable-sum games within work organizations (Dubin 1956, Tannenbaum 1968). To a greater or lesser extent these interpretations tend to follow Durkheim's theory which sees increases in the division of labour as creating greater interdependence and solidarity between different social groups or units. If one accepts this interpretation one would expect a variable-sum game to prevail in those organizations which exhibit a highly developed division of labour. Counter to this, are theories derived from Marx's ideas based on class antagonisms which stress the antagonistic nature of the division of labour within work organizations. These theories suggest the existence of a zero-sum game, at least between those organizational levels which represent the interests of labour and capital.

Our research design does not enable us to provide a direct and definite answer as to whether variable- or zero-sum games predominate in our 134 organizations. The reason why such an answer is not possible is that we did not examine processes of power distribution over time but only patterns (or structures) of power at a given point in time. When talking about zero or variable-sum games, therefore, we can only point to some synchronic trends which are evident from our data.[7] These trends are visible in Table 7.5 which reports the various influence correlations between all possible pairs of organizational levels. A brief inspection of this table reveals a variable-sum game across most organizational levels with the notable exception of games with top management. The influence of top management correlates negatively with the influence of workers, of supervisors, of corporate levels, and of external bodies. These negative correlations are not always statistically significant but they are nevertheless consistent across almost all levels. The only exception in this respect is the weak positive relation that exists between top and middle management. It is worth noting, however, that the influence of middle management is, at the same time, positively related to that of both workers and supervisors, and that these correlations are stronger than the one between top and middle management. It would appear, therefore, that top management plays a zero-sum game against all other levels and that there is no one level that creates power coalitions with top management.[8]

The influence of bodies at the corporate level also tends to be negatively related to that of lower levels within organizations. The position of such corporate bodies, however, differs from that of top management in that their influence, unlike that of top management, correlates positively with that of both representative bodies and external societal groups.[9] The influence of corporate bodies is negatively related to that of top management.

In other words, Table 7.5 suggests a tendency towards the formation of two main power coalitions in our organizations: one at the bottom of the organization where alliances between workers and supervisors are more or less supported by middle management, and another coalition at the top of the organization where alliances between representative bodies and external groups are partly supported by bodies at the corporate level. Top management lies between these two power coalitions, partly isolated, partly in opposition to them.[10]

Table 7.6 offers a more detailed picture of the relationship between top management's influence and that of other levels, by presenting the results of the analysis for each cluster of decisions separately. The general picture which emerges from this table is similar to the one discussed above: top management's influence correlates negatively with that of almost all other levels across short-, medium- and long-term decisions. Top management creates only very specific coalitions over limited sets of issues: with middle management and supervisors over long-term decisions, and with representative bodies and corporate levels over short-term decisions. It seems that these particular coalitions are the only bridges linking top management to other organizational levels. Narrow as they are, however, such co-operative links are important since they reduce top management's isolation and its need to rely on the use of coercive power.

Table 7.5
Inter-level correlations of Influence for all decisions

Levels	Influence (PO1a)						
	Workers (A)	Foremen (B)	Middle managers (C)	Top management (D)	Level above plant (E)	Representative bodies (F)	External groups (G)
Workers (A)							
Foremen (B)	.44						
Middle managers (C)	.17	.37					
Top management (D)	−.32	−.02	.02				
Level above plant (E)	.07	−.04	−.01	−.18			
Representative bodies (F)	.37	.08	−.08	−.05	.26		
External groups	.35	.06	.10	−.15	.23	.43	

Note: $p \leq .05$ if r > .15.

Table 7.6
Inter-level correlations of Influence by decision-type

	Influence (PO1a)					
Clusters of decisions	Foremen (B)	Middle managers (C)	Top management (D)	Level above plant (E)	Representative bodies (F)	External groups (G)
Workers (A)						
ST[a]	.48	.23	-.34		.17	.07
MT	.43	.15	-.34		.38	.40
LT	.47	.30		.21	.66	.37
All decisions	.44	.17	-.32		.37	.35
Top Management (D)						
ST	-.32	-.24			.20	
MT	-.28			-.27	-.17	-.18
LT		.32	.24	-.21	-.18	-.16
All decisions	-.32			-.18	-.15	-.15

Note: $p \leq .05$ if $r > .15$.

[a] ST = short-term; MT = medium-term; LT = long-term.

From Table 7.6, we can see that the relation between workers' influence and that of other levels also varies across different clusters of decisions. The most stable relations are those between the influence of workers and that of supervisors and middle management. These correlations are significant and positive across all clusters of decisions thus confirming the impression that the coalitions which form among lower levels within organizations tend to be relatively stable in nature. Workers' relations with higher levels, on the other hand, appear to be more variable. The general pattern of these relations could be characterized as follows: the more strategic the decision, the stronger the positive correlation between the influence of workers and that of representative bodies and external groups.

It would appear, therefore, that workers' participation in medium-and long-term decisions tends to be facilitated by the development of some kind of coalition with both local representative bodies and external groups. Such coalitions, however, may not be so necessary in the case of short-term decisions. When it comes to influencing these types of decision what appears to be more important is for workers to obtain the support and backing of supervisors and middle management.

In this connection, special attention should be directed at the relationship between direct and representative democracy or, let us say, between workers' influence and the influence of representative bodies. In accordance with Lammers' hypothesis we expected to find little or no relationship between these two types of democracy (Lammers 1967), although we also took note of the opposite results found by Qvale (1970). Our results support both contradictory expectations. We found a very low correlation between the influence of workers and that of representative bodies in relation to short-term routine decisions, and a very significant positive correlation between these two levels with respect to medium- and long-term decisions. What this suggests is that some form of segmentation between direct and representative democracy is likely in cases where industrial democracy is less developed, while such segmentation becomes less likely where industrial democracy is more developed. This interpretation is congruent with the suggestion made in Chapter 8 to the effect that direct and indirect participation seem to be better integrated in Yugoslavia and in the Scandinavian countries—that is in those countries where industrial democracy is relatively more developed (see IDE 1980, chapters 2, 3, 4, 5 and 12).

Our findings concerning the role played by external bodies are also important from the point of view of the development of industrial democracy. It is evident that the influence of these outside groups is consistently and positively correlated to the influence of both workers and representative bodies while it is negatively correlated to the influence of top management. Greater control by groups representing the wider social environment appears to have a positive effect on the degree of internal democratization of work organizations. The case of Yugoslavia provides a clear example in this respect. This finding can also be formulated from an organizational perspective: the more organizations become open systems, the more influenced they are by the wider society and therefore the more democratized they tend to become. This suggestion is similar to Crozier's argument that the most efficient way of de-bureaucratizing organizations is to increase their openness to wider societal influences (Crozier 1963).

A similar bivariate analysis of inter-level influence relations was carried out for each of our sixteen decisions separately. We again found that in most cases negative inter-level relations are connected with top management and with bodies at the corporate level: 49 out of a total of 65 negative correlations involved one of these two levels.

Finally, a similar inter-level influence analysis was carried out for each country separately: Because of the number of cases within each particular country no significant relationships can be reported. In spite of this shortcoming we can say that countries differ quite substantially in terms of the number of negative inter-level correlations as well as in terms of the level that is most frequently involved in negative correlations. For instance, in the U.K., Sweden, and Yugoslavia almost half of all possible inter-level correlations are negative, while in Belgium, Norway, and Denmark, less than one-fifth of them are negative. We believe that quite different reasons lie behind the negative inter-correlations to be found in the various countries, but at the same time we would suggest that higher frequencies of negative correlations indicate less stable power systems, perhaps systems which are in transition.

Although the U.K., Sweden, and Yugoslavia are similar in terms of the number of negative inter-level correlations they differ in terms of which level is most frequently involved: in the U.K. it is bodies at the corporate level; in Sweden top management; while in Yugoslavia, it is the Workers' Councils. The level most frequently involved in zero-sum games is perhaps one of the best indicators of the basic problems confronting industrial democracy in a particular country.

Patterns of Influence Distribution and Conflicts

Although organizational conflicts might have great explanatory power in relation to questions about zero- and variable-sum games, our instruments are too weak for a thorough analysis of their nature. Unfortunately we have no precise information about the nature of such conflicts, about their intensity or about the actors involved in them. The only dimension of conflict measured in this research is the occurrence of 'disagreements' over the sixteen decisions.[11]

The basic information about the distribution of conflicts between countries is presented in Table 7.7. It seems that the overall trend over the whole sample of organizations is that the more strategic the decisions are the more conflictual they tend to be (see the last column of the table). This trend is not very marked but it is quite consistent for the whole population and also for majority of the countries. Since influence relations under conflict conditions emerge as power relations we should conclude that relations between participants in long- and medium-term decisions are more likely to take the form of power relations than those between participants in short-term decisions.

However, the frequency of conflicts varies remarkably across the countries. Organizations in Norway and Yugoslavia tend to be the most conflict-ridden. If we take into account the fact that workers in these two countries have more influence than workers in other societies and that both these countries have

Table 7.7
Conflicts by country

| | Percentage of key respondents who reported disagreements | | | | | | | | | | | | |
Decisions	Belgium	Denmark	Finland	France	Germany (West)	U.K.	Italy	Israel	Holland	Norway	Sweden	Yugoslavia	All countries
Short-term	62	20	20	23	26	23	43	31	39	63	38	51	37
Medium-term	59	10	33	32	22	26	49	62	25	60	48	62	40
Long-term	58	46	23	35	32	41	44	43	42	68	51	50	47
All decisions	61	20	20	24	21	23	44	37	39	60	42	56	38

relatively higher degrees of democratization and decentralization, then we can suppose that conflicts will tend to be most common where there is the greatest equalization of power. Similar results emerged from a longitudinal research study exploring long-term decision-making processes in three European countries. According to the preliminary results of this research, Yugoslav enterprises have less unequal power distributions but are more conflictual than either British or Dutch enterprises (Rus 1978).

The fact that Belgium appears to have the most conflictual decision-making processes seem to contradict the findings and hypotheses discussed above. Workers in Belgian enterprises exercise very little influence—less than workers in other countries, and the concentration of control in the hands of top management is relatively high. Belgium, therefore, is at the other extreme of the scale relative to Norway and Yugoslavia. Since these countries, with extremely different patterns of influence distribution, also have very high levels of conflict, we have reason to suppose that, besides patterns of influence distribution, there are other sources of conflict in decision-making.[12]

Table 7.8

Inter-correlations between the amount of Influence of different levels and the frequency of conflicts

| | Conflicts over: | | | |
Amount of Influence	Short-term decisions	Medium-term decisions	Long-term decisions	All decisions
Workers (A)				
Foremen (B)	−.24	−.15		−.25
Middle managers (C)	−.25			−.25
Top management (D)		−.14	−.15	
Level above plant (E)		.18		
Representative bodies (F)	.22	.24		.26
External Groups (G)		.17		.17
All levels	−.17			−.18
VARPO1 to[a]		.22		.15
EQPO1 to (A)[b]	.18	.21		.22
EQPO1 to (F)	.31	.28		.36

Note: $p < .05$ if $r > .15$.

[a]VARPO1 to = Variance in Influence regarding total set of decisions over all groups in the organization.

[b]EQPO1 to (A) = Differences in Influence for the total set of decisions between workers and other groups in the organization.

In this connection, Table 7.8 shows that there are fairly consistent correlations between these two sets of variables. If we look first at the relation between conflict and the total influence of particular levels, the data presented in this table suggest the following three basic conclusions:

i. There is no relation between the influence of workers and the level of conflict in decision-making;

ii. There are quite consistent negative correlations between the amount of influence exercised by low, middle, and top management and the frequency of conflicts: the greater the influence of lower, middle, and top management, the less conflict there tends to be;

iii. There are quite consistent positive correlations between the influence of higher non-hierarchical levels and the frequency of conflicts: the greater the influence of representative bodies (and to some extent also of external groups), the more conflictual the decision-making process tends to be.

The absence of any significant correlations between the influence of workers and the frequency of conflicts over the 16 selected decisions could be explained by the generally low levels of control exercised by workers, or by the fact that workers tend to exercise their influence in a negative way through resistance and not through direct confrontation. We suppose also that, in most cases, workers can positively influence these decision-making processes only indirectly through their representatives or through external groups. The significant positive correlations to be found between the influence of representative bodies and the frequency of conflicts indirectly confirms this hypothesis. Representative bodies do not have a substantially greater amount of influence than workers, but their influence is significantly correlated with the level of conflict.

In contrast, the concentration of power in the hands of management seems to reduce significantly the likelihood that conflicts will surface or find expression in the decision-making process. What this suggests is that management tends to use its influence to prevent conflicts from arising during decision-making processes.

The above discussion can be summarized by reference to the results reported at the bottom of Table 7.8. The correlations at the bottom of this table point to the existence of a negative relationship between our different measures of power inequality and the frequency of conflicts: the greater the inequality in the distribution of influence across managerial and non-managerial levels, the lower the frequency of conflicts.[13] One of the consequences of internal democratization, or, let us say, of a greater degree of power equalization is, therefore, an increase in the level of organizational conflict and uncertainty.

Conditions and contingencies of patterned influence distribution

In the following sections, we will explore the extent to which patterns of influence distribution are conditioned by organizational context (CON variables) and by the institutionally or formally prescribed normative system (PS variables). In the following multivariate analyses, both sets of variables will be taken into account as co-predictors of patterned influence distribution.

Theoretically, we will treat institutional or normative regulations (PS) as conditons and organizational characteristics as contingencies. The first set of variables, are, in most countries, legal regulations governing participation and as such represent a kind of meta-power to which *de facto* participation in organizations is submitted. The organizational characteristics are less institutionalized and are more the outcome of the circumstances in which organizations operate and try to survive. These organizational characteristics will be treated as contingencies or as moderators between the normative and actual participative systems. However, we do not have sufficient information to be able to distinguish between conditions and contingencies as is demonstrated at the end of Chapter 4. Therefore, we will limit our multivariate analyses in such a way that both sets of variables will be treated as co-predictors of the influence distribution in organizations.

Country, sector, and size as predictors of influence distribution

The most complex predictors of patterned influence distribution are countries, sectors in which organizations are situated, and size. Size of organizations usually

Table 7.9
*Analysis of variance and multiple classification: country,
sector and size as independent variables and influence
as the dependent variable[a]*

Dependent variable	Independent variables						
Influence	Country	Sector	Size	Interactions			Multiple R square
Workers (A)	.77	.07	.10	.16	.07	.59	.59
Foremen (B)	.57	.25	.10	.11	.04	.69	.40
Middle managers (C)	.42	.15	.12	.86	.61	.98	.20
Top management (D)	.57	.19	.33	.63	.54	.58	.45
Level above plant (E)	.62	.13	.10	.96	.97	.89	.39
Representative bodies (F)	.89	.01	.03	.09	.02	.34	.78
External Groups (G)	.69	.13	.07	.01	.04	.02	.50
All levels	.50	.13	.18	.65	.40	.81	.31
Difference D–A[b]	.71	.13	.24	.65	.46	.79	.56
Variance A–E[c]	.70	.25	.25	.82	.44	.58	
EQP01 to (A)[d]	.71	.11	.21	.44	.38	.84	.55
EQPO1 to (F)	.84	.02	.14	.79	.52	.89	.75

[a]Values in first three columns are adjusted beta coefficients, values in the next three columns are significance of F values, and in the last column are multiple R^2. There were 134 cases.

[b]Difference in Influence between top management and workers.

[c]Difference in variance of Influence between workers and the level above plant.

[d]EQPO1 to (A) = Differences in Influence for the total set of decisions between workers and other groups in the organization.

conditions a very great number of other organizational characteristics (Blau and Schoenherr 1971). The predictive power of these three variables can be seen in Table 7.9. If we compare the values in the columns, we can see that country is a far better predictor of influence distribution than sector or size. Interaction effects are, in almost all cases, non-significant so that the amount of explained variance presented in the column reflects mainly the independent effects of country, sector, and size of organization. Moreover, in almost all cases much of the explained variance can be attributed to the predictive power of the country variable (cf. IDE 1980).

Table 7.9 shows that country has different effects on the influence of different levels. It has the greatest effect on the influence of workers, representative bodies, and external bodies. The strong relationship between country and influence which exists for these three levels cannot be easily explained since country as a predictor contains an extremely large number of implicit dimensions. It could be variables related to culture, political structure, economy, or institutional arrangements which make 'country' a strong predictor of influence distribution. Some authors regard culture as a synonym for country and therefore suppose it to be a main determinant of power relations within organizations (see, for example Hofstede 1976). We do not share this belief since the concept of culture in its complexity, escapes strict operationalization and is difficult to relate to power distribution in organizations.

Our hypothesis is that the very great power of country as a predictor of influence distribution is a consequence of the country's institutional arrangements. These are closely related to power relations within organizations and also legally determine those relations. The fact that country is the best predictor of influence for workers and for representative bodies, suggests that our hypothesis is correct. However, the amount of influence of top management is relatively less well explained by country differences and relatively better by the size of the organization. It seems that the amount of influence of top management is less institutionally determined and more conditioned by organizational structure.

Top management is the only group whose influence is explained more by the size of the organization than the other two variables. The fact that size and sector appear as very weak predictors of the influence of workers and representative bodies, and the fact that the interaction effects of size and sector are non-significant, create an impression that the influence of these two levels is not anchored in organizations but in the environmental social setting. It seems that the influence of these two levels—and accordingly industrial democracy—is an externally-based phenomenon which does not have a supportive framework within the organization.

If we also examine the results of the analysis of variance and multiple classification regarding our equality measures at the bottom of Table 7.9 we find similar results as have been found for particular organizational levels: all measures of inequality are much better explained by country than by sector or size of organization. Interaction effects are also non-significant here, as in the cases mentioned above. The fact that the degree of inequality of the distribution of influence is best and largely explained by country suggests that national institutional characteristics are more relevant predictors of the distribution of influence than culture which may be similar in various countries (c.f. IDE 1980, ch. 14).

Institutional norms as predictors of influence distribution

The circular explanation of *de jure* and *de facto* participation would be the most appropriate framework for our interpretation in this section (Nagel 1969). This kind of theory conceives the process of the institutionalization of participation as a reciprocal process in which legislation promotes structural and behavioural changes and in which these changes in turn modify and develop legislative activity. However such an explanation requires a longitudinal research design which we have not been able to undertake. Therefore, a more voluntaristic (and more one-sided) interpretation of these relations will be presented: by means of cross-sectional analysis we are going to test the extent to which positive law and formal regulations contribute to structural and behavioural changes in organizations.

Table 7.10 contains a set of multiple regressions in which the dimensions of the institutional framework are taken as predictors and basic dimensions of the actual distribution of influence as dependent variables. The last three columns give an overview of the effects which the institutional framework has on the actual distribution of influence. It is evident that institutional rules significantly affect the distribution of influence: the more developed are institutional or other formal regulations for participation for workers, representative bodies, and bodies above plant level, the lower becomes the difference of influence between workers and top management. Greater overall power equalization, measured by the variance of influence across all levels, is also conditioned by legal regulations at the corporate level. We are not able to interpret this rather surprising effect. It seems that these regulations limit power at the corporate level and in this way contribute indirectly to greater overall influence-equalization.

The total amount of influence in organizations is not conditioned by formal regulations. The explanation for this finding, contained in the last column of Table 7.10, lies in data presented in the first 12 columns of the Table. The columns show the different effects of formal regulations on the influence of workers, top managers and representative bodies: formal regulations have different effects on the influence of different levels. The combination of these opposite effects results in a non-significant overall relation between the total amount of influence and formal regulations.

However, if we look at the table horizontally we can see the multi-level regulative function of the *de jure* system. What is perhaps one of the most interesting findings contained in this table is that the *de jure* system works directly by promoting the influence of workers and representative bodies and indirectly by inhibiting the influence of competing levels within organizations. For instance, the formal regulations for workers' participation do not facilitate their influence only but also the influence of representative bodies while they inhibit the influence of top management. Formal regulations for the participation of top management do not facilitate the influence of this level but inhibit to some extent the influence of workers and representative bodies. The effects of formal regulations are therefore multiple, and they are not located only at the level for which they are established.

We assume that these effects on other levels are usually not planned or controlled and therefore represent a kind of side-effect of institutional regulations. However, these apparently confusing effects can easily be theoretically interpreted if we relate them to dependence theories of power according to which relative power relations are not only the outcome of the absolute power possessed by one level but are also the outcome of the power of other levels in an organization.

So far we have described only the effects of formal regulations on the influence of workers, top management and representative bodies. One reason for this is that these three levels are crucial for understanding how the processes of democratization develop in organizations. Another reason is that preliminary analysis has shown relatively weak effects of formal regulations at other organizational levels. However, even within these three levels the predictive power of formal regulations varies considerably. This is evident from the bottom lines of Table 7.10 where it is seen that formal regulations explain about 50 per cent of all the variance of the influence of representative bodies, a similar amount of the variance of workers' influence over medium- and long-term decisions, and substantially less for top management. If we compare the data on the bottom lines of Table 7.10 we realize that the predictive power of formal regulations becomes greater the more strategic are the decisions and the higher is the level of participation: workers' influence on short-term decisions is weakly explained by formal regulations but their influence upon long-term decisions is greatly explained by them.

One suggestion seems to follow from the above findings: it is not possible to expect more developed forms of industrial democracy without the further development of formal regulations. Regulations should be primarily oriented towards workers' influence over medium- and long-term decisions and toward the influence of representative bodies over all kinds of decision. At the same time, these regulations should not be oriented only towards encouraging the growth of workers' influence and that of representative bodies. They should also take into account indirect effects which can be produced by increasing the influence of external bodies or through regulations which restrict the influence of top management upon short- and medium-term decisions.

Still considering the impact of formal participatory rules we may now ask questions about the differential effects of different norms on the distribution of influence. Two questions may be pursued. The first is which formal sources (Bases)—possibly in interaction with their respective Modes—produce the highest levels of participation? Two-way analysis of variance helps to answer this question. The three main Base categories (laws, collective bargaining agreements, managerial policies) and their Modes[15] for each of the sixteen decisions are treated as independent variables and the *De Facto* Influence scores (PO1) of workers and representative bodies as dependent variables.

Significant F-values ($p = < .05$) for the differences of worker Influence scores in relation to the three Base categories were only found in six out of our sixteen decisions: transfer, pay level, assigning tasks, dismissals, work study, and holidays. For decisions regarding pay level and holiday dates it is managerial policies which 'produce' the highest worker Influence scores (3.0 and 3.6 respectively), for dismissals it is the law (Influence score: 1.8). If we consider

Table 7.10
Multiple regressions; different dimensions of influence regressed by institutional norms (PS)[a]

Institutional norms (PS)	Influence (PO1a)									Levels			Difference Variance		
	Workers (A)			Top management (D)			Representative bodies (F)			(A)	(D)	(F)	D-A[c]	A-E[d]	Total
	ST[b]	MT	LT	ST	MT	LT	ST	MT	LT						
Workers (A)															
ST															
MT		.51*								.34					.32
LT			.29		-.32	-.34			.39						
Foremen (B)															
ST	-.47														
MT															
LT			-.40			-.43				-.41		-.30			
Middle managers (C)															
ST				.40							-.39				
MT															
LT						.43									
Top management (D)															
ST	.41						-.32					-.21			
MT		-.38													
LT			-.61												
Level above plant (E)															
ST										.39			-.47	-.59	
MT		.32													
LT			-.19	-.33								-.15			

	1	2	3	4	5	6	7	8	9	10	11	12	13	14	15
Representative bodies (F)															
ST			.20		.34	.24	.56	.66							
MT															
LT															
External Groups (G)															
ST			.21								-.41		.59		
MT								-.25	.37			-.18			
LT								.22	.14			.22			
Multiple R	.549	.705	.804	.511	.568	.546	.733	.788	.757	.659	.543	.809	.658	.494	.468
Adjusted R²	.17	.40	.58	.12	.19	.16	.45	.55	.49	.32	.16	.59	.32	.10	.07
F	2.3	5.2	9.7	1.8	2.5	2.2	6.2	8.7	7.1	4.1	2.2	10.1	4.1	1.7	1.4
P	003	000	000	001	001	003	000	000	000	000	004	000	000	.03	.09

[a] Values in table are standardized beta coefficients with $p \leq 0.7$, Df = 21, 112.

[b] ST = short-term decisions, MT = medium-term decisions, LT = long-term decisions.

[c] Difference in Influence between top management and workers.

[d] Difference in variance of Influence between workers and the level above plant.

also the non-significant relationships we find that collective bargaining is associated with the highest Influence scores for twelve out of our sixteen decisions—the exceptions being the three decisions mentioned above and investment decisions (the highest Influence score for legal bases is 1.4). Only in the case of dismissal decisions do we find a significant interaction between Base and the prescribed level of participation (Mode).

A similar analysis of variance for the data regarding representative bodies yields a somewhat less clear picture. F-values of differences between the Influence scores for the three Base categories are significant only for decisions regarding capital investment (management policy with the highest Influence score), assigning tasks (collective bargaining highest), holidays (management policy highest) and working hours (laws highest).

The second question asks how effective are the different Base categories in assuring high levels of compliance with the norms for participation. Again we consider the three Bases as independent variables, this time in a one-way analysis of variance. The dependent variable is now the difference between the respective Mode and Influence scores (separately considered for workers and representative bodies). The scales for Mode scores (based on the six-step Mode scale) and Influence scores (based on the five-point Likert-type scale of PO1) are, of course, not strictly comparable due to the difference in the nature of scales. However, for our purposes we can assume that lower difference scores imply higher compliance with existing rules and vice versa.

Using Scheffe's procedure to determine significant differences in the average Influence scores of workers or representative bodies based on laws, collective bargaining agreements, and managerial policy we find a relatively homogeneous picture emerging. In the majority of the decisions where we find significant differences ($p = < .05$) it is formal rules based on collective bargaining contracts that are associated with the smallest differences between norms and *de facto* participation. In other words, compliance with given participative rules and regulations seems to be best guaranteed if such rules stem from collective bargaining. This is consistently the case for representative bodies, and for the three decisions where, for workers, highest levels of norm compliance are found on the basis of law or managerial policies we can find plausible explanations (see Table 7.11).

To be sure, our data must be interpreted with caution. We have analysed the impact of different formal Bases on the *de facto* Influence of workers and representative bodies across all of our 134 organizations, thus neglecting country, sector and other factors that might possibly confound this relationship. However, a conservative interpretation suggests that among our three Base categories it is collective bargaining contracts that might be of primary importance in the promotion of worker and representative body influence as well as in attempts to guarantee that such norms have a chance of being implemented by the groups in question. While laws may set global frameworks, collective bargaining agreements may serve as the choice instrument to fill these frames with content.

Contextual variables as predictors of the distribution of influence

Although contextual variables figure in our research model as contingencies which have the function of moderators between *de jure* and *de facto* participation,

Table 7.11
*Different types of formal participatory rules in their impact
on compliance with formal participative norms*[a]

Decision relating to:	Bases 'producing' significantly higher levels of norm compliance for:	
	Workers	Representative bodies
Working conditions	C.B.[b] > M.P.[c]	
New department head		C.B. > L
Training courses	C.B. > L.[d], M.P.	C.B. > L.
Investment	C.B. > L.	C.B. > L.
New product		C.B. > L.
Personal equipment	L. > C.B.	
Reorganization	M.P. > C.B.	
Dismissals	L. > C.B., M.P.	
Holidays		C.B. > L.

[a]$N = 134$ organizations.;
[b]C.B. = Collective bargaining.
[c]M.P. = Managerial policy.
[d]L. = Laws.

we will test these contextual variables in this section as predictors of the pat-terned distribution of influence.[14] Since the contextual variables included in this research design are numerous and quite heterogenous, for the purposes of our subsequent analysis we have grouped them in five clusters slightly different from those in Chapter 5. These are:

i. *Personal variables* or attributes of employees which have been aggregated at the level of hierarchical groups; in this cluster of contextual variables we include Skill-level of employees (CO 5), Stability of Work-force (age and tenure of employee CO 14), Male Domination (CO 15), and Employee Mobilization (their membership in unions and representative bodies (CO 16));

ii. *Technological contingencies* which contain the following contextual variables: the Level of Automation of work (CO 6), Technological Interdependence or work flow continuity (CO 7) and Product Complexity (CO 8);

iii. *Structural contingencies* which contain variables of organizational structure: the (1g) Size of organizations (CO 19) which is expected to be the main condition for other structural variables,[16] Functional Differentiation based on division of labour (CO 9), vertical differentiation or Vertical Span which indicates the number of hierarchical levels in an organization (CO 10), Formalization of organizational roles at different levels of the organization (CO 11), the Span of control of Top Managers (CO 12) which indicates the extent of functional concentration at this level, and finally the Intensity of managerial Control (CO 13);

iv *Economic contingencies* which indicate the success of the organization and contain the following contextual variables: evaluation of Organizational Success (CO 17), and Growth Rate of organizations (CO 18);

v. *Environmental contingencies* which contain contextual variables of the environment in which the organization is situated: the Formal Independence of the organization (CO 1), Competitive Position (CO 2), Political Instability (CO 3), and the Sector in which the organization operates (CO 4).

In Table 7.12 the effects of these contextual variables on the distribution of influence in organizations are presented in a set of multiple regression equations in which contextual variables are predictors and the influence of workers, top management, and representative bodies are dependent variables. Data presented in this table are limited to the influence of the three most important levels as we have tried to avoid too complex a presentation.

i. Personal variables as predictors of the distribution of influence

We did not expect that personal variables would have a great effect on influence distribution since we treat patterns of influence distribution as structural variables which are not substantially conditioned by interpersonal relations among employees. Data in Table 7.12 generally confirm our expectations: Skill-level, the Stability of the Workforce and sex evidently do not have great effects on influence distribution.

The frequent expectation that more highly educated employees will have greater influence and that therefore a higher educational level among employees in organizations will coincide with a more equalized power distribution does not have great support from our findings. It seems that higher education and/or skill does not by itself represent a sufficient, but only a necessary, condition for higher influence; if an employee does not have the relevant status in the organization, his skill does not contribute significantly to greater influence.

From this point of view we can also interpret the data contained in Table 7.12. Education has a significant effect on the influence of representative bodies but no significant effect on the influence of workers themselves; the first have the status for participation, the second do not. However, if we look only at workers' influence on long-term decisions we see that it is significantly affected by their own skill. One possible explanation for this exception can be found in Table 7.10 where it was evident that the influence of workers on long-term decisions depends largely on the relative influence of different levels inside and outside the organization.

Although sex, age, and tenure incorporated in CO 14 and CO 15 do not have a great effect on patterned influence distribution one can see the very great and very consistent effect of employees' mobilization upon influence distribution at all levels and within all clusters of decision-making. If we take into account that this contingency is a composite of employees' membership in representative bodies and of employees' unionization, and that, according to some preliminary computations, unionization as a predictor has a minor role in relation to past and present membership of representative bodies, then we should conclude that the greatest effect on the distribution of influence comes from membership in representative bodies; this involves not only a kind of activity but also higher status.[17] We suppose that the mobilization of employees has such a great impact on influence distribution primarily because it leads to higher status. It looks as if membership of representative bodies contributes much more to power equalization than do all the other personal characteristics.

Multiple regressions; dimensions of influence are regressed by contextual variables[a]

Contextual variables	Influence (PO1a)											
	Workers (A)			Top management (D)			Representative body (F)			Levels		
	ST[b]	MT	LT	ST	MT	LT	ST	MT	LT	A Σ	D Σ	F Σ
Formal independence of enterprise						.26	−.24	−.17				−.19
Market domination of enterprise		−.19*			−.27		.21			.20		.16
Political instability							−.17	−.16	−.18			−.19
Sector	.27							.26				
Skill						−.27	.19					.17
Automatization			.23									−.19
Technological interdependence			−.22					−.22	−.17			
Product complexity		.18		.20			.26	.26		.22	.17	
Functional differentiation		.29	.25						.30			.33
Vertical span						−.30						
Formalization					−.24						−.23	
Span of top management		−.16										
Intensity of control												
Stability of work force			−.19						−.17			
Male domination												
Mobilization	.19	.45	.42	−.20	−.30	−.19	.35	.33	.50	.33	−.27	.43
Evaluation of success												
Growth of enterprise												
Log size												
Multiple R	.396	.613	.617	.529	.501	.585	.558	.531	.631	.479	.554	.606
Adjusted R²	.006	.05	.26	.14	.10	.21	.17	.14	.28	.08	.16	.24
Σ = all decisions, influence of respective level	.96	3,11	3,17	2,01	1,78	2,69	2,33	2,02	3,42	1,54	2,17	3,00
P	.50	.000	.000	.01	.04	.001	.004	.01	.000	.08	.007	.000

[a]Values in the table are standardized beta coefficients with p < .07

[b]ST = short-term decisions, MT = medium-term decisions, LT = long-term decisions.

Mobilization has multiple effects: it affects the influence of workers and representative bodies to a great extent and, at the same time, limits the influence of top management. Beside this the effects of Mobilization on medium- and long-term decisions are greater than on short-term decisions, which means that mobilization represents one of the best ways to encourage the long-range development of industrial democracy in organizations.

ii. Technological contingencies as predictors

Technology and organizational structure are frequently treated as the main predictors of social phenomena and of the amount of participation and distribution of power in organizations (Evan 1977). However, these expectations are based on investigations which have been mainly oriented towards management behaviour or employees' behaviour on the job. Research which overcomes this very narrow scope of employee activity and which attempts to uncover relationships between more complex kinds of participation and technology has found no evidence for a close relationship between technology and workers' participation (Jacob and Jacob 1978), or that technology has restrictive effects on participation only in extreme cases i.e. in the case of assembly-line work (Mohr 1971). In the light of these findings the results contained in Table 7.12 are not surprising. What is rather unusual is the greater effect of automation on the influence of representative bodies than on workers' influence. It seems that the level of technological interdependence of the work-flow does not have any significant effect on influence distribution while the level of automation does. We suppose that the effect of automation on the influence of representative bodies is not a direct one but is perhaps mediated by the greater independence of the organization or by some other contingency which is connected with higher automation.

The complexity of production affects the distribution of influence in the expected way, since it is usually supposed that greater complexity creates greater unpredictability and therefore the need for greater participation by employees in all areas of activity.

iii. Structural contingencies as predictors of influence distribution

According to the findings of Blau and Schoenherr (1971), the size of the organization correlates highly with vertical, horizontal, and professional differentiation of the organizational structure. As such it should be one of the most important contingencies for the distribution of influence in organizations. Contrary to these expectations, size does not significantly affect any dimension of the distribution of influence which is included in Table 7.12 although the other variables of organizational structure do. According to the data we can say that vertical differentiation (measured by the number of hierarchical levels) is in fact nonsignificant for influence distribution, while horizontal differentiation (measured as functional differentiation) is the second-best predictor of influence distribution: the greater the functional differentiation, the greater the influence workers have on medium- and long-term decisions and representative bodies have on all kinds of decision. It seems that greater functional differentiation demands much greater effort for co-ordination and in this way creates more opportunities and also more need for participation (see Chapter 5). It is also possible that the concentration of power is decreased by functional differentiation which facilitates greater participation and greater power-sharing.

Among the structural variables Formalization has also quite a major effect although in a rather unexpected way. Formalization is usually taken as an indicator of bureaucratization and alienation (Aiken 1966). However, some recently published discussions have turned attention to the multiple character of formalization and to the possibility that subordinate levels are more protected by formalization of management power (Gustavsen 1972). Our results demonstrate exactly this effect. Formalization does not coincide with less Influence for workers or representative bodies but with less Influence for top management. Formalization in this case contributes to the greater equalization of power in organizations.

iv. Economic contingencies as predictors of the distribution of influence

Organizational growth and economic effectiveness are sometimes seen as outcomes, sometimes as conditions of industrial democracy. Since direct causal relations between industrial democracy and economic efficiency have never yet been proved, this dilemma is becoming less relevant. According to our data, economic efficiency and the growth of organizations have no significant impact on the distribution of influence.

v. Environmental contingencies as predictors of the distribution of influence

All four environmental contextual variables have some—although not very great—effects on the distribution of influence in organizations. Greater formal independence of organizations coincides with greater influence for top management and with less influence for representative bodies. Independence therefore does not contribute to the democratization of organizations as is usually expected. While unexpected, this result has some connection with our previous results in which it was found that the influence of external bodies encourages internal democratization in organizations. The traditional liberal hypothesis about the necessary coincidence of external autonomy and internal democracy of organizations should be modified at least by the sub-hypothesis that, under certain circumstances, the opposite might be true: internal democratization cannot increase without greater openness and less external autonomy for organizations.

The effects of the market position of the organization on the internal distribution of influence are also rather surprising: a better position in the market leads to more influence for workers and representative bodies and less influence for top management. As in most other cases we do not believe that these effects are direct. It is much more probable that a better market position increases the security of employees and decreases the need of top management for close control over medium-term decisions.

Finally, the effect of Sector is in line with expectations and coincides with previous findings. It seems that in non-industrial organizations there are more opportunities for democratization than in industrial organizations. Whether this is an effect of the less conflictual relations between employees and employers, or of the better economic positions of banks and insurance companies, or of a less developed division of labour than in industry, or of the greater skill structure is a question which we have not yet explored, but it seems that there are greater chances for the development of 'industrial democracy' in non-industrial settings.

In summarizing the findings presented above we can say that only one contextual variable has a great, and perhaps also a direct, effect on the internal distribution of power: Mobilization of Employees. This contingency, however, is not by nature an economic, structural, or personal variable. It is more an activity supported by either social or political agencies. To this finding should perhaps be added the findings from Table 7.10 where we found that the legal structure had a great effect on the distribution of influence within organizations. Taking these two findings together we can tentatively conclude that industrial democracy in our 134 organizations is not primarily personally, structurally, technically, or economically conditioned. It is mainly conditioned by the socio-political and institutional environment of an organization.[18]

Institutional norms and contextual variables as co-predictors of the patterned distribution of influence

In Table 7.13 institutional norms and contextual variables are taken as co-predictors of the distribution of influence in organizations. Institutional norms are selected according to the results of multiple regressions presented in Table 7.10 and contextual variables according to the results of multiple regressions in Table 7.12. While the contextual variables are constant for all three levels as co-predictors of influence distribution, the institutional norms as co-predictors vary across the three levels.

The results presented in Table 7.13 do not provide any substantially new insight into relations between influence distribution and its co-predictors. They do allow us a more synthetic insight into these relations.

The most general conclusion which can be derived from Table 7.13 is the much greater predictive power of institutional norms in comparison with contextual variables. The standardized beta coefficients for institutional norms, are, for all three levels of influence, much greater than the beta coefficients of the contextual variables. However, there are some other differences in relation to the influence of particular levels: institutional norms are better predictors for the influence of workers and representative bodies than for the top management, while contextual variables are the best predictors for top management and predict the influence of the other two levels less well.

This is quite an important finding and suggests perhaps that our studies of industrial democrary should be re-oriented. These studies are perhaps too much oriented towards explaining the main sources of variation in participation, influence, and power with contingencies, whether derived from the personal abilities of participants or from the structure and technology of organizations. While such research was perhaps appropriate enough for examining managerial behaviour, it seems—according to our results—that it becomes less appropriate, the more we are investigating the influence and involvement of employees in contemporary organizations. While the freedom of action of management is obviously quite strongly determined by the structure of the organization the activities of employees and representative bodies are much more determined by social and political factors outside the organization. The very high amount of explained variance, especially for the influence of representative bodies, adds even more significance to this conclusion.

If we now turn our attention to the regression equation for each level, we can establish that workers' Influence is mainly predicted by (i) institutional norms which promote workers' participation in medium- and long-term decisions and (ii) by norms which facilitate the participaton of external bodies in short-term decisions. All the contingencies such as Skill-level, Employee Mobilization, and Sector do not have such a considerable impact on workers' Influence. The same could be said for inhibiting factors: institutional norms facilitating top management involvement represent quite strong restrictions on workers' Influence, more important than Level of Automation or other contextual variables.

Institutional norms also appear to be strong predictors of the Influence of top management, but in this case they do not act as facilitators. Institutional norms facilitating workers' involvement in medium-term decisions have quite a strong negative effect on the Influence of top management. These negative effects are a specific feature of this level: most of the other institutional norms and even contextual variables demonstrate negative rather than positive effects on top-management's Influence. Such negative effects are evident, for example, for the Formalization of organizational rules and for the Mobilization of Employees. Product Complexity appears to be the only predictor with a consistently positive effect on the Influence of top management.

Among the strongest predictors of influence we should mention the following three: (i) the Functional Differentiation of organizational structure, (ii) the Mobilization of Employees and (iii) institutional norms which facilitate the involvement of members of representative bodies in medium-term decisions.

It appears that institutional norms which regulate the involvement of workers, managers, and representative bodies have the major impact on power equalization. These institutional norms have great positive effects on workers' influence on medium- and long-term decisions and on the influence of representative bodies and they inhibit the influence of top management (see Table 7.13). When they are established as facilitators of the Influence of top management they have a negative effect on the influence of workers. All these results point to the conclusion that the establishment of institutional norms relating to medium-term decisions seems to be the most important instrument of power equalization and of further democratization of those work organizations involved in this research.[19]

Besides the institutional norms which regulate the participation of internal groups those related to the involvement of external bodies should not be neglected. The role of external bodies was frequently mentioned as an important facilitator of a more even distribution of influence within organizations. In Table 7.13 their role does not appear in its complexity since we did not include these predictors in most of our regression equations. But if we consider the only beta coefficient presented in the table—those of institutional norms which regulate the involvement of external bodies in medium-term decisions, their impact on the influence of representative bodies is quite significant.

In summarizing these analyses, we should stress the voluntaristic character of industrial democracy. It seems to be much more conditioned by human

Table 7.13

Multiple regressions: dimensions of Influence (PO1) are regressed by selected contextual (CON) and De Jure Participation (PS) variables[a]

CON and PS	Influence (PO1a) Workers ST[b]	MT	LT	Σ	Top management PS variables	ST	MT	LT	Σ	Representative bodies PS variables	ST	MT	LT	Σ
Formal independence of enterprise	.18*			.15			−.22							
Political instability														
Sector	.20													
Skill			.24											
Automatization			−.16											
Product complexity		.13		.15		.29		.18	.30					
Functional differentiation		.17						.17	.17		.20	.14	.14	.22
Formalization						−.16	.20	−.29	−.24		−.15			−.11
Mobilization		.21				−.21	−.17		−.21		.19	.13	.33	.24
PS A3[c]		.59	.63	.48	PS A3		−.33	−.26	−.21	PS A4	−.20			−.13
PS B2			.18		PS B2					PS B3				
PS B3			−.18		PS C2		.22	.35		PS D2	−.34	−.21		−.29
PS D2					PS C4					PS F3	.64	.73		.67
PS D3		−.32	−.28		PS E4	−.22				PS G3			.41	
PS E3	.32			.18	PS F4		.21		−.24					

Multiple R	.513	.753	.752	.637	.583	.586	.653	.594	.744	.768	.754	.824
Adjusted R²	.15	.50	.50	.32	.18	.25	.34	.26	.49	.53	.51	.63
F	2.5	9.1	9.1	4.8	2.8	3.6	5.2	3.8	9.3	10.8	9.9	15.9
P	.003	.000	.000	.000	.001	.000	.000	.000	.000	.000	.000	.000
	Df = 16, 112				Df = 16, 112				Df = 15, 113			

[a] Values in table are standardized beta coefficients; CON predictors are the same for all PO1 variables while PS predictors are different for each level of PO1.

[b] ST = short-term decisions, MT = medium-term decisions, LT = long-term decisions, Σ = all decisions.

[c] PS A3 means *De Jure* Participation of Level A (Workers) cluster 3 (medium-term decisions) while PS B2 means level B (foremen) cluster 2 short-term decisions etc.

action than by technological, structural, and economic conditions. According to the results of our research, there is sufficient reason to question prevailing 'reificatory' theories of industrial democracy. These theories persistently relate industrial democracy to 'objective' environmental restrictions such as technology, organizational structure, etc. However, our findings provide little support for the basic paradigm of such theories. It is therefore time to begin more critical investigations of reificatory theory and to develop a more voluntaristic theory of industrial democracy.

Predictors of conflicts in decision-making

Using analysis of variance and multiple classification we have first analysed the extent to which the variation in the number of conflicts across organizations is explainable by country, sector and size. This is evident from App. Table 7.1 in Appendix F. Country is a much greater source of variance than are Sector or Size of organization. We believe that institutional norms at the national level are one of the strongest predictors of the frequency of conflicts. And since institutional regulations vary much more at the level of countries than at the level of sectors or organizations, countries are a major source of conflict variation.

This hypothesis is partly supported by the results of multiple regression which are presented in Table 7.14. Here again institutional norms appear as the strongest predictor in relation to the others included in the regression equation. Besides institutional norms, amount of Influence and expectations in relation to influence are also significant predictors. The other predictors relating to organizational structure and to organizational climate are not at all significant for the frequency of conflicts in decision-making; it is clear that conflicts are not structurally conditioned. According to our results we can say that they are closely connected with power and institutional regulations and that they are socially and not structurally or functionally based. However, the amount of explained variance is relatively low in these equations, therefore we suppose that there are other significant predictors which are not included in our equations such as general industrial relations climate, union militancy, global stratification etc.

Among power predictors the Influence of representative bodies is the strongest. Greater influence for these bodies contributes significantly to more frequent conflicts, while greater influence for workers has the opposite effect. The effect of the influence of representative bodies was expected and is in accord with our previous findings, but the effect of workers' influence is rather surprising and not congruent with previous findings. We can speculate, however, that greater influence for workers promotes their interests and therefore produces anticipatory behaviour among management and representative bodies in decision-making processes. Unfortunately, we do not have any appropriate instruments to test this hypothesis.

The same is true for the unusual negative effect of the expectations of members of representative bodies; Most sociologists would expect that greater expectations increase relative deprivation, so that more conflictual situations could be expected in decision-making processes. In our case the result is opposite and we do not have any adequate explanation for this finding.

Table 7.14
*Multiple regressions; dimensions of conflict are
regressed by a number of predictors*

Predictors	Conflict (PO1b)			
	Short-term decisions	Medium-term decisions	Long-term decisions	All decisions
Market domination of enterprise				
Skill				
Functional differentiation	.17			
Vertical span				
Formalization				
Mobilization				
CLIM-S[a]				
CLIM-R[b]				
Influence:				
Workers (A)	−.29		−.25	−.30
Top management (D)				
Representative bodies (F)	.32		.26	.34
Involvement:				
Workers (A)				
Representative bodies (F)			−.18	−.20
OPART-D[c]				
De Jure Participation:				
Workers (A)				
Top management (D)				
Level above plant (E)	.40	.26	.37	.36
Representative bodies (F)	−.34			−.32
External groups (G)	.27			.20
Multiple R	.537	.454	.496	.529
Adjusted R^2	.16	.06	.11	.15
F	2,33	1,46	1,86	2,23
P ≤	.003	.10	.02	.005

Df = 19,109

[a]CLIM-S = Organizational Climate (Structure).
[b]CLIM-R = Organizational Climate (Relations).
[c]OPART-D = Leadership style

Among institutional norms the best predictors are those norms which facilitate the involvement of bodies at company level, the involvement of representative bodies, and the involvement of external agents. Institutional norms which facilitate the involvement of representative bodies are associated with fewer conflicts, which corresponds with theories about the rationalizing function of organized conflicts: the more involvement is institutionalized the less conflict appears in decision-making. The effects of institutional norms regulating the participation of external bodies and bodies at the corporate level are the opposite: they are associated with a greater frequency of conflicts in decision-making processes (see Table 7.14). It is possible that the greater involvement of these two levels intensifies the confrontation between 'organi-centric' and 'socio-centric' orientations.

We can conclude from these analyses that the promotion of institutional regulations contributes to a greater amount of conflict and that greater influence for groups which are directly involved in decision-making processes has the same effect. The development of industrial democracy, whether formal or informal, is therefore connected with more frequent disagreements. These disagreements can contribute to greater uncertainty but also to a higher quality of decision-making. Finally, we should note that leadership style does not affect the frequency of disagreements in decision-making processes. Although this result was not expected, it is understandable: a non-participative management style might contribute to worse inter-personal relations with employees but it might not have any direct effects on relations within decision-making processes.

Summary

Hierarchical patterns of influence distribution are found across all countries, sectors, and also over almost all sixteen decisions; in all these cases workers have the lowest amount of influence and top management the highest. Correlations between the amount of influence across the organizational levels are mainly positive with one very consistent exception: top managements' influence is negatively related to the influence of most of the other organizational levels.

A more equal distribution of influence appears to be best promoted by institutional norms and by the mobilization of employees. Personal and organizational predictors have generally minor effects on influence distribution and therefore we can conclude that a less unequal distribution of power in organizations could be achieved primarily by political and institutional changes.

A greater total amount of influence and more conflict within organizations seem to be the correlates of a more even distribution of influence.

INVOLVEMENT AND ITS RELATION TO INFLUENCE

Involvement of employees

As is described in Chapter 4, the Involvement of employees was measured with different instruments than those used to measure Influence distribution, and these instruments were also employed on a different sample of respondents. Respondents in this case were only workers, and low and middle managers who were asked to indicate their own mode of involvement in each of the sixteen decisions. Data collected on the basis of self-evaluation by individual respondents were then aggregated in averages which indicate the extent of involvement per level, per cluster of decisions, per organization, and per country.

Aggregations of individual self-evaluations per level and per organization were made primarily for the following reasons:

i. Data regarding involvement and obtained through self-evaluation can be used for individual units of analysis or for more complex units, groups, levels, organizations, and countries (Comstock 1977); aggregating the data at the organizational level does not, therefore, contradict their nature and at the same time reduces error variances associated with the individual units;

ii. Data about individual involvement refer to decision-making processes. These processes take place at the level of the group rather than the individual and therefore aggregation of individual data to the group level does not create group means as a statistical artifact, but corresponds to the group nature of problem-solving activity (Lord 1977) as a real framework for involvement in decision-making;

iii. The aggregation of individual data at group level corresponds also to the nature of organizational behaviour which is closely connected with the organizational setting, especially with norms and rules which regulate the involvement of participants (Pfeffer 1976). Although involvement is primarily inter-personal behaviour, it is also organization-specific and substantially conditioned by organizational norms, roles, and assets;

iv. The aggregation of individual data has also been done for reasons of comparison. Since data on institutional norms and influence are collected only at the organizational level, the comparison of involvement with institutional settings and with the patterned distribution of influence can only be done at the organizational level of analysis.

Involvement of employees across levels and decisions

Aggregate scores of the actual involvement of organizational members across levels and decisions are presented in Table 7.15. The results in this table were remarkably similar to the results in Table 7.1 in which we presented responses of key persons as to the amount of influence of different groups. This shows that the evaluation by key persons of the distribution of influence across levels does not substantially deviate from the self-evaluations of respondents with reference to their own involvement in decision-making, although different scales and different samples of respondents have been used. The main similarities refer to the vertical distribution as well as to the horizontal one. They can be summarized as follows:

i. In Table 7.1 and in Table 7.15 the consistent hierarchical distribution of influence and involvement is evident. Workers have the lowest degree of involvement and middle management the highest. In addition, there is almost perfect equidistance between workers, foreman, and middle management in relation to the amount of involvement.

ii. In both tables there are consistent trends of lower influence or involvement in long-term decisions;

iii. In both tables the amount of influence or involvement is relatively low and is particularly low for workers. According to the scale used for measuring involvement, workers are merely informed about decisions.

iv. A similarity between both tables also exists as to the kind of decision in which workers are most and least involved or on which they have most or least influence; the maximum participation of workers in both cases is in decisions

Table 7.15

Actual Involvement over levels and decisions

| Decisions | Involvement (PO2a) | | | |
	Workers (A)	Foremen (B)	Middle managers (C)	Total
Working conditions	2.4[a]	3.3	3.6	3.1
New department head	1.4	1.6	2.3	1.7
Hiring procedures	1.4	2.6	3.0	2.4
Training courses	2.2	2.9	3.6	2.9
Transfers	2.3	3.1	3.6	2.9
Investment	1.3	1.8	2.4	1.9
New product	1.4	1.8	2.4	1.9
Appointment own superior	1.4	1.5	1.7	1.5
Pay levels	1.6	2.0	2.6	2.1
Personal equipment	2.6	3.5	4.0	3.4
Reorganization	1.5	2.2	2.9	2.2
Task assignment	2.5	4.2	4.6	3.8
Dismissals	1.5	2.9	3.5	2.6
Work study	1.5	2.4	2.7	2.2
Holidays	3.5	3.9	4.2	3.8
Working hours	2.2	2.5	3.2	2.6
Short-term	2.3	3.3	3.8	3.1
Medium-term	1.5	2.2	2.7	2.1
Long-term	1.4	1.8	2.4	1.8
All decisions	1.9	2.6	3.2	2.6

[a] 1 = not involved.
  2 = informed beforehand.
  3 = informed beforehand and can give opinion.
  4 = opinion is taken into account.
  5 = take part in decision with equal weight.
  6 = decide on my own.

about work environment, personal equipment, and holidays, while the minimum participation is in decisions about the nomination of new department heads, investments, new products, and the appointment of immediate superiors. The first set of decisions refers to work and the second to personal and financial policy.

Beside these similarities, some differences exist between the distribution of influence and the amount of involvement across levels and decisions. The main difference lies in the sharper division of involvement between organizational groups across decision-areas as compared to the division of influence and power.[20] Differences in the involvement of workers and supervisors in decisions which refer to work and which refer to broader issues such as reorganization (or work-study technique) are sharper than are differences in the amount of influence of these two levels in the same areas. The same could be said for middle management: its level of involvement in long-term decisions is relatively lower and in work-related issues relatively higher than when we compare its amount of influence over these two areas.

Together with the relative differences described above we also find almost perfect co-variation of involvement of lower levels in organizations: each of the three lower levels—workers, supervisors and middle management—have the lowest mode of involvement in personnel and economic decisions and the highest mode of involvement in work-related decisions. Such strong co-variation of involvement for these three levels should have some implications for relations between them and the higher hierarchical levels—especially with top management. Although we do not have any data about the variation of the involvement of top management, it can be assumed that, according to the involvement of lower levels, the segmentation between them and top management will be higher than when we look at the unequal distribution of influence.

After describing these similarities and differences between the distributions of influence and involvement, we refer again to the beginnning of the chapter where we discussed the relation between these two variables. Recalling their initial ambiguity we could regard these similarities and differences in two ways:

i. as instruments for the cross-validation of our variables only; or

ii. as indicators of real similarities and differences between the distributions of influence and involvement.

In the first case, all the similarities found above are looked upon as indicators of validity. In the second case, these similarities are looked upon as indicators of authentic participation since greater involvement more or less corresponds with greater influence for participants. The differences found above could be interpreted in the opposite way, as indices of non-validity or as indices of manipulated participation.

In the last section of this chapter we will try to resolve this ambiguity to the extent possible with our type of investigation.

Desired involvement of employees across levels and decisions

In this research expectations of involvement are treated as complementary to, and relevant predictors of, social actions. According to our conceptualization social reality can not be reduced to actual behaviour, but also involves desired behaviour. The complex notion of social reality can therefore be derived from the relation between actual and desired behaviour.

Thinking in terms of such a concept of social reality, it is clear that the distance between actual and desired involvement will affect the behaviour of employees. If distances between actual and desired involvement are very great or very small, the social effects will be less salutary than in the case when they are moderate: very great differences will frustrate participants and provoke cynical reactions among employees, while very low differences will evoke self-satisfaction and passivism. Contrary to these two extremes, we expect that moderate differences between actual and desired involvement will have the greatest mobilizing effects on employees. Desired Involvement has been measured with the same type of instruments as Actual Involvement using the same sample (see Chapter 4). Data about Desired Involvement are presented in Table 7.16 for decisions, clusters of decisions, and for three organizational levels: workers, supervisors, and middle management.

The main differences between Desired and Actual Involvement are quantitative: respondents want a generally higher mode of involvement than they actually have (compare Table 7.15 and 7.16). These differences are absolutely consistent: the amount of Desired Involvement is greater than the Actual Involvement across all decisions and across all three levels. However, the desired amount is not very much greater than the actual amount of involvement: there is no case where the Desired Involvement is two points greater than Actual Involvement. If one compares the bottom lines in Table 7.15 and 7.16 it becomes clear that, taking the levels together, the differences for any decision, cluster of decisions, and for the total set of decisions do not exceed one point—in a six-point scale— which means a relatively small difference. It seems that aspirations are very strongly connected with the existing amount of involvement.

This hypothesis is confirmed by the structural similarity between the distributions of Actual and Desired Involvement. If these two differ in amount, they do not differ by profile. The following similarities exist between them:

i. Equi-distant hierarchical distribution between levels;

ii. Consistent decrease in the amount of Actual and Desired Involvement from short- to long-term decisions: workers, supervisors, and middle management desire less involvement in long-term decisions than in medium-term and less in medium-term than in short-term decisions;

iii. Actual and Desired Involvement for all three levels is the greatest on decisions 10, 12, and 15 (replacement of personal equipment, task distribution and working time) and smallest on decisions 2, 6, 7, and 8 (appointment of managers, investments, introduction of new products, nomination of supervisors).

The data described above suggest that the respondents do not desire any structural change. Their desired involvement is a copy matrix of their actual involvement. It can be said that they desire more of the same thing. Our results show that the aspirations of employees for direct involvement can be characterized as very pragmatic and oriented toward daily work problems. However this orientation towards the work environment rather than towards policy issues was expected since it has frequently been found in previous empirical investigations (Blumberg 1969, Možina 1971).

Although this interpretation of employee aspirations is correct, we should also take into account the representative aspirations of employees. These are presented in Table 7.17; they show that employees prefer to delegate policy-making decisions to representative bodies. This tendency of employees to delegate more important decisions to other levels was found in many previous studies and was an expected outcome of our research as well (Wall and Lischeron 1977).

What should be stressed at this stage is the complementary relation between aspirations of employees for direct and indirect involvement. Data in Table 7.17

Table 7.16
Desired Involvement over levels and decisions

| Decisions | Desired Involvement (PO2b) | | | |
	Workers (A)	Foremen (B)	Middle managers (C)	Total
Working conditions	3.4	3.8	4.2	3.5
New department head	2.6	2.7	3.2	2.7
Hiring procedures	2.3	3.4	3.7	3.0
Training courses	3.2	3.6	4.1	3.3
Transfers	3.4	3.7	4.1	3.4
Investment	2.3	2.7	3.3	2.5
New product	2.4	2.7	3.3	2.6
Appointment own superior	2.7	2.7	3.0	2.6
Pay levels	2.9	3.1	3.5	3.0
Personal equipment	3.6	4.1	4.4	3.7
Reorganization	2.7	3.2	3.8	3.0
Task assignment	3.5	4.6	4.8	4.0
Dismissals	2.8	3.6	4.0	3.2
Work study	2.9	3.2	3.5	2.9
Holidays	4.3	4.4	4.7	4.2
Working hours	3.5	3.5	4.0	3.4
Short-term	3.4	3.9	4.3	3.5
Medium-term	2.7	3.1	3.5	2.9
Long-term	2.3	2.7	3.2	2.5
All decisions	3.0	3.5	3.9	3.2

show very clearly that representative and direct involvement are inversely related: in decisions and clusters where they have relatively smaller aspirations for direct involvement, they have greater aspirations for representative involvement. The complementary character of employee aspirations in relation to direct and representative involvement can be summarized as follows:

i. All levels have the lowest aspirations for involvement of the representative body in decisions 10, 12, and 15, where there exists at the same time the greatest amount of desired direct involvement;

ii. All levels would like the representative body be more involved in long-term and medium-term decisions than in short-term decisions: the trend is therefore reversed in comparison with the trends in desired direct involvement;

iii. A reversed trend of aspirations exists between direct and representative participation across the three levels although its intensity varies: middle management want the most direct involvement and workers the least; in relation to desired representative involvement, middle management has the lowest aspirations and workers have the highest.

When both types of aspirations are compared, a more complex, more differentiated, and also less pragmatic picture of employee expectations, appears: direct desired involvement is oriented more to local work-flow arrangements while representative desired involvement is oriented more to medium- and

Table 7.17

Desired representative participation by decisions and levels

Decisions	Desired Representative participation			
	Workers (A)	Foremen (B)	Middle managers (C)	Total
Working conditions	88[a]	80	73	80
New department head	73	58	43	58
Hiring procedures	72	57	52	60
Training courses	67	53	46	54
Transfers	67	59	51	58
Investment	80	72	63	72
New product	74	59	52	62
Appointment own superior	65	50	38	51
Pay levels	86	76	66	77
Personal equipment	50	40	31	40
Reorganization	81	72	63	72
Task assignment	42	26	24	31
Dismissals	89	82	72	81
Work study	80	72	67	73
Holidays	45	35	31	38
Working hours	75	72	70	73
Short-term	65	55	49	56
Medium-term	78	67	57	67
Long-term	76	67	57	67
All decisions	71	61	52	61

[a]Values in tables are % of 'yes' responses to question: Would you like the main representative body to have a say in this matter?

long-term decisions (on issues such as work environment, wages and dismissals). The latter orientation is certainly more political, although it is still quite defensive. The representative body is not conceived by respondents as a co-management body which should be involved in financial, constitutive, and organizational issues. It is desired that a representative body functions similarly to a union, promoting and defending employee interests, primarily related to a good work environment, better pay, and to greater job security.

Although employee aspirations are very complex, they are still relatively low on so-called taboo decisions, which are the more or less exclusive prerogative of the top management or bodies at company level. Employees do not have high aspirations to be directly or indirectly involved in the nomination of managers or their supervisor although more than 50 per cent of employees want representative bodies to have a say in these matters. Here the differences between levels are the highest: more than two-thirds of the workers desire the involvement of the representative body, while only one-third of middle managers desire it. It is obvious that middle management voluntarily refrains from expressing aspirations regarding prerogatives of top management.

Another possible way to evaluate differences between Desired and Actual Involvement can be developed by using the Alutto–Belasco measure (1972) or by using a modified and improved version of these measures (Conway 1976).[21] If we apply the 'continuum of participation' to data presented in Tables 7.16 and 7.17 we can say that, in our organizations, there is no case of equilibrium or saturation since all differences have negative value; across all decisions and levels participative deprivation exists. If we take differences or rather 'deficits' smaller than 1.0 as indicators of relative equilibrium, differences equal to 1.0 as indicators of slight deprivation, and differences larger than 1.0 as indicators of deprivation, then two kinds of decision are at the extreme ends of this scale:

i. Decisions referring to holidays where we see overall participative equilibrium at all three levels;

ii. Decisions referring to the nomination of superiors where we can see overall deprivation at all three levels.

Dahrendorf's formulation, mentioned above, still seems highly relevant, although it was developed fifteen years ago; according to employee aspirations, industrial democracy should be conceived as an enlargement of political rights into economic organizations. Since the basic right is the right to elect leaders, it is not surprising that most deprivation occurs in this area of decision-making for all three levels of respondents (see also Katz and Kahn 1966).

If we estimate the relationship between Actual and Desired Involvement according to Conway's criteria workers are slightly deprived across all decisions, supervisors are slightly deprived for medium-term decisions only, and middle management is saturated across all decisions. However, this estimate refers only to individual decisions. A comparison of total scores, which represent average deprivation over all decisions, and scores for particular decisions allows a substantially different evaluation. High deprivation on one or only a few decisions, even if they are strategic, should not have such a strong effect on an employee as does a relatively modest deprivation over all decisions in the organization. In the first case, some compensatory involvement could be undertaken, which allows indirect promotion of some vital interests through side channels, while in the second case, no such possibility exists.

Actual and desired involvement of employees across countries

The distributions of Actual and Desired Involvement have some patterns which exist across all the organizations in the countries studied. These general patterns are evident in the data presented in Table 7.18 and App. Table 7.2 in Appendix F. In all countries we find:

i. that workers have the lowest and middle management the highest average mode of Involvement in decision-making;

ii. that in all countries the Actual Involvement of middle management is also the highest within each particular cluster of decisions;

iii. that in all countries middle management desires the highest and workers the lowest average mode of direct Involvement; and

iv. that in all countries aspirations for indirect Involvement are reversed: the aspirations of workers for the Involvement of representative bodies are the highest in all countries and the aspirations of middle management the lowest.

Table 7.18
Actual and Desired Involvement by country

Actual Involvement (PO2a)

Level	Belgium	Denmark	Finland	France	Germany (West)	U.K.	Italy	Israel	Holland	Norway	Sweden	Yugoslavia
Workers (A)	1.8	2.0	1.7	2.0	1.9	2.1	1.7	1.7	2.1	1.8	1.8	2.7
Foremen (B)	2.5	3.7	2.6	2.5	2.5	2.4	2.5	2.4	2.7	2.6	2.6	3.1
Middle managers (C)	2.8	3.7	3.5	3.1	3.5	3.0	2.6	2.9	3.5	3.2	2.8	3.2
Total	2.3	3.2	2.6	2.6	2.6	2.5	2.2	2.3	2.8	2.5	2.4	3.0

Desired Involvement (PO2b)

Level	Belgium	Denmark	Finland	France	Germany (West)	U.K.	Italy	Israel	Holland	Norway	Sweden	Yugoslavia
Workers (A)	2.9	3.1	2.9	3.1	3.1	2.9	2.7	2.9	3.1	2.7	2.9	3.7
Foremen (B)	3.4	4.0	3.4	3.4	3.5	3.3	2.9	3.5	3.6	3.2	3.4	3.8
Middle managers (C)	3.7	4.0	4.0	3.9	4.2	3.7	3.2	4.2	3.7	3.7	3.6	3.9
Total	3.1	3.4	3.1	3.2	3.4	3.1	2.8	3.1	3.2	2.9	3.1	3.8

These four patterns, spread across all countries, reveal a very consistent hierarchy in all organizations. The patterns exist even in Yugoslav enterprises although this country has a substantially different political and social environment than do the other countries. It seems that such consistent hierarchical patterns of actual and desired involvement are not conditioned primarily by political, economic, or other social characteristics of the environment, but by the existing technical division of labour, which is still quite similar for all organizations in all 12 countries, including Yugoslavia. We found in previous sections that *de jure* participation, which reflects to some extent the political and economic environment, can significantly modify the hierarchical patterns in organizations, but it obviously cannot dissolve the hierarchy itself as a pattern.

Differences among the countries appear if we look more specifically at differences in Actual Involvement by decisions and clusters of decisions. The twelve countries could be classified into four quite distinctive groups, according to differences in involvement across the clusters:

i. countries where the Actual Involvement of the three levels is high in all clusters, such as Denmark and Yugoslavia;

ii. countries where the Actual Involvement of the three levels is low in all clusters of decisions, such as Belgium and Israel;

iii. countries where the Actual Involvement of the three levels is relatively high for short-term decisions and low for long-term decisions, such as France and Holland; and

iv. countries where the Actual Involvement of all three levels is relatively low in short- and relatively high in long-term decisions such as Italy and Norway.

From the global political point of view, perhaps, the distinction between the first and second group of countries is the most relevant. But from the more specific point of view of industrial democracy, the last two clusters are more interesting, since they demonstrate two main strategies of democratization: in countries under (iii) industrial democracy revolves around daily problems of the work environment and in countries under (iv) it revolves around policy issues. It seems that different social forces stand behind such different strategies of democratization: strong external forces in the case of Italy and Norway, and stronger internal forces in a case of France and Holland.

Another trend should be mentioned in relation to Actual Involvement: the variation in workers' involvement across countries is the greatest for short-term decisions, and the smallest for long-term decisions. Yugoslavia is an exception: workers' involvement in short-term decisions in Yugoslav enterprises is not higher than in Denmark and only slightly higher than in some other countries, but the actual involvement of workers in medium- and long-term decisions is more than 100 per cent higher than in other countries. We suppose that the organizational context is the most important factor determining the actual involvement of Yugoslav workers in short-term decisions and that institutional legislation prevails in determining their involvement in medium- and long-term decisions.

In connection with the data presented in Table 7.18 another trend should be mentioned. Differences of Actual Involvement between workers, supervisors, and middle managers are not equal in all countries: in seven countries, differences are lower between supervisors and middle management than between workers and supervisors, while in the other five countries the relations among the three levels might be seen as relations among employees. For instance, we can expect that in the first seven cases supervisors would be more identified with management than with workers, that conflicts would be less frequent, and that resistance would be higher, etc.

Relationships between Actual and Desired Involvement are presented in Table 7.19. This table contains inter-correlations between measures of Actual direct Involvement and correspondent indicators of Desired Involvement for four levels and four clusters of decisions. A correlation of Actual and Desired Involvement for an inequality measure (between groups C and A) is also given.

The correlations of Actual and Desired direct Involvement are very strong across levels and clusters. Such strong correlations might be the outcome of mutually dependent dimensions of social activity. Of course, this mutual interdependence between Actual and Desired Involvement could, in specific stages of development or in specific circumstances, have different directions: in some cases Actual Involvement might increase Desired Involvement while in other cases the direction might be reversed. However, the direction of this correlation is not of primary importance for our analysis. What is important is the overall strong inter-dependence between Actual and Desired Involvement which seems to be the main internal source of the participative dynamic, and which should constitute a self-reinforcing process. This circularity of 'cause-effect' relations between actual and desired involvement seems to create a kind of *'perpetuum mobile'* of industrial democracy. Of course it could be inhibited or excited by external circumstances, but, in a stage when it becomes rather strong, it should be able to promote industrial democracy primarily by its own internal dynamic.[22]

In the following chapter, a similar finding supports this interpretation. Table 8.14 presents correlations between the overall Direct Involvement of workers and attitudes concerning representative participation. These correlations show that the interest and motivation of representatives are, in most cases, related to the amount of involvement they have through participation in a representative body. This means that the more influence they have, the more they are inclined to be interested in, and to remain participants in, these bodies. Here, at the level of individual analysis, we find similar self-reinforcing processes as were found at the aggregate organizational level.

Conditions of Actual Involvement

In this section, we will mainly analyse conditions and contingencies of Actual Involvement. Desired Involvement appears to be so closely connected with Actual Involvement that we do not expect it to be associated with substantially different conditions and contingencies. However, we expect differences between Involvement and Influence. Since Influence is treated more as a structural variable and Involvement more as a behavioural variable, we expect Actual Involvement to be more closely connected with personal or group attributes and less with organizational context. In the next three sections we will present the results of the multivariate analysis of predictors and co-predictors of actual

Table 7.19
Inter-correlations between Actual and Desired Involvement

	Actual Involvement (PO2a)				Decisions			Difference: Middle managers— workers	All decisions
	Level								
Desired Involvement (PO2b)	Workers (A)	Foremen (B)	Middle managers (C)	Representative bodies (F)	Short-term	Medium-term	Long-term		
Correspondent Desired Involvement (for level, cluster, or difference)	.67	.63	.66	.40	.65	.58	.67	.65	.74

involvement. This analysis will be displayed in the same way as was done for predictors of Influence distribution.

We have first used analysis of variance combined with multiple classification where Actual and Desired Involvement were regressed on country, sector, and size as predictors. These results may be found in Appendix F (see App. Table 7.3). We will mention here only that the results are quite comparable with those presented in Table 7.9 for Influence distribution: Country is again a much greater source of variance than Sector or Size of organization for all dimensions of Actual and Desired Involvement which have been included in the analysis. Another similarity lies in the fact that Country explains workers' Involvement better than the Involvement of the other two levels (supervisors and middle management). We would argue that similar factors lie behind the strong explanatory power of Country: the institutional norms which facilitate workers' actual and desired involvement.

Different results from those of Table 7.9 have been found only for representative bodies: Involvement of members of representative bodies is less well explained by Country than Involvement of other levels, while the Influence of representative bodies was best explained by Country. This difference is perhaps due to the fact that we did not ask members of representative bodies about their specific involvement in representative bodies but for their general involvement in decision-making processes.

Institutional norms as predictors of involvement

Table 7.20 contains significant standardized beta coefficients which are predictors of employees' Actual Involvement. If we compare these results with those in Table 7.10 it can easily be concluded that the determining function of institutional norms is quite similar in both cases.

If we first analyse the effects of institutional norms upon Involvement at different levels, we see that these norms are far better predictors of workers' Involvement than of the Involvement of the other levels. Institutional norms explain almost 50 per cent of all the variance of workers' Involvement, which is similar to the explained variance found for workers' Influence. This is a rather unexpected outcome of our multiple regression equations. We have thought that institutional norms directly affect the amount of workers' Influence and through this only indirectly their Involvement. According to the obtained results it seems that the relationship between institutional norms and workers' Involvement is no less direct than the relationship between institutional norms and workers' Influence.

A further similarity is found to the very complex relationship between institutional norms and workers' Influence. As is evident, workers' Involvement is not only determined by corresponding institutional norms which facilitate their participation, but is also determined by institutional norms which regulate the Involvement of top management, representative bodies, bodies at corporate level, etc. However, the determining power of those institutional norms which regulate the Involvement of representative bodies and top management is greater than the determining power of those institutional norms which regulate workers' Involvement. The indirect effects of institutional norms, which have been characterized earlier as 'side-effects', seem to become 'main effects' in spite of the fact that they have not been intended as such.

The indirect effects of institutional norms are significant also for the Involvement of members of representative bodies. The overall effects of institutional norms on their Involvement are, however, substantially lower than the overall effects of institutional norms on the Influence of representative bodies. But their effects on the Involvement of members of representative bodies within particular clusters are quite significant. Institutional norms regulating the Involvement of other levels have the same or even stronger effects on representatives' Involvement as have their own institutional norms.

Table 7.20 shows the most general and strongest indirect effects in relation to those norms which regulate the Involvement of workers, top management, and external bodies. The norms which regulate the Involvement of top management within medium-term decisions have the largest and strongest negative effects on the Involvement of all the other levels.

Finally, some effects of institutional norms on Involvement within particular levels are similar to the effects on Influence distribution. In both cases the effects are greater the more strategic are the decisions. The effects of norms are greater on workers' Involvement for long- and medium-term decisions than for short-term decisions. The same is also true for effects on the Involvement of members of representative bodies. In relation to these results we suggest that short-term decisions are determined more by organizational contingencies while medium- and long-term decisions are determined more by the institutional and broader socio-political framework.

Contextual variables as predictors of actual involvement

According to our theoretical hypothesis, patterns of influence distribution have been treated as structural and actual involvement as behavioural characteristics. Following this postulate, we expect that patterns of influence distribution will be more determined by organizational structure and its environment, while modes of actual involvement should be more determined by technology and the personal attributes of participants.

If we now compare the results of multiple regression for modes of Involvement (Table 7.21) with corresponding results for patterns of influence distribution (Table 7.12) we see that the above expected differences are only partly confirmed. The most general conclusions based on results contained in these two tables are:

i. that modes of Involvement are slightly better predicted by personal variables, especially by Educational Level of employees than are patterns of Influence distribution;

ii. that technology, or more specifically Level of Automation, is a better predictor of Involvement than of patterns of Influence distribution;

iii. that the environment of organizations does not influence the mode of Actual Involvement and that the same can be said for economic contingencies.

However, these conclusions are correct only for the comparison of the Influence and Involvement of workers. If we look at the determining

Table 7.20
Multiple regressions: dimensions of Actual Involvement (PO2a) are regressed by dimensions of De Jure Participation (PS)

De Jure Participation (PS)	Workers (A) ST[a]	Workers (A) MT	Workers (A) LT	Foremen (B) ST	Foremen (B) MT	Foremen (B) LT	Representative bodies (F) ST	Representative bodies (F) MT	Representative bodies (F) LT	Decisions Total ST	Decisions Total MT	Decisions Total LT	All decisions Workers (A)	All decisions Foremen (B)	All decisions Representative bodies (F)
Workers (A)															
ST	.41			−.41	−.52	−.38							.33	−.43	
MT		.28		.23									.25		
LT															
Foremen (B)															
ST													−.35		
MT								.37	.31			.38			
LT								−.50	.36						
Middle managers (C)															
ST									.69						
MT									−.51						
LT															
Top management (D)															
ST	−.57	−.37	−.51				−.32		−.41	−.50	−.36	−.56			
MT					.24					.28	−.47	.29			
LT												−.54			
Level above plant (E)															
ST	−.40								−.41				.37		
MT									.28						
LT			.30							.34					

Representative bodies (F)																
ST	−.70													−.46		
MT	.54	.30												.58		
LT	.29		.32					−.31	.33					.25		
External groups (G)																
ST		.19	.20			.33			.32							
MT			.20										.32			
LT														.16		
Multiple R	.604	.763	.808	.384	.482	.553	.447	.539	.662	.480	.413	.540	.601	.760	.438	.496
Adjusted R^2	.24	.50	.58	−.01	.08	.17	.05	.15	.33	.08	.01	.15	.24	.49	.04	.10
F	3.0	7.4	10.0	.9	1.6	2.3	1.3	2.1	4.1	1.6	1.0	2.2	3.0	7.3	1.2	1.7
P	.000	.000	.000	.56	.05	.002	.16	.005	.000	.06	.36	.004	.000	.000	.21	.03

Df = 21, 112

[a] ST = Short-term decisions, MT = medium-term decisions, LT = long-term decisions.

Table 7.21

Multiple regessions: Actual Involvement regressed by contextual variables

| | Involvement (PO2a) | | | | | | | |
| | Workers (A) | | | Representative bodies (F) | | | Level A F | |
Contextual variables	ST[a]	MT	LT	ST	MT	LT	All dec.	
Formal independence of enterprise								
Market domination of enterprise								
Political instability								
Sector	.31			.33				.30
Skill		.23	.20	−.31				−.24
Automatization	−.22	−.20				−.20	−.27	
Technological interdependence								
Product complexity								
Functional differentiation		.27	.33			.27	.20	
Vertical span	.23						.27	
Formalization	.16							
Span of top management			−.14					
Intensity of control								
Stability of work force			−.16					
Male domination								
Mobilization	.19	.35	.40	.21	.26	.22		
Evaluation of success	.15							
Growth of enterprise								
Log size								
Multiple R	.535	.566	.607	.434	.389	.485	.527	.395
Adjusted R^2	.14	.19	.24	.03	−.01	.08	.13	−.008
F	2.07	2.43	3.02	1.19	.93	1.59	1.98	.95
P	.01	.002	.000	.27	.55	.07	.01	.51

Df = 19, 980

[a]ST = short-term decisions, MT = medium-term decisions, LT = long-term decisions.

effects of contextual variables on the Influence and Involvement of members of representative bodies, to some extent we find different results. We are inclined to explain these unusual results by the fact that members of representative bodies were not asked specifically about their Involvement in representative bodies but very generally for their Involvement in the organization. Therefore it is quite possible that they combined their experience from sessions of representative bodies with their everyday experiences at the level of their work group. In spite of this, the conclusions under (i) and (iii) hold also for representatives.

Turning our attention from the general effects of contextual variables on Influence and Involvement toward analysis of the specified decision-clusters, we first look at the role of personal variables. Personal variables, with the exception of education, have approximately the same effect on workers Involvement as they have on workers' Influence: Employee Mobilization is the best predictor of their Involvement, while sex, tenure, and age do not influence their Involvement. Educational Level appears as a significant predictor for Involvement of workers in medium- and long-term decisions, and for the Involvement of workers' representatives in short-term decisions as well.

Since the low, or in some cases even negative, effects of Educational Level on Involvement were not expected by many members of the research team, a more specific analysis of the relationship between Educational Level and Involvement was made. Some results of this analysis are presented in Appendix F (App. Table 7.4). They confirm the low correlations between the education of workers and their involvement in decision-making processes. Only three quite weak positive correlations between workers' Educational Level and their Involvement were found: in decisions relating to the reorganization of departments, assigning tasks, and holidays.

The first reaction to these findings was that perhaps there is such a low variation of Educational Level and of Involvement within the workers' level that co-variations could not be significant. This might be at least partly true since all significant correlations appear within those decisions in which the degree of workers' Involvement is above average. However, when we look at the significant but frequently negative correlations between workers' Educational Level and the Involvement of supervisors and middle management, the above hypothesized interpretation does not seem to be the best or the only possible explanation. It is evident that workers' education does not increase their own Involvement but that it significantly limits the Involvement of superiors.

It seems that organizations function in such a way that workers can use their knowledge only as negative power or, let us say, as an instrument for greater resistance, while they do not have the opportunity to use their knowledge as an instrument of greater co-operation.

The correlation matrices which contain per country analysis of relations between the Educational Level of workers and their Involvement also reveal an absence of significant correlations (see App. Table 7.5). Within the Service sector there are only three exceptions: Sweden, Finland, and Denmark. In these three Scandinavian countries, significant positive correlations exist between Educational Level and Involvement of workers in banks and insurance companies. Within industrial organizations, only Yugoslavia and West Germany are exceptions (and Scandinavian organizations for involvement in short-term decision-making) where significant positive correlations between Educational Level and workers' Involvement exist across almost all types of decision.

These correlations could in fact be treated as indicators of skill utilization. The correlations are significant only in Yugoslav, West German, and Scandinavian organizations, that is, only in organizations in which power inequality is relatively lower than in other organizations. It seems that greater power equalization might contribute much more to greater skill utilization than other apparently more sophisticated psychological and organizational changes. According to these findings we are inclined to treat problems connected with skill utilization primarily as political problems and not so much as psychological and functional issues.

Expectations that technology would be one of the main predictors of involvement were based on previous research which demonstrated a close relationship between technology and participation in decisions regarding work-flow issues (but a weak relationship between technology and the overall distribution of power) (Hickson 1969, Perrow 1970). As stated earlier, these expectations have not been completely confirmed: while automation seems to be a significant obstacle to greater work involvement, the other variables of technology do not have a significant impact on workers' involvement. We are particularly surprised that greater work-flow interdependence does not have any effect on workers' involvement, although quite significant effects have been found in some previous empirical investigations (Mohr 1971). We supposed that functional interdependence unavoidably increases the necessity for more frequent co-operation between workers, although a greater amount of co-operation and participation does not necessarily increase influence. It seems that such greater co-operation and participation is not necessary, and that the mechanical integration of work-flow can substitute for greater human co-operation.

Among structural variables Functional Differentiation within the organization again has a greater effect on workers' Involvement than any other variable of organizational structure. Besides Functional Differentiation, Vertical Span or hierarchical differentiation also has a positive effect on workers' Involvement. The effects of vertical differentiation are not as significant as the effects of horizontal differentiation, but they are surprising because they are positive and not negative. However, we have already found similar results in a Yugoslav study (Rus 1977). We attempted to interpret this positive relationship between vertical differentiation and the involvement of workers by suggesting the possibility that a greater number of hierarchical levels decreases the concentration of power in the hands of top management, and that this provides more space for all kinds of activity. The negative effects of the Span of Top Managers on workers' Involvement support this hypothesis.

The almost complete absence of any effects of economic efficiency or organizational environment on the involvement of employees was expected and argued at the beginning of this section. It is our belief that these contingencies are too far removed from involvement, so that they may, perhaps, have some very mediated effects which are not registered by our analysis. However, the effects of Sector are quite significant and even greater on workers' Involvement than on their Influence. We suppose that these effects are also indirect and that they are connected with some other contingencies which were not included in our regression equations.

Finally, some additional words should be said about the non-existent effect of the Size of the organization upon the Involvement of employees. It seems that size is not a serious obstacle to the promotion of industrial democracy, although in traditional organizational theories it is treated as such: Tinbergen should be mentioned in relation to this hypothesis (Tinbergen 1971). He predicted, for instance, that Yugoslav self-management would only be efficient during the early steps of industrialization, and would become less feasible with higher concentrations of capital and greater integration of work organizations into large companies. The reactions of radicals as well are usually based on this premise; therefore they call for small organizations and simple technology (Gorz 1973). Our results, however, confirm some trends which were evident in

Tannenbaum's study (Tannenbaum et al. 1974) as to the shortcomings and advantages of big organizations. In relation to the problems connected with size and its effect upon democratization, it should be mentioned that workers in large Yugoslav enterprises experienced less powerlessness than those in small organizations. It seems that in big organizations the countervailing power supporting workers' interests becomes greater at the same time as the power of top management becomes greater. Equilibrium in big organizations is therefore created in a different way than in small organizations, where power-sharing is perhaps achieved mainly through greater direct co-operation between workers and management.

Institutional norms, contextual variables, and other copredictors of actual involvement

In Tables 7.22 and 7.23 different dimensions of Actual Involvement are regressed on a very complex set of predictors. These results are therefore only partly comparable with the results of multiple regression presented in Table 7.13 where different dimensions of Influence have been regressed only on contextual variables and institutional norms. Such a partial comparison only allowed us the following conclusions:

i. as in the regression of Influence, in regressions of Actual Involvement, institutional norms appear as better predictors than contextual variables;

ii. like Influence the Involvement of workers is better predicted than are corresponding dimensions at managerial levels;

iii. the Involvement of workers' representatives is much less well predicted by selected variables than was their Influence.

However, many new predictors included in the multiple regression in this table substantially alter the entire picture of the determination of Involvement. Three new kinds of predictor are involved in the regression equations:

 i. the Influence of workers, top managers, and representative bodies;

 ii. Leadership Style across all levels;

iii. social climate related to the structure and to interpersonal relations in the organization.

The inclusion of these new predictors already means some modification of our initial research design, because Influence was not treated as a predictor of Actual Involvement. However, the relationship between Influence and Actual Involvement is still very ambiguous. The same should be said for the other two sets of predictors: Leadership Style and social Climate were treated at the beginning of our investigation as outcome variables by which we would measure the effects of Involvement. Later the members of the research team became increasingly inclined toward the hypothesis that Leadership Style and Climate should be taken as contextual variables for Actual Involvement.

It may be that these new sets of predictors represent the so-called 'specification error'. In a case of specification error the results presented in Tables 7.22 and 7.23 would be meaningless or even misleading, since the statistical model would not correspond to the real system of relations. However, our hypothesis is reasonable if we consider the very low level of workers' Involvement. Such an embryonic state of workers' involvement is more likely to be conditioned by

Table 7.22

Multiple regressions: Actual Involvement of workers and representative bodies regressed on a number of independent variables

| | Involvement (PO2a) | | | | | | | | |
| | Workers (A) | | | | Representative bodies (F) | | | | |
Predictors	ST[a]	MT	LT	Σ	Predictors	ST	MT	LT	Σ
Sector	−.15	−.23	−.21				−.19		−.19
Automatization									
Functional differentiation									
Vertical span									
Mobilization									
PS A2[b]					PS A4				
PS A3			.26					−.45	
PS B2					PS B3			.33	
PS D3	−.24	−.21	−.16	−.23	PS C2			.50	
PS F2					PS C3				
PS F3					PS E2				
PS F4					PS F3				
PS E4		−.15		−.16	PS G2			.19	
OPART−D[c]	.52			.32					
Influence									
Workers (A)		.22	.16	.15					
Top management (D)									
Representative									
bodies (F)							.24		
CLIM−S[d]	−.16		.21						
CLIM−R[e]			−.18			.22			
Multiple R	.767	.757	.779	.755		.544	.524	.587	.527
Adjusted R²	.511	.49	.53	.49		.16	.14	.22	.14
F	7.8	8.4	8.5	7.3		2.3	2.0	2.9	2.12
P	.000	.000	.000	.000		.003	.008	.000	.007

Df = 20, 110

[a]ST = short-term decisions, MT = medium-term decisions, LT = long-term decisions,
Σ = all decisions.

[b]PS A2 means *De Jure* Participation of Level A (workers) cluster 2 (short-term decisions) etc.

[c]OPART−D = Leadership style

[d]CLIM−S = Organizational Climate (Structure).

[e]CLIM−R = Organizational Climate (Relations).

leadership style and social climate than to be itself the condition of them. Also, if we take into consideration the cross-sectional nature of our research, and the impossibility of measuring feedback effects it is less risky to test Leadership Style and social Climate as contingencies than as outcomes of Involvement.

If we now turn to the analysis of effects which the selected predictions have

Table 7.23
Multiple regressions; Actual involvement of foremen and all levels regressed on a number of independent variables

| Predictors | Involvement (PO2a) | | | | | | | |
| | Foremen | | | | All levels | | | |
	ST[a]	MT	LT	Σ	ST	MT	LT	Σ
Sector	−.28	−.34	−.31	−.32		−.23	−.22	
Automatization		−.17					−.14	
Functional differentiation								
Vertical span								
Mobilization			.19					
PS A2[b]								
PS B2								
PS D3						−.21		−.20
PS D4						.21		
PS F3								
PS G2							.14	
OPART-D[c]	.30	.31	.26	.35	.32	.23		.29
Influence								
Workers (A)	.17	.22	.38	.23		.26	.38	.24
Top management (D)								
Representative bodies (F)								
PO1 D								
PO1 F					−.27			
CLIM-S[d]								
CLIM-R[e]			−.21					
Multiple R	.513	.548	.605	.535	.577	.582	.660	.578
Adjusted R²	.18	.22	.30	.21	.22	.22	.23	.34
F	3.5	4.2	5.6	3.9	3.1	3.0	3.1	4.7
P	.000	.000	.000	.000	.000	.000	.000	.000

Df = 17, 111

[a]ST = short-term decisions, MT = medium-term decisions, LT = long-term decisions.

[b]PS A2 means *De Jure* Participation of level A (workers) cluster 2 (short-term decisions) etc.

[c]OPART-D = Rating of Direct Participation.

[d]CLIM-S = Organizational Climate (Structure).

[e]CLIM-R = Organizational Climate (Relations).

on the total amount of Involvement (last column of Table 7.23) we see that only three of the twenty-one predictors have significant effects on the total amount of Actual Involvement:

i. institutional norms regulating the participation of top management;

ii. Leadership Style; and

iii. the amount of workers' Influence.

It seems that Leadership Style represents the strongest predictor of employee

Involvement. This outcome of our multiple regression corresponds with Heller's hypothesis (Heller 1973) that democratic leadership style is a more decisive factor in the overall democratization of work organizations than is public ownership, representative participation, or formal regulation of workers' participation. According to our results, we can at least assume that there is no democratization of organizations without democratization of management practice. Perhaps this democratization of leadership is not a sufficient condition but it is evidently the most elementary one for the overall democratization of organizations.

This general statement can be made more specific by looking at Involvement within each particular cluster. If we compare the effects of predictors on particular clusters we can conclude that Leadership Style has dominant effects only on Involvement relating to short-term decisions; its predictive power in relation to involvement in medium-and long-term decision-making becomes lower, while the predictive power of workers' influence becomes greater. The effects of institutional norms and Sector also become more significant.

If we try to put together all of these findings we can say that democratic leadership style is more important when the involvement of workers is less developed and focussed mainly on short-term decisions (work-related issues), but it becomes less relevant when workers' involvement becomes more oriented towards medium- and long-term decisions. In this case the distribution of power and institutional norms become more relevant stimuli of actual involvement.

The effects of the predictors become more clear and also stronger when we analyse the Involvement of workers, supervisors, and workers' representatives separately. Workers' Actual Involvement is predicted primarily by:

i. institutional norms governing the Involvement of top management which have consistently negative effects on the Involvement of workers;

ii. Leadership Style which seems to be the strongest predictor of workers' Actual Involvement in Short-term decisions;

iii. the Influence of workers which is a significant predictor for medium- and long-term decisions; and

iv. Sector as a dimension of organizational environment.

Companies belonging to the insurance sector and norms regulating top management involvement have negative effects on workers' Actual Involvement within all three clusters, while Leadership Style and the Influence of workers seem to be interchangeable: when democratic leadership does not have any effects on involvement the effects of workers' influence become more significant.

The Involvement of workers' representatives is conditioned in a very different way and is mainly predicted by institutional norms and only in some very specific cases also by social Climate or their own Influence. Leadership Style does not have significant effects on their Involvement, and the same could be said for organizational context.

The Actual Involvement of supervisors is again differently conditioned. The main predictors of their Involvement are:

i. Sector;

ii. Leadership Style; and

iii. the Influence of workers.

The Influence of workers does not have negative but positive effects on supervisors' Involvement: it means that greater Influence for workers coincides significantly with the Involvement of supervisors and does not limit it, as does the Educational Level of workers.

In Appendix F we present the multiple regressions in which the Actual Involvement of workers is regressed for those decisions in which we have found the highest average mode of workers' Involvement (App. Table 7.6). Workers' Involvement in these decisions is quite well predicted by the same predictors as were included in Tables 7.22 and 7.23. Since the decisions in which workers have the highest involvement are all of the short-term type, it is understandable that a democratic leadership style appears as the best predictor. But, apart from this, normative regulations seem to be stronger predictors for workers' Involvement in two out of the five decisions.

It seems that, at the present level of development, the institutional framework and democratic leadership are the most important promoters of workers' involvement. The combination of an appropriate institutional framework with changes in the practice of local management could, perhaps, provide the best support for workers' influence and involvement at the present stage of development (see IDE, 1980, chs. 1 and 14).

DISCUSSION: UNSOLVED PROBLEMS RELATING TO THE RELATIONSHIP BETWEEN INFLUENCE AND INVOLVEMENT

Some theoretical and methodological problems connected with the relationship between Influence (PO1) and Involvement (PO2) have already been discussed above. In these sections we have described the cognitive problems related to the nature of this relationship and its direction, the methodological problems connected with the validity of the measuring instruments, and the methodological problems connected with the different samples we used in our research.

In order to make this discussion more complete, we should mention at least two additional problems which contribute to the ambiguity of the data on influence and involvement. The first of them is connected with the different scales used in our research: while the scale measuring Influence (PO1a) is a Likert-type attitudinal scale, the scale measuring Involvement (PO2a) is Guttman-type behavioural scale. The differences are considerable. In spite of them we have found relatively high correlations between scores for Influence and Involvement (see Table 7.24).

These relatively high correlations are surprising if we take into account another possible difference between the measurements of Influence and Involvement: it is possible that the first instruments measure only or primarily the actual amount of influence and the second set of instruments primarily the attempted amount of influence. If this is true, the amounts of influence and involvement should vary, even if we had the same scales, same samples, and same wording. Since, in spite of differences in scales, samples, and wording, we have high correlations, one can assume that they measure something common.

However, if we compare all these correlations, one particulary interesting trend should be noted. For all three levels, the correlations becomes higher the

Table 7.24
Inter-correlations between Influence and Involvement scores

	Involvement (PO2a)										
	Workers (A)	Foremen (B)	Workers (A)			Foremen (B)			Middle managers (C)		
Influence PO1a	All dec.	All dec.	ST[a]	MT	LT	ST	MT	LT	ST	MT	LT
Corresponding levels and clusters of decisions	.46	.53	.30	.62	.68	.46	.52	.58	.16	.18	.42

Note: $p \leqslant .05$ if $r > .15$

[a]ST = short-term decisions, MT = medium-term decisions, LT = long-term decisions.

more strategic the decisions are: within any particular level they are higher for medium-term decisions than for short-term decisions. This general trend suggests another interpretation: it is possible that higher correlations between Influence and Involvement for medium- and long-term decisions reflect some real social effects; for instance in those organizations in which workers have more influence in long-term decisions they are also more involved. However, the same explanation can be turned around: it is equally possible that the greater the involvement of workers in medium- and long-term decisions the stronger is their influence.

Taking into account the cross-sectional nature of our research, it is obvious that we are not able to decide which interpretation should be taken as the more appropriate. This relationship cannot be postulated as asymmetrical, but further clarification can be obtained by analysing scores of both Influence and Involvement in relation to the other variables in our research.

Institutional norms are the first set of variables which should be looked at in this analysis of the relationship between influence and involvement, because they are the best predictors of Influence and Involvement (Tables 7.10 and 7.20). Using the results of these two tables, we would like to suggest that institutional norms (PS) are a common predictor for Influence (PO1) and Involvement (PO2a) (see Figure 7.1 Institutional model).

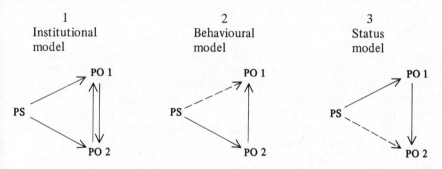

Figure 7.1 Possible models of industrial democracy

This model (the institutional model) becomes less acceptable if we take into account the partial correlations between Influence and Involvement scores controlling for scores of institutional norms: the values of the partial correlation coefficients are only significantly lower in two cases and only close to zero in one case (see App. Table 7.7). Significantly lower partial correlation coefficients are found only for representative bodies and for clusters of medium-term decisions at the workers' level. Only for these cases, can we assume that the institutional model in Figure 7.1 is the appropriate interpretation.

An alternative model is presented in Figure 7.1 under 2: this model suggests institutional norms as predictors, Involvement as an intervening variable, and Influence as an outcome variable. The implicit logic behind this model is that norms influence greater involvement which in turn produces greater influence for employees. With the intention of finding some empirical support for this interpretative model we have computed partial correlations between institutional norms and Influence scores controlling for Involvement scores (see App. Table 7.8). As we can see, in almost all cases the partial correlation coefficients are lower than the zero-order correlation coefficients but in most cases they are also far from zero. The results suggest that model 2 would be most suitable for long-term decision processes.

However, the data in App. Table 7.9 suggest a third, 'status' model, since the correlations between normative regulations and Influence for short- and medium-term decisions are stronger than the correlations between normative regulations and Involvement. According to the third model, institutional norms will affect organizational behaviour, only when the influence of workers is already relatively high; if workers are powerless no normative regulation can help them to be involved in decision-making processes.

Summarizing the above analysis, we should first stress again the complexity of organizations. It seems that not only each organization but even each level or each cluster of decisions might have different predictors and different patterns of relations. According to our analyses we must draw the temporary conclusion that none of the above proposed models of interpretation can be taken as a general one and as proper for explaining all relations in organizations.

According to the results obtained, we can suggest that the institutional model is the most appropriate for the explanation of the relationships between institutional norms, influence, and involvement related to medium-term decisions. We suppose that the institutional model is the most appropriate for this type of decision because they are more institutionally regulated than the others. The second, behavioural model is the most appropriate for long-term decisions. It is possible that these decisions are less regulated by institutional norms and that therefore personal involvement is a more significant mediator of influence over them. The third, status model seems not to be specific to a particular cluster of decisions. In spite of this it is potentially relevant because of the consistently greater correlation between institutional norms and Involvement.

If we try to generalize the above suggestions we can, perhaps, develop a systematic, hypothetical typology of systems of industrial democracy, where we take into account the fact that such systems can be different for different levels, clusters of decisions, sectors, and, primarily, for countries. For instance we can assume that institutional interpretative models are more appropriate for West Germany and Yugoslavia where the institutional norms are most developed, that the behavioural model is most appropriate for countries with highly-skilled manpower where the personal bargaining power of the employee is high, and that the status model is most appropriate for countries where institutional regulations are not developed, but where the countervailing power of unions and their informal pressure on organizations is high (c.f. IDE 1980).

Such a contingency-based typology of industrial relations might lead to a great improvement in our investigations since it would be based on very complex relations between institutional norms, the distribution of influence, and involvement modes rather than only on the distribution of power in organizations.

NOTES

1 Many useful improvements were suggested by all of the members of the IDE group who discussed and reviewed the first and the second draft of this chapter. Especially thorough criticism and detailed comments have been provided by Erik Andriessen, Pieter Drenth, Frank Heller, Cornelis Lammers, Vesna Pusić, Thoraef Qvale, Jörg Rayley, Bengt Stymne, Malcolm Warner, and Bernhard Wilpert. Finally, Riccardo Peccei is to some extent the co-author of this chapter: he has rewritten part of it and stimulated discussion about the possible alternative relations between influence and involvement. The outcome of this discussion is contained in the last section of the chapter.

2 Further discussion of theoretical and methodological issues related to the concepts of 'power' and 'involvement' is not necessary at this point since it is presented more completely in Chapter 2. In fact the previous theoretical introduction to this chapter was later included in the Chapter 2.

3 If the absolute amount of influence of top management is examined, the concentration of influence does not appear too great since in most countries top management's influence is close to 'much' then to 'very much' influence. However two points should be added to this fact:

i. First, 'much influence' of the whole level of top management does not exclude 'very much' influence of narrow managerial circles upon critical issues. This hypothesis is frequently suggested in the organizational literature: in critical situations, this trend toward concentration of decision-power in small groups of managers is even reinforced, as is shown by Smart and Vertinsky (1977).

ii. The second point which should be mentioned refers to the so-called dependence theory of power. According to this theory, the power of one person, group, or organization over another does not depend so much upon the absolute power of a powerful group but much more upon the powerlessness of other groups. In fact, we find that almost all organizational groups in almost all countries do not exceed a small amount of influence. The only exception is middle management which never has a great amount of influence, although in the majority of countries it has a moderate amount of influence (see Table 7.2).

4 However in some countries, as will be discussed in chapter 8, representative bodies are less efficient in promoting workers' interests than bodies at the corporate level as well as external bodies. The composition of representative bodies is in some countries such that they are to a greater extent promotors of managerial rather than of workers' interests. But in spite of these shortcomings, representative bodies are at least partly composed of workers' representatives and may be therefore used as agents of democratization.

5 However when only medium- and long-term decisions are taken into account, the relationship between democratic and decentralized patterns of influence distribution becomes closer. It seems that the more important the decisions are the less likely is it that decentralization will have a compensatory function.

6 Some members of IDE team argued that the correlations contained in this table represent some kind of statistical artifact since the variance of difference scores overlaps with the variance of one of the constituent variables (for instance the variance of influence of level A with the variance of differences between levels D and A). Although this critical comment should be taken into account, it does not refer to the all negative correlations which are contained in this table. In addition one can see that negative correlations between differences and

the amount of influence of workers also appear when this level is not a constituent part of the differences measure:

	Workers' Influence			
Differences of influence between levels	All dec.	ST[a]	MT	LT
Differences middle managers—foremen	−.21	−.21	−.25	−.09
Differences top management—foremen	−.55	−.51	−.47	−.41
Differences top management—representative bodies	−.44	−.41	−.45	−.53

Note: $p < 0.5$ if $r > .15$. a

[a]ST = short-term decisions, MT = medium-term decisions, LT = long-term decisions.

7   Negative correlations by themselves certainly do not give enough informations about zero-sum games. Besides obtaining negative correlations we should also control the total amount of influence—it should be constant across organizations and countries. As we could see from Table 7.2 the total amount is in fact almost equal across the countries and not too different across the organizations.

8   One possible explanation of the fact that top management is involved in zero-sum games is its relatively high amount of influence. Only top management exceeds the value 4 and approaches 'very much' influence. In such a case there is little chance for power-sharing since the relative differences are such that all the other groups are heavily dependent on top management.

9   The supervisory board at corporate level is not necessarily the headquarters of a company. In some countries it consists of employee representatives (West Germany) and in others (Yugoslavia) exclusively of workers representatives. This may explain ambivalent inter-level relations which are in some cases positive in others negative.

10 Positive correlations between levels are a necessary but not sufficient indicator of a power coalition, as on the other side negative correlations do not necessarily mean hostile relations between levels. For instance negative correlations (or a zero-sum game) might reflect either the process of delegation, or an extremely open fight for power between two hierarchical levels. Positive correlation could be the outcome of close co-operation between two levels (and therefore some kind of coalition), or could just be the result of a general expansion of the whole organization which allows a synchronic increase of the influence of different hierarchical levels which are in conflict.

11 Conflictual and non-conflictual decisions have been measured in terms of the responses of key persons to the question: 'Is a decision usually reached through disagreement? (See Chapter 4). We have used this word 'disagreement' in order to avoid giving too narrow an idea of conflict as referring only to open and direct confrontations between participants in decision-making processes. The word disagreement also implies less articulated contradictions which in the literature are usually treated as 'latent conflicts'. At the same time we should mention that according to the reports of researchers open conflicts are not necessarily more radical or more intransigent than latent ones.

12 Non-democratic leadership style could be another source of conflict especially in the field of short-term decision-making which is usually controlled by low and/or middle management. As one can see in Chapter 8, Belgium and Italy (which have a higher frequency of conflicts) have relatively less developed democratic leadership than the other countries.

13 More detailed insight into relations between levels' differences and the frequency of conflict is provided in the table below: the greater are power differences between top management and representative bodies, the lower is the frequency of conflicts in decision-making processes.

Differences of Influence (D–F)	Amounts of conflicts			
	short	medium	long	All dec.
Short-term decisions		−.17	−.21	.23
Medium-term decisions	−.14	−.21		−.20
Long-term decisions		−.23		−.19
All decisions	−.13	−.24		−.22

Note: p ≤ .05 if r > .15

14 Methodological reasons for such a procedure were discussed earlier in chapter IV.

15 The six-step Mode scale was collapsed to three categories: 1 = no information, 2 = information in general and *ex ante*, 3 = obligatory consultation, veto right, group has final right of decision.

16 Size and sector were analysed above as co-predictors with country, while here they are analysed as co-predictors of structural or environmental contingencies.

17 However in some countries it is difficult to distinguish between level of unionization and membership in representative bodies, since shop stewards are at the same time members of representative bodies for instance in Scandinavian countries and in the U.K. In these countries representation on boards is perhaps completely conditioned by the level of unionization.

18 We should keep in mind that there is almost no variation of *De Jure* Participation within a particular country. Hence these differences reflect country differences. What is apparently conditioned by PS differences might also be conditioned by all kinds of other country differences. Another problem connected with this kind of analysis is that in some countries we have obtained quite different results about relationships between PS and PO1a indicators.

19 A tentative explanation for the centrality of medium-term decisions might be as follows: short-term decision areas (like safety, work environment) are already fairly well treated by establishments. At the same time the decisions are treated as concerning mainly individuals or local work-groups and not joint issues. On the other hand long-term decisions (investments, new products) are perhaps treated as professional prerogatives of top management. Medium-term decisions (like wages, dismissals) are perhaps seen as realistic targets of workers' participation.

20 This could be due to the fact that we have a six-step involvement scale, but only a five-step influence scale.

21 These measures compare scopes of Actual and Desired Involvement. The situation in which the number of decisions in which respondents want to participate exceeds the number of decisions in which they actually are involved is called participative deprivation; the situation in which the numbers are equal is called participative equilibrium, and the situation in which the number of decisions in which they want to participate appears to be lower than the number of decisions in which they are actually involved is called participative saturation. This third case is also treated as over participation, and according to the

hypothesis and results of empirical investigation it has similar negative effects on satisfaction as under-participation.

22 This circular cause–effect relationship between Actual and Desired direct Involvement might be conditioned by participation being a learning process (Mulder 1978).

8

WORKERS' EVALUATION OF DIRECT AND REPRESENTATIVE PARTICIPATION

ATTITUDES TO PARTICIPATION

Outcomes of participation

The actual functioning of participation structures and patterns of influence distributions are not isolated phenomena, nor are they goals themselves. Participative decision-making is most often introduced because of its supposed consequences. Various models appear—implicitly or explicitly—to be the bases for propagating one or another form of participation (e.g. Dachler and Wilpert 1978). Chapter 4 refers to the fact that, according to some models, participation leads to more satisfaction and a greater feeling of involvement (this might be called the 'human relations' model), or to a better use of knowledge and abilities (the 'human resources' model), or to greater legitimization of decisions for more efficient organization and higher productivity. Lammers (1973) calls developments of this sort 'functional democratization'.

Other models refer to power equalization as a valued outcome in itself. Processes of participation which change the distribution of power in favour of the lower-level participants in a hierarchical organization are called 'structural democratization' by Lammers (1973). Efforts in the direction of structural democratization often increase dissatisfaction and conflict because traditionally-subordinate people make greater claims for satisfaction of their own interests, claims which often cannot be met.

In actual practice pure models are seldom realized. The distinction points however to groups of possible outcomes of participation. One can distinguish several of these groups:

i. Primary individual-level outcomes, such as: satisfaction with the job or company in general; feelings of identification and involvement; feelings of power and political efficacy or of powerlessness, frustration, and alienation; better information concerning the company.

ii. Secondary individual-level outcomes through the 'primary' outcomes: higher or lower motivation; higher or lower absenteeism, turnover, and lateness; desire for more or less participation and influence.

iii. Company structure and process outcomes: more conflict because of incompatible interests; less conflict because different interests are better-tuned to each other; power equalization; more control through information and anticipation of employee behaviour; mutual trust; better information-sharing and communication; more efficient decision-making through better skill utilization; better implementation of decisions.

iv. Company reward system: (expected) changes in working conditions, pay, etc; (expected) equalization of material conditions and privileges.

All these outcomes can contribute, positively or negatively to: the promotion of the interests of top management and company (efficiency, flexibility, etc.), the promotion of the interests of workers and unions, and changes in societal norms and values concerning participation or the distribution of influence.

The discussion in this chapter will be confined to evaluation of, and (dis)satisfaction with, direct and representative participation by individuals. The levels of conflict attached to certain decision-issues have been dealt with in the previous chapter. Economic 'outcomes' (profit, etc.) as indicators of the efficiency and effectiveness of the orgnization are not considered as outcome variables in this context, but as contingency variables.

The literature concerning participation and attitudes shows that few, if any, consistent and generalized relationships appear to exist. This is attributable to various sources:

i. Moderating variables—the effect of these is that the relationship between two variables is different for different sub-populations. One very important moderating variable is the level of aspirations or expectations of individuals. To participate or to have influence may give satisfaction to some people who desire participation. However, it may have no effect or even cause dissatisfaction for those who do not aspire to participate. Several well-known studies refer to the bases of these aspiration-levels such as sub-cultural norm patterns and power distance. Concerning norm patterns, Hulin and Blood (1968) suggested that workers from rural areas and small towns have much more desire for, and satisfaction with, participation because their Protestant work ethic stresses responsibility and autonomy. Workers from highly industrialized areas have a much more instrumental orientation towards participation and are therefore not interested in it. Mulder (1970) has argued that the main satisfying and motivating element in participation situations is not the level of infuence itself, but the 'power distance' between people. The smaller this distance, the greater the dissatisfaction of the less powerful with their own level of influence and the more they are motivated to reduce the distance.

ii. Conceptual and methodological complexity—lack of consistent relationships is also due to the fact that often quite different concepts are indicated by the same term. The term 'participation' is, on the one hand, applied to a more or less formalized system of decision-making in which various groups of people are involved to some extent and on the other it is used as a synonym for 'having actual influence or power'. In this study the term 'participation' is used as a very general concept, which covers both *de jure* and *de facto* participation. A growing literature is devoted to the study of contingent factors (moderating variables) such as education level, experience, motivation, value-orientation, trust, type of decision-area, the existence of rewards for participative behaviour, and the existence of particular (protective) procedures and regulations. The effects of these factors depend, however, on the relationships which are investigated; those between *de jure* and *de facto* participation (in this study: PS and PO) those between *de jure* participation and outcomes (PS and O) or those between *de facto* participation and outcomes (PO and O).

Lastly, we want to draw attention to the fact that 'consequences' or 'outcomes' include a very heterogeneous set of variables. Satisfaction with the control one has over one's own work does not necessarily lead to satisfaction with other aspects of the job or company. Or, as Nicholson et al. (1977) have shown, casual absenteeism can be a function of the lack of involvement in decision-making a person has, while turnover can be a function of the difference between actual and desired involvement.

Empirical evidence

Blumberg's classic book on industrial democracy (1968) is very outspoken in its conclusion that participation in decision-making decreases alienation and increases satisfaction. Wall and Lischeron (1977) also examine quite thoroughly the evidence concerning the relationships between participation and satisfaction. They discuss two groups of studies. The first group consists of correlational studies, particularly of the relationship between participative leadership and satisfaction. In most cases both concepts are measured through individually-administered questionnaires. The correlation between the variables is generally positive. A few criticisms concerning this evidence should however be given.

i. The direction of causality might be other than the one assumed. Perhaps leaders show participative behaviour because their group is satisfied and co-operative. Another explanation might be that satisfied workers attribute desirable, i.e. more considerate and participative, behaviour to their boss (a kind of halo effect).

ii. Participation is often only one element in a scale, such as the Ohio State leadership questionnaire, and satisfaction with leadership style might stem from other elements in the scale such as openness, trust, attention to personal problems, and so on.

iii. Questionnaires measuring types of leadership can hardly avoid measuring satisfaction with the leadership style. Leadership scales are meant to be descriptive in nature, but they cannot avoid including evaluative terms. This might result in measuring two types of satisfaction rather than relating leadership style and satisfaction.

iv. Tannenbaum (1974), moreover, argues that the relationship between influence and satisfaction might be explained by a third variable which determines both of them, such as hierarchical level. People at higher hierarchical levels often have more influence and show more motivation, identification, and satisfaction than people at lower hierarchical levels. Higher satisfaction and motivation are, however, not only consequences of the amount of influence one has, but also of the higher status, interest, and secondary benefits and privileges connected with the job.

These criticisms of the correlational evidence are supported by the inconsistent evidence coming from other sources. First, relationships between participation and absenteeism and turnover are not the same in different studies (Argyle 1958, Nicholson et al. 1977) although the relationship is more often positive than non-existent.

Second, the results of participation experiments also appear to be divergent. People taking part in participation experiments are, at least in some cases, no more satisfied (with the job, the supervision, or with the company in general) than before the experiment or than control groups. Wall and Lischeron (1977), who obtained these results in their experiments, give three possible explanations for the lack of relationship. First, the introduction of the experiment might result in an unrealistically high expectation-level. Second, the increase of influence in the experiment might actually be negligible. Third, in participation experiments people may try to tackle more difficult and time-consuming problems, which often results in frustration.

In their own experiments the qualitative evidence pointed to the third explanation. Frustration with problems encountered does not mean, however, that participation should be avoided or stopped. Despite the dissatisfaction, or at least lack of much satisfaction, people often point to actual or expected positive results of participation. In quite a few studies people appear to keep asking for direct and for representative participation.

Wall and Lischeron's interpretation is particularly applicable to situations where participation is introduced in an institutionalized way and is still in an experimental phase. In these situations participation often takes place in regular, formal meetings where issues outside the daily experience of the workers are discussed. It is, however, quite possible that the permanent participation of workers in the day-to-day setting (which is often tapped by the traditional approaches using questionnaires about leadership styles) results in a more positive attitude on the part of the people involved than the institutionalized experiments.

The desire for, and evaluation of, direct participation depend on several factors of which a few have already been mentioned. Other factors to be found in the literature, either as important determining (of desire for participation) or moderating variables (in the relation between participation and satisfaction) are sex, age, educational level, hierarchical level, membership of union, type of work (white/blue collar, staff–line, production–non-production), and work orientation. The following conclusions are generally drawn:

i. white-collar and maintenance workers often have more influence and autonomy and more satisfaction than blue-collar production workers;

ii. female workers in our male-dominated society generally have less desire for influence and are nevertheless more satisfied than male workers;

iii. older workers appear to (perceive themselves to) have more influence, and they are also more satisfied (or adapted?) than younger workers;

iv. employees with more education have more opportunities for exerting influence, but they also have higher aspirations, which often leads to less satisfaction than employees with less education have.

Attitudes related to representative participation

To a large extent, the previous discussion is applicable to both direct and representative participation. There are, however, some problems particular to representative systems. They have to do with:

i. The attitude of workers to 'distant' decision-making in general. Various studies have shown that people are generally more interested in participation in decision-making concerning their own situation than in general policy decision-making. (Blumberg 1968). Wall and Lischeron (1977) however show both in their review of relevant literature and through their own research, that (*a*) many employees consider that the participation of non-managerial personnel in decision-making concerning general policy issues is too small;

(*b*) employees rarely desire the right of veto concerning these issues, but often ask to be informed and to have the opportunity to discuss them;

(*c*) industrial workers (nurses, for example, much less so) want this participation to be realized through representatives, although there are different preferences concerning the type of representation;

(*d*) individuals and groups show marked differences in their opinions on the extent to which their representatives should be involved and the types of decision they should participate in making.

The extent to which the level of (representative) participation in distant decision-making influences the satisfaction of workers is unclear. One might expect that the more people are interested in these distant decisions, the stronger the relationship between participation in this area and the evaluation of the system will be. The evidence, however, is not very systematic or consistent. Obradović (1970) found a relation between the level of (representative) participation and job satisfaction for handicraft and mechanized workers, but not for workers in automatized production processes: Wall and Lischeron (1977) found the relationship between participation in 'distant' decisions and satisfaction with organization, job, and other aspects to be positive for skilled male workers, zero for female workers, and negative for unskilled male workers. Tannenbaum et al. (1974) in their study of five nations showed that, in Yugoslavia, the representatives had more influence, but the workers did not have more satisfaction, trust, sense of responsibility, or work-motivation, than in the other countries. Inevitably many other factors play a role in these relationships, an important one being the type and functioning of the representative system.

ii. The attitude of workers to a representative system and to their representatives. Attitudes of employees towards representative systems are widely divergent. From various reviews and studies (Batstone and Davies 1976, Emery, Thorsrud, and Trist 1959, Wall and Lischeron 1977) one can draw the following tentative conclusions:

(*a*) Rank and file employees generally do not know much about the work of their representatives;

(*b*) They often show a lack of interest in the work of their representatives;

(*c*) The influence of the representatives on policy decision-making is often considered quite marginal;

(*d*) Both cases of negative and positive attitudes and evaluations are found. When asked about the system as such and its merits people show a positive attitude i.e. they do not want to lose their representatives. This might also explain why participation in elections is often quite high.

Wall and Lischeron (1977) comment on these findings in the following way:

(*a*) Systems of representative participation are often established by management or by legal provisions; the lack of interest of workers might therefore be due to the fact that the functioning of these bodies is not geared to their own interests, and to the fact that the implementation of these bodies was quite authoritarian.

(*b*) Representatives rarely have much influence on policy decisions in organizations; this is perceived by workers and might be the cause of dissatisfaction and lack of interest.

In some countries, e.g. Scandinavia, representative bodies are based on collective agreements where union initiative has been dominant. In those countries workers probably see these bodies as instruments for promoting their interests, particularly when they are actually involved in higher-level decision-making (e.g. Engelstad and Qvale 1977). However that may be, a lack of personal and regular interest does not imply that workers want to do away with these systems; they delegate the work to their representatives.

iii. The problems of the representatives. The great problem for representatives lies in role conflict between, on the one hand, involvement in policy decision-making and, on the other, their relationship with the electorate. Various studies mention this role conflict for works' council members (Drenth 1973), shop stewards, worker directors (Brannen et al. 1976) and other representatives (Fürstenberg 1953). Such role conflict is often accompanied by a sense of powerlessness and alienation. Obradović (1970) and Arsenz (1977) found that alienation was higher for representatives than for workers in general. Emery, Thorsrud, and Trist (1969) consider the influence of worker directors quite marginal, and Drenth (1973), in his study concerning Dutch works' council members, found strong evidence of dissatisfaction among representatives because of this role conflict. On the other hand, some studies (e.g. Emery, Thorsrud, and Trist 1969, Brannen 1974) point to the growing professionalization of representatives, the emergence of new career patterns, and other factors as possible explanations for the fact that members of representative bodies have more interest in the work of these bodies than the average employee does.

Research questions in this study

The previous discussion touches only a few problems concerning research into the effects of participation. It illustrates, however, that it is hardly possible to formulate general hypotheses, particularly when dealing with so many different countries and social settings. The approach in this chapter will therefore be mainly exploratory in nature.

The main research questions to be dealt with in this chapter are the following:

i. What are the major patterns of attitudes towards direct and indirect participation in the various countries?

ii. What relationships exist between attitudes to direct and to indirect participation?

iii. What are the differences in attitudes between various subgroups of employees? Important sub-grouping criteria are, according to the literature, hierarchical level, job-type, sex, age, education, and membership of a union. Members of representative bodies form a special group themselves. To what extent do their opinions deviate from those of non-members? Differences between sub-groups might be due to differences in the desire (need) for participation. Can this be traced by differentiating respondents on the basis of professed importance of participation?

iv. To what extent are attitudes concerning direct and indirect participation related to actual involvement in decision making?
v. To what extent are attitudes concerning direct and indirect participation related to organizational characteristics?

THE OUTCOME VARIABLES: STAGES OF ANALYSIS

The outcome variables discussed in this chapter can be categorized into five sub-groups (the questionnaire is presented in Appendix A).

i. Attitudes concerning representative participation.

(a) Rating of the consequences of the representative system (OROC-R). The scale consists of five questions concerning the actual consequences of the representative body; for each respondent a mean scale score over these five items is computed.

(b) Evaluation of the representative system (OPART-E). A scale consisting of four questions concerning evaluation of, and satisfaction with, the functioning of the representative bodies.

(c) Interest in the representative system (OPART-I). This scale contains four questions conerning contact with, and interest in, the functioning of the representative bodies.

ii. Attitudes concerning direct participation.

(a) Rating of consequences of direct participation (OROC-D). This scale contains the same items as OROC-R, but they refer in this case to direct and daily participation in decision-making

(b) Rating of direct participation (OPART-D). There are five items based on a scale concerning participative leadership; four questions pertain to the amount of direct participation and autonomy allowed by the superior. One item asks for the level of satisfaction with direct participation.

iii. Attitudes concerning the job and the company in general. This is a thirteen-item scale resulting in a general satisfaction score (OSAT) and two scores, each based on four items, concerning satisfaction with the job (OSAT-W), company, and management (OSAT-C).

iv. Desired own involvement (PO2b) and desired influence of representative bodies (PO2c). These variables have been discussed in Chapter 7 but some attention is also given to these issues in this chapter.

v. Behavioural outcomes.

(a) Absenteeism. For each company an index of absenteeism is calculated i.e. percentage of working hours lost in 1976 due to absenteeism.

(b) Turnover. For each company the percentage of employees leaving the company in 1976 is calculated.

The last two outcome variables can only be used in organization–level analysis.

Although financial and judgemental indicators of effectiveness, profit etc. are available, they will not be discussed in this chapter. In Chapter 5 it is argued that these data should be used as conditional characteristics rather than as out-comes. It should be remembered that, in the various countries, the instructions and/or the scale items, refer to different representative bodies and systems.

Table 6.1 in Chapter 6 contains detailed information (see also IDE 1980). It should be noted that in some countries a single body is referred to:

France, West Germany[1], Italy, Holland: works' council

Israel: workers committee

Yugoslavia: workers council

U.K.: the main internal representative body

Finland: the internal participation body

In other countries, a more complex system is referred to in which unions have various strengths and roles:

Norway, Denmark, Sweden: bodies of joint consultation and co-determination including works' councils, Boards, and other joint bodies.

Belgium: representative bodies e.g. works councils, safety committees, and union delegations.

The plan of this chapter is as follows. First, the basic results concerning the three scales of representative participation are presented, followed by an analysis of their relationships with individual characteristics. The next section covers the attitudes of representatives themselves. Then the basic results concerning attitudes to direct participation and to work and the company in general are presented and related to individual characteristics. The effects of a few moderating variables on the relationship between involvement and attitudes are then discussed. Then the results of an analysis with organizations as the basic units are presented. This section considers the relationships between organizational characteristics in the area of influence distribution, technology, and structure, on the one hand, and attitudes, as discussed in previous sections, on the other. Finally, attitudes concerning direct and representative participation are compared, and some concluding remarks concerning this chapter are made.

ATTITUDES TOWARDS REPRESENTATIVE PARTICIPATION

Opinions about the consequences of the work of the Representative Bodies

People probably base their evaluation of representative bodies to some extent on the effects these bodies are perceived or presumed to have. Five questions were therefore asked concerning these possible effects:

i. Do people through the work of the (main representative body) know more about what is going on here?

ii. Do people accept decisions easier because of the work of the (main representative body)?

iii. Has the quality of decisions increased because of the work of the (main representative body)?

iv. Are the interests of employees better represented because of the work of the (main representative body)?

v. Do employees because of the work of the (main representative body) have a greater say in what's going on in this firm?

In all the countries the responses to these questions appeared to be quite strongly related to each other.[2] Table 8.1 presents the mean scores on the total scale. The results for a few separate questions will be presented in Figure 8.1.

When comparing the results from the various countries it should be kept

Table 8.1

Rating of the Consequences of representative participation (OROC-R) by country[a]

| Country | OROC-R | | |
	Workers (A)	Foremen (B)	Middle managers (C)
Norway	29[b] (3½)	29 (5)	29 (4)
Sweden	27 (10)	30 (3½)	28 (7)
Denmark	29 (3½)	30 (3½)	29 (4)
Finland	28 (6½)	27 (8½)	29 (4)
U.K.	28 (6½)	2 (8½)	27 (10)
Germany (West)	31 (2)	31 (2)	32 (2)
Holland	27 (10)	27 (8½)	28 (7)
Belgium	28 (6½)	28 (6)	27 (10)
France	28 (6½)	27 (8½)	28 (7)
Italy	27 (10)	26 (11½)	27 (10)
Yugoslavia	33 (1)	34 (1)	34 (1)
Israel	26 (12)	26 (11½)	25 (12)
Mean	28.4	28.5	28.6

[a]Mean scale scores and rank order (in brackets).

[b]Minimum score = 10, maximum score = 40.

in mind that the 'systems of representative participation' to which the questions refer are often quite different. Particularly important is the difference between complex and simple systems. Another point to be kept in mind is that, according to other results, many people do not know precisely, or even at all, how the representative bodies are functioning in actual practice. This might imply that the scale measures a global opinion on the basis of hearsay rather than precise knowledge about the actual functioning, a conclusion which is supported by the high correlations between the responses to the various items.

As will be shown later the responses to these questions were hardly, if in any way, systematically related to individual characteristics (and to hierarchical position, as Table 8.1 shows). As was expected the responses did vary, however, between countries and between companies. This suggests that the (perceived) effects of representative bodies are, at least to some extent, due to the opportunities given by the system as such (explaining the differences between countries) and to the actual functioning of the system (explaining the differences between companies). The differences between the countries are, however, not very substantial. In most countries the average scale score is quite near the overall mean. The Yugoslav data for both workers (level A) and management show by far the highest score, followed by the West German data. It appears that the Yugoslav workers' council, which has much more formal authority than any of the other representative bodies, is, as far as our sample is concerned, also perceived to achieve, on the whole, better effects than the other systems. Although the other means are quite close to each other, the data suggest that, on the whole, combining results for the three hierarchical groups, the means from countries with complex systems are the highest (see e.g. IDE 1980, ch. 7 and 12).

The relationship between characteristics of the participation system and the attitudes of employees will be discussed later in more detail. Here the data suggest that the general effects of representative participation are, on average, perceived to be (slightly) better in those countries where the system provides for workers' participation at more than one level.

Table 8.1 gives an overall indication of perceived effects. It is, however, interesting to see whether the results on the separate questions present a different picture. In Figure 8.1 the results for items 2 (acceptance of decisions), 4 (representation of interests), and 5 (greater say) are presented. The results on the two other items are omitted, because the figure would become too complex. The scores for these two items generally fall between those of items 2 and 5. Figure 8.1 suggests that, in most countries, but particularly in Holland, Belgium,

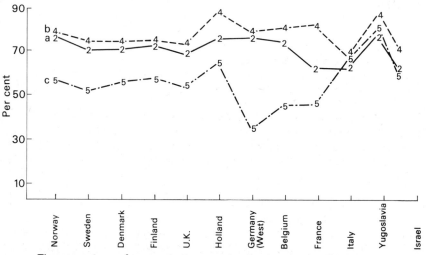

a. The percentage of respondents at worker level endorsing ('definitely' or 'maybe') item 2–accept decisions easier
b. The percentage endorsing item 4–better representation of interest
c. The percentage endorsing item 5–greater say for employees

Figure 8.1 The effects of participation (workers) by country

and France, the representative system is generally perceived as representing employee interest rather than as a system which gives workers influence and 'say' in the general decision-making. This is in line with those who maintain that most representative bodies cannot really participate in (policy) decision-making because of lack of power, information, or of other commodities.[3] The best a representative body can hope for is to present the interests of the workers *vis-à-vis* the management. Nevertheless, in most countries the proportion of respondents which does perceive the representative bodies as giving greater say for employees is larger than 50 per cent.

The representative system might have another role, which is indicated by the results on item 2. Between 60 and 80 per cent of the respondents believe that people in the organization accept decisions more easily because of the representative bodies. The data for the three items together might indicate that these bodies are often perceived as functioning as part of the control structure of the organization, i.e. as integrative devices.

Evaluation of and interest in representative bodies

The terms Evaluation and Interest refer to two groups of questionnaire items (see Appendix A2, Form 1.5–OPART).

The Evaluation scale contained the following items:

Do you think, in this company, the Works' Council is given a real chance by management?

Do you think that, in this company, the right people are available to represent the interests of the employees?

How satisfied are you with the functioning of the Works' Council?

Do you think your interests are represented by/in the Works' Council?

The Interest scale consisted of these four items:

How much do you usually hear about what goes on in the meetings of the Works' Council?

How interested are you personally in the work of the Works' Council?

If your colleagues asked you to become a candidate for the Works' Council in the elections would you be interested in accepting a candidacy?

How easily can you get in touch with your representatives in the Works Council?

The items were grouped together on the basis of a factor analysis, separately performed on the data for each national sample. The interrelationships of the responses to these items are, however, generally only moderately high.[4] Results on a few separate items will be presented later. In Table 8.2 the mean scores of workers, and supervisors, and middle management are presented for each country.

Evaluation of, and interest in, representative bodies is often related to individual characteristics. In particular, the differences due to the fact that people belong to different hierarchical levels are sometimes quite large. To give some impression of the endorsement of the items by respondents at the four levels, the overall means per level will be presented for all items. The data in table 8.3 are overall mean percentages. The general trend—at higher hierarchical levels more people have a positive evaluation and interest than at lower hierarchical levels—is only consistently present in the Scandinavian and Yugoslavian samples. Generally speaking the Evaluation of Representative Bodies by workers is again highest in the Yugoslav and West German samples, followed, in this case, by the Danish and French samples. It is clear that the more complex systems are not consistently evaluated as best: on this scale the Norwegian and Swedish systems receive quite moderate evaluations. Moreover, the West German and Danish questionnaires refer in these items only to the works' council.

Table 8.2
Evaluation of (OPART-E), and Interest in (OPART-I), participation by country[a]

Country	Evaluation			Interest		
	Workers (A)	Foremen (B)	Middle managers (C)	Workers (A)	Foremen (B)	Middle managers (C)
Norway	32[b] (6)	32 (7)	34 (5)	30 (9)	32 (8½)	35 (5)
Sweden	31 (8½)	34 (4)	32 (9)	30 (9)	35 (3)	35 (5)
Denmark	35 (2½)	37 (2½)	35 (3½)	33 (2½)	36 (2)	36 (3)
Finland	30 (11)	30 (10½)	29 (12)	30 (9)	33 (6½)	35 (5)
U.K.	32 (6)	32 (7)	33 (6½)	31 (6½)	32 (8½)	31 (9½)
Germany (West)	36 (2½)	37 (2½)	37 (2)	33 (2½)	34 (4½)	28 (11½)
Holland	31 (8½)	32 (7)	32 (9)	31 (6½)	34 (4½)	33 (8)
Belgium	32 (6)	30 (10½)	30 (11)	32 (4½)	31 (10)	37 (2)
France	34 (4)	33 (5)	35 (3½)	32 (4½)	33 (6½)	34 (7)
Italy	30 (11½)	29 (12)	32 (9)	28 (12)	28 (12)	28 (11½)
Yugoslavia	37 (1)	39 (1)	40 (1)	36 (1)	40 (1)	40 (1)
Israel	30 (11½)	31 (9)	33 (6½)	29 (11)	30 (11)	31 (9½)
	32.5	33	33.5	31.2	33	33.6

[a]Mean scale score and rank order in brackets
[b]Minimum = 10, maximum = 50.

Table 8.3

Mean percentage of respondents per country giving affirmative answers to questions concerning Evaluation of and Interest in representative bodies

	Workers (A)	Foremen (B)	Middle management (C)	Top management[a] (D)
Evaluation				
item 3 Is the Representative Body given a real chance?	37[b]	45	54	61
5 Are the right people available	45	49	48	59
12 Are you satisfied with the Representative Body?	46	49	44	57
13 Are your interests represented?	37	37	35	
Interest				
item 1 Do you hear much of the Representative Body?	25	30	37	64
2 Are you strongly interested?	42	50	51	69
4 Would you be a candidate?	27	32	40	
6 Can you get in touch easily?	69	76	74	

[a]Data for top management are based on samples from only seven countries: Belgium, Denmark, U.K., Israel, Sweden, Yugoslavia, Finland; The number of top management respondents in other countries, and for items 13, 4, and 6 respondents at all levels, was insufficient.

[b]The figures in the table represent the percentage of respondents giving affirmative responses ('very much' or 'much').

The results on these scales are complemented by the data on three separate items (Figure 8.2). These figures show, firstly, that, except for a few cases, less than 50 per cent of workers and supervisors in each country is positive about the functioning of the representative body particularly about the chances it is given by management and the extent to which it represents their interests. The very low scores for Finland in item 3 might be due to the attitudes of the unions, which generally have a strongly negative attitude towards works' councils. While middle managers are always more positive than workers about the chances given to the representative body (item 3), their average response to the other items of this scale are generally no different from those of workers or supervisors. As far as differences between the two sectors are concerned, the results are not consistent. Representative bodies are evaluated significantly lower in service than in metal companies in the Belgian and Italian samples and significantly higher in service than in metal in the Yugoslav, French, and British samples.[5]

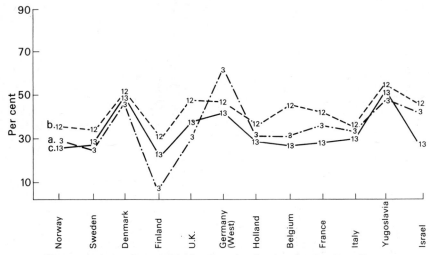

a. The percentage of respondents at worker level endorsing item 3–
   representative body is given a real chance

b. The percentage endorsing item 12–satisfied with representative body

c. The percentage endorsing item 13–representative body represents your
   interests

Figure 8.2 Attitudes to representative body by country

The results relating to the Interest scale (see Table 8.2) show a slightly different picture. Although the differences between countries in workers' responses are generally quite small the differences between levels and sectors are sometimes quite substantial. In almost all countries supervisors show more Interest than workers. And in the countries where data for top managers are present these show much higher Interest than middle managers or supervisors.

The middle management group, however, shows some marked deviations from the general trend. In four samples (Norway, Finland, Belgium, and France) they follow the hierarchical trend, i.e. they show more interest than the supervisors. In the Danish, Swedish, Yugoslav, and Israeli samples their mean score is not, or hardly, higher than that of supervisors. And in the samples from Holland, the U.K., and particularly West Germany middle managers show less interest than supervisors.

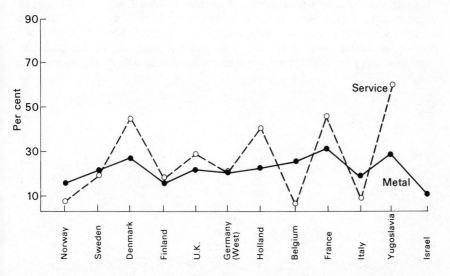

Figure 8.3 Per country the proportion of respondents (worker level) from metal and service industries usually hearing (very) much about meetings of representative body

Sector differences concerning this scale are also quite important. The overall mean score for the metal firms is the same as the mean score for the service firms (both in case of workers and supervisors). In some samples, however, (Norway, Belgium, the U.K., and Italy) respondents sampled from the service companies score significantly lower, while in other samples (Denmark, France, and Yugoslavia) they score significantly higher than respondents from metal companies.

The response of workers to the question on information received about the work of the representative body is presented in Figure 8.3. It appears that, so far as the workers sampled from the metal companies are concerned, at least two-thirds or more do not get much information about the meetings of the representative bodies. The differences between the countries for these sub-samples are not very substantial. They are much larger for the workers from the service companies, varying between 60 and 70 per cent. These differences suggest that in metal companies the situation is more or less fixed and the same in all countries, perhaps due to the type of organizations and/or the education level of the workers. In service industries, however, one encounters a much more heterogeneous situation. So far as hierarchical differences are concerned the previously-mentioned trends hold generally i.e. each higher hierarchical level is better informed: from level A 24 per cent of the respondents; level B 31 per cent; level C 41 per cent; and from level D 62 per cent. Comparing the various country patterns the picture is, however, not consistent: in some countries the major differences are found between levels, in other countries between sectors; in some countries the differences are very large, in other countries negligible.

Another interesting item concerns the extent to which people are willing to be candidates in the elections for representatives. In this case the differences between sectors are generally quite small except in the U.K. where only 5 per cent of workers in the service companies reacted positively to this question. More interesting are the differences between levels as shown in Figure 8.4. The

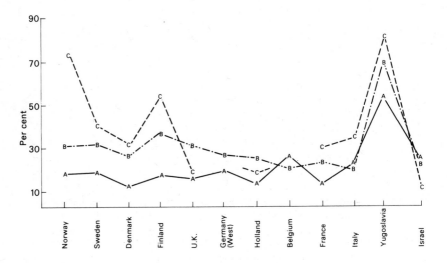

Figure 8.4 Per country the proportion of workers, foremen, and middle managers willing to be a candidate for the representative body ('definitely' or 'probably').

overall proportion of respondents willing to become a member is (excluding Yugoslavia) 20 per cent for workers, 28 per cent for supervisors, and 36 per cent for middle managers. The differences between the countries are, however, particularly substantial in the case of middle managers. The explanation for the positive reactions of the Norwegian middle managers is probably due to the recent interest of their union in representative participation in general, and board representation in particular (Engelstad and Qvale 1977).

Taking together a few central points presented in this section it appears that, when asked about the effects of the representative bodies in general, people are quite positive in their reactions. However, so far as their own involvement, contact, satisfaction, and motivation with respect to the representative system is concerned, in most countries the workers, and often also the supervisors, are less positive. This goes together with the fact that, in most countries, relatively few people think the representative body is given a real chance by management. The Yugoslav sample is, in most cases, an exception to these conclusions, although even there often little more than 50 per cent of the workers is positive about the above-mentioned issues.

DIFFERENCES AMONG ORGANIZATIONS AND INDIVIDUALS IN ATTITUDES TO REPRESENTATIVE PARTICIPATION

In the previous section it was shown that attitudes towards, and evaluations of, representative systems are different for different countries. Possible reasons for these differences have been mentioned already and will be dealt with more thoroughly later. Differences in these judgements and attitudes might be due, however, to two other groups of factors— system characteristics and individual characteristics. For example, it is quite probable that the perceived effects of the representative system (OROC-R) are related to the opportunities or constraints present in certain types of organization. It is also possible that, for example, some people are much more interested in representative participation than others.

To study these questions we will analyse the data in three steps:
i. An analysis of the relative importance of differences across Country, Sector, Size of organizations, and Level (analysis of variance over all data).
ii. An analysis of the extent to which differences between companies are relevant (analysis of variance per Country).
iii. An analysis of the importance of inividual differences in age, sex, union membership, etc. (multiple regression and analysis of variance per country).

Importance of country and organization differences

Table 8.4 presents the results of an analysis in which the four basic stratifying factors in this research project—Country, Sector, Size,and Level—are the independent variables. These results show that, among the four stratifying variables, Country differences are the most important. The fact that, on the whole, respondents at different hierarchical levels hardly differ systematically in their effect rating (OROC-R) and evaluation (OPART-E) of the representative system in their firm, suggests that these instruments are measuring the actual functioning of the bodies concerned, and less an individual view on these bodies. It is, on the other hand, likely that different sub-groups in the organization, e.g. different hierarchical levels, will have varying interests and motivations concerning the work of the representative systems, and the significant effect of differences in level (.17) on the Interest scale is therefore quite understandable.

The main effects of Sector and Size are not, or hardly, significant. The results in the last two columns, however, do show interaction effects, which are in all cases significant but also quite small. Summarizing, one can state that differences between countries account for 6 to 9 per cent of the variance in the outcome variables, while differences between industrial Sectors and in organizational Size account for only 1 to 3 per cent of the variance. This means that one

Table 8.4

Multiple classification analysis and analysis of variance of variables concerning representative participation[a]

Dependent variables related to representative participation	Independent Variables				Interactions	
	Country	Sector	Size	Level	C*Se	C*Si
Rated effects (OROC–R)	.27[b]	–	.07	.04	5.4[c]	8.0
Evaluation of (OPART–E)	.29	–	.06	.07	5.4	2.8
Interest in (OPART–I)	.24	–	–	.17	6.6	3.4

[a]Country has 12 categories; Sector has 3 categories; Size has 3 categories; Level has 4 categories.

[b]The figures are adjusted beta coefficients, i.e. adjusted for the effect of the other 3 variables. For the interpretation of these beta coefficients in multiple classification analysis see Andrews et al. (1973).

[c]The figures in these columns are the F-values of the interaction between Country and Sector, and between Country and Size.

finds very few consistent differences between (respondents from) metal companies or service companies, and between small or large organizations, in the rated effects, evaluation of, and interest in the participation system of these organizations. This conclusion does not necessarily imply that the rest of the unexplained (reliable) variance in outcome variables has to be attributed to individual respondent variance. There might be organizational characteristics other than Sector and Size responsible for variance in the outcome variables, e.g. characteristics of the distribution of Influence, of the technology or environment.

We will deal with these issues in more detail later in the chapter. Here, however, we can make a rough estimate of the importance of these characteristics. We can estimate the amount of variance which might be explained by organizational characteristics if we could have measured all of them. This is done through another analysis of variance, this time by Country. The independent variable in this case is the company. Generally the results of this analysis indicate that within each country, differences between companies account for about 10 to 12 per cent of the variance in the outcome variables.

Relevance of personal characteristics

In this section we will study the relationships between attitudes *vis-à-vis* representative participation[6] and the following set of personal characteristics.

   i. actual involvement in decision-making

  ii. desired involvement in decision-making

 iii. department type (production vs. non-production)

  iv. sex

   v. age

  vi. tenure

vii. education

viii. being a member of a representative body

  ix. having been a member of a representative body in the past

   x. union membership

  xi. need for direct participation (score on ORON–item 3)[7]

In the various analyses the specific firm is also included as a predictor. This allows for a distinction between genuine individual-level determinant or antecedent variables and differences which are due to organizational characteristics.

The effects of all these variables were analysed in several stages. First, according to the model, the correlations between individual Actual and Desired Involvement and the dependent variables were calculated. However, the results might be spurious due to the effect of antecedent variables which are related both to Involvement and the dependent variables. Moreover, it is also interesting to know the extent to which the dependent variables were determined directly by personal characteristics. The second step consisted, therefore, of a multiple regression analysis in which variables (i) (ii) and (iv) to (x) were included as predictors. Differences between the two department types had to be calculated separately because this distinction was only applicable in metal firms. Thirdly, a reduced set of independent variables (age, education, union membership, the need for participation, and firm) together with two co-variates (Actual Involvement and Desired Involvement) were included in an analysis of variance.[8]

Basic to all these analyses is a model of the following form:

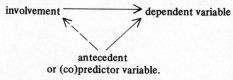

In a later section we will analyse the possible *moderating* effect of some of these individual characteristics. In that case the model tested has the following form:

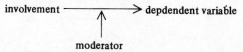

In Table 8.5 a summary overview of all these analyses is presented. The most consistent predictors concerning differences in the ascribed effects of, evaluation of, interest in, and desired power for the representative bodies are, on the one hand, the individual involvement variables (Actual and Desired Involvement) and, on the other, organizational differences (the latter being the strongest predictor of the three). This implies that, in most countries, attitudes concerning representative participation differ between firms (and this is not, or hardly, due to Sector and Size differences). Later we will try to discover which company characteristics might be responsible for these different attitudes.

Apart from firm differences (and differences due to other personal characteristics) we find that a higher level of direct Involvement of workers in decision-making is related to a higher Evaluation of, and Interest in, representative participation. In some countries not only Actual, but also Desired Involvement

Table 8.5
Summary table of relations between organizational or personal characteristics and attitudes concerning representative participation[a]

	Dependent variables			
	Rating of Consequences			Desired-Representative Influence PO2cto
Independent variables	OROC-R	Evaluation OPART-E	Interest OPART-I	
Over all respondents				
1. Country	strong	strong	strong	strong
Sector				N.A.[b]
Size	weak	weak		N.A.
Level	weak	weak	strong	N.A.
Over workers, per country				
2. Firm	8[c]	9	8	7
Age		1		
Education	2	2	3	1
Union membership		2	7	6
Need for participation				
Actual Involvement (PO2ato(A))	9	9	5	10
Desired Involvement (PO2bto(A))	3	7	7	8
3. Department		1		8
Sex	3		5	N.A.
Tenure	2	3	3	N.A.
Member of representative body	1		10	N.A.
Past member of representative body			4	N.A.

[a] The results of the table are based on an overall analysis of variance (on the first four independent variables, see Table 8.4), a multiple regression per country, (on all variables in (2) and (3) except Firm and Need for participation) and an analysis of variance per country (on variables in (2) where the first five variables were factors and the last two co-variates).

[b] N.A. = Not available. PO2cto was only later included in the analyses.

[c] Number of countries where the effect of this variable is significant (p < .05).

is related to the Evaluation of, and Interest, in the Representative Body. The following trend, which exists in most countries, is particularly interesting: as far as actual involvement is concerned it is mainly involvement in short- and medium-term decision-making which is related to attitudes to representative participation, while for desired involvement it is most often the desire to be involved in medium- and long-term decision-making. In other words: the more involved you are in shop-floor decisions and the more you desire to be involved in policy decisions, the higher your evaluation of, and interest, in the functioning of the representative body, and also the more influence you want this body to have. Production and non-production departments do not differ consistently so far as the evaluation of representative systems is concerned. However, when asked whether the representative bodies should have a say in short-term or medium-term decisions, in most countries production workers desire influence for these bodies to a greater extent than other employees. This is probably due to the fact that workers outside the direct production departments often have much more autonomy in their own tasks than workers in production departments. And, obviously, the more you can make your own decisions, the less you feel the need for distant groups, such as representative bodies, to have a say in these matters. For production workers, it is mainly the boss who decides about the job and its environment. One can understand that they would like this monopoly in decision-making power to be shared by a body which, at least to some extent, represents their interests.

These conclusions are generally not true for supervisors and middle managers, that is one does not find consistent differences between higher-level employees from production and non-production departments. Obviously these respondents are more homogeneous in their ideas about representative participation.

As far as sex is concerned, it appears that, particularly in some of the northern countries (i.e. Finland, Norway, West Germany, Holland, and Belgium), female employees are less 'interested' (as measured on the Interest scale) in the representative system than male employees. This finding has been reported more often. It might, in some cases, be due to the fact that female workers have less commitment to the company because their stay is often much shorter. It might, however, also be due to more complex processes of differential alienation. In Finland, where female employees constitute a large proportion of the work-force, it was shown (Enbom 1969) that women are passive in unions where men are in the majority, and men are passive in unions where women are in the majority. This phenomenon suggests that at least part of the lack of interest of female employees which was encountered in some countries can be attributed to feelings of powerlessness *vis-à-vis* the male-dominated representative system.

Current membership of a representative body is a relevant predictor of interest. Representatives in most countries are more interested and motivated to participate (again) in this representative work than other employees. This phenomenon will be elaborated upon below.

The last relevant distinction is that between union members and union non-members. It appears that union members are often more interested in representative bodies, even to the point of accepting a candidacy for membership, then workers who are not unionized.[9] And union members also desire more influence for these representative bodies than non-unionized workers. Several explanations for this difference can be thought of. The first is based on the 'general activity' theory concerning union membership: it is a particular, active type of worker who looks beyond his own individual situation, who becomes a member of a union, and who is also keen on such activities of general interest as representative participation. A second explanation follows from the supposition that unions might have an explicit strategy of gaining influence in representative bodies. The fact that in several countries (e.g. Finland) unions are quite opposed to what they sometimes call the manipulated role of representatives seems to refute this explanation. However, the opinion of the average union member might be different from official union policy (see IDE 1980, for context).

The remaining variables—age, tenure, education, past membership of a representative body, and expressed need for participation—do not appear to be very relevant in the prediction of attitudes concerning representative participation. Except for age, the same applies to the prediction of attitudes towards direct participation or job and company in general.

Comparing the various dependent variables one can roughly distinguish two phenomena. So far as the rating of Consequences of representative bodies and the general Evaluation of the work of these bodies are concerned, the major differences appear to be found between countries, and within the countries between firms. This finding might suggest that the way in which workers evaluate the functioning of these bodies depends on the general characteristics of the systems (of the various countries) and on the actual functioning of these bodies (within each country). This idea will be pursued further below. The Interest in (participating in) these bodies, and the extent to which one desires these bodies to have influence, are, however, not only dependent on system and organization characteristics, but also on characteristics of the individual, such as hierarchical level, type of work, union membership, and, last but not least, the extent of the desire for involvement.

MEMBERS OF REPRESENTATIVE BODIES; A SEPARATE GROUP

Members of representative bodies have the right to be considered separately. Previous research studies (e.g. Arzenszek 1976, Drenth 1969) have shown that their position is often a most difficult one, because their electorate, on the one hand, and management, on the other, have quite different expectations concerning their role. For this reason they might feel more alienated than other employees. Some studies however, (e.g. Drenth 1973) have also shown them to derive satisfaction from their position, or at least to desire its prolongation because it provides them with opportunities they do not normally have in their job.

In the present study some of the questionnaires were also presented to representatives, which allows us to compare the attitudes and evaluations of these respondents with those of other employees. The discussion here will be limited to a comparison of workers and representatives from the ranks of the workers. Figures 8.5 to 8.7 present the differences between the mean scores of representatives and non-representatives on the three scales related to

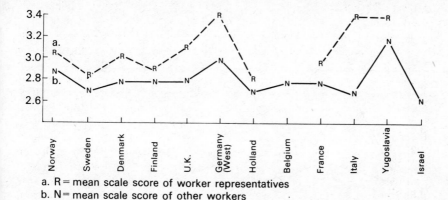

a. R = mean scale score of worker representatives
b. N = mean scale score of other workers

Figure 8.5 Rated Consequences of the Representative System by country

representative participation. So far as the ratings of the effects of indirect representation are concerned (Figure 8.5) it appears that, in all countries for which data are present, representatives are, on the average, slightly more positive than other workers. Figure 8.6 shows that, by and large, the same phenomenon holds for the Evaluation scale, although the differences between countries are larger than in the previous case.

Differences between representatives and workers are again largest in the cases of the West German and Italian sample. And again the German and Yugoslav representatives are the most positive about their representative systems. The most interesting and remarkable differences are found when one analyses the responses to the Interest scale (Figure 8.7). In most countries,

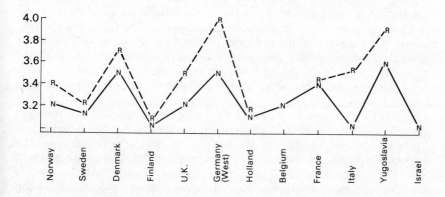

Figure 8.6 Mean scale per country of representatives (R) and other respondents (N) (both of worker level) concerning Evaluation of the Representative System (OPART-E).

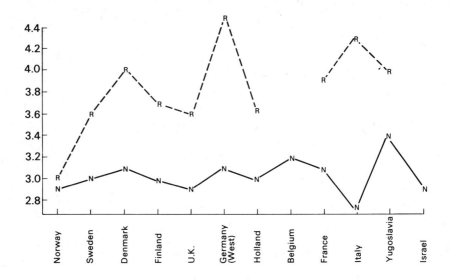

Figure 8.7 Mean scale score, per country, of representatives (R) and other respondents (N) (both of worker level) concerning Interest in the Representative System (OPART–I).

but again particularly in West Germany and Italy, the differences between the two groups of respondents are quite large. This is also reflected in the responses to the separate items, of which item 4—willingness to be a candidate—is particularly interesting.

Why are representatives more interested in, and motivated to participate in representative bodies than other workers? It might be related to the possibility of being able to have a say in all kinds of decision-making processes. This interpretation is supported by results presented in Table 8.7. In this table representatives and other workers are compared as to the relation between direct involvement and attitudes toward representative participation. The table shows that the interest of representatives in most cases is related to the amount of involvement they have themselves—inter alia through their participation in a representative body. This means that the more involvement the representatives have the more they are inclined to be interested in, and stay as participant in, the functioning of these bodies.

Summarizing the results presented in this section, it appears that members of representative bodies are, on average, slightly more positive about the effects and general functioning of these bodies than other employees. This phenomenon might be explained by assuming that representatives generally know better than their employees that these participative bodies do indeed have positive results. An alternative explanation might be in terms of the cognitive dissonance theory: most representatives would not be able to live with the conflicting cognitions of working in a body which is not successful. More remarkable, however, are the large differences when it comes to interest in,

Table 8.6
Willingness to be a candidate for the representative body by country

Percentage of respondents willing to be a candidate

	Norway	Sweden	Denmark	Finland	U.K.	Germany (West)	Holland	Belgium	France	Italy	Yugoslavia	Israel
Representatives	21	20	14	19	17	21	15	28	15	24	55	25
Non-representatives	31	38	51	56	48	88	45	67	88	75

Table 8.7

Correlations between overall direct Involvement (PO2ato) and attitudes concerning representative participation[a]

Country	Rated effects (OROC–R)	Evaluation (OPART–E)	Interest (OPART–I)
Norway			
Sweden			
Denmark	Repr.[b]		Repr.
Finland	Repr.		Repr.
U.K.		Repr.	Repr.
Germany (West)		Repr.	Repr.
Holland			
Belgium[c]	–	–	–
France	Repr.	Repr.	Repr.
Italy			Repr.
Yugoslavia			
Israel[c]	–	–	–

[a]Correlations were calculated separately for representatives and other worker (level A) respondents.

[b]Repr. means that the correlation between PO2ato and the column variable is significantly (p < .05) higher for representatives than for other workers.

[c]Too few representatives in the sample.

and motivation to participate again in these bodies. It might be explained in several ways:

i. role conflicts exist but the advantages are even greater;

ii. the growing professionalization of representatives decreases role conflicts i.e. new career patterns develop;

iii. role conflicts are small because representatives have chosen to identify with one of the parties.

The first explanation is supported by the finding that the motivation of representatives to keep participating is often related to the amount of influence they think they have. In Mulder's (1977) words, having influence is addictive; the more you have, the more you want.

PERCEPTION AND EVALUATION OF DIRECT PARTICIPATION, JOB, AND COMPANY

In this section we discuss results relating to the rating of the Consequences of Direct Participation (OROC-D), Attitudes to Direct Participation (OPART-D), and the three Satisfaction indices (OSAT, OSAT-W, OSAT-C). The relationships between the actual decision-making processes and the attitudes tapped by these indices should be considered as being slightly different in nature from the relationships between decision-making processes and the indices discussed above. Not only because of the type of research (a cross-sectional study) but also conceptually it is difficult to think in terms of cause and effect. The index for 'Attitudes to Direct Participation' can be considered as reflecting both the managerial style in a department and an evaluation of this style by the employees. A relationship with Involvement indices (PO2) might therefore be explained in several ways. The same applies to a relationship between the Satisfaction indices and Involvement. In this section particularly, the interpretation of results will therefore be very tentative.

Opinions about the Consequences of Direct Participation

The five questions presented to the respondents were identical to those discussed above for OROC-R, but this time they referred to the consequences of *direct* participation.[10] Table 8.8 presents the mean scale scores per country while Table 8.9 gives some results for separate scale items. Ranking the countries in terms of either workers' data or management data results in almost the same picture: Yugoslavia and Norway have the highest mean scores; Italy and Israel the lowest.

The results for the separate items of this scale again are quite similar to those of the scale concerning representative participation. It seems that a much greater proportion of respondents indicates that direct participation leads to easier acceptance of decisions and better representation of interests than to a greater say for employees. The only exceptions to this conclusion are Yugoslavia and Italy where the percentages for the three items are almost the same. The overall picture is therefore essentially similar to the one represented in Figure 8.1. And for each item the same is true as for the total scale: the higher the hierarchical level the more positive a respondent is (see Table 8.9). Sectoral differences are small. In most countries workers from service industries give either the same or a slightly more positive evaluation than those from metal industries. The striking exception is Italy where both workers and supervisors in service companies are much more negative about direct participation than respondents in metal industries (c.f. IDE 1980, ch. 11).

Attitudes to Direct Participation or Participative leadership (OPART-D)

This scale purports to measure the leadership style of the direct leader of respondents. This means that it is supposed to be specific to leader and work-group or department. Table 8.8 shows that differences between hierarchical Levels are rather large. This is to be expected since supervisors and managers are generally more involved in the decision-making of their superior than workers are in the decision-making of their supervisor. It is also clear that the major differences are found between workers on the one hand and supervisory and managerial personnel on the other. As far as differences between Sectors are concerned practically all samples show slightly more participative leadership for workers in service than in metal manufacturing companies. For supervisors the differences are hardly worth mentioning.

Generally these results accord with expectation: particularly in low-skilled metal manufacturing companies workers' jobs are of such a routine nature that there are less opportunities for a participative leadership style, than in service industries.

Table 8.8

Ratings of Consequences of Direct Participation (OROC–D) and of Direct Participation/Participative Leadership (OPART–D)[a]

Country	Rated Consequences (OROC–D)			Rating of Direct Participation (OPART–D)		
	Workers (A)	Foremen (B)	Middle managers (C)	Workers (A)	Foremen (B)	Middle managers (C)
Norway	32 (2½)	32 (2)	33 (2½)	33 (3½)	39 (4)	42
Sweden	27 (7)	30 (5)	30 (8½)	31 (7½)	39 (4)	40
Denmark	28 (6½)	29 (7)	31 (6)	38 (1)	45 (1)	44
Finland	26 (9)	27 (10½)	29 (10)	30 (10)	37 (7)	42
U.K.	25 (11½)	28 (8½)	30 (8½)	32 (6)	37 (7)	38
Germany (West)	29 (4½)	31 (3)	32 (4)	33 (3½)	39 (4)	–[b]
Holland[c]	29 (4½)	30 (5)	33 (2½)	33 (3½)	40 (2)	42
Belgium	30 (3)	30 (5)	31 (6)	31 (7½)	36 (9½)	–[b]
France	26 (9)	28 (8½)	31 (6)	30 (10)	37 (11)	41
Italy	25 (11½)	26 (12)	26 (12)	29 (12)	36 (9½)	–[b]
Yugoslavia	33 (1)	35 (1)	34 (1)	33 (3½)	37 (7)	39
Israel	26 (9)	27 (10½)	27 (11)	30 (10)	33 (12)	35
Mean	28	29.4	30.6	31.9	37.9	39.9

[a]Mean scale scores and rank order (between brackets) per country. OROC–D: min. = 10, max. = 40. OPART–D: min. = 10, max. = 50.

[b]Insufficient number (< 15) of responses.

[c]The OROC–D scale was only presented in the five companies which had some kind of institutionalized job consultation system.

Table 8.9

Percentage of respondents (all countries together) endorsing five statements on this effects of direct participation[a]

Effects of direct participation	Percentage of respondents:		
	Workers (A)	Foremen (B)	Middle managers (C)
1. people are better informed	65	77	82
2. decisions easier accepted	65	78	80
3. decisions are better	72	75	78
4. interests better represented	70	77	81
5. greater say	52	60	66

[a]Members of representative bodies are included.

Evaluation of work and company

As discussed before, three indices were constructed on the basis of a 13-item scale: overall Satisfaction, Satisfaction with Work (OSAT-W) and Satisfaction with the Company (OSAT-C).[11] As Table 8.10 shows, over all countries there is a positive relationship between hierarchical Level and Satisfaction. This does not apply equally to all countries, the main departure from a linear relationship being that, in some countries, managerial personnel have the same or even less satisfaction than supervisory personnel. It is noteworthy that, on average, in practically all countries satisfaction with job and work is greater than satisfaction with the company. Sector differences are hardly worth mentioning as

Table 8.10

Overall mean Satisfaction scores per level[a]

	Workers (A)	Foremen (B)	Middle managers (C)
General satisfaction	3.45	3.7	3.8
Satisfaction with Work	3.6	3.95	4.0
Satisfaction with Company	3.5	3.7	3.8

[a]min = 1, max = 5.

far as general Satisfaction and Satisfaction with the Work is concerned. However, Satisfaction with the Company is generally higher for workers in service than in metal companies.

ORGANIZATIONAL AND GROUP LEVEL ANALYSIS OF ATTITUDES TOWARDS PARTICIPATION

The analysis of possible 'determinants' of variation in attitudes relating to direct participative leadership, job, and company will deal with:

i. The relative importance of differences in country, sector, size, and level (an analysis of variance over all data);
ii. The extent to which differences between companies are relevant (analyses of variance per country);
iii. The relative importance of individual characteristics (multiple regression and analysis of variance per country).

Importance of country and organization differences

Table 8.11 presents the results of an analysis in which the four basic stratifying factors are used as independent variables (in a statistical sense). The results in Table 8.11 confirm what was discussed in the previous section i.e. there are significant differences between countries. Also differences between hierarchical levels have already been shown to be important. They are much more so in this case than in the case of the perceptions of, and attitudes towards, representative bodies. The same is true for sector differences.

To analyse the extent to which these attitudes and opinions differ between organizations, an analysis of variance was performed per country. A summary of the results is presented in Table 8.12. Although these results show that differences between organizations are relevant, it is also clear that, apart from Satisfaction with the Company, these attitudes and opinions do not vary so much between companies as attitudes concerning the representative system. To some extent the differences between companies are due to Sector and Size differences. The relations with other organizational characteristics are discussed below. It will be shown that few relationships are worth mentioning. This is quite understandable assuming that direct participation is much more a department and group phenomenon than a general organization phenomenon. And general or work satisfaction is probably much more an individual characteristic than an organization phenomenon.

Relevance of personal characteristics

In this section we will analyse the relationships between personal characteristics and attitudes concerning participation, job, and company. The stages in the analysis are identical to those applied to the attitudes concerning representative participation. The summary data are presented in Table 8.13. The most consistent and important predictors of the attitudes under consideration are current (PO2a) and desired (PO2b) Involvement in decision-making. This is particularly relevant in view of the questions discussed earlier concerning the relationship between participation and satisfaction. Table 8.13 shows that, even when differences between firms or between certain sub-groups of employees are taken into account, the relationships between the level of Involvement and satisfaction with aspects of the decision-making process (OROC–D and OPART–D), job, and company in general (OSAT–indices) holds.

The relatively strong relationship between Actual Involvement and the participative leadership index is not unexpected. The meaning of these indices overlap. One interpretation of the OPART–D scale is that it measures the

Table 8.11
Analysis of variance of attitudes concerning direct participation, job, and company[a]

Dependent variables related to direct participation	Independent variables				Interactions	
	Country	Sector	Size	Level	C*Se	C*Si
Rating of Consequences of Direct Participation (OROC–D)	.32[b]	.05	–	.16	5.2[c]	3.6
Rating of Direct Participation (OPART–D)	.21	.10	–	.35	5.3	2.8
General Satisfaction (OSAT)	.25	.08	.06	.22	7.1	3.7
Work Satisfaction (OSAT–W)	.23	.14	–	.22	6.6	3.9
Company Satisfaction (OSAT–C)	.22	.10	.07	.18	7.1	5.7

[a]Country has 12 categories; Sector has 3 categories; size has 3 categories; Level has 4 categories.

[b]The figures are adjusted beta coefficients, i.e. adjusted for the effect of the other 3 variables.

[c]The figures in these columns are the F-values of the interaction between Country and Sector, and Country and Size.

Table 8.12
Company differences in attitudes concerning direct participation, job, and company

Dependent variables	Mean % of variance explained by company differences, in responses of:	
	Workers	Foremen/middle managers
Rating of Consequences of Direct Participation (OROC–D)	6[a]	13
Rating of Direct Participation (OPART–D)	9	14
General Satisfaction (OSAT)	8	9
Work Satisfaction (OSAT–W)	6	8
Company Satisfaction (OSAT–C)	12	14

[a]Figures are means of squared adjusted beta coefficients in a multiple classification analysis per country.

Table 8.13
Summary table of relations between organizational and personal characteristics and attitudes concerning direct participation, job and company[a]

Independent variables	Dependent variables				
	Rating of Consequences OROC-D	Rating of Direct Participation OPART-D	General Satisfaction OSAT	Work Satisfaction OSAT-W	Company Satisfaction OSAT-C
Over all respondents					
1. Country	strong	strong	strong	strong	strong
Sector	weak	weak	weak	weak	weak
Size	–	–	weak	–	weak
Level	strong	strong	strong	strong	strong
Over workers, per country					
2. Firm	6[b]	9	9	–	11
Age	1	1	6	6	1
Education	2	1	–	1	–
Union membership	–	1	2	1	2
Need for participation	–	1	–	–	–
Actual Involvement (PO2ato(A))	7	11	12	10	11
Desired Involvement (PO2bto(A))	3	8	11	8	11
3. Departments	2	8	6	4	7
Sex	–	2	2	1	–
Tenure	–	1	–	2	2
Member of representative body	3	2	1	1	1
Past member of representative body	1	–	–	–	1

[a]The results of this table are based on an overall analysis of variance (on the first four independent variables), a multiple regression per country (on all variables in (1) and (2) except Firm and Need for participation), and an analysis of variance per country (on variables in (2) where the first five variables were factors and the last two co-variates).
[b]Number of countries where the effect of this variable is significant (p < .05).

managerial style in the company. However, the fact that this participative leadership index varies between firms in different sectors, or between production and non-production departments can be explained on the basis of differences in task structures which exist between these sectors or departments. Moreover, the correlations (at the individual level) between Involvement and the participative leadership index suggest that participative leadership even varies between individual group members. If this is true one can hardly speak of the general managerial style of a company. A third argument in this analysis arises from the fact that, in eight countries, the participative leadership style is also and separately (negatively) related to the index of Desired Involvement in decision-making (PO2b). This means that, even when the Actual Involvement (PO2a) is constant, the higher the Desired Involvement is, the lower the participative leadership of the boss is (perceived to be). It is unlikely that workers with the same Actual Involvement vary in their descriptions of the extent to which their boss is participative, nor that the more their boss is participative, the less increase in involvement they desire. There are even a few good arguments for reversing the causal arrow: the more workers are involved in decision-making (PO2a) the more they perceive their boss as participative (OPART-D).[12] And, the more workers desire an increased involvement in decision-making (PO2b) the less they perceive their boss to be participative.

However, in view of the fact that all three instruments are of the questionnaire type, responded to by the same respondents, the most cautious stand is to leave out any causal interpretation. The conclusion is then that the measurements are inter-related, which implies that workers who rate themselves as relatively more involved in decision-making, also perceive their boss to be participative.

The results concerning the satisfaction indices are interesting. First, in most— though not all—country samples we find a positive correlation between level of Involvement and Satisfaction. This applies particularly to involvement in a sub-set of the 16 issues—the short-term work-place issues. Even more interesting is the fact that this relationship between Involvement in work-place issues and satisfaction is stronger for satisfaction with company and management as a whole than with the job, particularly so in the Scandinavian and Yugoslavian samples. Table 8.14 gives more information on this phenomenon. These data suggest that involvement, particularly in one's daily work, has more effect on the attitude towards company and management than on attitudes towards the job. Possibly, participation generally does not change the content of the job itself, but it changes the relationship with one's superiors. The fact that this phenomenon is particularly present in the Scandinavian countries and Yugoslavia deserves further study.

Satisfaction is not only related to Actual Involvement in decision-making (PO2a), but also, negatively, to the Desired Involvement (PO2b): the more the increase in involvement one desires, the less the satisfaction, particularly with the company.

The long-standing discussion concerning the meaning of satisfaction measurements points to another possible interpretation of these correlations. Satisfied workers have a more positive perception of their involvement than less satisfied

Table 8.14

Mean correlation coefficients of Involvement and Satisfaction indices

Involvement in:	General satisfaction OSAT	Work satisfaction OSAT-W	Company satisfaction OSAT-C
Short-term decisions	.23[a] (.30)[b]	.15 (.16)	.19 (.28)
Medium-term decisions	.14	.10	.11
Long-term decisions	.14	.10	.12
All decisions	.23	.15	.20

[a]Figures are means (via z-transformation) of PM correlations per country.

[b]Figures between brackets are means based on Scandinavian and Yugoslavian data.

workers. This question will be considered again later—the same outcome variables (aggregated per organization) will be correlated with the index of Influence (i.e. expert rating instead of self-description of involvement).

In quite a few cases attitudes found in production departments are different from those found in other departments. The results concerning the participative leadership index are quite consistent. Generally leadership style is perceived as more participative in non-production departments than in production departments. This stands to reason, assuming that employees in other than production departments (e.g. maintenance, R & D, administration, etc.) have generally much less restricted and routinized jobs, and are therefore often consulted by their boss, and allowed autonomy. It appears, however, that this does not include a more positive rating of the effects of this participativeness (OROC-D).

A further variable worth mentioning is age. In quite a few countries the older employees are more satisfied with—or should one say more adapted and accustomed to—their work, and their company.

Lastly, the effect of differences between hierarchical levels appears to be interesting. Supervisors and managers are, as was expected, more positive about their participation, their work and company.

However, there also appears to be an interesting moderating effect of hierarchical level on the relationship between Involvement (PO2a) and Satisfaction. The correlation coefficients are generally higher when computed over all respondents together than for the workers or for the supervisors and managers separately. This supports the suggestion of Tannenbaum et al. (1974) that a positive relationship between participation and satisfaction might partly be due to the effect of a third variable i.e. hierarchical level: supervisors are generally more involved in decision-making than workers, and they are also, for different reasons, more satisfied; their satisfaction is however due not only to involvement itself, but also to other factors.

OTHER DIFFERENCES BETWEEN SUB-GROUPS OF RESPONDENTS

In the previous sections it was shown that sub-grouping respondents on the basis of job or personal characteristics appeared to be quite relevant when studying attitudes to direct or representative participation. It was made clear that sub-groups vary as to the mean score on attitude scales. It is, however, quite possible that sub-groups vary also in other aspects, particularly in the relations between variables. Younger employees are often more interested in participation and are disappointed when they do not find opportunities to participate, while older workers often derive their satisfaction from other sources. The existence of similar differences is suggested for other sub-groups such as men and women, individuals at different levels of the hierarchical ladder, or people with different professions or jobs. More generally one might expect differences in reactions to participation between those individuals who do and those who do not value participation (see Turner and Lawrence 1965).

In this section we will investigate this phenomenon through a series of sub-group analyses. In each country workers are divided into two or three sub-groups according to the value of various moderator variables. A similar type of analysis has already been performed when these correlation coefficients were calculated separately for workers and managers: the correlation patterns for representatives and other employees were also compared earlier. In this section we will compare the correlations between direct Involvement (PO2a) and the outcome variables separately for the following sub-groups (of workers)

i. younger (< 35) and older (> 35) respondents;

ii. union members and non-unionized employees;

iii. those who value direct participation relatively highly (ORON–3 score 3) and those who value direct participation less highly (ORON–3 score 1).[13]

The results of the first sub-grouping, distinguishing between younger and older workers, are presented in Table 8.15. It is clear that in only a very few cases are the differences between older and younger persons significant. The only case where a trend might be discernible is the relationship between direct Involvement and Satisfaction with the Company (and management). Although the difference is significant in only three countries, in all countries a difference in the same direction is present, however small. These results might suggest a more general trend that younger workers' satisfaction with company and management is slightly more strongly related to involvement in decision-making than older workers' satisfaction. Apart from this trend the number of cases where the differences are significant is hardly greater than might be expected on the basis of chance alone. It is possible that another split or a trichotomy would give better results. Secondary analysis at a later stage might give more insight. At this stage we are left with the conclusion that older and younger workers do not differ substantially in their reaction to involvement in decision-making.

Second, we distinguish between union members and non-unionized employees. The results are given in Table 8.16. Again the pattern is not clear or consistent enough to draw general conclusions. In a few cases (the Swedish, U.K., West German and Dutch samples) it is particularly for union members that the evaluation of the representative bodies is related to the extent to which they participate directly. It is, however, difficult to explain this phenomenon.

Third, workers were split according to the importance they attributed to having 'the opportunity to influence decisions about my own job'. (ORON item 3) A first inspection of Table 8.17 reveals that the ORON item 3 variable is a

Table 8.15

Differences between older (> 35) and younger workers concerning the correlations between overall direct Involvement and outcome variables

| | Outcome variables (attitudes) concerning | | | | | | | | N | |
| | Representative Participation | | | Direct Participation | | Work Situation | | | | |
Country	OROC-R	OPART-E	OPART-I	OROC-D	OPART-D	OSAT	OSAT-W	OSAT-C	Older	Younger
Norway		young[a]							160	180
Sweden									490	520
Denmark									150	150
Finland				old[b]					170	400
U.K.									160	190
Germany (West)	old	old							170	170
Holland								young	220	250
Belgium									100	250
France				young					150	250
Italy						young	young	young	110	215
Yugoslavia					young				100	210
Israel	old					young		young	100	115

[a] 'young' means the P.M. correlation coefficient is significantly higher (p < .10) for younger than for older respondents.

[b] 'old' means the P.M. correlation coefficient is significantly higher for older than for younger respondents.

Abbreviations: OROC-R Rating of Consequences of Representative System, OPART-E Evaluation of Representative System, OPART-I Interest in the Representative System, OROC-D Rating of Consequences of Direct Participation, OPART-D Rating of Direct Participation, OSAT General Satisfaction, OSAT-W Work Satisfaction, OSAT-C Company Satisfaction.

Table 8.16
Differences between union and non-union members concerning the correlations
between overall direct Involvement and outcome variables

| Country | Outcome variables (attitudes) concerning | | | | | | | | N | |
| | Representative Participation | | | Direct Participation | | Work Situation | | | | |
	OROC-R	OPART-E	OPART-I	OROC-D	OPART-D	OSAT	OSAT-W	OSAT-C	Union	Non-union
Norway	N.U.[a]		N.U.			N.U.			280	55
Sweden	U.[b]			U					900	80
Denmark[c]	—	—		—	—	—		—		—
Finland			—			—			500	75
U.K.	U.	U.							220	130
Germany (West)	U.	U.							150	190
Holland					N.U.				160	290
Belgium								N.U.	230	140
France						N.U.	N.U.		120	265
Italy									240	80
Yugoslavia									217	85
Israel[c]	—		—		—			—		—

[a] Non-union (N.U.) means the P.M. correlation coefficient is significantly higher (p < .10) for union non-members than for union members.
[b] 'Union' (U.) means the P.M. correlation coefficient is significantly higher (p < .10) for union members than for union non-members.
[c] Insufficient number of union non-members in sample.

Abbreviations: OROC-R Rating of Consequences of Representative System, OPART-E Evaluation of Representative System, OPART-I Interest in the Representative System, OROC-D Rating of Consequences of Direct Participation, OPART-D Rating of Direct Participation, OSAT General Satisfaction, OSAT-W Work Satisfaction, OSAT-C Company Satisfaction.

Table 8.17

Correlations between overall direct Involvement index and outcome variables, separately for workers who do and those who don't consider direct Involvement important

| | Outcome variables (attitudes) concerning | | | | | | | | N | |
| | Representative Participation | | | Direct Participation | | Work situation | | | | |
Country	OROC-R	OPART-E	OPART-I	OROC-D	OPART-D	OSAT	OSAT-W	OSAT-C	Important	Unimportant
Norway		Imp			Imp	Imp	Imp		80	90
Sweden	Imp[a]	Imp	Imp	Imp	Imp	Imp	Imp	Imp	260	250
Denmark				Imp		Imp	Imp	Imp	80	70
Finland			Imp			Imp			150	170
U.K.					Imp				50	150
Germany (West)	Unimp[b]	Unimp	Unimp	Unimp					80	140
Holland						Imp		Imp	130	140
Belgium		Imp	Imp			Imp		Imp	60	140
France				Imp	Imp	Imp	Imp		30	130
Italy				Imp	Imp				60	30
Yugoslavia				Unimp			Unimp	Unimp	65	95
Israel						Unimp		Unimp	40	110

[a] 'Imp' means the P.M. correlation coefficient is significantly (p < .10) higher for those who value direct participation, than for those who consider direct participation relatively unimportant (ORON–3 score 3 vs score 1).

[b] 'Unimp' means the correlation coefficient is significantly higher for those who consider direct participation relatively unimportant.

Abbreviations: OROC–R Rating of Consequences of Representative System, OPART–E Evaluation of Representative System, OPART–I Interest in the Representative System, OROC–D Rating of Consequences of Direct Participation, OPART–D Rating of Direct Participation, OSAT General Satisfaction, OSAT–W Work Satisfaction, OSAT–C Company Satisfaction.

much more relevant moderator than age. In other words, those who value direct involvement in decision-making often have different reactions to variations in actual involvement than those who do not value this so much. Particularly relevant for the relationship is this distinction between direct involvement and satisfaction. In seven out of the twelve countries the relationship between involvement and satisfaction is particularly high for those who value involvement.

Summarizing the results presented in this section and comparing them with some of the results presented in previous sections, the following very tentative conclusions can be drawn:

i. While previous sections show that, in various cases, older workers differ from younger workers, and union members differ from non-unionized workers in the extent to which they evaluate effects of representative or direct participation positively, this section shows that there are hardly any consistent differences between these groups so far as relationships between the level of direct involvement and evaluation are concerned. This suggests that older workers and union members do not react very differently from younger and non-unionized workers to the extent of personal involvement in decision-making.

ii. Within all these sub-groups there are workers who do and those who do not value having influence in their own work situation. It appears that this difference is more relevant than the previous ones, where the relationship between involvement and attitudes or satisfaction is concerned, although the same patterns are not found in all countries. There are indications that satisfaction, particularly with the company and management, is much more strongly related to the extent to which one is involved in decision-making for those who consider participation important than for those who do not.

WHICH ORGANIZATIONAL CHARACTERISTICS ARE IMPORTANT?

Although in previous sections opinions and attitudes concerning participation were shown to vary between companies, it was not yet clear which company characteristics (apart from Sector) were related to these differences. In this section we will analyse the relationships between outcome variables (aggregated to company means) and company characteristics, such as aspects of influence distribution, and features of the organization such as technology, personnel distribution, or market position. This analysis will be done over all 134 companies in the twelve countries together. It is however quite possible that relationships found in this way are actually due to differences between countries and not to differences between companies. For example, we might find that in those companies where the formal authority of the representative bodies is relatively high (PS) the effectiveness of these bodies is on average also rated quite highly by the respondents (OROC–R). This however is probably not a company phenomenon but a country phenomenon. In the countries where representative bodies have relatively more formal power the effectiveness of these bodies is also rated as relatively high. To overcome this possible confusion of levels of analysis, analyses over countries or per country will be added wherever feasible.

In Table 8.18 the major results of the analysis are presented. The following points can be made concerning the results presented in this table. First, one can conclude that workers' satisfaction with work and company in general, whether measured through questionnaires or through behavioural indices such as turnover and absenteeism, is not consistently related to any organization-level characteristic, or the distribution of influence.[14] Although differences in average satisfaction-levels between types of company and between countries do exist (see tables 8.4 and 8.11) they are not related to the overall level of influence workers have, to inequality in the distribution of influence, or to technological, structural, and other organizational characteristics (see Table 8.19) at least so far as these variables are measured in this study.

The coefficients in the last two columns of Table 8.18 are the exception to this trend. One has to be very cautious in interpreting these results. The negative relationship between the level of *De Jure* participation for workers and Absenteeism might be due to a country effect: some countries which have more prescribed participation for workers, for some reason or other happen to have a lower average absenteeism than other countries. This might also apply to the other coefficients. Still it is attractive to hypothesize that companies or countries where the total amount of *De Jure* Participation (TOPSto) and personal Involvement (TOPO2ato) is high experience a lower absenteeism.

However this may be, the relationship, sometimes found in other studies and again in this one, between actual involvement and satisfaction can be considered to be mainly an individual-level phenomenon resulting from the fact that both depend on individual perceptions. For these variables a causal interpretation— being involved causes satisfaction with work and company is therefore not suitable. One can say that those individuals who perceive themselves as more involved in decision-making are usually also the more satisfied individuals. However it is not true that, in those organizations where the involvement of workers —either directly or through their representatives—is higher, the overall satisfaction is also higher. This conclusion does not apply to attitudes and opinions concerning participation through representatives or direct personal participation which will be discussed later.

A second observation is that indicators of total amount of Influence (comparable with Tannenbaum's 'total amount of power' (1968) are of much less importance for the outcome variables than the absolute amount of influence itself. The 'total amount of power' appears to be mostly unrelated to the outcome variables. This result is quite contradictory to Tannenbaum's data. Not only general satisfaction with work and company, but even attitudes to participation itself, appear not to be related to the total amount of influence but only to the level of influence of the group of employees concerned. The differences between these and Tannenbaum's results might be due to differences in methodology. Tannenbaum based his 'total amount of power' index on responses of a sample of respondents to a very global question concerning the influence of other levels in general. This is comparable to our perceived Involvement instrument (PO2a) which is, however, focused on specific issues. The results concerning this instrument show positive correlations with Satisfaction and Evaluation indices but, again, these can be attributed to individual-level perceptual phenomena.

The 'total amount of influence' indices in this study, which are based on

Table 8.18

Relations between (organization mean score for) outcome variables and aspects of Influence and Involvement distributions in the organization

| | Attitudes of workers towards | | | | | | | | | |
| | Representative participation | | | Direct participation | | Work situation | | | | |
	OROC-R	OPART-E	OPART-I	OROC-D	OPART-D	OSAT	OSAT-W	OSAT-C	Turnover	Absenteeism
Direct Involvement of Workers (A)	.31[a]	.44	.44	.33	.53	.25	.23	.27		
Involvement of representatives (F)					.34					
Influence of Workers (A)	.21	.26	.20	.26	.23					
Influence of representatives (F)	.33	.43	.38	.28						
De Jure Participation of workers (A)	.38	.32	.30	.46	.20					-.22
De Jure Participation of representatives (F)	.30	.42	.40	.32	.21					
Total amount of:										
Involvement	.20	.25	.25	.19	.34				-.18	
Influence					-.26				.19	-.18
De Jure Participation				.33						-.18
Inequality:										
Influence: PO1to(D–A)[b]				-.24	-.28					
Influence: EQPO1to(F)[c]	.30	.41	.37	.33						
De Jure Participation: PSto(D–A)							.22			
De Jure Participation: EQPSto(F)		.34	.35							
Total Involvement[d]	9×	9×	5×	7×	11×	12×	10×	11×		

[a]Figures are Pearson product-moment correlation coefficients calculated over 134 companies. In case of missing values variable means are substituted.

[b]PO1to(D–A) = Inequality in Influence regarding all decisions between top management and workers.

[c]EQPOto(F) = Differences in Influence for the total set of decisions between representatives and other groups in the organization.

[d]The figures in this row indicate the number of countries where the PO2ato(A) index is a significant predictor—in individual level analysis—of the respective column variable; (based on Tables 8.5 and 8.13).

Abbreviations: OROC–R Rating of Consequences of Representative System, OPART–E Evaluation of Representative System, OPART–I Interest in theRepresentative System, OROC–D Rating of Consequences of Direct Participation, OPART–D Rating of Direct Participation, OSAT General Satisfaction, OSAT–W Work Satisfaction, OSAT–C Company Satisfaction.

descriptions of actual influence processes by key figures are, however, not related to the outcome variables as discussed in this chapter. Is the expanding power theory less applicable to European than to American companies, perhaps because, in general, the decision-making processes are more of a bargaining (i.e. zero-sum game) than of a problem-solving nature? Or is the variance in Tannenbaum's 'total amount of power' index mainly due to differences in, for example, satisfaction. Some critics of Tannenbaum's theory (e.g. Perrow 1972) hold the opinion that the control graph instrument measures all sorts of individual biases, attitudes, and feelings. The lack of confirmation of Tannenbaum's results when using a more objective measure focused on specific issues, supports this interpretation. It is clear anyway that the concept of the 'total amount of power' is quite ambiguous in nature and meaning.

Third, the indices of inequality appear to add very little to the explanation of variance in the outcome variables. The correlation coefficients that are presented in Table 8.18 seem to contradict this conclusion. The inequality variables are, however, highly correlated with the absolute influence variables to which they refer:

$$PO1to (D-A) \text{ correlated with } PO1to (A) = -.77$$
$$PO1to (D-A) \text{ correlated with } PO1to (D) = .86$$
$$EQPO1 to (F) \quad \text{correlated with } PO1to (F) = .81$$
$$EQPSto \quad (F) \quad \text{correlated with } PSto (F) \quad = .69$$

Consequently, the correlations with the inequality indices decrease to a non-significant size when, through partial correlations, the respective influence variables are controlled for. On the basis of these data it is impossible to conclude whether attitudes to participation are the effect of the absolute, or the relative, level of influence. They are too strongly correlated with each other to distinguish separate effects.

In Table 8.19 we have presented correlation coefficients between the outcome variables and objective organizational characteristics referring to technology, size, formal structure, personnel composition, and environment.[15] Taken together these results suggest that evaluation of the effects and general functioning of representative bodies is related to certain organizational characteristics. Representative bodies appear to function better (at least according to the evaluations of lower-level employees) in complex organizations—organizations with high functional differentiation and more formalized in task descriptions and procedures.

Another interesting finding is the relationship between Mobilization and attitudes concerning representative participation. Mobilization refers to the proportion of workers and managers who are union members and/or who have been representatives. The correlations indicate that the functioning of the representative bodies is more highly evaluated the more the employees are mobilized in this way. These correlations are not due to a country effect because the variables concerned did not correlate when aggregated at country level. The relationship is therefore a true company-level phenomenon indicating that in those companies where the union is more strongly represented, and where more employees are, through previous membership, familiar with the functioning of the representative system, this system is more positively evaluated.

Table 8.19

Relations between organization characteristics and (aggregated) attitudes toward participation, job, and company[a]

	Rating of Evaluation of									
	OROC-C	OPART-E	OPART-I	OROC-D	OPART-D	OSAT	OSAT-W	OSAT-C	Turnover	Absenteeism
Market domination of enterprise		.19								−.19
Sector	.21[b]			.16	.30	.15		.35		
Automatization							−.16	.16		
Technological Inter-dependence	.21	.22								
Product Complexity					.21			−.20		
Functional Differentiation	.32	.29	.25							
Intensity of Personal Control				.19						
Male domination							.17	−.20	.21	
Mobilization	.24	.26	.26	.16	.18					
Evaluation of success			.17							
Log size	.17	.17	.20					.17		

[a]The aggregated attitude variables are based on the data from workers.

[b]The figures are PM correlation coefficients over 134 firms. In case of missing values variable means are substituted. Only coefficients with significance level < .05 are given; coefficients higher than .18 have p < .01.

Abbreviations: OROC-R Rating of Consequences of Representative System, OPART-E Evaluation of Representative System, OPART-I Interest in the Representative System, OROC-D Rating of Consequences of Direct Participation, OPART-D Rating of Direct Participation, OSAT General Satisfaction, OSAT-W Work Satisfaction, OSAT-C Company Satisfaction.

It is reasonable to hypothesize that the relationships between these organizational characteristics and attitudes to representative bodies are mediated by the actual power of these bodies, that is, in functionally specialized companies the influence of the representative bodies is higher and therefore the evaluation of the (effects of the) representative system is more positive. It appears that, when controlling (through partial correlation analysis) for the possible intervening effect of actual influence, only the correlations with the Mobilization index drops to a low level ($p < .10$). This means that the higher evaluation of representative participation in companies with a more mobilized work force is probably due to the fact that, in such a company, the actual influence of the representative system is relatively large.

However, the other correlation coefficients hardly decrease in size. The relationship between organizational characteristics and attitudes seems to be a direct one. The conclusion at the end of this section is, therefore, that workers in organizations characterized by functional differentiation, formalization, technological interdependence of production units, and market strength, have more positive evaluations of their representative bodies than workers in other organizations, independent of the actual influence of these bodies.

Influence distribution and attitudes to participation

Table 8.18 showed that attitudes concerning participation are quite strongly related to indices of *De Jure* Participation and *de facto* Influence. One would expect that the relationships between the *De Jure* Participation structure (PS), the actual distribution of Influence (PO), and outcome variables would be structured according to the following specification of the basic IDE model:

$$PS (F) \longrightarrow PO (F) \longrightarrow O (F)$$
$$PS (A) \longrightarrow PO (A) \longrightarrow O (A)$$

This means that attitudes referring to representative participation (OROC-R, OPART-E, and OPART-I) would be mainly related to the influence of the representative bodies (level F), while workers' attitudes concerning direct participation (OROC-D and OPART-D) would be mainly related to their own direct influence (level A).

The boxes in Table 8.20 contain the relevant coefficients. The basic IDE model is supported by the fact that the boxes are filled with significant correlation coefficients.

Another and most remarkable finding is that the indices of *De Jure* Participation (PS) correlate as strongly or even more strongly with the outcome variables than the indices of *de facto* Influence (PO). This does not accord with the IDE model in its most simple form, which assumes that attitudes to participation are affected by the actual decision-making processes and not (or less) by the formalized, prescribed, procedures. To check whether the relationships with PS indices are only due to the intervening effect of PO indices, partial correlations have been calculated and presented between brackets in Table 8.20. It is clear that the partial correlations are far from zero, which implies a direct relationship between

Table 8.20

Relations between Influence (PO1) and De Jure Participation (PS) and average workers' attitudes towards participation[a]

	Influence		De Jure Participation	
	Workers (A)	Representative bodies (F)	Workers (A)	Representative bodies (F)
Representative participation				
OROC–R	.21	.33	.38 (.33)[b]	.30 (18)
OPART–E	.26	.43	.32 (.24)	.42 (.24)
OPART–I	.20	.38	.30 (.24)	.40 (.25)
Direct participation				
OROC–D	.26	.28	.46 (.40)	.32 (.21)
OPART–D	.23	–	.20 (.11)	.21 (.19)

[a]N = 134. In case of missing values variable means are substituted.

[b]Between brackets: partial correlations, the parallel PO1-index partialled out (see text).

Abbreviations: OROC–R Rating of Consequences of Representative System, OPART–E Evaluation of Representative System, OPART–I Interest in the Representative System, OROC–D Rating of Consequences of Direct Participation, OPART–D Rating of Direct Participation, OSAT General Satisfaction, OSAT–W Work Satisfaction, OSAT–C Company Satisfaction.

De Jure Participation and the evaluation of the functioning of participation no matter what the distribution of *de facto* Influence.

The relationships between *de jure* and *de facto* influence on the one hand and outcome variables on the other might be due to other variables at two levels: organization (CON-variables) and country. In other words, attitudes to participation might be more positive not because the participative systems in the companies are functioning better but either because attitudes and actual influence both happen to be higher in certain companies (characterized by some characteristics) or because attitudes and actual influence both happen to be higher in certain countries.

The first explanation is investigated by computing partial correlations controlling for the relevant organization characteristics i.e. those organizational variables which are presented in Table 8.19. The results in Table 8.21 show that, even when taking into account the differences in organizational characteristics, the relationships do not disappear altogether. We will therefore investigate the second explanation (the variation is due to country differences rather than company differences) by analysing the relationships between the indices of *De Jure* Participation and Influence on the one hand, and the outcome variables on the other, both within countries and over countries. In the latter case the data per country are aggregated to form a country mean score.

One has to keep in mind that an analysis per country is based on a very small number of units—about nine. In Table 8.22 only mean coefficients are therefore presented. In Table 8.23 correlations between the same variables are presented, but this time calculated over country mean scores. The number of

Table 8.21
Zero and first order partial correlaion coefficients between De Jure Participation, Influence, and outcome indices, contextual variables partialled out[a]

	Influence		De Jure Participation	
	Workers (A)	Representative bodies (F)	Workers (A)	Representative bodies (F)
OROC-R	— (.21[b])	.17* (.33)	.29*** (.38)	.21** (.30)
OPART-E	.19* (.26)	.30*** (.43)	.23** (.32)	.39*** (.42)
OPART-I	— (.20)	.29*** (.38)	.19* (.30)	.36*** (.40)
OROC-D	.22** (.26)	.17* (.28)	.44*** (.46)	.26** (.32)
OPART-D	.23** (.23)	—	— (.20)	— (.21)

[a]The contextual variables partialled out are those presented in Table 8.19.
[b]The coefficients between brackets are the zero order correlation.

$*$: p < .05 $**$: p < .01 $***$: p < .001

Abbreviations: OROC-R Rating of Consequences of Representative System, OPART-E Evaluation of Representative System, OPART-I Interest in the Representative System, OROC-D Rating of Consequences of Direct Participation, OPART-D Rating of Direct Participation, OSAT General Satisfaction, OSAT-W Work Satisfaction, OSAT-C Company Satisfaction.

Table 8.22
Average within-country correlation between participation and outcome indices (based on attitudes of workers)

	De facto influence		De Jure Participation	
	Workers PO1ato (A)	Representative bodies PO1ato (F)	Workers PSto (A)	Representative bodies PSto (F)
Representative participation				
OROC-R	.01	.20	.10	.01
OPART-E	.18	.31	.10	.11
OPART-I	.11	.10	—.09	—.19
Direct participation				
OROC-D	.10	.05	.16	—.01
OPART-D	.04	.03	.18	—.02

Note: N per country is ± 9; data for Italy and Israel are excluded because n < 5.

Abbreviations: OROC-R Rating of Consequences of Representative System, OPART-E Evaluation of Representative System, OPART-I Interest in the Representative System, OROC-D Rating of Consequences of Direct Participation, OPART-D Rating of Direct Participation, OSAT General Satisfaction, OSAT-W Work Satisfaction OSAT-C Company Satisfaction.

Table 8.23
Correlations between participation and outcome indices calculated over country mean scores[a]

	Influence					De Jure Participation				
	Workers	Representative bodies				Workers	Representative bodies			
	All decisions	All decisions	ST[b]	MT	LT	All decisions	All decisions	ST	MT	LT
Representative participation										
OROC-R	.33[c]	.11	.20	.13	.42	.70**	.26	.32	.25	.38
OPART-E	.0	.33	.32	.38	.50	.36	.55*	.28	.61*	.33
OPART-I	.0	.09	.29	-.02	.21	.13	.57*	.70**	.45*	.41
Direct participation										
OROC-D	.10	.12	.02	.17	.65**	.60*	.36	.28	.50*	.48*
OPART-D	-.05	.03	.0	.04	.48*	.03	.24	.08	.60*	.43

*: p < .05. **: p < .01.

[a]the attitude variables are based on the responses of workers.

[b]ST = short-term decisions, MT = medium-term decisions, LT = long-term decisions.

[c]Figures are Spearman rank correlation coefficients (N = 12). Country scores are calculated in such a way that differences between the samples in terms of number of respondents, sector, age, and gender are taken into account; the actual scores were derived from an SPSS-multiple classification analysis with country, sector, sex, and age as factors.

Abbreviations: OROC-R Rating of Consequences of Representative System, OPART-E Evaluation of Representative System, OPART-I Interest in the Representative System, OROC-D Rating of Consequences of Direct Participation, OPART-D Rating of Direct Participation, OSAT General Satisfaction, OSAT-W Work Satisfaction OSAT-C Company Satisfaction.

observations is therefore twelve. Comparing Tables 8.22 and 8.23 it is clear that, in some cases at least, variation of the outcome variables within countries is related to PO variance, that is to differences in the actual distribution of Influence. Variation in outcome variables between the countries is more related to PS variance—i.e. differences in *de jure* participation structures.

For one of the variables concerned (OPART-E) this phenomenon is visually presented in Figure 8.8. Figure 8.8 shows visually that, while differences in the

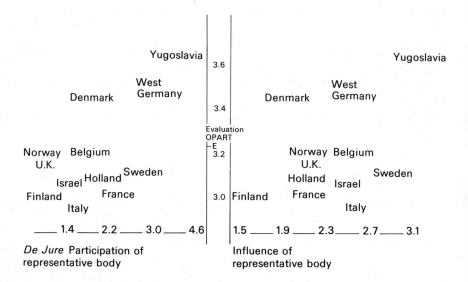

Figure 8.8 The relationship between Evaluation of the Representative System (OPART–E) and the *De Jure* Participation (PS) and Influence (PO) of the representative bodies (scale scores of worker-level respondents aggregated per country)

de jure authority of the representative systems in the various countries are associated with differences between countries in the evaluation of these systems (by workers), differences in the actual influence of the bodies are not.[16]

These results suggest the following conclusions. In some countries (e.g. Yugoslavia and West Germany) the *de jure* participation system assigns more opportunities for influencing decision-making to the representative bodies than in other countries, and therefore employees in those countries are more positive about these representative bodies (not necessarily because these bodies actually have more influence). Within countries however evaluation of, and interest in, the representative bodies is affected by the way these bodies exert actual influence. As Table 8.23 shows, the relationships between the formal system and Evaluation or Interest are particularly strong when one considers, not the overall PS index, but only the PS index referring to cluster 2 (short-term issues) or cluster 3 (medium-term issues). This suggests that whether representative bodies have formal rights to be involved in policy issues does not strongly affect the evaluation and interest of workers.

The trend visible in Figure 8.8 is also present in the case of the Interest variable (OPART-I), but not in the case of the rated effects index (OROC-R). This however, makes our previous conclusion even more clear. The OROC-R index is considered to measure the effects of the functioning of the representative system, and it is quite plausible that the actual results of a participative system are more or less independent of the formal opportunities provided (except when the opportunities are really great such as in Yugoslavia and, to some extent, West Germany). We conclude therefore that differences between countries in their formal participation structure (PS) do not determine the (perceived) effects of the systems (OROC-R) but they do result in differences so far as the general evaluation of, and interest in, the system are concerned. Part of people's happiness about their representative bodies is due not to what they actually achieve, but to what they may achieve.

Similarly, aspects of the direct involvement of the *de jure* rights of workers (PS-A) are related to attitudes (OROC-D), although one would have expected this index—like the OROC-R index—to reflect the actual functioning of direct participation rather than its *de jure* provisions. Less easy to explain is the relationship between the *de jure* provisions for the direct participation of workers (PSto-A) and the rated effects of the representative system (OROC-R: s = .85). Perhaps we have to consider a carry-over of satisfaction with one's potential individual influence to the system as a whole.

Summarizing the main points in this section we can conclude that characteristics of the *de jure* system, of the actual distribution of influence, and of technology and structure are related to employees' attitudes (perception, evaluation, and interest) concerning both representative and direct participation, but not to satisfaction with the job and company in general.

ATTITUDES TO REPRESENTATIVE AND DIRECT PARTICIPATION COMPARED: A SUMMARY

General patterns

In this chapter attitudes to representative participation, direct participation, job, and company in general, and their relations to personal and organizational characteristics are studied. It appeared that for all attitude-indices differences between countries and between companies within each country are significant. However, while the perception people have of the effects of the representative bodies is not very different for respondents from various hierarchical levels or other sub-groups—which suggests that it is determined by the actual functioning of these bodies—the other attitudes (interest in representative participation, and evaluation of direct participation, job, and company) are often related to personal characteristics.

Comparing the perceived effects of the two types of participation—representative (OROC-R) and direct participation (OROC-D)—it appears that the patterns are quite similar, although on average in most countries slightly fewer respondents were positive about the various effects of direct participation. In both cases, however, the outcome 'greater say' was the least endorsed by the respondents. Apart from 'greater say', the other effects were perceived by the majority of the respondents in all countries to be quite positive. Among these effects is 'representation of the interests of employees' and 'people accept decisions more easily'.. This might be so because employees perceive the direct or indirect participation structures to function adequately. It might, however, also be interpreted as a sign of the fact that these structures function as part of the control structure of the organization. However this may be, respondents are generally quite positive about the effects of representative and direct participation. On the other hand, personal interest and involvement (as measured by the Evaluation and Interest scales) for more than half of the respondents are quite low. Particularly when asked whether they would accept a candidacy for these bodies an average of only 20 per cent professed to be willing. The Yugoslav sample is an exception—about 50 per cent would accept a candidacy. Combining this with the fact that the majority of the workers desires the representative bodies to have a say in all sorts of decision, particularly the more important ones, we come to the conclusion that most people support their representative bodies although only a minority feels itself motivated or able to be an active member.

It is possible to compare the countries as to attitudes concerning the two types of participation. Combining the above scales into two indices which measure the evaluation of representative and direct participation,[17] the countries can be compared as to the mean score of workers on the two dimensions. (Figure 8.9)

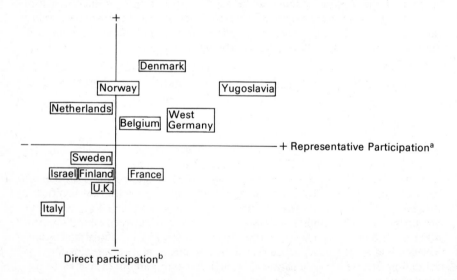

[a]representative participation index = OROC−R + OPART−E + OPART−I

[b]direct participation index = OROC−D + OPART−D

Figure 8.9 Workers' evaluations (mean) of representative and direct participation by country.

There appears to be a positive relationship between the two dimensions: respondents from countries like Yugoslavia, Denmark and West Germany are relatively positive about both types of participation. Respondents from countries such as Italy, Israel, Finland, and the U.K. are relatively negative about both. There are, however, countries which deviate from this general line. In the French sample we find that representative participation is more positively evaluated than direct participation, while in the Dutch sample the reverse is true.

Differences between sectors, organizations, and groups of individuals

So far as attitudes to the representative system are concerned sector differences are sometimes significant although not often consistently in the same direction in all countries. With regard to direct participation we find slightly more positive reactions in service companies than in companies in the metal industries. It is interesting to compare this with the indices concerning the desire for direct or representative involvement in decision-making (PO2b and PO2c). It appears that, on average, the workers in low-skilled metal companies desire more influence for their representatives than those in the high-skilled metal companies, while the respondents in service industries have the lowest desires in this respect. This is probably related to the fact that more workers in production departments (in metal companies) ask for more influence for representative bodies than workers in non-production departments, while the reverse is true for the desire for direct participation.

The effects of age, tenure and sex are not very consistent or strong so far as the outcome variables are concerned. In some of the northern countries it appears that female workers are less interested in representative participation than male workers. The effects of age and tenure might be curvilinear. Turning to the desire for individual involvement or influence for one's representatives, the picture is more consistent. On the whole, male, lower-level employees, and union members prefer the participation of workers to be realized through representative bodies. Younger and more highly educated workers prefer personal participation.

Hierarchical level differences are often quite large. Supervisors and managers are generally more positive about the representative system than workers. They are also more willing to participate in these bodies although, compared with workers, they desire less influence for these bodies. They themselves prefer, much more than workers, to have influence through personal participation.

It appears that in some countries a more positive evaluation of, and, particularly, a higher interest in, the functioning of the representative bodies is displayed by workers who have a relatively higher personal involvement in decision-making. In those countries the interest in representative participation is also greater for workers who desire an increase in involvement, particularly in medium- and long-term issues. These phenomena are present in most of the northern countries and in Yugoslavia. One might speculate that in these countries both types of participation are, to some extent, integrated, which implies that having some personal involvement and desiring more personal involvement might be combined with, and realized through, representative participation. In the Southern European countries the two systems might be more independent of each other, perhaps because the representative bodies are perceived more as a platform for representation of interests and as an arena for confrontation.

Attitudes related to organizational characteristics and the distribution of influence

A major finding in this chapter concerns the determinants (in a statistical sense) of satisfaction with job and company. Although at the individual level satisfaction and perceived involvement are related, the actual influence of workers or representative bodies—as measured in more objective ways through expert judgement about specific decision-processes—is not related to satisfaction with job or company.

Evaluation of, and interest in, the work of the representative system, is, however, relatively strongly (positively) related not only to characteristics of the production process and the formal structure of the organization, but also to the actual influence and, remarkably, to the *de jure* authority, of the representative bodies. The effect of *de jure* authority seems to be partly due to differences between countries. It appears that the attitude of workers is due, not only to what the representative system actually does achieve, but also to what it, according to *de jure* regulations, may achieve (c.f., IDE 1980).

NOTES

1   The German questionnaire refers in the OROC–R scale to the whole system of co-determination.
2   The alpha-coefficients of homogeneity range between 0.76 and 0.90 (see Appendix B.2).
3   A Norwegian study (Engelstad and Qvale 1977) shows that 41% of shop stewards and members of representative bodies give as the main obstacle the fact that the laws provide for too little power.
4   Homogeneity coefficients are: for Evaluation 0.50–0.81, and for Interest 0.40–0.73.
5   Differences between sectors were not analysed for middle managers because the number of respondents was sometimes too small.
6   At some stage in these analyses the 'desired representative influence' was included. This variable—the overall summary score concerning the issues one desires the representative body to have a say in—has already been discussed in a previous chapter, which, however, does not contain individual-level analyses.
7   ORON item 7—the importance of having good representatives—might have been another candidate for inclusion in this analysis; however, respondents hardly differed in judging this item as less important.
8   The computer programme for this analysis of variance allows for only five independent factors.
9   This conclusion is not valid for the Scandinavian countries.
10   The five items constitute a homogeneous scale in all countries; alpha co-efficients range from 0.69 to 0.90.
11   Appendix B shows alpha coefficients ranging from 0.59 to 0.85.
12   Several studies have shown that this type of scale, although it tries to elicit descriptions of a situation, often measures evaluation of that situation. One

might therefore rephrase the statement as: the more workers are involved in decision-making the more they are satisfied with the extent to which their boss is participative.

13   The respondents giving ORON item 3 a score of 2 are excluded from this analysis.

14   The fact that the satisfaction scores are related to the first variable—aggregated overall involvement index—is obviously due to the individual-level correlation of these variables (see also the last row).

15   Of the nineteen CON indicies discussed in Chapter 4 only the ones with correlation coefficients > 0.16 are presented in this table.

16   Comparable results are found for the Interest scale.

17   Scores on the OROC–R, OPART–E, and OPART–I scales are added to get an overall index of evaluation of representative participation; the evaluation of direct participation is indicated by a sum-score of OROC–D and OPART–D.

9

CROSS NATIONAL PERSPECTIVES

OVERVIEW[1]

This chapter is concerned with four tasks. Firstly, we will briefly review the literature of the relevant multi-country studies in our area of research. Secondly, an attempt will be made to test for country groupings by means of multivariate statistical methods without pre-setting country clusters. Thirdly, pre-set profiles of countries, based on previous research, will be tested. Finally, our twelve-country data, described in previous chapters, will be reviewed and analysed for consistency, using bivariate diagrams. This last method will be seen to be the most relevant for the data at our disposal. Using historic, political, and social information for each country, quite meaningful explanations of the major variations can be made. The reader who is not particularly concerned with methodology and cross-cultural theory could ignore the next three sections.

Previous chapters have made it clear that the objectives of the present research required a multi-country sample since it was intended to measure the impact of country-specific legal and quasi-legal structures on variations in *de facto* participation. However, the study was not designed to test other cross-country differences or the effect of 'culture'. With such an objective in mind, one would have looked for much greater variations in the geographic distribution of countries, while our industrial democracy sample concentrated only on Europe with the addition of Israel. Nevertheless, since very few multi-national studies have this data for twelve countries, it is appropriate that we should try to relate the findings to the existing growing literature on cross-national organization research.

PROBLEMS RELATING TO CROSS-NATIONAL STUDIES

Cross-national research into organizations and the behaviour and attitudes of their members is of relatively recent origin. The topic attracted very little research before 1960 (Harbison and Myers 1959) but a survey of the comparative research literature 1962–1967 discovered about 500 moderately relevant publications (Roberts 1967).[2] Most of the comparative work up to now has consisted of samples from two or three countries and this is insufficient for making broad generalizations about groupings based on similarities or differences. There are good reasons for the reluctance of researchers to enter this area of scientific inquiry. Apart from the obvious expense of time and money, there are profound, and some will argue, intractable methodological problems which have to be faced (Merritt 1975). While a growing volume of literature has addressed itself to the methodological and theoretical problems, they have not been solved (Schweitzer 1975, Triandis 1972, Rokkan 1968, Landsberger 1970, Przeworski and Teune 1970, Schenk 1966, Brislin et al. 1973).

It is not intended to review these problems in any detail, and we do not claim to have improved substantially on previous research in this respect. However, as was demonstrated in Chapter 4, we have reason to be satisfied with the instruments and the validity of the scales derived from them; we have a larger sample than most previous research and we have gone to a great deal of trouble to ensure comparability of our data.

It is therefore appropriate that we should use the research to address a number of current controversies, for instance the examination of the so-called culture-free versus the culture-bound hypothesis. The use of the term culture immediately adds to our problem since it is difficult to define operationally and carries a varied number of value-determined overtones. The word culture was adapted in French from the Latin *cultura* which is related to the Latin *cultus*— cult or worship. In ordinary language the major meaning of the term[3] is closely associated with socially elitist concepts like refinement of mind, tastes, and manners based on superior education and upbringing. It has also been identified with the intellectual side of civilization, particularly in its German spelling.[4]

In comparative research on organizations, culture is rarely isolated as a defined category and separated from other variables as an integral part of the research design. It is more usually treated as a residual entity and as an afterthought. This problem has been scathingly analysed in a seminal article by Roberts (1970) who reviewed 526 publications and found that only 54 per cent based their arguments about culture on empirical data. She came to the conclusion that, even where data were available, the conceptualization was usually descriptive, vague, and ignored the impact of alternative factors like technology or structure which probably accounted for a larger percentage variation of the dependent variable. Child (1980) has made similar criticisms.

Explanations of cross-country differences vary and some authors are content to describe the existence of differences without offering reasons for them. We argue that, if significant country or societal differences emerge repeatedly in different studies, causal explanations should be sought in the form of measurable independent variables. Major candidates for such analysis are child-rearing practices, educational systems, socio-structural factors like class and religious practices, economic factors and legal-political systems (see for instance Ajiferuke and Boddewyn 1970).

A BRIEF REVIEW OF SOME RELEVANT STUDIES

A considerable variety of cross-national studies and comparative theories relating to them have recently been described and analysed (Lammers and Hickson 1979, Child 1980). We will therefore confine ourselves to a selection of studies particularly relevant to the present research.

After a few early, but mainly impressionistic, studies (Harbison and Myers 1959, Granick 1962), a large-scale comparison of managerial attitudes in fourteen countries attracted a great deal of attention (Haire, Ghiselli, and Porter 1966). These authors grouped their sample into four clusters: (i) Nordic European (Denmark, Germany, Norway, Sweden), (ii) Latin European (Belgium, France, Italy, Spain), (iii) Anglo-American (the U.K. and the United States), and (iv)

Developing Countries (Argentina, Chile, India). Japan did not fit into any of the clusters. Other large-scale comparative studies have found substantial national differences in variables like managerial objectives (Bass and Eldridge 1973), managerial values (England 1975), and decision-making styles (Heller and Wilpert forthcoming 1980), but without the neat country clusters suggested by the Haire et al. research.

Managers, as well as social scientists, find the possibility of categorizing organizational differences by 'culture' clusters very appealing and recent evidence suggests that it is worthwhile to re-examine some of the clusters postulated by Haire et al. One part of the evidence comes from a large multi-national high-technology company, which, from time to time, conducts surveys on its employees in about forty countries. Some of these results have been analysed by Hofstede (1976, 1977). One of Hofstede's measures is called a Power Distance Index (PDI) based on three questions.[5] He finds that this measure correlated with the Gross National Economic Product of the employee's country and with its geographic location. The countries that are closer to the equator have larger PDI scores than the more northern countries. His ranking of countries on the PDI index can also be arranged into two broad clusters very similar to the Haire et al. clusters described above. Hofstede's first group includes: Nordic countries (Denmark, Sweden, Norway, Finland), Germanic countries (Austria, Switzerland, Germany, Holland), and Anglo-American countries (New Zealand, Ireland, the U.K., Australia, Canada, and the U.S.A.). The second broad cluster is made up of Latin European and Mediterranean countries (Italy, Spain, Greece, Portugal, Belgium, Turkey, and France).

In a recent book on comparative organization studies Lammers and Hickson (1979) put forward a strong case for clustering countries according to cultural affinities based on a similar division into two main country clusters and supported by evidence from a variety of studies, including Hofstede's. The authors define culture as the 'pattern of norms and roles embedded in certain paramount values as professed by organization participants' (Chapter 21: 402). A distinction is made between two types of bureaucracy, the 'classic' or Latin type and the 'flexible' or Anglo-Saxon type. Latin bureaucracy is characterized by centralization, a large number of hierarchical levels, rigid stratification, high bureaucratic control, low total amount of control, low morale, low co-operativeness, and a preference for routine rather than innovative decisions. The Anglo-Saxon bureaucracy is pictured as having the reverse of these characteristics (Chapter 22).

We have mentioned earlier that a number of two- or three-country comparative studies have been carried out. Several are very interesting for organizational research (Ruedi and Lawrence 1970, Dore 1973, Wilpert and Heller 1973, Gallie 1978, Child and Kieser 1979, Maurice et al. 1980), but do not lend themselves to the kind of systematic comparision we are attempting to carry out here.

In an eight-country comparative study of influence- and power-sharing practices at the top levels of 129 organizations, significant differences between countries emerged (Heller and Wilpert 1979, 1980). However, the variation between countries could not be explained by reference to clearly identifiable predictors and the differences were less important than the support for a number of hypotheses which were substantiated in each country. One important conclusion relevant to the present study shows that, in every country, influence- and power-sharing increases when subordinates are more highly trained or when they are perceived to be competent.

An important five-country study on participative practices (Tannenbaum et al. 1974) at various organizational levels in 52 plants covers three of the countries in our sample: Yugoslavia, Israel, and Italy. The Israeli sample, however, is entirely of Kibbutzim plants, while our study is of Histadrut-owned enterprises only. Differences between the five country samples are explained by different forms of ownership, formal decision-making structures, and reward systems. On these three dimensions the Kibbutzim and Yugoslav enterprises stand out as being considerably more participative, while the Italian plants fall close to the non-participative end of the continuum. In Italian plants, workers have little influence over decisions and are not encouraged by their foremen to contribute suggestions. It will be seen that some of the findings of this study in respect of participation in Yugoslav and Italian enterprises are almost identical to our own.

Two other very recent multi-country studies of participation will be mentioned, although most of the data have not been published at the time of writing. Both were co-ordinated through the Vienna Centre.[6] One was a follow-up of the previously mentioned research (Tannenbaum et al. 1974) extended to seven other countries, including three from Eastern Europe (Bulgaria, Hungary and Rumania) and two from South America (Brazil and Mexico). The two European countries were Germany and Ireland (Tannenbaum and Rozgonyi forthcoming).

One of the main conclusions from both studies is that many important aspects of organizational life are equally present in all samples despite substantial differences in ownership, formal structure, reward methods, and socio-political systems. While the follow-up research was not so carefully matched between countries for method and sample as the previous one, the authors believe that certain generalizations about participation, hierarchy, job satisfaction, alienation, and perceptions about how the organization operates could be universal, since many of the likenesses replicate results of earlier research elsewhere. However, while remuneration gradients are sloped in each case, these are a good deal less steep in socialist nations than in the others.

Within-country variance is also important. In Hungary, for instance, co-operatives and small plants practise more participation than other enterprises; they also have higher morale and a greater sense of responsibility. In Hungary, as in the other countries, all groups within plants want more participation and control. The difference between the amount of participation they have and the amount they would prefer is much greater among workers than at higher levels. The Hungarian researchers conclude that the 'organizations function more like it should be in the view of managers than in the view of workers' (Tannenbaum and Rozgonyi forthcoming). This conclusion is an interesting confirmation of Haraszti's (1977) classic case study of factory life in Hungary. However, from the point of view of comparative analysis, the interesting fact is that the conclusions reached by the Hungarian team could also have been extracted from the control graph data of the other samples, for instance from West Germany.

Confirmation of this presumably unexpected finding of east–west similarity comes from another study using different samples and methods. The research on 'Automation and Industrial Workers' in six socialist and nine non-socialist countries was co-ordinated by the Vienna Centre.[6] The questionnaire contained a section on the extent of current participation, the extent of influence workers have on different managerial decisions, the opportunities workers should have to participate, and their own willingness to participate. In other sections there were measures of job satisfaction, technology, etc.

One of the questions the research asked was whether the socio-economic or management system in which a man worked, affected his participatory behaviour (Jacob and Ahn 1978). They found statistically significant differences in amount, kind, opportunities, and commitment to participation among the workers and managers in the fifteen countries, although these differences do not relate directly and consistently to differences in the national-economic system. More specifically they found great differences between one nation and another, but few of these differences depended on whether the countries are socialist or capitalist. One of these few differences relates to the extent workers thought they ought to participate in all or most decisions affecting their plants. Workers in the socialist countries believed in this very extensive participation (the U.S.S.R. 85 per cent) but workers in other countries, most notably the U.S.A. did not (only 10 per cent said that workers should have this all-embracing participation).

It seems that the crucial condition for actual participation in all fifteen countries is the 'opportunity workers see open to them to influence decisions'. The more the opportunity, the more they are likely to make use of it. From the point of view of the research we report in this book, the two most interesting opportunities relate to trade unions and legislative support for participation. Workers who consider their unions effective see greater opportunities and participate more. Incidentally, they also have a higher appreciation of their company. But the finding of the Automation study which most closely supports our own, related to the impact of formal legal provision for participation. While they do not measure this variable empirically, as is the case in our own research, they assessed the differences descriptively. They conclude 'officials and workers themselves agree that workers exercise greater actual control over management decisions in countries where the law provides for maximum participation' (Jacob and Ahn 1979: 66).

TESTING FOR COUNTRY CLUSTERS AND PROFILES

From our brief review of the literature, it will be seen that, while some researchers have found country clusters based on national, cultural, or geographic distinctions, others have not found any meaningful patterns of country differences. It seems certain that a great deal more research will have to be carried out to resolve this issue. A worthwhile attempt to reconcile the existing divergence of findings and steer academic inquiry towards a more eclectic analysis of country differences has recently been put forward by Child (1980). Incorporating the data and theoretical positions of a variety of approaches, including Lammers and Hickson (1979), he argues for a three-prong attack. He would use a theoretical framework with pre-specified variables covering contingencies (i.e. size, technology, level, etc.), culture (social institutions, labour movements, expectations about norms, etc.), and economic system variables (ownership of means of production, economic centralization, etc.).

The method we adopt below is, apart from pre-specification, not incongruent with Child's suggestion. However, to begin with we will test the simpler and, some may feel, more rigorous, hypothesis that coherent country clusters or profiles do exist. A considerable number of taxonomic and multi-variate techniques are available for analyses of country comparisons. Two approaches were chosen. One is based on the theoretical, but possibly contentious, assumption that, if data contains statistically consistent and reliable country differences, these should emerge by what can be termed 'blind' methods. Blind methods are analogous to the use of factor anaysis for discovering empirically homogeneous cognitive or personality structures. The second approach was more deductive and used country clusters that had emerged from previous research. It will be seen that neither method yielded very convincing results, although the second approach produced some support for the Latin versus non-Latin country hypothesis.

Using Multi-variate Techniques

Our first approach was to test the global theory of country groupings by a number of multi-variate statistical techniques devised to arrange data into hierarchies and clusters depending on their statistical proximity.[7]

The results of these inductive statistical methods can be summarized briefly. One major consistency emerges from all analyses. Yugoslavia stands apart from the other countries on all major variables. The results from the other eleven countries do not fall into any consistent pattern. For each variable, for instance, satisfaction, organizational climate, consequences of participation, or involvement, different groupings emerge. Typically, the clusters also differ for service and manufacturing industry and for large and small companies. They form groups or clusters which are not consistent from one analysis to another. When countries are grouped according to their scores for Involvement (PO2) for instance, they form different clusters in the metal and service sectors, and different clusters again if we separate them by size. This lack of consistency of country groupings could be due to a number of reasons which do not necessarily relate to our main objective.[8]

Given the current state of knowledge about the subject of our research, such particularistic groupings are of limited theoretical and practical importance. If different country profiles emerge for most of our variables and contingencies, then broad conclusions about the impact of country or culture are not possible.

Testing for *A Priori* Clusters

Our twelve-country sample does not include the U.S.A. nor developing countries, but in other respects it is similar to the Haire et al. sample and covers many of the Latin and Nordic groupings found in the other research we reviewed earlier.

Our preliminary computer-analysis, as well as visual inspection of the available results, showed that the Finnish sample in this research did not seem to fit into the Nordic cluster. We also leave out the Yugoslav sample because it could not be included in one of our two clusters on theoretical grounds. Israel is left out for the same reason.

To make country comparisons easier, all data was converted to standardized Z scores ($x = 0$, $SD = 1$). We started with three *a priori* groupings: a Latin cluster (Belgium, France, and Italy), a Nordic cluster (Denmark, Norway, and Sweden) and an Anglo–German cluster (West Germany, the U.K., and Holland).[9] For most purposes, however, we used only two clusters by merging the Nordic and Anglo–German (Nordic-Anglo–German abbreviated NAG).

The analysis, with standard scores, is available for twenty variables covering all main PS, PO and O dimensions. We will confine our report here to a discussion of those variables where the two or three country clusters are clearly separated by Z-score values. Figure 9.1 shows the results when the aggregate scores are divided into three country clusters: Latin (L), Nordic (N), and Anglo–German. The Nordic cluster is fairly consistently above the Anglo–German and both substantially above the Latin cluster, for all but one of the six variables shown.

The difference between countries can be analysed separately for the two sectors in our sample. Figure 9.2 shows the service sector divided into Nordic–

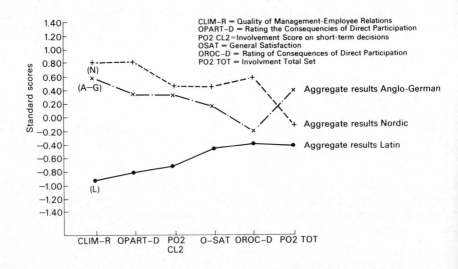

Figure 9.1 Country cluster differences—aggregate results (standard scores, Nordic, Latin, and Anglo–German)

Anglo–German and Latin. Consistently large differences between these two groupings exist on all six variables. The Nordic–Anglo–German cluster shows very much higher scores than the Latin cluster. However, for the metal sector the difference is smaller and less consistent (see Figure 9.2). We only show the results for the low-skill sub-sample of the metal sector; the results for the high-skill metal sector are similar.

Discussion Relating to Country Clusters

The findings reported above give the culture–cluster thesis tentative support. The term tentative is used for three reasons. In the first place, as we have seen, a statistically neutral, that is to say inductive, method of analysis finds no country clusters. For those scientists who, with Popper, believe in the superiority of a hypothetico-deductive approach, this negative finding is of little importance.

The second argument for caution relates to the possibility that differences in country results on selected variables could be due to cultural differences in 'response-set' to specific linguistic stimuli. This argument is similar to that which applies to any instrumental research design and is usually called the 'social desirability' effect (Phillips 1973). In the case of differences between countries, the possibility exists that what is socially desirable in, say Norway, is different

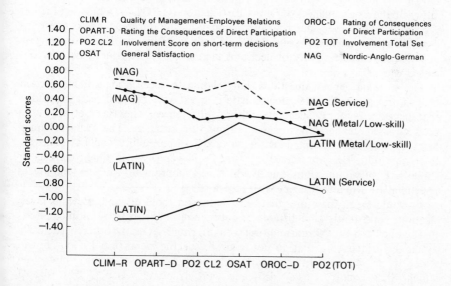

Figure 9.2 Country cluster differences in the service sector and high–low skill samples in the metal sector companies (standard scores: Latin and Nordic–Anglo–German)

from what is socially desirable in Italy. The causes of differences in social desirability may, of course, be culturally determined but these cultural factors could
be independent of the particular variables under investigation. However, this
explanation would not be acceptable to some social scientists and, of course,
it could not apply to cluster differences based on structural variables and those
not derived from questionnaire responses (see Lammers and Hickson 1979,
Maurice et al. 1980).

The third reason for caution is due to the finding that sector differences are
substantial on some variables although country differences remain (see Figure
9.2). To this we must add that our Latin cluster is made up of only three countries
and the Italian results are, in some cases, responsible for pushing the mean
cluster value much lower than might be the case with a larger sample of Latin
countries. Using tests of significance, the differences of only two of the six
variables in Figure 9.1 were statistically significant.

A culture–cluster thesis, however, receives some support from the finding that
the biggest and most consistent Nordic–Latin differences show on the two
variables for which the questions are couched in very general terms. The variable
Climate of management–employee Relations (CLIM-R) consists of three broadly
worded statements, one of which reads: 'In general, I find the situation in this
plant relaxed and easy-going'. The rating of Direct Participation (O PART-D)
consists of four questions, one example being: 'To what extent does your
superior give you the opportunity to decide on your own?' General Satisfaction
(O-SAT) could be called a broad variable, while the other variables in Figures
9.1, 9.2, 9.3, and 9.4 (with the exception of Involvement (PO2)) and those not
shown on these figures, tend to ask more specific questions. For instance, the
rating of the Consequences of Direct Participaton (O ROC-D) which, on Figures
9.1 and 9.2, shows very much smaller country–cluster differences, asks questions
like: 'As a consequence of your direct and daily participation in what is going on
in this firm, has the quality of decisions increased because issues have been discussed widely?'

Fairly broad general questions, not relating to specific identifiable current
behaviour, have tended to predominate in questionnaire-based research studies
that have found fairly clear-cut cultural differences. The Haire et al (1966)
research used deliberately broad questions, for instance: 'The average human
being prefers to be directed, wishes to avoid responsibility and has relatively
little ambition. Do you agree?' Hofstede's Power Distance Index consists of
three fairly broad questions, one of which asks subordinates whether 'employees
in general are afraid to disagree with superiors'.

It would seem, therefore, that our results and those of some previous investigations consistently find differences between respondents from Latin countries
on the one hand and Nordic and Anglo-Saxon countries on the other, particularly
in answer to questions that do not relate to specific events or behaviour, but to
wider issues. A different explanation, however, must be sought for research
which finds country–cluster differences on structural variables. The role of
'organizational choice' influenced by socio-historic factors mediated by country-
specific managerial literature and consultancy practice cannot be ruled out.

Some additional computations have been carried out using contextual variables described in Chapter 5. They are roughly in line with the findings we have reported and will be tested in secondary analysis.[10] While further research is necessary to discover the causes for country-cluster differences, the findings reported here give some support to the idea that aspects of bureaucratic attitudes in Latin countries like values relating to centralization and morale, are different from bureaucratic attitudes in non-Latin countries.

ECLECTIC COMPARATIVE ANALYSIS

In reviewing the cross-cultural results from the data of previous chapters in this book, we will use our theoretical framework. This begins with an analysis of the relationship between *De Jure* Participation (PS) and *De Facto* Participation (PO1 and PO2). In the second place, we will look at the relationship between participation (PO) and outcomes (O). Finally, contingency variables like the degree of Unionization, Formalization in terms of procedures and rules, and Conflict, etc. will, where possible, be related to the main aspects of the model.[11]

It will be seen that some countries[12] consistently come high, others low on most dimensions and bi-variate comparisons. We end this chapter with an explanation of these differences in terms of specific industrial relations and socio-political circumstances in the high- and low-scoring countries. In conclusion, we put forward the theoretical notion of 'choice' which illuminates the position of countries like West Germany, the U.K., and Finland, and points towards the role of policy and change in future developments in this field of industrial relations.

De Jure and *De Facto* Participation

One of the main conclusions from Chapter 7 is that institutional rules (PS) contribute significantly to greater equality in the distribution of Influence between top management and workers (PO1 D–A). While many of the analyses in previous chapters were carried out at the level of organizations, the country-level results are shown in Figure 9.3 and fully support this conclusion. Yugoslavia has the smallest difference in Influence between top management and workers, and Israel has the largest. These two countries also came out top and bottom on the measure of institutional rules (PS) applicable at worker level.

The relationship between institutional rules and Influence both measured at worker level, shows a complementary trend but the correlation is weaker. Figure 9.4 presents the results for the Influence measure derived from Cluster 2 (routine decisions) but it is similar for the aggregate of all sixteen decisions. Once again, Yugoslavia is high on both variables and Israel is low on both. West Germany and Norway are quite high on both variables but the other countries coalesce in the centre. It will be seen that several other country analyses follow a pattern similar to Figure 9.4.

It is tempting to predict a correspondence between Modes of formal participation as they apply to the permanent representative bodies of a country (PSa level F) and the average level of Influence enjoyed by workers (PO1 level A). Figure 9.5 shows that there is no such correspondence. While Yugoslavia is high

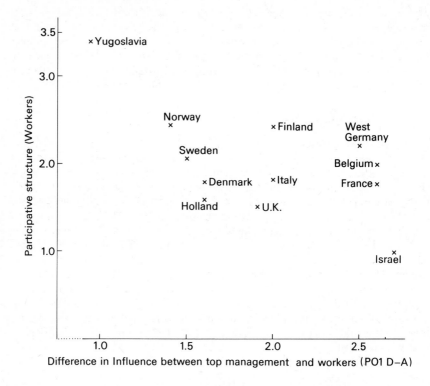

Figure 9.3 Formal participation of workers and inequality in the distribution of Influence (PO1D–A)

on both dimensions, Norway is high on Influence but very low on institutional norms, while Germany is high on institutional norms but relatively low on Influence at worker level. The other countries show no clear association between the two variables.

A similar unclear pattern emerges when we compare Modes of formal participation at worker level (PS level A) with Actual Involvement of workers (PO2 level A). This is shown in Figure 9.6. The hypothesis of such an association might be supported by Yugoslavia at the high end and Israel at the low end but the other countries cluster in the centre and almost show a contrary relationship between these two variables. Finland and Norway are relatively high on institutional norms but low on involvement, while the U.K. and Holland are relatively high on involvement but low on institutional norms.[13] However, the picture changes substantially when we move from an analysis of the worker level to that applicable to the representative system (level F) (Figure 9.7). Now a fairly strong correlation emerges. This is a clear pointer to the attention paid by our sample of countries to *de jure* participation structures to support the permanent representative body. As we saw in Chapter 7 with the analysis at organizational level it seems that *de jure* structures at representative-body

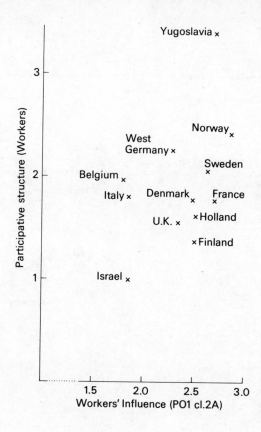

Figure 9.4 Formal participation (PS) and Influence (PO1) over short-term decisions at worker level

level are, in some respects, more effective in increasing influence than *de jure* structures at worker level. Comparing Figures 9.3 with 9.4 and 9.5 suggests that *de jure* structures at worker level act by reducing the difference in influence between senior managers and workers more than by increasing the influence of workers as such. Comparing Figures 9.5 and 9.4 with 9.7 also demonstrates how difficult it is for formal measures alone to assure that influence actually reaches the lowest level of organization, that is to say workers.

We can summarize this part of the country comparisons by saying that the relationship between *de jure* and *de facto* participation is strong at the level of representative bodies and when we compare *de jure* rights for workers with an index of Influence Inequality between the top and bottom of the hierarchy (Level D–A). However, a comparison of Figures 9.3 and 9.7 shows that, while Yugoslavia's position remains the same, the position of other countries on these variables varies. This means that, in addition to registering a significant general

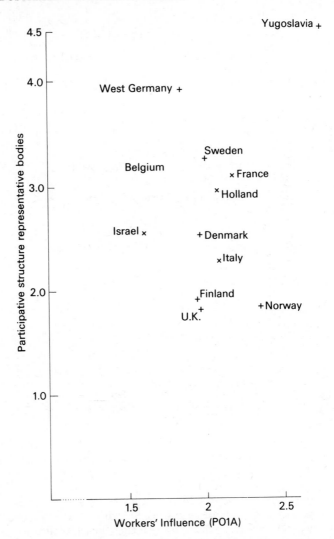

Figure 9.5 Formal participation of representative bodies and workers' Influence

trend, we have to be prepared to look for supplementary country-specific explanations. We come to this later.

De Facto Participation and Outcomes

Several interesting cross-national results were reported in Chapter 8. Even a cursory examination of Figures 8.1, 8.2, 8.5, 8.6, and 8.7 demonstrates that Yugoslavia and West Germany consistently show more positive results on outcome variables than the other ten countries,

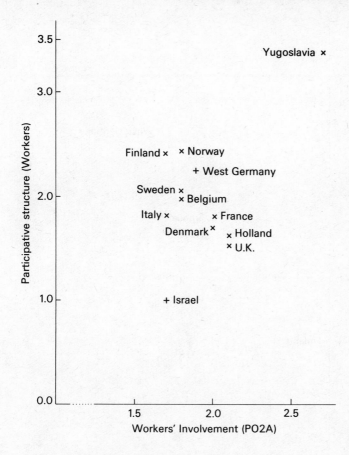

Figure 9.6 Formal participation of workers and their Involvement

A useful index is the assessment of the Consequences of Representative Participation (OROC-R). It uses questions like: 'Do people know more about what is going on here as a result of the work of the main representative body?' 'Do people accept decisions more easily?' 'Has the quality of decisions improved?' Yugoslavia ranks first and West Germany second. Norway also comes very high. Israel and Italy come lowest (see Table 1 in Chapter 8). It is also interesting that workers, supervisors, and managers are largely in agreement on this overall assessment.

The relationship between the assessment of the Consequences of Representative Participation (OROC-R) and Influence at worker level (PO1a) is shown in Figure 9.8 (the statistical data can be found in Table 8.23. Once again Yugoslavia is highest on both variables and Israel is lowest. West Germany is relatively high on both but most other countries occupy an undifferentiated middle position.

If in Figure 9.8 we substitute an assessment of the Consequences of Direct Participation, (OROC-D) the relationship, while not shown here, virtually

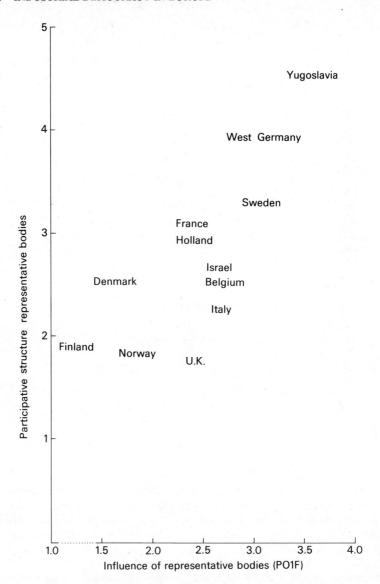

Figure 9.7 Formal participation and the Influence of representative bodies

disappears (see Table 8.23). Yugoslavia still comes highest on both variables and Israel comes fairly low. The second highest association on both variables, however, is now occupied by Norway instead of West Germany.

Two other questionnaires gives us an employee evaluation of the representative system and their interest in it (OPART-E and OPART-I). Yugoslavia and

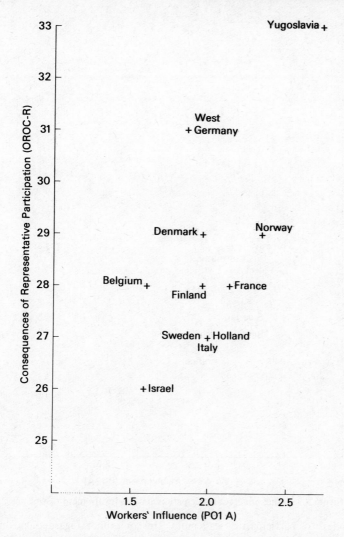

Figure 9.8 The Consequences of Representative Participation and the Influence of workers

West Germany occupy the first two ranks while Italy and Israel share the lowest two ranks on both.[14]

The percentage of people who are willing to be candidates for the representative body provides us with a good indication of interest and motivation. In Yugoslavia, 55 per cent of respondents who are *not* representatives are prepared to take on this task (in West Germany it is 21 per cent). Of those who are or were representatives, 88 per cent in West Germany and 75 per cent in Yugoslavia want to be candidates again. In most other countries, the percentages are substantially lower.

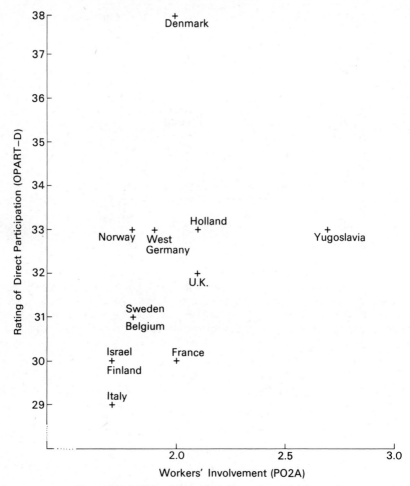

Figure 9.9 Rating of Direct Participation and the Involvement of workers

Attitudes to participative leadership are sometimes regarded as outcome variables but can also be treated as contingencies. We asked questions like: 'How often does your superior consult with you?' 'If you have an opinion different from your superior, can you say so?' (OPART-D). Yugoslavia, West Germany, Norway, and Holland achieve equally high scores on this variable, while Italy, Israel, France, and Finland have low scores.[15] Results from Chapter 7 (see Tables 21 and 22) show that participative leadership is, at the company level of analysis, one of the main predictors of the extent of actual involvement at worker level. We illustrate this correlation at the country level in Figure 9.9.

We can sum up by saying that, while substantial country differences in outcome variables exist, the largest correlation between participation and outcomes was that shown in Chapter 8, Figure 8, which followed a pattern fairly similar to Figure 9.7 above. The pattern is familiar and repetitive but this characteristic is itself of some importance, as we shall see.

Contingency Variables and Participation

One can regard the number of disagreements or conflicts in the decision-making process either as a contingency or as an outcome variable in an analysis of participation. Most of the literature in this field leads to the prediction that as participation increases, disagreements will decrease. It must be stressed that our measure of disagreement or Conflict, is a judgement based on what happens in relation to our set of sixteen decisions and has nothing to do with overt behaviour like strikes. For instance, the U.K. which has a high rate of strikes has one of the lower indices of disagreement as measured on our decision-set. When countries are plotted on numbers of disagreements and workers' Influence (PO1a), an apparently ill-defined picture emerges (Figure 9.10). However, some interesting observations can be made. Norway and Yugoslavia are very high on both conflict and Influence and Israel is relatively moderate to low on both. Italy, Sweden, and Holland fall in between. Belgium is an exception. It shares with Israel the lowest score on Influence but has a very high rate of disagreement on our decision-set. One possible explanation is in terms of the complexity of the present industrial relations system in Belgium. Unions there appear to be deeply divided by religious and political differences and the industrial relations climate has been 'characterized by a latent tension' based on a very high rate of unemployment, a rapidly deteriorating economic situation, and closing down of enterprises (IDE 1980, 171).

The complex relationship between participation and Conflict (disagreements) is of theoretical interest and we have obtained similar evidence elsewhere (Rus et al. 1977). In that project, conflicts were carefully analysed longitudinally over a two-year period in seven different enterprises in three countries. The findings give a clear indication that greater involvement in participative decision-making is accompanied by increased levels of conflict, although, once again, the conflicts are related to specific decisions and do not correlate with overt behaviour like strikes.

Among the semi-structural contingency variables, formalization is of potential interest in view of the finding in Chapter 7 that it contributes to greater equalization of the influence of management and workers when company is the unit of analysis. The country-level analysis is shown in Figure 9.11. Plotting the difference in influence between senior management and workers against the degree of formalization (that is to say, the number of written rules, procedures, and instructions), one finds a moderate to weak correlation. Yugoslavia, which has the highest degree of Formalization, also has the highest worker-management equalization of influence. Italy and France, which have low influence-equalization, also have little Formalization of rules and procedures. Belgium, Norway, and Holland deviate somewhat from this pattern.

One could hypothesize that countries which prescribe a high degree of formal participative structure for the permanent representative body (PS level F) would also tend to have organizations with more formal written rules and procedures

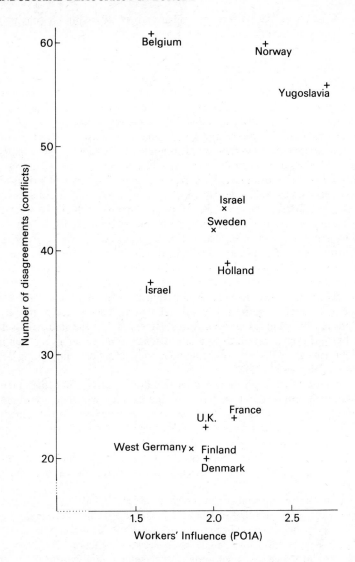

Figure 9.10 Conflict and the Influence of workers

(see Figure 9.12). It is, of course, quite possible that the direction of causation goes the other way. This explanation is particularly likely when one correlates Formalization with the extent of workers' Actual Involvement in decision-making (PO2a). This relationship, though not illustrated separately, follows a very similar trend to that shown in Figure 9.12 Yugoslavia and Israel are respectively very high and very low on both dimensions; Norway, West Germany, Denmark, and the U.K. follow this trend very closely at in-between levels.

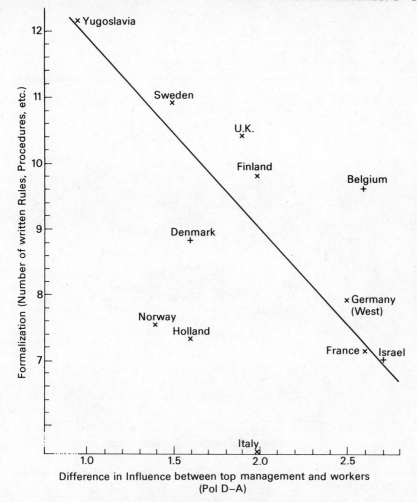

Figure 9.11 Formalization in the organization and inequality in the distribution of Influence

Previous research on the relationships between formalization, participation, and group autonomy support this finding (Payne et al. 1971, Pheysey et al. 1971, Warner 1972). The authors argued, on the basis of their findings, that formal regulations, rules, and procedures aid, rather than inhibit, participation, group relations, and innovation. It seems that managers may find it easier to share influence with lower levels when conditions and limits for influence-sharing are sanctioned within the formal rules and procedures laid down by policy. However, such a correlation between dimensions of participation rather than for systems with extensive self-management at lower levels. Autonomy probably requires flexibility which pre-determined rules and regulations inhibit.

Finally, we look at a contingency variable called Mobilization. As was explained

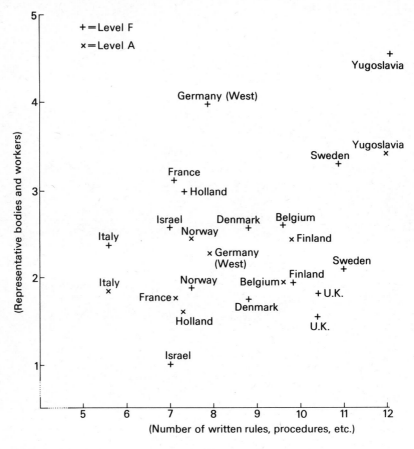

Figure 9.12 Formal participation of both representative bodies and workers and Formalization in the organization

in Chapter 7, this index is a measure which combines the extent of unionization with the number of employees who have been representatives on participative committees. At the level of organization, Chapter 7 showed that Mobilization has a strong and consistent effect on the Influence of representative bodies (see Table 7.12). We plot this relationship at the country level in Figure 9.13 but it fails to show any clear trend. Countries that are very low in Mobilization, like France and Holland, have the same amount of representative body Influence as countries with very high levels of Mobilization like Denmark and Norway. This position changes very significantly, however, if we assume that trade union strength and representative membership must be supported by formal participative structures. In Figure 9.14 for each country we have multiplied the index of Mobilization by the measure of formal participative structure (PS(F)) and related it to the Influence of the main representative body (PO1(F)). A very

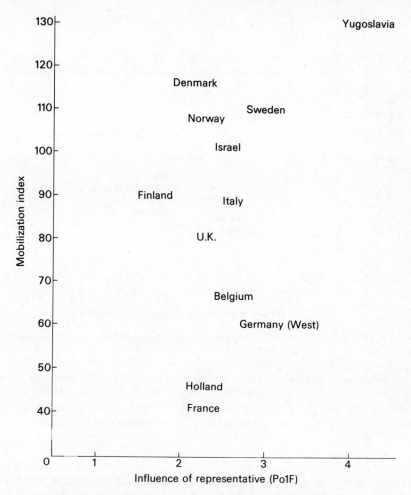

Figure 9.13 Mobilization and the Influence of representative bodies

clear correlation emerges. The relationship between PO1(F) and this combined index of Mobilization and PS(F), in fact, is stronger than the relationship between PO1(F) and either one of the other two variables taken separately (compare Figure 9.14 with Figures 9.7 and 9.13). When comparing Figures 9.13 and 9.14 it is particularly instructive to observe the changes in the position of Finland, the U.K., and West Germany. Finland and the U.K. are relatively high on Mobilization alone but take up a much lower position relative to other countries when this index is weighted by formal structural support, while West Germany moves up from tenth place to fifth when legislative support is included in the combined index. We will argue later that this is a good example of the phenomenon of choice which appears to emerge from this research. In this particular example, Finland's 'choice' not to support high mobilization with formal measures

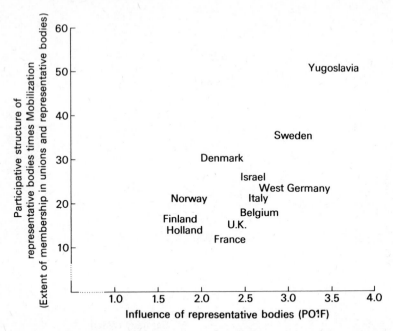

Figure 9.14 Mobilization (weighted by formal structural support for representative bodies) and the Influence of representative bodies

leads to a loss of effectiveness if we define this term to stand for influence of, or on behalf of, workers. West Germany, on the other hand, faced with low mobilization, has 'chosen' to strengthen the effectiveness of influence by giving formal legislative support to participation at the representative-body level.

OVERVIEW

We must now attempt to give an explanation of the results presented above. To help achieve this objective in Figure 9.15 we have drawn a simple descriptive picture of the theoretical framework on which this research is based (see IDE 1976 and Chapter 2 in this book). In each box, representing a group of variables, we have placed six countries. Countries placed towards the top end of each box achieve high scores on the variable in question while those at the bottom end have low scores. The interrelations between the major variables described by the boxes in this figure have been shown in Figures 9.3 to 9.14. We have shown only six countries to keep the situation fairly simple. We chose five of them because they tend to come high or low on many of the variables and the sixth, Britain, because it occupies an interesting in-between position which we will analyse later. We have concentrated our comparative analysis at the level of the main representative body and the worker level.

A reasonable explanation of the overall results just presented is as follows. In our twelve-country sample one country stands out with almost completely

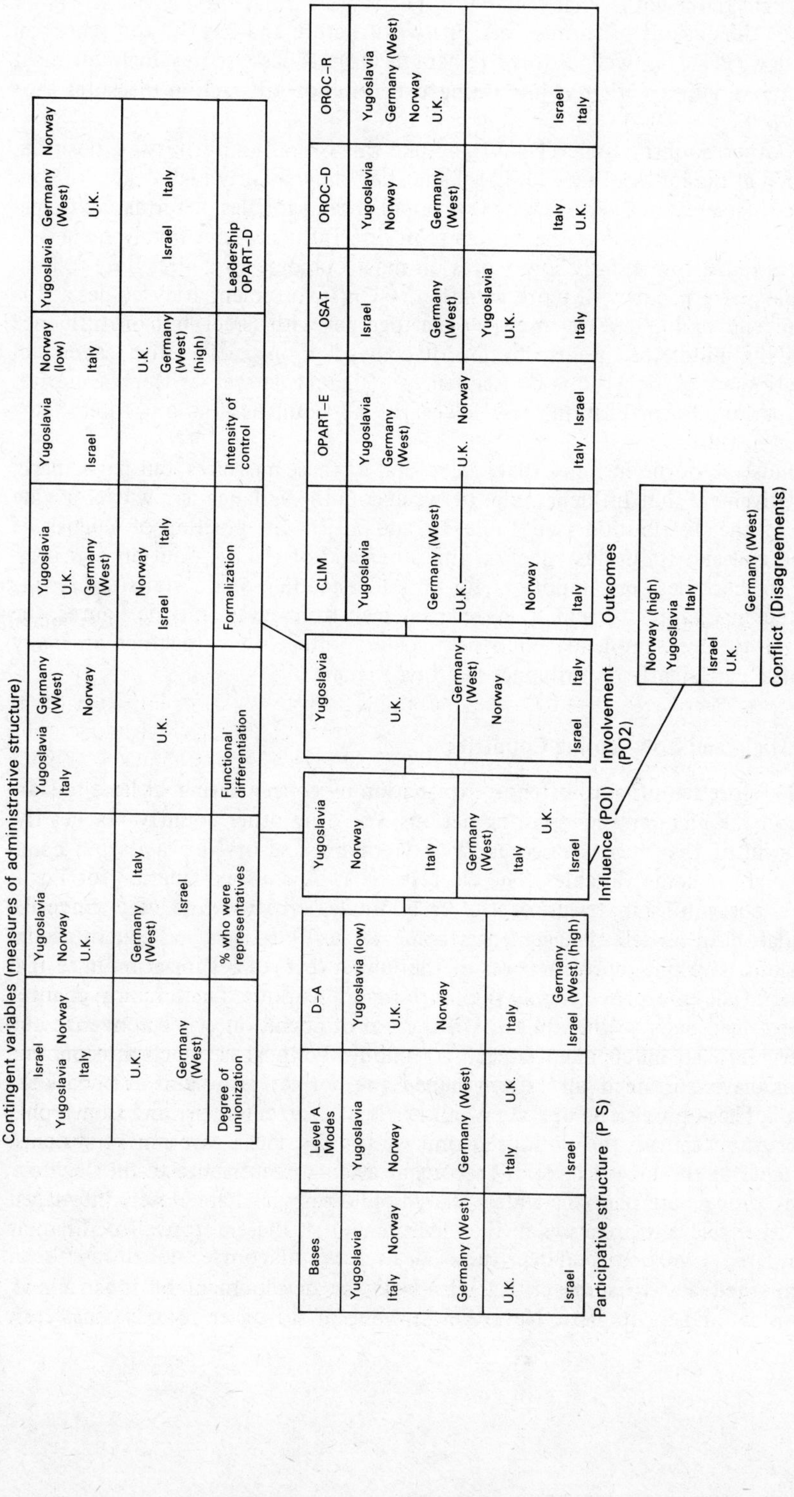

Contingent variables (measures of administrative structure)

	Israel Yugoslavia Norway Italy	Yugoslavia Norway U.K.	Yugoslavia Germany (West) Italy	Yugoslavia U.K. Germany (West)	Yugoslavia	Norway (low) Italy	Yugoslavia Germany (West) U.K.	Norway
	U.K. Germany (West)	Germany Italy (West) Israel	U.K.	Norway Israel Italy		U.K. Germany (West) (high)	Israel Italy	
	Degree of unionization	% who were representatives	Functional differentiation	Formalization	Intensity of control		Leadership OPART–D	

Participative structure (P S)

Bases	Level A Modes	D–A			
Yugoslavia	Yugoslavia	Yugoslavia (low)			
Italy Norway	Norway	U.K.			
Germany (West)	Germany (West)	Norway			
U.K.	Italy U.K.	Italy			
Israel	Israel	Germany Israel (West) (high)			

Influence (POI)

	Yugoslavia	Yugoslavia
	Norway	
		Italy
	Germany (West)	Germany (West)
	Italy	Norway
	U.K.	U.K.
	Israel	Israel Italy

Involvement (PO2)

Norway (high)
Yugoslavia
Italy
Israel
U.K.
Germany (West)

Conflict (Disagreements)

Outcomes

CLIM	OPART–E	OSAT	OROC–D	OROC–R
Yugoslavia	Yugoslavia Germany (West)	Israel	Yugoslavia Norway	Yugoslavia Germany (West) Norway U.K.
Germany (West)	U.K. Norway	Germany (West)	Germany (West)	
U.K.		Yugoslavia U.K.		
Norway				
Italy	Italy Israel	Italy	Italy U.K.	Israel Italy

Figure 9.15 Overview: Selected country results for workers and representative bodies

consistent results and with very high scores on all the main variables in our theoretical framework. That country is Yugoslavia. It has the highest scores on all three dimensions of formal participative structure and has the top scores on Influence (PO1) as well as Involvement (PO2). It also scores high on most outcome variables with the interesting exception of satisfaction measures (not shown in Figure 9.14).

No other country achieves anything like this overall uniformity of position, although at the low-scoring end, Israel and Italy show a fairly high degree of consistency. Israel scores very low or low on all three variables of formal participative structure. It also has the lowest scores on Influence and Involvement and achieves fairly consistently low scores on most outcome variables. Italy follows a similar pattern but with more variation.[17] On Involvement Italy comes at the bottom end of our twelve-country scale together with Israel, but on Influence it is in the middle of the distribution. It comes low on participative leadership, Evaluation of participation, Consequences of Direct, as well as Representative, Participation, Formalization, and lowest of all countries on our three Satisfaction measures.

It must be borne in mind that, on several of these measures, but particularly on Involvement and Influence, the between-country variance is low over a wide range of the distribution (see Table 7.2 and 7.17). The position of Yugoslavia on one end and Italy plus Israel on the other end of the distribution of scores, therefore becomes very important for an understanding of the statistical results reported in Chapters 7 and 8. As can be seen from several of the figures, the majority of our sample of countries cluster quite closely together on many variables, particularly on Influence and Involvement.

High- and Low-scoring Countries

It is therefore tempting to offer an explanation by concentrating, at least to start with, on the high- and low-scoring nations. While no other country reaches the high level of the Yugoslav scores, West Germany and/or Norway often come fairly high on some variables. The clearest, most obvious explanation for Yugoslavia's position is in terms of the early implementation and very extensive formulation of its self-management scheme. Since 1950, legal and constitutional provisions have put representatives of the lowest level of organization in formal control of all enterprises employing more than 5 workers. These radical changes can be traced back to the upheaval of the war of liberation which converted the country into an independent socialist republic. Political as much as economic reasons have sustained and strengthened the formal provisions for workers' control. These provisions operate at all levels of each enterprise and isomorphic support comes from the political, community, and local government systems. The rights of the lowest level of the organization to contribute to the decision-making process are part of a widely-shared philosophy and are closely integrated with other relevant processes in the environment of the enterprise (see Chapter 12 in IDE, 1980). In practice, these ideals have, of course, not always been implemented and to some critical observers the development has been excessively slow and incomplete. Nevertheless, none of the other countries has such an extensive scheme, or has had quite such a long time to develop it.

In several respects, West Germany is closer to Yugoslavia than any of the other countries. In the first place, the motivation for its co-determination legislation can also be traced back to the upheaval suffered by trade unions during the Hitler regime, although in this case historic precedents for movements to increase the rights of workers goes back a long time before 1945. Secondly, as in the case of Yugoslavia, legislative provision for a form of industrial democracy started in 1951 and had therefore had twenty-five years of continuous development by the time our research was carried out. The West German system of co-determination was relatively uncontroversial when it was first introduced[18] but, in more recent years, legal extensions of the scheme have been increasingly opposed by employers' organizations. The biggest difference between the West German and Yugoslav systems of industrial democracy, however, is in West Germany's much less radical and less integrated provisions for workers' influence over all aspects of enterprise decision-making (see Chapter 7, IDE 1980).

Norway, which frequently achieves high scores on our variables, has had an extensive tradition of collective bargaining, including local-level worker representation. However, although advisory committees of worker representatives were set up as early as 1945 and were then 'seen as an important step towards socialism' (IDE, 1980, 26), there has been little legislative provision until quite recently. The public debate about the advantages and disadvantages of putting workers on the Board of Directors has been going on for many years. There was, and is, a tendency for many Norwegians, including social scientists, to prefer voluntaristic national and company-based schemes aimed at promoting worker autonomy and bargaining rights over work-place issues, instead of putting worker representatives into positions of influence at higher levels. Consequently, a law to give employees one-third representation at Board-room level was only passed in 1973. However, the position of unions is very strong and they expect to be consulted by Governments on most major economic policy issues.

The country-specific descriptions we have just given are probably an adequate explanation for the position of Yugoslavia and, to a lesser extent, West Germany, but many of the industrial relations characteristics typical of Norway are to be found also in other countries, for instance in Sweden.

In our twelve-country sample, Israel has the lowest scores for formal participative structures (PS), both in terms of the number of Bases, that is to say, legislative and other provisions, and in terms of Modes, that is to say the degree and extent of support for these structures. In terms of our major hypotheses, these facts alone would, of course, adequately explain why our sample of Israeli companies achieve such low scores on Influence (PO1) and Involvement (PO2), On many of our contingency measures, as well as outcomes, Israel also comes low (see Figure 9.15).

It is important to stress at this point that companies in our Israeli sample do not come from the Kibbutz part of the economic sector. This was a deliberate choice, although most previous research into participation in Israel concentrated on these more innovative institutions (for instance, Tannenbaum et al. 1974). Our findings are, therefore, in no way comparable to this other research. However, the Histadrut sector of the economy, from which our sample was drawn, has its own interesting history of political involvement, trade union ideology, and worker-participation objectives. Until 1977 the Histadrut (Jewish Federation of Labour) was closely inter-linked with the then-dominant political party and played a leading role in all major social and economic decisions for nearly fifty years. However, during a large part of the country's history, Israel, then Palestine, operated under the British Mandatory Authority. This influence has to some extent survived to the present day and may account for the circumstance that, except for state-owned companies, there is no legal support for worker participation in the management of Israeli companies.

The Histadrut has the uneasy task of combining social ownership of industry with trade union principles and social democratic values. Over the last thirty years it has adopted resolutions favouring the introduction of participation programmes and in 1956 formally adopted a programme of Plant Councils to be established by all their enterprises. The scheme was not successful and 'ended for all practical purposes in 1961 when the last councils disappeared quietly' (Rosenstein 1973). Thus, a scheme of Joint Management for involvement at higher levels of the individual enterprise met with continuous difficulties. It was conceived in the early 1960s but was formally introduced only in 1968. Implementation of the scheme was very slow and was often faced with the objections of managers and the indifference of workers in the Histadrut-owned enterprises, which had to be overcome in each case before the scheme could be introduced. In many enterprises of the Histadrut the joint management programme was introduced on the initiative of the central bodies of the Histadrut rather than resulting from a perceived need for it by the managers and workers concerned. It should also be remembered that in the past employees of the Histadrut-owned enterprises were in many cases ideologically motivated and their identification with the Histadrut's policy and approach was strong. In recent years, however, ideological identification has weakened and many employees see little difference between an enterprise which is owned by the Histadrut and those which belong to the private sector or are state-owned enterprises. One should also bear in mind that, within the small Israeli sample of enterprises, two of the larger ones did not have joint management when the data were collected (a further analysis of individual plants would, therefore, be of special interest). A combination of the circumstances we have just described would account for the consistently low scoring of the Israeli sample.

While the Italian situation is quite different from Israel's in most respects, they share two circumstances which are very important for our research theme. In the first place 'there is no legally defined, detailed institutional framework for participation at plant level (and) there is no system of co-determination, nor are there Works' Councils or other legally defined bi-partite (labour-management) bodies at company level' (IDE 1980, 208). Secondly, there was an attempt after 1945 to establish a type of co-determination scheme but it 'failed and was abandoned by the early 1950's' (Zanzardo 1977, quoted in IDE 1980, 208). This negative experience has led to a widespread disappointment with the notion of influence-sharing by way of participative schemes. It has also consolidated the trade unions' opposition to such schemes.

The major Italian legislation in support of worker and union rights came as late as 1970 and even now there remains some doubt about the validity of the as-yet-unrepealed Fascist civil code which gives employers and managers 'the exclusive power to manage, organize, and run the productive activities within the enterprise' (IDE 1980, 204). On the positive side, the unions have been able to achieve a substantial degree of unity and co-operation in recent years, particularly at plant level. This greater unity, combined with the establishment of the Factory Councils in the early 1970's, has enabled the unions to strengthen and consolidate their position at plant level, while at the same time enabling them to enlarge substantially the area or scope of work-place bargaining.

These various idiosyncratic aspects of the Italian industrial relations scene go a long way towards explaining the findings in our research. Compared to other countries Italy has a relatively high PS Base score, i.e. formal rules regulating participation in decision-making tend to be particularly prevalent in Italy. More often than not, however, these regulations derive from, or are grounded in management norms rather than legislation or collective bargaining agreements (see Chapter 6, Figure 6.2). The degree or intensity of the given participation (PS Mode) prescribed by these formal rules for both workers and representative bodies is among the lowest in our sample. The Influence (PO1) of representative bodies in Italy is, nevertheless, relatively high when compared to that of similar bodies in other countries (Figure 9.5). When it comes to workers, however, as Figure 9.15 shows, Italy comes low on Influence (PO1) and even lower on Involvement (PO2) and low also on participative leadership (OPART–D). The Italian sample scores uniformly low on all outcome variables.

A Middle Position: the U.K.

When this research started, it was thought that the inclusion of the U.K. would give the multi-national comparison a useful limiting case. Alone among the twelve countries the U.K. has neither legislation for any aspect of industrial democracy nor a strong centralized collective bargaining system. If formal participative structures (PS) were the only determining factor in producing high levels of worker influence or involvement, then U.K. companies would score lower than others. It was thought possible, however, that even if formal industrial democracy structures were to account for a significant part of the variance of *de facto* participation, other compensating factors might intervene. The major difference between the U.K. industrial relations system since 1945 and that of the other countries is the considerable decentralization of trade union collective bargaining to local and factory levels. This is backed up by a strong, and at times even aggressive, shop steward system based on individual factories (IDE 1980).

In the 1950s there was an upsurge of management-initiated schemes of consultation, most of which died out within a decade. They tended to deal with very marginal issues like the proverbial chipped tea-cups in the works canteen; some cut across the union machinery and were seen as antithetical to it and many appeared to have been started as a deliberate way of weakening plant-based collective bargaining.

The official position of the Trade Union Congress is to favour a scheme of genuine industrial democracy in which unions would occupy half the seats on a single-tier Board of Directors, linked up with established channels of plant-based trade union negotiating machinery. This is unlikely to happen in the near future. At the time the research took place, and at the time of writing, most British firms in the sectors covered would experience influence-sharing or involvement as occurring primarily through plant-based trade union or *ad hoc* machinery. Nevertheless, the extent of unionization in the U.K. (as well as in the U.K. sample of companies) is lower than in Yugoslavia, Norway, or Italy, though higher than in West Germany (see Figure 9.15 and Table 5.5 in Chapter 5). This factor might reduce some of the impact of nationally- or regionally-based collective bargaining efforts and might help to explain the U.K.'s relatively low position on Influence (PO1).

However, the main reason for the U.K.'s low score on Influence, given the hypothesis underlying this research, is the virtual absence of formal participative bases, particularly for main representative bodies (see Chapter 6, Table 6.2). Among the twelve countries only Israel has lower scores on the number of formal supporting structures (Bases) as well as on their participative intensity (Mode). Given these facts, it might seem surprising that the U.K.'s workers come fairly high on Involvement (PO2), higher than Norway's West Germany's, or Sweden's.

It will be remembered that Involvement is measured by asking every employee to describe how much he is able to participate on each of the sixteen different decisions. The range of alternatives which he can endorse follow a Guttman-type scale from 'not being involved at all' to 'being able to decide on his own'. It seems likely that the respondents to these questions described involvement in the decision-making process which did not depend on the formal structural support given by legislation or nationally-based norms. From Figure 9.15 it can be seen that U.K. employees gave relatively low scores to their evaluation of the Consequences of Direct Participation (OROC–D) but relatively high scores to their assessment of representative participation. In the U.K., representative participation in nearly all cases in our sample operates through the plant-elected shop steward system. It seems likely, then, that the relatively high scores on Involvement are due to the U.K. worker's judgement of his own impact on company-based decisions through the shop steward system.

If this explanation is accepted, it follows that effective participation in organizations can be achieved by a combination of different circumstances. Minimally, one can suppose that compensating factors exist which can make up for the deficiency of a given determinant. Maximally, one could postulate a theory of equi-finality in which a number of different determinants have equal opportunities for producing a given outcome. The evidence available to us from this research suggests something substantially less than equi-finality. It looks as if even the most robust locally-based shop steward system does not achieve the same Influence (PO1) in the U.K. as the more norm-based schemes in other countries. We would not wish to argue that involvement is more or less desirable than influence but it is an alternative.

THE CONCEPT OF CHOICE

The evidence and arguments we have presented point towards the existence of compensating mechanisms giving organizations and countries a useful measure of choice. Choice does not have to be conscious or recognised. The data presented in Chapters 7 and 8 have already stressed multicausality, for instance in regression analyses. It was pointed out that, at the current stage of development of industrial democracy schemes, a human resources theory operationalized through participative leadership practices is probably complementary and supportive rather than inimical to power-devolution philosophy and practice.

The concept of choice is becoming increasingly important in the study of organizational behaviour. It can be developed at various levels. In studying the relationship between machines and social motivation at the shop-floor level, the joint optimization of both the social and technological 'imperative' was held to be superior to traditional attempts at maximizing either factor (Trist and Bamforth 1951). The precise relationship between sub-optimal variables gives designers of socio-technical systems a wide measure of choice (Emery 1969). At higher systems levels, Child (1972) has argued for a choice model in opposition to the more prevalent deterministic theories.

Contingency theories are widely misunderstood, in part because there are many quite distinct conceptualizations (Heller et al. 1976, Heller and Wilpert forthcoming). They have been criticized for being excessively normative and rigid, for opposing change, and for denying the existence of choice (Millar 1978). Where they postulate a form of environmental determinism, as in recent theories by Pfeffer and Salancik (1978), this criticism is probably justified. Moreover, the validity of many deterministic contingency models has been challenged (Pennings 1975). In other contingency models, as in the present research, the possibility of change and the opportunity for choice are highlighted. Variables are examined to see whether they increase predictability or moderate the relationship between two or more sets of conditions.

We have already given several examples. The correlations between Mobilization and Influence (Figure 9.13) and between institutional norms and Influence (Figure 9.7) were substantially increased by weighting Mobilization with institutional norms (PS) and vice versa (Figure 9.14). It was shown that substituting an Evaluation of Direct for Representative Participation reduces the correlation with Influence (Figure 9.8). The relationship between participative structure and participative practice shifted substantially when we substituted measures for the representative body for worker-level measures (Figures 9.6 and 9.7). The example of the U.K. provides a particularly good illustration of the notion of choice at higher system levels.

Choice also exists within a given set of variables, for instance participative structures (PS). This was illustrated in Chapter 6 in relation to the variety of Bases or norms used in each country. Our measures distinguish ten possibilities from constitutional norms via national, regional or sectoral collective bargaining to management policy. Figure 6.2 in Chapter 6 presents a very condensed summary; the fuller analysis will have to be left for later publications, but it shows interesting differences between countries. France and Holland, for instance, use no managerial norms, while Italy and Belgium use this method predominantly. Holland and France both rely mainly on legal norms but the Mode score for both countries at worker level, that is to say the intensity of the prescribed involvement at that level, is very low (see Table 6.4). Italy and Belgium achieve higher Mode scores at worker level with less legal prescription and more managerial norms. Yugoslavia is probably a special case but it achieves its very high Mode and participation scores largely through management norms.[19]

The choice element becomes even clearer when we try to explain the impact of different formal structures (PS) on countries that achieve high influence for workers. Yugoslavia and Norway achieve the highest scores on worker Influence (Figure 9.15) but by diametrically different formal structures. Yugoslavia uses a lot of management norms and very little legal provision while the exact reverse is the case in Norway (Chapter 6, Figure 6.2).

Even at the global level of analysis, we saw in Chapter 7 that different formal structures (laws, collective bargaining, and managerial policies), or combinations of structures, account for high levels of Influence (PO1) and high levels of compliance with norms (see for instance Chapter 7, Table 7.10). Generalizing over the whole sample of twelve countries, it seems that legal structures exert a major impact on dismissals decisions but management norms are more important in bringing about high levels of influence on levels of pay and holiday dates. Finally, collective bargaining structures are important in increasing influence over the remaining twelve decisions.

In each case the norms we have mentioned as primary are backed up by at least one other norm which also exerts a significant effect. This means that, for any one country faced with a policy decision in this field, the possibility of substituting a different combination of norm structures to achieve a given outcome should not be ruled out. Choice, based on the kind of evidence presented here, presents opportunities for policy-making.

SUMMARY

In the last three sections we have used the theoretical model to compare the position of countries on most variables. By concentrating on countries that consistently show high or low correlations between major dimensions of the model, we were able to confirm the association between participative structures and participative behaviour as measured by one or both influence and involvement variables. The contingency and outcome variables also follow the high-low trend.

These explanations are meaningful for five countries. The remaining seven countries do not follow any very consistent pattern, but it seems likely that these apparent 'inconsistencies' can also be adequately explained by drawing on a knowledge of historical social and economic circumstances. Even the high-low scoring countries show some 'inconsistencies' which benefit from situationally-derived analysis.

Within and beyond the consistent correlations one can identify important areas of choice where substitution of alternative arrangements appears to lead to comparable outcomes. Analysis of these choices should be increased because it speaks to the situation facing the real world and facilitates the implementation of desirable social changes.

In an earlier part of this chapter we submitted our data to several statistical analyses to see whether a stable cluster or profile of countries emerged. We could only find significant differences between Nordic and Latin 'cultures' on two variables.[20] A review of some recent literature revealed the existence of findings to support both the culture-cluster and the more situationally- or contingency-oriented theories. We hope that by our methods of analysis we have contributed to the discussion relating to these opposing positions. It can be argued that the culture-cluster approach is simple and elegant while the contingency approach is complex and ungraceful.

At the level of pragmatism and the contribution of social science research to social policy, the relatively inelegant findings analysed above have advantages. For instance, as we have said, by identifying the existence of choices, one facilitates the design of policy options. Some of the options operate at the level of companies or industrial sectors, others at the macro-level of countries and legislative provisions. Adjustments of this kind can take place within a relatively short period of time. On the other hand, most definitions of national culture, or even socio-economic factors like class structure or Gross Domestic Product assume societal forces that are not easily influenced by organizations and Governments.

Interpretation of cross-national findings should not be influenced by some pre-determined preference for elegance versus pragmatism. The evidence must speak for itself.

NOTES

1 Many members of the international team have made valuable suggestions towards the text of this chapter. In particular the help of Cor Lammers, Riccardo Peccei, and Bengt Stymne is gratefully acknowledged. The Belgian team, Pol Coetsier and Marnix Ryckaert, were joint planners of the multi-variate computer analysis and the Ghent Applied Psychology Computer Centre carried out the calculations. Marc Buelens was attached to the Tavistock Institute for an academic year during which time he contributed very usefully to our work.

2 Not all, of course, are cross-national, but the methodological problems are similar.

3 According to the Shorter Oxford English Dictionary.

4 During the 1930s in Europe the term 'Kultur' was used by some authors to justify theories of racial superiority.

5 The three questions relate to (i) greater or less perceived fear to disagree with superiors, (ii) subordinates' perception of their boss's decision-making behaviour, and (iii) subordinates' dependence or counter-dependence needs.

6 This refers to the European Co-ordination Centre for Research and Documentation in Social Science based in Vienna.

7 Two computer programmes were chosen from a range available to us at the Applied Psychology Laboratory of the University of Ghent. One called HICLUS produces simple hierarchical clusters of all variables fed into the data matrix. Since this data reduction technique uses absolute difference scores for each set of variables, only homogeneous data like the various output variables were used for each analysis. In this way each major group of variables (PS, PO, and O) were analysed separately. In each case, the result was a hierarchical ordering of countries. Separate analyses were carried out for each sector, size, and skill dimension.

The second major programme used is called CORRESP. It is a multi-variate technique appropriate for the analysis of contingency tables. It compares in one analysis column and row profiles, and both dimensions of the table have an equivalent contribution to the final solution. Correspondence analysis standardizes row and column entries in order to correct for artificial differences in row or column size (e.g. because of sampling variation or differences in accessibility). Each row is then treated as a point in a space with as many dimensions as there are columns; through principal components analysis this space is reduced to a meaningful number of dimensions. Using a non-euclidian metric, closely related to Chi-square, one reaches a final solution that is identical to a solution found on a basis of treating each column as a point in a space with the rows as dimensions. The interchangeability of rows and columns is the major characteristic of the method.

8 One can raise the question whether the techniques were suitable for our data. Within the range of blind inductive methods using mechanistic search or structuring techniques, HICLUS and CORRESP constitute an appropriate choice, as the former analyses means and the latter profiles. Further support for CORRESP stems from the fact that the technique shows clear and meaningful clusters in the variables. One has to bear in mind, however, that the absence of consistent clusters for aggregate data does not imply an absence of clusters for subsets of variables, or at least substantial differences for some variables between pre-set clusters (see later).

In retrospect we would argue that in a field with heterogeneous data, the purely mechanistic techniques are not very suitable because they do not allow, to any great extent, the identification of the variables on which to concentrate in the search for meaningful clusters. Semi-mechanistic techniques (e.g. discriminant analysis, which presupposes certain clusters) could be attempted for secondary analysis. The problem arises then, of course, which part of the results can be attributed to information stemming from the data and which part to the predefined structure.

The difference between 'blind' and 'pre-set' methods of analysis raises many issues of research epistemology to which we cannot address ourselves here.

9 It is, of course, arguable that the name Anglo-German does not fit Holland. In terms of language, history, and tradition, however, the grouping can be defended.

10 The work was done by Cor Lammers and used non-parametric statistics separated for sector and size on thirteen variables. By leaving out Israel, Finland, and Yugoslavia, a result similar to that shown in Figure 9.1 is produced.

11 Conflict is a complex variable. Many definitions of power assume that conflict of interest must exist before power is exercised. As was seen in Chapter 7, our measure is of the number of disagreements between the parties concerned on our sixteen decision issues. This measure of disagreement conflict can be regarded as an intervening variable or as an outcome.

12 While we use the term 'country' for simplicity, we should really refer to our country sample, that is to say, the companies making up a particular country sample.

13 It must be remembered that, as we saw in Chapter 7, the analysis at the level of companies, showed a significantly positive relationship between these two variables.

14 See Chapter 8, Table 8.2. Denmark and West Germany actually share the second and third rank between them but, at this stage, we are not analysing the Danish position in the sample.

15 See Chapter 8, Table 8.8. We take these results from the workers' level. Denmark has the highest scores; only Sweden of the Scandinavian countries occupies a relatively low position on this assessment of participative leadership.

16 It may be relevant to remember that Israel is the only country in our sample which, at the time of the research, was virtually in a state of war with its neighbouring countries. It is possible that this external factor led workers to minimize their disagreements with management.

17 In particular, its participative structure Base score is very high while its Mode score is low. This means that in Italy a large number of the decisions in our set are supported by laws, collective agreements, etc. (See Figure 6.2 in Chapter 6) but the extent of influence available through these formal measures is limited (see Table 5.4 in Chapter 5).

18 The Communist Party was one of the main opponents of co-determination at that time. The churches and the main political parties, backed by the Allied Control Commission, gave it a reasonable measure of support.

19 Yugoslavia is a special case because self-management norms came about through a process that is different from other countries. Management norms are backed by constitutional provision.

20 The two variables on which t-test analysis revealed significant statistical differences were the Quality of Management-Employee Relations (CLIM-R) and the Rating of Direct Participation (OPART-D). The culture cluster differences on the other variables did not reach statistical significance but we have already mentioned that further analyses are planned to examine these controversial issues.

10

THE SOCIAL SCIENTIFIC SIGNIFICANCE
OF THE IDE STUDY

In this chapter we review, from the perspective of the development of the social scientific study of participation, what we believe to be the most significant findings and lessons learned from the IDE project. The chapter is, thus, not an exhaustive review of the findings and methods used—these are provided at various places in the text—but rather a selective interpretation of the importance of the study in the context of received ideas. The chapter is divided into three broad sections; the first concerns the organization of the research, the second covers methodological issues, and third matters of theory and associated empirical findings. The practical significance of our findings are discussed in the next chapter.

ORGANIZATION OF THE RESEARCH

The IDE project involved some thirty researchers, from a variety of intellectual and disciplinary backgrounds, over a period of 7 years. In terms of size (research on 134 organisations with over 8,000 individual interviews spanning twelve nations) it is perhaps the largest collaborative inter-disciplinary piece of social science research ever conducted (other pertinent large scale international comparative studies are reviewed in Chapter 9). There are, of course, no intrinsic virtues in a large project unless the subject-matter warrants it—but surely in the case of international comparisons of industrial democracy the merits of exhaustiveness are immediately evident. Much of the strength of the IDE project does, in our opinion, rest with the breadth of its coverage. International research has been carried out before in this field but not very often across anything approaching twelve nations. Despite efforts to involve researchers, some Western European countries were unfortunately not represented in the study; nevertheless, we have, whatever the limitations of our chosen research methods, managed to embrace the major European systems of participation. What is more, a set of internationally cross-validated research instruments have, we believe, proved their worth in countries often very different culturally, politically, and economically. There was a certain audacity in mounting such an enterprise but the results do enable us to answer the basic question posed at the outset of the research as to the impact of PS (formally prescribed participation schemes) upon actual participation practice (PO) in selected organizations.

It is perhaps worthwhile, therefore, to ponder the organizational and administrative lessons we have learned over the seven year period for which the project has so far lasted:

i. The research was conducted on an international comparative basis but each national team, though committed to the core of the study, was free to make additional studies which they thought made sense in terms of their particular national systems. Thus we had, at the end of the research, not only the material for the international comparisons but twelve studies viable in their own right. This strategy had three advantages; first, it permitted a relatively high level of commitment and motivation on behalf of the national teams who may have had certain reservations about the international study; second, it allowed part of the study to reflect the different national standards and styles of research, method and theory; third, it effectively spread the risk—if the international comparative project had failed then the national studies were, at least in part, retrievable. This, particularly for the younger and less well-established researchers, held out the advantage of publications in nationally based social science journals with their own standards and traditions. We emphasize that all this was accomplished without putting into jeopardy the validity and comparability of the core instruments.

ii. The research was organized on a mixed centralized-decentralized basis. It became clear, because of intellectually divergent tendencies, that a strong administrative centre had to be established with clear authority over administrative matters. This was found to be entirely compatible with a highly participative intellectual style. All matters of design, theory and method were extensively debated between and amongst all national teams and, though universal agreement was not always arrived at, the sense of fair play, tolerance, and mutual concession established grounds upon which a centralized administrative structure (with its inevitable 'power') became acceptable to all.

iii. The analysis of the core international comparative data was largely carried out centrally—some effort at decentralized parallel analysis proved rather messy and unsuccessful. As it turned out the analysis was carried out at the administrative centre of the study (The International Institute of Management) but there is perhaps no necessary reason why this should have been so.

iv. The IDE research team elected an analysis sub-group both to oversee and to *partially initiate* details of the analysis. Although this necessarily reduced the level of participation and amounted to a certain centralization, it seemed inevitable given the way the analysis of the data was never as straightforward as one would have liked.

v. The project was financed both centrally, for international overheads, and at the level of each nation to cover the national research effort. Given the total cost of ventures on the scale of the IDE project, financing from one source seems unrealistic but, furthermore, the responsibility of national teams to their local sponsors had an obvious motivating effect.

In sum we believe that, through a certain amount of trial and error, we evolved suitable organizational principles upon which a large international collaborative study can be based. They amount to administrative centralization with extensive intellectual participation and establishing a core study embodying mutual concessions complemented by national studies which enhance the core study and are viable in their own right.

METHODOLOGICAL ISSUES

There is a profound sense in which a group of researchers coming from different intellectual backgrounds will, in settling their differences, tend to adopt a conservative posture. It is difficult for such a group to be methodologically innovative, the tendency always being to fall back on the tried and the true—to play safe. Despite this tendency, however, the IDE project has, we feel, been methodologically innovative in at least two respects.

First, our attempt to 'measure' the normative framework of participative systems (PS) comprises potentially an important step forward in social science research. Although there are many claims in the literature that the normative/legal framework of enterprises exerts a significant effect on their internal structure, to our knowledge there have been scarcely any systematic attempts to study this impact. What we have been able to do is (i) select a series of decisions (ii) locate these in terms of·formal Bases and Modes of prescribed participation in each national industrial relations system, and (iii) show the impact they have on the decision-making of the enterprise. The reader may wish to object to our selection of decisions but it would be difficult to deny the utility of our method. What we claim to have done is to provide a relatively easy and cheap method of reducing very complex participative systems to a relatively simple, but analytically-revealing, set of dimensions. Again the reader may wish to query some of the categories we have employed for the Base and Mode scales, but we think this would, in all probability, lead to an extension or reformulation of the categories rather than to a rejection of the overall method. Needless to say the proof of the validity of any set of instruments lies ultimately in their correlation with a given criterion variable.

Second, as we argued in Chapters 2 and 4, our measures of PO were, in the final analysis, reputational in nature and they may thus suffer from the cognitive and ideological biases identified in these chapters. There is also a very clear sense in which we are indebted to Tannenbaum (1968) and his colleagues. However, we have made a number of small innovations:

i. We have distinguished between Influence (PO1) and Involvement (PO2). The former is measured on a ranked 'influence scale' entirely parallel to Tannenbaum's. PO2, however, uses a 'behavioural scale' which we believe is probably less susceptible to cognitive biases. Furthermore, we based PO1 on responses from key personnel while PO2 was a self-rating scale applied to a sample of enterprise members. This strategy has a number of advantages. First we were able to study the relationship between PO1 and PO2. Clearly PO1 is quicker and cheaper to administer and, in the face of a high correlation between the two (i.e. high cross-validity), might have been regarded as the preferred instrument. Of course the response categories on the two scales differed (there is no intrinsic reason why this should be so but, as we pointed out above, with PO1 we were to a large degree replicating Tannenbaum's scale, while with PO2 we experimented with a behavioural scale). In practice, however, we interpreted PO1 and PO2 as measuring different aspects of participation (see Chapter 8) because the interrelation was not of the order of magnitude that would have warranted regarding them as alternative operationalizations of the same concept.

ii. We have used PO1 and PO2 as scales of participation (Influence and personal Involvement) over sixteen decision-making areas rather than inviting the respondent to generalize across all decisions (c.f. Tannenbaum). We would want to claim that this—especially when the decisions are further categorized into 'short-, medium-, and long-term'—gives a much better picture of the participation structure of an organization.

Thus, though the methodological innovations in the IDE study may be considered as modest, they were significant and their limitation was largely determined by pragmatic considerations. Aspirations to study decision-making over time and *in situ* and to draw fine conceptual distinctions—particularly in relation to 'power' and 'influence' had to be curtailed if the research was to be manageable for twelve countries. However, three countries, the U.K., Holland, and Yugoslavia, conducted a longitudinal study (Drenth et al., 1979).

THEORETICAL AND EMPIRICAL RESULTS

The IDE study was primarily designed to provide an answer to a politico-scientific question: 'What impact do the various European participation schemes (PS) have on the participation (Influence PO1 and personal Involvement PO2) of different groups in organizations?' In addition we were also concerned to see if PS, PO1, and PO2 affect attitudes.

At the most general level our salient conclusions may perhaps be expressed thus:

i. PS (Mode) though by no means explaining all the variance in PO1 and PO2 has a more significant effect than any other variables we measured. This is true for all groups (A to G) within and outside the organization and the effect is particularly significant for workers (Group A);

ii. PO1/PO2 have distinct 'effects' on selected outcomes (O);

iii. PS (Mode) has a distinct 'effect' on selected outcomes (O);

and following from (i):

iv. the characteristics of the enterprise ('technology', size, sector, etc) are relatively weak moderators (CON$_1$ Figure 2.2) or additional determinants (CON$_7$ Figure 2.2) of PO.

v. The characteristics of the individual organizational participant seem to be better predictors (additional determinants) than organizational characteristics.

These rather bold statements need, however, both interpretation and placing in theoretical context.

The International 'Sample'

Although we use the term international sample it should be emphasized that the 134 organizations studied were *not* randomly drawn stratified according to nation, though the 8,000 individual respondents were selected on a sampling basis (see Chapter 4) within each organization. Any inferences from our results to 'The Nations of Europe' should therefore be made with due caution. However, this said, our careful selection of organizations from two sectors should facilitate reasonably safe inferences at least for these sectors in each country. In addition, the analysis presented in Chapter 5 gives us reasonable assurance that the organizations selected were not atypical for the country in question and, furthermore, that they were reasonably uniform across nations. For instance Table 5.1 shows that the percentage of workers (group A) in the organizations averaged 82 per cent and varied only between 90 per cent (Yugoslavia) and 71 per cent (Norway). The proportions of supervisors (Group B) and managers (Groups C and D) were a little more variable but not dramatically so. The proportion of female respondents in the international 'sample' was 27 per cent—somewhat higher than the international average of women in the workforce—but this is attributable to the selection of the service sector. The degree of Unionization amongst the respondents in each country is strongly correlated with national figures (Spearman's Rho = 0.85, Table 5.5). Respondents at lower levels in the organizations were younger, had less tenure, less education, and comprised a lower proportion of men (again because of the service sector) than the corresponding population. The age distribution in the 'sample' seems reasonably representative.

When we turn to organizational characteristics it should be emphasized that the majority of the organizations studied were 'part' of a larger unit. Only 23.9 per cent were independent, the rest being either dependent branches or subsidiaries (Table 5.7). This may well colour our findings concerning the level of participation particularly of levels E (level above the plant), G (external groups), and D (top management). The countries were not evenly distributed with respect to 'dependence' and the service sector was more 'dependent' than metal manufacture. There is some additional evidence that the organizations selected were 'representative'; a national random household survey in the U.K. gave very similar results to the 'organizational' sample.

The Distribution of PS (Base and Mode)

Our instruments enabled us to obtain a measure of the degree of formalization (Table 6.2) of the various national participatory systems (i.e. the average number of the sixteen decisions for which some kind of formal prescriptions were made for all levels A to G). This, we believe, is important, for it gives some overall estimate of the impact of law and regulation on industrial relations systems. The results show Yugoslavia leading the list running down to the U.K. at the bottom. The ranking, especially at the extremes, is entirely in accord with more qualitative estimates (see IDE 1980) and gives us confidence that the method employed (see earlier remarks) captured the essentials of the various systems. The socio-political debate concerning the 'desirable' level of legal and quasi-legal penetration of industrial relations schemes is relevant here; there seems, however, to be no significant correlation between the rank order of the country in the 'degree of formalization of participation list' and their rank order for GDP per capita (Rho = 0.12) (1978). This effectively refutes any simple explanation connecting national economic performance and 'formalization of the industrial relations system'. Furthermore, (Table 6.2) it enables us to study the relative importance of 'legal norms', 'collective bargaining norms', and 'management norms' as legitimizing bases for participation (and thus formalization). It

incidentally shows that, for the majority of the countries, 'legal norms' i.e. laws are the major source (Base) of legitimation, though this varies from level to level. The ranking for the incidence of 'legal norms' across countries is: Holland > Norway > France > West Germany > U.K. > Finland > Denmark > Sweden > Belgium > Israel > Italy > Yugoslavia
The ranking for 'collective bargaining norms: is: Israel > Finland > Sweden > Norway > France > U.K. > Italy > Belgium > West Germany > Holland > Denmark > Yugoslavia (see IDE 1980 for descriptive detail).
The ranking for 'management norms' is: Belgium > Italy > Yugoslavia[1] > Sweden > Denmark > West Germany > U.K. > (Norway = Finland = Holland = France = Israel).

The rank-order correlation between the incidence of legal norms and collective bargaining norms is 0.21, that between legal norms and management norms is −0.5, and that between management norms and collective bargaining norms is −0.6. Thus, not surprisingly the different bases are, to a degree, complementary to each other across countries (c.f. IDE 1980, ch. 14).

Again, the relationship between each of the above rankings and the ranking of GDP per capita (1978) are zero except for legal norms which do appear to be marginally significant (Rho = 0.49). There is (see Chapter 9) a certain amount of evidence that Yugoslavia and Israel 'dominate' our data as polar styles. (Note their position in the above rankings). If these two countries are dropped from the rankings there is some effect on the rank correlations with GDP per capita. The correlation (Rho) with 'legal norms' increases from 0.49 to 0.6 with 'collective bargaining norms' from zero to 0.2, and with 'management norms' from zero to 0.4.

Our very tentative (recall the limitations of our sample) conclusion must be that there is no strong relationship between either the degree of formalization or the source of legitimation of national participatory schemes and global economic performance, though the use of legal norms does correlate with performance (it would, however, be of interest to pursue these issues either at the level of the enterprise or with genuine national samples). The weakness of the relationship points to factors in national tradition etc. as of overriding importance—law may 'work' (economically-speaking) in one place and not in another.

The analysis of 'Modes' (Table 6.4 and Figure 6.3) enables us to distinguish four different patterns for *de jure* participation across all groups A to G. (There seems, incidentally, to be little overlap between these and the country 'clusterings' of other variables analysed in Chapter 9). It may be noted that the four patterns are, in effect, *de jure* control graphs across all sixteen decisions, which extend the distribution to groups outside the organization. This extension has some theoretical significance because the low-profile pattern (Belgium and the U.K.) would have not have looked materially different from the 'representative one-peak pattern' (Yugoslavia) if groups E, F, and G had not been included in the analysis. The same is true for the 'hierarchical one-peak' and 'hierarchical two-peak' patterns—these could not easily have been discriminated either. It is thus clear that, in future research when 'control graphs' are constructed, the number of levels or groups studied should be extended beyond the formal boundary of the organization. A couple of questions arise here in relation to the received finding that the area under a control graph (in Tannenbaum's terms 'total control' (1968) but see Abell (1976a) and Gundelach and Tetzschner (1976)) is related to organizational performance. Would this finding hold if 'external groups' were included? Second, would the finding hold for 'de jure' as opposed to 'de facto' distributions (see below)?

The Distribution of Influence PO1

Table 7.1 demonstrates some quite remarkable uniformities. Across all twelve countries studied and all sixteen decision-types the gradient in Influence (PO1) from Group A to Group D is impressively smooth. It also shows that representative bodies have significant influence (c.f. PS above). The high levels for group E (level above plant) may reflect the high 'dependency' in the sample also noted above. External groups have the lowest influence—even lower than workers. Furthermore, the patterns for short-, medium-, and long-term decisions all show a positive gradient with hierarchical level (A–D), though the long- and medium-term decisions show a sharp jump from middle to top management. There is, of course, nothing controversial in these findings and they are in accord with expectations (c.f., IDE 1980, chapters 1 and 14).

When the pattern is broken down by country (Table 7.2) the same sort of picture emerges, except for Yugoslavia where representative bodies have relatively high Influence (c.f. Yugoslavia's one-peak pattern for PS).

If we now turn to 'total Influence' we note a fairly constant value for all countries around 2.4 to 2.6 except, once again, for Yugoslavia where the value is 3.0 (bottom line Table 7.2). Table 7.2 shows that the total amount of Influence does not vary significantly for long-, medium-, and short-term decisions.

Inequality of Influence (PO1):

Inspection of Table 7.4 reveals a very clear pattern of negative correlations between the amount of Influence for all groups, except top management and Inequality in the distribution of Influence (PO1). The correlation for top management is positive. What is the theoretical significance of this strikingly consistent result?. Something along the following lines seems reasonable and consistent with the finding. A traditional (i.e. low-participation) organization is characterized by (i) much inequality in 'Influence' and low 'total Influence'— that is to say concentration of influence in the hands of top management. But, as the participation/influence of subordinate groups increases, inequality decreases, if the influence of top management remains approximately constant or even decreases. This sort of reasoning, if correct, seems to hint at a 'zero-sum' conception of influence and to suggest that the influence scale is probably tapping something rather stronger than mere 'participation'—a patently variable-sum concept (Chapter 2, Wright Mills 1956). We can explore this possible conclusion further by examining the inter-level correlations of amount of Influence. Table 6.5 reveals a fairly consistent pattern of (i) positive correlations between the amounts of Influence of all pairs of 'subordinate' groups (A, B, C, E, F), (ii) negative correlations between top management and all groups except middle management. These results remain essentially intact when the correlations are computed separately for long-, medium-, and short-term decisions (Table 6.6). We have drawn the conclusion that Influence (as measured by PO1) is distributed in a 'zero sum' fashion between the subordinate groups and top management. Higher influence for top management is associated with lower levels of influence for the other groups.

Now we have argued in Chapter 2 that the operational Influence scale (PO1) is ambiguous with respect to the distinction between 'power' (roughly the ability to get one's way in situations of conflict) and 'participation' (being involved in decision-making in one way or another). The former is 'zero sum' the latter not. The problem is what do respondents have in mind when they refer to amounts of 'influence'? Our results tend to demonstrate that the Influence scale is, at least to a certain degree, picking up some conception of 'power' between top management and a 'coalition' of the other groups. Putting it another way a positive correlation between the amount of influence of a pair of groups may indicate one of two things; first, that the scale of influence is tapping a non-zero sum concept of participation or, second, that the groups act in concert (they have identical objectives) that is to say they form a 'coalition'. It is significant in this respect that external groups and representative bodies show a positive correlation between themselves and with workers, foremen, and middle managers and a negative correlation with top management. Thus, if our reasoning is correct, these groups form a 'coalition' with the subordinate internal groups against top management. This finding is not surprising for representative bodies but is less explicable for external groups.

We should introduce a word of caution here; a perfect negative correlation does not guarantee a zero-sum relationship only that as one variable increases the other decreases in a predictable (linear) manner. One requires a stronger relationship to draw an unequivocal zero-sum conclusion: namely that as one variable increases by a unit the other decreases in a predictable linear manner by the same unit value (i.e. the regression coefficient is -1). However, the pattern of correlations in Table 7.5 is very consistent and impressive and, in the absence of a clear metric for influence, we have tentatively drawn the zero-sum conclusion.

This caveat aside, the relationships between top management and the other groups in our organizations are zero-sum. If this finding is generalizable then variability of the area under the control graph which correlates with effectiveness, must arise from the simultaneous increase in 'power' of the subordinate groups. Alternatively, it may be that respondents partially 'think' in terms of 'participation' when comparing subordinate groups with other subordinate groups but 'power' when comparing them with top management. These results, however, could be interpreted in an alternative way, for instance, the negative correlation between the amount of Influence of top management and other levels may merely be attributable to the delegation of influence by top management rather than other levels wresting it from top management. Only more detailed studies could settle the precise nature of the mechanisms. Further detail in the other volume may help here (IDE 1980). What we can say though is that it would be wrong to draw the conclusion that the 'power' of top management and subordinate groups can be increased at the same time.

The function of conflict

We pointed out in Chapter 2 the significance of 'conflict' for an adequate conceptualization of 'power'. Our instruments were unfortunately inadequate to do full justice to this conceptualization. However, there are two competing theories concerning the incidence of conflict and participation. On the one hand it has been suggested that increasing the level of participation will decrease the level of conflict. The idea here is that participation will increase the comprehension of the problems facing the enterprise and thus reduce conflict (Batstone and Davies 1976). On the other hand, it has also been suggested (Mulder 1977) that precisely the reverse will occur. Increasing participation could bring into the open conflicts which were previously latent (non-decisions one might say—Bachrach and Baratz 1970).

Our results tend to suggest that the more strategic the decision (i.e. long-term as opposed to short-term) the more likely is it to generate 'disagreement'. Furthermore, the ranking of countries for the incidence of disagreement across the sixteen decisions (Table 7.7) is: Belgium > Norway > Yugoslavia > Italy > Sweden > Holland > Israel > France > U.K. > West Germany > Finland = Denmark. This ranking first of all bears no relationship to the rank order for total Influence (bottom line Table 7.2) under the PO1 curve averaged over all organizations per country—nor does it bear any significant relationship to the ranking of countries on PS (Base). In Table 7.8, however, we find some evidence of a negative correlation between the amount of Influence of supervisors and middle and top management and the incidence of 'Conflict', whereas the correlates for level above establishment, representative bodies, and external bodies are positive and there is no correlation for workers. The same table shows a positive correlation between equality in the distribution of Influence and the incidence of disagreement or Conflict (this finding is incidentally entirely congruent with the findings of the 'Decision-making in Organizations' project (Drenth et al. 1979). These various findings, when taken together, seem to point quite clearly to three rather important conclusions: (i) that increased representation brings conflict or disagreements out into the open, (ii) that strong 'traditional management' tends to reduce conflict, and (iii) that increasing the direct involvement of workers has no discernible effect on levels of conflict.

This leads us to modify the two opposing 'theories' we mentioned above concerning the incidence of conflict and representative democratization. It appears to be the case that conflict does increase when participation is increased through the agency of representative bodies—though not through increased participation by workers; the latter has no effect on conflict. The results thus effectively discount the 'decrease in conflict theory' but point to a modified version of the increased conflict theory' (Mulder 1977). These findings also have important implications for the theoretical interpretation of 'control graphs'. It will be recalled that the area under a control graph (total control) almost invariably shows a positive relationship with the effectiveness of the enterprise. What our results; in encapsulated form, show is that, as representative participation increases, there is a tendency for conflict to increase and thus increase use (i.e. scope) of bargaining power (as we have defined it in Chapter 2). Putting it another way conflict is brought into the open—that is to say more decisions generate conflict than before. It is thus the *scope* of 'power' relations (Chapter 2) that increases. Now, in so far as the area under a control graph (or at least the part of it relating to representative bodies measures 'power' relationships, then its variability across organizations (i.e. its variable-sum characteristics) is attributable to the increased scope of power relations. If this reasoning is correct then, in the face of a positive relationship between effectiveness and the area under the control curve, we must assume that the increased use of conflict must be functional for the enterprise. This is theoretically interesting, for a number of authors have questioned the sometimes explicit, often implicit, assumption in organizational theory that intra-organizational conflict is dysfunctional (Coser 1966, Abell 1976b).

Explaining the Variation in Influence (PO1)

The contents of Table 7.9 demonstrate quite clearly that 'Country' is a better predictor of the amount of influence of most groups than Sector or Size of organization. Interaction effects also seem, on the whole, to be of poor predictive value. The one exception seems to be that the Size of the organization is a fair predictor of the amount of Influence of top management. A similar picture emerges for inequality in the PO1 distribution—once again 'Country' is the dominant predictor. Since Country and PS are largely coincidental these predictions amount to a vindication of the policy of introducing 'participation' through *formal* normative procedures (Edelstein and Warner 1975). This implication is entirely born out by inspection of Table 7.10 where Influence scores for each group are regressed on to PS (Mode) scores. The multiple correlation coefficients are relatively high (not so high in adjusted form). Furthermore, they increase in value from short- to long-term decisions for all groups; so the more strategic the decision the better PS predicts PO1. *De Jure* Participation has the most significant effect at the levels of worker, top management, and representative bodies but these results may vary from country to country. The multiple correlation coefficients rank as follows: representative bodies (0.809) > workers (0.65) > top management (0.54). Inspection of the standardized regression coefficients reveals some interesting patterns; the distribution of negative, positive, and 'zero' values seems to suggest that (i) the value of PS for a given group is the best predictor of the PO1 value of that group (except for top management), and (ii) PS for representative bodies reduces the value of PO1 for top management. There appears, therefore, to be some evidence for the assertion that formal participation norms not only promote the influence of their corresponding level in an organization (with the exception of top management) but inhibit the influence of competing levels.

We have made various attempts to augment this simple picture by introducing contextual variables (CON_7-type variables in Figure 2.2, Chapter 2—Tables 7.11 and 7.12). Our findings do not seem to point to any systematic effects of any magnitude. Of course, since *De Jure* Participation is not a perfect predictor of Influence, there must be additional predictors that our research has not detected despite the incorporation of a very wide ranging list of variables.

Influence (PO1) and Involvement (PO2)

The Influence and Involvement scales are scored differently and were administered to different samples (Chapters 4 and 5). Nevertheless the distributions are remarkably similar, as a comparison of Tables 7.1 and 7.14 demonstrates. This shows that the estimates of key personnel regarding the 'amount of Influence' across levels does not substantially deviate from the self-evaluations of respondents concerning their own amount of 'Involvement'. Table 7.23 further emphasizes the similarity of the distributions showing the interrelations between amounts of Influence and Involvement of workers, foremen, and middle management over short-, medium- and long-term decisions. The correlations, it should be noted, are stronger the more 'strategic' the decision. As we have repeatedly noted in earlier chapters the interpretation of the relationship between Influence and Involvement is problematic. If, however, we interpret them as measuring different aspects of participation the high correlation calls for explication in terms of PS (Mode). In·Chapter 2 we described some alternative models of possible relationships between these three variables, and these were explored in Chapter 8 where certain tentative but theoretically radical conclusions were drawn. Namely, that the evidence suggests that different sorts of model are probably appropriate for both (i) different groups in organizations and (ii) short-, medium-, and long-term decisions. These matters will be explored in more depth in a subsequent publication.

Desired Involvement (PO2b)

Tables 7.14 and 7.15 seem to demonstrate that there is a universal but moderate desire for more involvement than the level currently experienced. This holds for all groups and all decisions; it is moderate because the excess of aspiration over the actual situation is never (on average) more than two points on the Involvement scale. There is a strong correlation between Actual and Desired Involvement (Table 7.18) for all groups and the pattern of Desired Involvement through representation and directly (i.e. by personal involvement) are inversely related (compare Tables 7.15 and 7.16). There seems to be clear evidence that all groups would prefer the representative body to be more involved in long- and medium-term decisions.

The patterns of Actual and Desired Involvement show remarkably consistent patterns when compared across nations (Table 7.17) and the inverse interrelation between aspirations for representative and personal involvement remains intact within each nation.

These findings gain their theoretical significance in terms of two competing theories; first, the satiation thesis 'the more involvement people have the point arises where the less they want', second, 'the more involvement they have the more they want'. It would perhaps be unwise to generalize these competing hypotheses across all groups since they are in fact usually directed at the behaviour of workers or groups traditionally subordinate in hierarchies.

It seems clear from our very wide-ranging results that, at least within limits, the second theory is the more correct—namely the more involvement people have the more they want, either personally or through representation. Of course the point may be reached where the tendency is stopped or reversed. It will be interesting, in a future volume, to study the pattern of aspirations in relation to the point on the involvement scale actually experienced for it would appear to be qualitatively discontinuous in nature—the first three points concern provision of information, the last two the ability to determine the outcome of decisions. As to the 'causal' direction of the relationship between 'aspirations' and 'experience' of involvement we cannot say anything definitive, though a reciprocal cause-effect model (Mulder 1977) may well be the most appropriate.

Explaining the Variation in Involvement PO2

A comparison of Table 7.9 and App. Table 6.3 demonstrates that the pattern of predictors of 'Influence' and 'Involvement' are very similar indeed. Again country dominates the picture, and thus PS, which is born out by a comparison of Table 7.10 and 7.19. Again notice from the latter table that the multiple correlation coefficients increase from short- to long-term decisions for workers, foremen, and representative bodies (there is no data for top management). The pattern of negative, zero, and positive coefficients, though not as clear-cut as for the corresponding table for Influence (Table 7.9) tends to support our conclusion concerning the inhibition of involvement of competing levels. In particular the PS for top management seems to have a negative effect, particularly on workers. When contextual variables are introduced into the picture (Table 7.20), although there are minor differences to the similar exercise for Influence (Table 7.10), the results seem very similar and do not point to any particular variable as an additional salient predictor of Involvement, though personal variables are slightly better predictors of Involvement than of Influence for workers. The negative correlation between 'education' and Involvement, as we explain, is rather puzzling as previous researchers (Wall and Lischeron 1977, Heller and Wilpert forthcoming) seem to have almost invariably found a positive relationship between these two variables. A breakdown of the correlation by Country and Sector (App. Table 7.5) shows some positive relationships and some negative. The results seem to suggest that a positive relationship between these two variables only emerges in organizations with relatively equal involvement and influence distributions.

However, we recognise that our research has not been able to measure effectively what one can call competence (meaning experience and skill). Nevertheless we measure mobilization which depends heavily on workers gaining competence through experience with the participation system over time. We also measure skill at the worker level. These two variables make an impact on the amount of influence exercised by workers (see Tables 8.9 and 8.10). Mobilization also has a fairly consistent negative effect on the influence of level D (senior management). Taken together these findings could be pointers for the importance of competence on the amount of influence or involvement people have or wish to have. Very strong indications to support this argument have been found in a longitudinal study (Drenth et al. 1979) and in an eight country comparative study (Heller and Wilpert forthcoming).

The findings on 'technological' variables are on the whole weak; for instance 'work-flow interdependence' does not have any effect on workers' involvement (c.f. Mohr 1971). The depth (or Vertical Span) of the enterprise has a positive (but weak) effect on Involvement of workers which is rather surprising but is consonant with Rus (1977) and Lammers and Hickson (1979). Finally the Size of the organization has no effect one way or the other on the Involvement of employees.

A series of findings presented in Tables 7.21 and 7.22 suggest that the values of PS for top management and 'management leadership style' (OPART-D) have significant, but weak, effects on the amount of Involvement. 'Management leadership style' has the strongest effect on Involvement in short-term decisions attenuating with medium- and long-term decisions. The Influence of workers on Involvement also appears prominent, but this also attenuates as a predictor from short- to long-term decisions for the Involvement of workers, but increases in importance for the Involvement of foremen. These latter associations should be interpreted with a certain amount of caution because, by the very nature of the Influence and Involvement scales, there is a 'built in' correlation (logical entailment). It would be difficult to see how a given group could, for instance, have 'very much Influence' and 'no information' (the first point on the Involvement scale). But, alternatively, it should be remembered that Influence and Involvement are elicited from different samples. These remarks parallel our earlier ones concerning the interpretation of Influence and Involvement as either independent variables or as alternative operationalizations of the same underlying variable.

Outcomes

We now turn to the 'Consequences' of participation. Table 8.1 tabulates the answers to OROC-R—the rating of the Consequences of Representative Participation by respondents. It shows that the mean rating does not vary between workers, foremen, and middle managers. Furthermore, the spread around these means across countries is very small (the sole exception being foremen in the U.K.). Table 8.3 shows the proportion of respondents giving positive evaluations of the representative bodies (remember these vary from country to country). In general, but not universally, the proportions increase with hierarchical level, though the average positive evaluation across all levels (and 4 dimensions of evaluation) is only 46 per cent leaving 54 per cent giving negative evaluations. The countries with the highest level of evaluation of the representative system are Yugoslavia and West Germany, the lowest tend to be Finland and Italy, though the rankings of workers, foremen, and middle managers (Table 8.2) in this respect are not uniform.

Interest in representative bodies is slightly more positive—the average positive response (across 4 dimensions) is 49 per cent but this percentage is affected by high positive responses to one dimension 'Can you get in touch easily?'. Over two-thirds of the respondents felt they did not 'hear much of the representative body'. Again Yugoslavia dominates the ranking of Interest in the Representative Body with Italy at the bottom. The rankings of Interest (Table 8.2) generally confirm earlier hypotheses that the higher the hierarchical level, and therefore the more participation one has, the more interested one is.

When we distinguish between respondents who have experience of serving on representative bodies and others we find (Figures 8.6 and 8.7) that the representatives' Interest in, and Evaluation of, the Representative Body are always more positive than others. This suggests that, despite the role conflict (Batstone and Davies 1976) etc. which representatives often encounter, the experience of participation increases positive sentiments (Mulder 1977). Table 8.6 supports this interpretation: representatives in all countries are significantly more 'willing to be a candidate for the representative body' (see also IDE 1980).

As reported earlier we found that country (and thus PS (Mode)) is the best predictor of Influence and Involvement. Table 8.5 shows similar results for the prediction of OROC-R, OPART-E, OPART-I, and PO2-c (see Appendix D.1 for operationalizations—also see Table 8.18). In all cases Country is a better predictor than Sector, Size, etc. Interaction effects are significant but weak (Table 8.4). It follows, of course, that *De Jure* Participation (Mode) is also a good predictor of these various outcome variables. Organization seems to be important (c.f. PO1 and PO2) as do some personal variables, notably Union Membership and personal Involvement. Both these results seem to support our above conclusion concerning experience and positive evaluation and interest.

Turning now to direct participation (OROC-D and OPART-D), Table 8.9 shows a rather high positive appreciation of the benefits of direct participation. The average proportion of respondents endorsing five positive statements across all countries is 71 per cent. There is, for all five statements, a greater probability of a positive response with increasing hierarchical level. Table 8.8 gives the rates and rankings for OROC-D and OPART-D; again the mean rating increases for both scales with hierarchical level.

Turning to predictors of the various scales characterizing direct participation (Tables 8.11 and 8.13), again country (and thus PS—see also Table 8.18) is the most important predictor followed by 'firm' and 'department'. The personal variables of importance are Desired and Actual Involvement. The picture, though different in detail, is thus not materially different to that for the representative system. The only important moderator variable for the effect of direct Involvement on outcome variables appears to be the Need for Direct Participation (Table 8.17). The correlations between the amount of Involvement in decision-making and the indices of general Satisfaction are rather low (Table 8.14). Finally, Table 8.23 suggests a positive correlation between the evaluation of representative and direct democracy. In the light of our earlier remarks concerning control graphs, it is interesting to note that we found little or no relationship between either the total amount of Influence or Inequality of Influence and outcome variables.

One of the surprising findings is that *De Jure* Participation (PS-Mode) is more strongly correlated with outcomes than Influence. Attempts to partial out Influence in studying the co-variation of PS and O (in the spirit of Figure 2.1) leaves a 'direct effect' of PS on O. We have drawn the general conclusion that the characteristics of the *de jure* system are related to employees' attitudes (evaluation and interest) concerning both representative and direct participation but *not* to satisfaction concerning job and company. This is clearly an area for further analysis.

In this chapter we have suggested that the contribution of the IDE study to the development of social science has been made in three areas. First, we have developed a model for the conduct of large-scale international and inter--disciplinary research which appears to be effective. Second, we have worked out a way of measuring *de jure* participation which is both relatively simple and analytically revealing and applied more precise measures of *de facto* participation than have been used before. Thirdly, we have produced a number of very interesting findings which suggest that current theories relating to the determinants and consequences of industrial democracy need considerable revision, and which also suggest areas for future research.

NOTE

1   As pointed out in Chapter 6 this high rank for Yugoslavia is somewhat misleading, since 'management norms' are, to a large extent, 'self-management norms'.

PART IV

POLICY ISSUES

11

STRATEGY IMPLICATIONS

INTRODUCTION

For a practitioner who has read an empirical study of this kind, the natural question to ask is: 'Knowing all this, how can I *use* it in my work?' We shall try to address this and similar questions here. From the preceding chapters and from the second volume of this study (IDE 1980) it appears, however, that participation in decision-making for workers has been introduced in the various countries for different reasons, by different actors, in different forms, and most likely in many cases with different expectations about results. How our results may be used, therefore, will also depend upon what kind of effects from participation the particular practitioner is looking for.

Strategies and tactics at different levels

'Industrial democracy', 'workers' participation in management' and related concepts originate in most countries in political debates and are mainly promoted by the Labour Movement as a part of its struggle for the emancipation of the workers. However, other objectives may be behind the introduction of a particular scheme for participation within a country or a specific enterprise.

At the political level, the Labour Movement leaders, e.g. in Scandinavia, usually argue that the main objective for democratization of industry is the redistribution of power and influence between labour and capital. At the same time, however, at a more practical level within unions and management systems, schemes for democratization are supported (or counteracted) for their expected effects on workers' safety, satisfaction, efficiency, stability, flexibility of the organization, etc. This means that the various parties interested in participation may have a hierarchy of interrelated or independent means and ends to explain how they evaluate a particular system for participation.

In our study we have emphasized possible connections between the form and strength of arrangements for participation and the distribution of power and influence *within the enterprise*. And we have indeed shown that there is a link of this kind. In addition, we have been studying possible links between satisfaction with the job, the enterprise, etc. and participation, and here the connections are more complex, so that we can argue that these are partly independent phenomena. These effects are measured at plant level. Particular schemes for participation, however, are usually negotiated at a higher level (branch, industry, nation) by others than those expected to be directly involved in the scheme. Although it seems that most schemes are introduced with the purpose of creating their immediate (first order) effects at plant/establishment level, it should not be overlooked that we have at least one case where higher-level effects have been the *main* target, and several others where expected national effects are important (IDE, 1980). In Yugoslavia, the system of workers' self-management is part of a national strategy for decentralization in order to avoid a Stalinist type of political control. It is still, of course, legitimate, and also interesting both from a practical and theoretical point of view, to study the plant-level effects of this system. But one should not overlook the fact that effects at the national level have been the main target.

We also have a potential case of a *supra*-national strategy, i.e. the EEC proposal for harmonization of corporate legislation in Europe in order to facilitate international economic activity within the EEC, to secure equal conditions for competition, to provide some degree of employee board-level participation for socio-political reasons and to reduce friction within enterprises (Wilpert 1976).

It seems that, in the West-European countries, the schemes for participation/industrial democracy/co-determination have been introduced, amended, supplemented, and strengthened as an almost continuous process in the decades after World War II. We have seen a clear European trend towards industrial democracy where the national leadership in each country either have responded to this trend in a more passive way or have tried actively to promote it. It is in itself an interesting finding that party politics cannot have been very important for the general development in Europe. We have, for example, no case in our twelve countries of the discarding of arrangements for participation, although there are several cases of political shifts. On the contrary, there has been further systematic development and strengthening of participation arrangements rather than the return to a situation similar to the one prior to the introduction of new rules.

Some countries have led the development towards institutionalized arrangements for employee participation, (Kendall 1973, Mazzolini 1978, IDE 1980). Generally it seems that the others are following, or selecting consciously or unconsciously by themselves, very similar paths. This allows us to compare across country boundaries and make inferences about the effects of formal arrangements for participation as a function of time.

For the national leaders the simplest way to respond to the pressure from a cultural trend of this kind, is to use means that can be centrally controlled, like legislation or national collective agreements. Tactically, it may be necessary to show that something is being done—like the passing of a new law. Thus the symbolic value is important. Otherwise there may be a loss in popular support, or pressure for more drastic measures may arise. It is clear that in many countries the introduction of systems for participation has mainly been done as a defensive measure—to avoid something. In a few countries, however, at least ideologically, there is more of an active political strategy behind it. Such examples may be found in Scandinavia, where Social Democrats have seen the democratization of industry as one step in a strategy for the general democratization of institutions. Putting ideology aside, however, the solutions found show striking similarities.

For us, the fact that we are mainly studying plant-level effects, may make us overlook important national differences. Some of these have, however, been dealt with in chapter 9, and more are covered in 'European Industrial Relations' (IDE 1980). Further, if systems for participation are to be judged against their intended consequences, we should also look at levels higher than the individual company and search for criteria, models, strategies, and tactics different from those incorporated in the study. With these limitations, however, our study covers those possible outcomes of participation which are most commonly mentioned in the political debate (redistribution of power and influence) and in the social science 'and management literature (change in employee attitudes, satisfaction, effects on efficiency, stability, economy, etc.).

The time dimension, unfortunately, is still not well covered in our study. Any strategy for social or political change would have to incorporate ideas about effects over time. One would, for example, expect that the introduction of a participation scheme would immediately produce a kind of 'Hawthorne effect' (positive or negative) i.e. change attitudes. Changes in the distribution of power, however, would probably come more slowly—possibly with a time-lag of a year or more (Engelstad and Qvale 1977), and the process might, of course, also be affected by, for example, counter-measures and supporting activities (which may or may not be a part of the original strategy).

Further, any political party, union, or employers' confederation that want to increase employees' participation through reform will usually consider whether any single reform will facilitate a second step later. Thus, the main objective might only be to create conditions for later action towards the desired outcome, rather than giving other immediate, positive results. Or employers, feeling the political pressure for democratization, may agree to the introduction of a scheme for participation which is seen as relatively harmless compared with other alternatives. Thus bodies for joint information and consultation can be created to put off Labour demand for board representation (typical in Scandinavia in the 1950's and 60's). Or worker directors and other plant-level systems for joint information and power-sharing may be suggested to reduce central union control and pressure e.g. for nationalization of industry—which seem rather typical in the current debate in the U.K. (Jenkins 1978, Prior 1978, Macbeath 1978), as described elsewhere (see IDE 1980, ch. 6).

From such processes we see that tactics at one level can be aimed at stopping an initiative at another. It follows from this that assessing the efficiency of any national strategy for democratization is extremely complicated. Any particular arrangement for participation is usually, in itself, the result of bargaining and negotiations between various—and frequently conflicting—interest groups. The resulting compromise may lead to new dimensions being added, some of the original ones weakened or even thwarted, initiatives at other levels may be stopped, and the functioning of the system itself may be different from what was originally intended. Of course, experience with a particular form of participation frequently changes the concepts, ideas, and objectives associated with the reform. Still, there is a surprising similarity in the development of formal arrangements for participation in the countries taking part in the study. This lends support to the theory that systems for participation in industry in Europe should largely be seen as attempts to overcome problems associated with industry in the context of a common cultural development.

Different models of industrial democracy?

In the preceding chapters, and particularly in 'European Industrial Relations' (IDE 1980), we have shown that the *same* formal arrangement for participation in a company (e.g. a works' council system) can be introduced for widely differing reasons. In Scandinavia reforms have been brought about by the Labour Movement, against some resistance from employers, in order to increase workers' influence and improve productivity, this also being seen as a step twoards socialism. In the U.K. and on the Continent the same kind of formal arrangements have, to some extent, been promoted by employers and managers against union resistance. In spite of all differences in actors, levels, objectives, strategies, and tactics between the countries, the structures created at plant level to provide possibilities for participation are very similar (Chapter 6).

There are variations in the strength of the arrangements, and the configuration of bodies vary somewhat. Yugoslavia's self-management system in principle gives full workers' control at the board level. On the other hand, in West Germany there is parity representation in some companies in specific sectors at approximately the same organizational level. The repertory therefore seems limited to a small number of types:

i. Trade union bargaining/collective agreement system including shop stewards;

ii. Joint information/consultation/decision-making bodies created outside of, and as a supplement to, line management with participation by employee representatives from one or several levels plus management;

iii. Participation by representatives of employees from one or several levels in top policy-making bodies;

iv. Employee ownership;

v. Systems for participation in decision-making in one's own job (job enlargement, job redesign, autonomous work groups, matrix organization, etc.).

Employee ownership of one's own company exists indirectly in Israel, where the Labour Movement owns a substantial part of industry. Yugoslavia has a more direct form of employee control although this does not include ownership. On the other hand, private ownership of the means of production does not exist in Yugoslav industry. For our purposes, the interesting aspects are more related to what kind of organizational forms (including employee participation in decision-making bodies) follow from employee ownership. We see that types (i), (ii), and (iii) are being applied in these two countries in order to provide opportunities for participation.

Increased room for participation within the job, which has developed quite extensively during the last decade, can only partly be dealt with in this study. Only in the Dutch sample do we have a few cases where conscious efforts to improve conditions for direct participation have been made (a work consultation system). Of course, in the other establishments we also find different degrees of job autonomy for the workers. We have, unfortunately, no objective measure of their different levels of discretion. We only have data on the individuals' perceived level of direct participation. As demonstrated, the high/low skill classification of enterprises is too rough and is not directly linked to the characteristics of the individuals' jobs anyway.

We see that participation at board level on the one hand and autonomous work groups on the other are respectively indirect and direct forms of participation within the company hierarchy. Participation in the Works' Councils, Safety Committees, and similar are forms of indirect participation outside the company hierarchy. The shop steward system is also in principle outside the company hierarchy, but on the other hand it is inside the trade union system.

We would expect that the degree to which the established arrangements for participation have effects—and the types of effects they have (power equalization within company, on attitudes, on satisfaction)—might be contingent upon:

i. the degree to which the various bodies and arrangements are interlinked through a union system (Garson 1977);

ii. whether the arrangements provide for direct or indirect participation (Emery and Thorsrud 1969);

iii. whether the arrangements give participation within or outside the management hierarchy (Gasparini 1977).

From 'European Industrial Relations' (IDE 1980) it appears that the configuration into which any single new arrangement is to be fitted, will, to some extent, decide its effects.

In the following, we shall firstly discuss whether our data indicate any further need for democratization of industry, and if so, in which areas. Then we shall discuss the various means for democratization in some detail. Our discussion in this chapter has to be read with caution. The main reason for this lies in the fact that we cover only one cross-section of time, and that there is little variation in arrangements for participation within the same country. Thus we do not know whether changes in the rules for participation within the same country, will have the same consequences as those we infer when comparing across countries. This is a basic problem we cannot solve in this study.

THE CASE FOR INDUSTRIAL DEMOCRACY

Three general lines of argument are often advanced in favour of developing industrial democracy: the purely political argument, the human relations and the human resources arguments. From a practitioner's point of view it is important to confront these arguments with the main thrusts of our findings. Although we have chosen to focus on the effects of *de jure* participation on the *de facto* distribution of power and influence within the organization, this does not imply that this has been the primary target in the countries studied. The motivation behind the various schemes is different across nations and organizations. In some countries plant-level participation has been supported because it is expected to reduce central union control. In Yugoslavia and the countries dominated by Social Democratic parties political objectives linked to a desirable future have been important. In other countries copying of arrangements in neighbouring countries or avoiding or reducing concrete problems associated with industry have been the reasons behind initiatives.

If we assume, however, that democratization is associated with equalization of influence and power among hierarchical levels within the enterprise, then our data can indicate empirically the areas where there is a need for democratization.

The results are very clear. The hierarchical level of the individual's job is the best predictor of his level of involvement, his group's influence, and (much weaker) also of his attitudes to job, company, and so forth. Employees at the bottom of the organizational pyramid are very much at a disadvantage as far as individual involvement in decision-making is concerned and they themselves have quite high aspirations to change this. The distribution of involvement across organizational levels is perfectly hierarchical in all countries and in all plants within each country. Taking such data at face value leads to the conclusion that the arguments for democratization in terms of improving conditions for decision-making in the job at lower organizational levels are very strong. The individual's self-reported involvement in decision-making at shop-floor level is very low—almost nil where strategic decisions are concerned—getting systematically greater at higher and higher levels.

In terms of influence and power workers are not so clearly at a disadvantage in absolute and relative terms when we consider the influence of the level together with that of the bodies created for participative purposes. This is particularly true for personnel matters. Further, there is a correlation between the influence of the three lowest levels within the organization, i.e. there is not necessarily a conflict between increasing the influence of the lowest level and that of the two above.

Still, the purely political argument for democratization—that influence is unequally distributed to the disadvantage of lower white- and blue-collar workers—is generally supported. But here national differences occur so that (notably in Yugoslavia although also in other countries) workers may achieve rough equality with the other levels through the combined influence of their own level and what they achieve through the works' council and similar bodies in a number of areas (in Yugoslavia: all areas). But, generally, it can be said that the clearest argument for democratization of the enterprise comes from the existing inequality in possibilities for individuals to be involved in, and make decisions about, their own jobs.

Within the 'human relations' tradition the need for democratic reform should be indicated by dissatisfaction among employees. If workers and/or lower white-collar employees systematically have lower scores for satisfaction with the job, the company, or with management, than higher-level employees, this could point to the need for change. We find, however, no widespread dissatisfaction at lower levels, and the differences in the scores across hierarchical levels are fairly small. This is the case even in national samples where the workers' level of participation is relatively low. However, in many cases, satisfaction with the system of representation is rather low—and lower among shop-floor employees than in management. There is considerable variation between countries and between companies and individuals within countries. Still, people are not expressing direct dissatisfaction—rather lack of interest and the absence of positive attitudes.

These findings suggest that the human relations approach gives somewhat weaker arguments for increasing employee participation, but still indicates the need for change in the same direction as the 'political' model. On the other hand, the strong connection between a democratic leadership-style, and satisfaction with job and company gives some support to 'human relations' theories.

From a management perspective data can also be used to argue a need for democratization. The 'human resources' model (Miles 1965, Emery and Trist 1965) calls for a management strategy involving the mobilization of employees if the organizations's environment becomes too dynamic to be handled with traditional business strategies or tactics. According to this model the development of internal flexibility and commitment to the company in order to cope with variability in the environment is contingent on the involvement of employees in the job and the legitimacy of the leadership. Given the current recession in the European economy and rapid technological and commercial development, it seems likely that a number of the enterprises we studied face rather dynamic environmental conditions.

Our data on conflict, labour turnover, and absenteeism in the enterprises covered by our study do not, however, give any clear picture of a need for drastic internal change in order to overcome problems in these areas. A number of the enterprises, for example in the Norwegian sample, were running at reduced capacity, had recently laid people off, and were losing money. Still, it is doubtful whether these, or any of the other enterprises in our sample, were experiencing an environment with 'turbulent fields' in the Emery and Trist (1965) sense of the concept. It seems that the companies were experiencing problems they expected to be able to handle within the ordinary range of measures. Thus we have only a few cases where management were systematically incorporating employee participation into the overall business strategy for survival. In one of these, which was completely dependent upon state contracts, top management was working together with local union representatives, the works' council, and the worker directors to make internal arrangements (relating to participation, payment, personnel policy, etc.) to gain maximum internal support and thus legitimacy in the eyes of the external political environment.

Our finding that enterprises which are approaching a monopolistic situation have a more highly developed system for internal power-sharing (and a more equal distribution of power) may be interpreted as a sign of the higher political vulnerability of such organizations. A high level of internal participation makes the organization more acceptable in the environment, if the latter is dominated by a political culture which values participation and democracy. Assuming that there is a common genuine cultural trend in the twelve IDE countries making participation, involvement, and power-sharing more central, this would be the strongest management argument for developing internal democracy.

In total this discussion suggests that the human relations argument for democratization is weaker than the 'political' argument. The open systems' 'human resources' approach is somewhere between the two, linking internal arrangements and structures to the prevailing external value system and other aspects of the relevant external environment for each enterprise.

In the next sections we shall discuss, in more detail, various ways of increasing participation in the enterprise, their effects, and possible interconnections.

WAYS OF INCREASING PARTICIPATION

The choice of direct means for increasing participation within a given enterprise or in a country's industry generally will, as we have discussed above, be dependent upon possibilities (the political climate within and outside the enterprise), the objectives of the reform (political, human relations, human resources), the model behind them (assumed causal chains), and thus the strategy. The situations of the enterprise, the unions, and maybe individuals may also be important. There are a number of ways in which attempts may be made to increase participation within an enterprise including: breaking down or modifying the hierarchy; establishing a more democratic leadership style; mobilizing employees in unions; and trying to increase the involvement and influence of employees by introducing or extending rules for participation.

Break down The Hierarchy?

Hierarchical level is a stronger predictor of power distribution within organizations than size, type of industry, or country. Thus the internal hierarchical structure of work organizations seems to be a basic determinant of existing distribution of power and also a basic obstacle to a more egalitarian distribution of power in organizations. From this it logically follows that the most efficient way to equalize the power distribution within the organization should be to take away its hierarchical structure. Within our sample we have no example of a direct attempt to do this, although there are cases reported elsewhere (Emery and Thorsrud 1976, Herbst 1976) which ultimately aim at creating 'non-hierarchical organizations'. Our data clearly point to the need for further research and experimentation in this direction but, given the limitations of our sample, we cannot shed more light on this. In the following we have to take the hierarchy as given and discuss how various other measures and strategies may modify it or even, perhaps, reduce inequality between levels without removing the hierarchy.

Introduce more formal rules

Given the framework of the hierarchy, introducing more rules for employee participation is the most efficient way of increasing employee involvement, particularly that of employee representatives, and of equalizing the distribution of power. Further, we find that the levels below top management and external bodies seem to have a 'common cause' so that the power of each of them may increase simultaneously. From this we imply that new rules for participation do not necessarily have to benefit lowest-level employees exclusively. We find that the more widely (in terms of areas covered) and strongly (in terms of degree of participation for the three lowest levels) the prescriptions are formulated, the more democratic an organization appears. If the rules prescribe relatively strong top management participation there is usually low worker influence.

Internal dynamics; Involvement and influence

Our findings support the notion that workers as individuals are mostly concerned with being directly involved in, and having influence over, decisions closely associated with their own jobs and work situations. At the same time we found that these are the decisions in which they are already most involved. This points to one of the dynamic properties of participation. Actual and desired participation build a self-reinforcing cycle. Any strategy for democratization of the organization which aims at involving the employees in general, rather than just a few elected representatives, would have to use this mechanism. It can be seen as a learning process (Thorsrud 1978, Mulder 1977) in which individuals depart from areas they know well with their specific needs and aspirations, acquire new skills and can then become involved in more remote and far-reaching decisions later.

Also we found that individual workers want their indirect influence (through elected representatives in joint consultation or decision-making bodies) to increase in long-range policy decisions. The complementarity between direct participation by individuals and collective indirect influence has to be central in any strategy for democratization. So far the development of formal arrangements for participation in Europe has centred around collective agreements and laws giving (i) security to the individual and (in most countries) (ii) indirect influence over a wide range of issues. However, conscious efforts to increase the individual's freedom in the job have generally been limited to management-initiated organizational development efforts aimed at creating a 'democratic leadership style'.

Leadership style

There is a clear connection between employees' feelings of involvement in decision-making and the leadership style of their superior. Democratizing the leadership style in the work organization seems to be second only to stronger *de jure* regulation of participation as a means of promoting *de facto* participation. This implies, however, more than just 'a pat on the workers shoulder'. Even the traditional human relations approach of informing the worker about management decisions in a friendly way and also letting him voice his opinion (without changing the decision) seems to increase the 'feeling of participation' (Pateman 1970). Compared with the obvious alternative of not informing at all—just issuing orders—this is not so surprising. We would be likely to find effects of democratization within the organization following the introduction of such management practices because the supervisors will be socially and pscycho-logically influenced by the workers, understand their positions, and so forth (see Chapter 8).

The way we have defined a 'democratic leadership style', however, goes beyond the traditional human relations concept as exemplified by the well-known Coch and French (1948) study. Our concept encompasses (i) informing workers before the decision is made, (ii) consulting workers affected by planned change, (iii) asking workers for their opinions if they may be affected, and (iv) to some extent leaving the decision to workers. In order to meet the interest of workers' in more direct influence over decisions connected with their own jobs a plan for the democratization of the enterprise would have to include the development of a democratic leadership style. This is particularly so in the early stages of democratization. The effects of a democratic leadership style on workers' actual involvement in short-term, job-related, decisions are strong. At a later stage, when involvement in medium- and long-term decisions is at stake, the workers' *influence* as a group may take over in importance.

Employee mobilization: The role of the unions

It seems that the local union acts as an integrator of the specific bodies for participation, the employees in general, and the external environment. Thus, the bodies created are more efficient in democratizing if there are unions present in the plant, and these are represented on the bodies. In such cases, as in Scandinavia, the union is the power base for employee participation both in joint information and consultation bodies and for minority representation on the board of directors. Our finding that high worker influence coincides with relatively influential 'external bodies' reflects the same phenomenon. The workers as a group become stronger within the enterprise if the local union is linked to a strong national union system. This also partly explains why past and present membership of participatory bodies is the only strong individual determinant of influence. In several countries, being a member of, for example, the works' council, is the same as being a member of the local union committee, because the seats are allocated to local union representatives. Having such positions of course gives personal skills and knowledge but, more important, workers who have (or have had) positions in the union or in a body for participation are connected with an organization that gives influence. Improving the conditions for shop stewards and works' council members to carry out their functions, involving as many employees as possible in such work, and linking the system for participation with the local and national union systems, are ways of promoting internal power-sharing.

A high degree of unionization of supervisors and middle-managers coincides with a relatively equal distribution of power across organizational levels. This is because a majority of the members of the bodies for participation are recruited from these two levels. When they are unionized and thus, at least to some extent politicized, they will contribute to a reduction of dominance by senior management in areas where they want a larger say. We cannot from our study describe the process leading to white-collar unionization. It seems, however, to be rather country-specific, and could reflect social and political closeness on the part of blue- and white-collar workers. In Sweden and the U.K., recent industrial relations 'reforms' are contributing to closer contact and co-operation between different unions notably white- and blue-collar, while in Norway board representation has activated the white-collar unions without bringing them closer to the blue-collar ones (IDE 1980, ch. 2).

Generally it seems that democratization of the organization can be promoted through white-collar unionization. This again underscores the point already raised, that workers, supervisors, and middle managers in principle have common interests in power-sharing. The dividing line in terms of power inequality is between top management and all other employees, rather than (as traditional stratification theory would assume) between workers and white-collar employees in general. A strategy that strengthens any of the three lower levels of the organization therefore will benefit all three.

Modifying the hierarchy?

Any sudden change from the present hierarchically-organized company to a non-hierarchic, possibly completely 'democratized' system, is unrealistic at best, and also possibly undesirable for a number of reasons. In order to maintain economic viability and some level of internal social stability we see the problem more as a question of finding practical modifications that either change the hierarchy (its present division of labour, sanctions and rewards, information system, decision-making rules and so forth) or compensate for its short-comings e.g. through establishing participatory bodies.

However, in our study we do not detect much effect from structural dimensions, like intensity of control or degree of centralization, formalization, functional differentiation and specialization on employee involvement and the internal distribution of power. Small changes here (within the fairly modest range of the participating enterprises) will therefore not be an effective means of democratization. We expected particularly that a relatively high degree of decentralization would increase involvement and influence for lower levels but this does not seem to be the case. We presume this is mainly because the enterprises covered by the study have applied the same basic principles of organizational design so there is fairly little variance. Further, the relationships between organizational structure and internal democracy are complex. Under certain conditions employees may be more secure and feel more involved and influential in a highly structured, formalized, and centralized organization, than in a more decentralized, less structured system which may also be more open to management manipulation (Crozier 1963, Gustavsen 1973).

Exploring the conditions under which decentralization within the management hierarchy has democratizing effects stands out as an important practical research task. Job rotation across hierarchical levels, time-limited election by employees to managerial positions, 'elite circulation', and similar arrangements aimed at avoiding the negative effects of the organizational hierarchy, are not covered by our study. Such measures might detach personal attributes, including power, from those of a particular role in the work organization, and, under certain conditions, would probably contribute to democratization. We are, however, not in a position to specify those conditions, though it is clear from our results that neither decentralization alone nor a separate reduction in the intensity of control will have democratizing effects.

For a job-seeker it may be of interest to note that, within the same country, enterprises with the most highly developed system for participation are also the ones with the most democratic distribution of power. Companies that score highly on functional differentiation and are relatively dependent on customers are also more democratic. Within the range we cover on technology and other structural dimensions of the organization, there are no other important determinants of the distribution of power. In terms of individual involvement, however, smaller organizations give better opportunities to the workers. In the large organizations, on the other hand, representative bodies are more powerful and thus provide better opportunities for indirect participation.

Selection of people?

Personal attributes of employees such as age, sex, tenure, and education have fairly little influence on their level of involvement and influence. As demonstrated, the hierarchical level on which the job has been placed largely overrules personal attributes. Within the same hierarchical level, however, individual characteristics have some effect. Women are less involved in decision-making than men. Past or present membership of a participatory body makes the individual more involved. A high proportion of workers with such membership contributes towards power-equalization. The effects of personal characteristics increase at higher organizational levels. While higher education does not seem to be a sufficient condition or increased influence and involvement at the shop-floor level, such effects are observed at the supervisory and middle management levels. A higher level of education among workers tend to decrease the involvement of the supervisors.

Power is more equally distributed in the organization if supervisors and middle managers are young and female, than if they are old men. Thus systematic selection to supervisory and managerial positions will have some effect on the distribution of power, but these are generally marginal.

External support systems

External bodies like local authorities, political organizations, trade unions, and other agencies of the environment function as support for internal democratization of organizations. More open and socially-influenced work organizations will also become more participative and democratic. Building links between various levels and internal bodies in the organization to external agents, is therefore a way of promoting internal democracy.

The effects of the economy and technology

The economic environment of the enterprise does not seem to have much effect on the internal power distribution, at least within the range covered by our study. The same goes for the industrial sector in the sense that there is no systematic difference between the three groups of enterprises covered. Opportunities for personal involvement on the shop-floor are low in the sectors covered. The level of involvement does not seem to be affected by the profitability of the enterprise. Arguments that participation is something the enterprise can afford when the economy is good, have to be rejected.

Systematic changes in technology in order to promote employee involvement and participation were not taking place in any of the enterprises covered by the study. Other studies, however, show significant effects both in terms of employee participation in the design process, and in terms of better opportunities for involvement in the job later (Elden 1979, Jenkins 1973). Further, it has been argued, (Taylor 1972) and demonstrated in practice (Agersnap 1973, Butera 1975, Emery and Thorsrud 1976) that it is strategically advantageous to start a process of wider employee participation with technological change in the area immediately related to the workers' job situation. Our results clearly show that workers are primarily interested in greater involvement in issues fairly closely connected to their own work situation, thus confirming some of these arguments. There is certainly variance in job design and technology in the firms studied, but this is not reflected in the data on involvement. The explanation for this is partly that we have not made an analysis at the individual level with the contents of the job as an independent variable. Partly the reason is that workers tend to take the technology as given and adjust their aspirations for autonomy and involvement in relation to the concrete situation.

Summing up

One possible answer to a worker who wants to get a job in a democratic organization is, according to our study, 'Go to Yugoslavia'. If he is only seeking an influential position for himself, the immediate advice is to become a top manager. If that is unrealistic the advice is: 'Get elected as a shop steward or member of a representative body in your firm.' This sequence is highly illustrative of some of the basic problems involved when summing up results from an international comparison of this kind. Within any one country our firms show little variation in levels of involvement and participation. The main message from our study is that, although the formal systems for participation show striking similarities, industrial democracy is not just one thing, even within Europe. And the formal systems, in spite of being the best predictor, only explain part of the variance in the distribution of power.

Furthermore, any piece-meal discussion of the various means for democratization can very easily be misleading—that is if one really wants to equalize power within the organization. Clearly a major reason why reforms in this area seem so limited in effects is due to the piece-meal introduction of most of them. Electing individuals to the board of directors without allowing them to hold union positions, without adequate training, without allowing them to inform their electorate about board matters, while running the meeting as before, would seem a rather sure way of preventing any significant effects in terms of the redistribution of power, as is shown in a recent study of worker directors (Brannen et al. 1976).

The interaction of individual, company-specific and external factors is decisive for the end results both in terms of internal democracy, employee attitudes and efficiency. Thus, a strategy for democratization would have to involve the systematic manipulation of several factors either simultaneously or sequentially in order to have lasting effects on the distribution of power and on attitudes.

EFFECTS OF PARTICIPATION

We have so far discussed strategies for democratization seeing equalization of involvement in decision-making and power as the target. However, power equalization, apart from not being the objective for all interest groups, may also be seen as instrumental for achieving other objectives, like worker satisfaction, reduced conflict, productivity, better payment, an improved working environment, etc. In the following we shall briefly discuss (i) the most central connections between participation and effects (outcomes) and (ii) limited strategies that aim directly at achieving one particular effect or a set of closely-related effects.

Participation and efficiency

There is no universal agreement on criteria for organizational efficiency, nor do we have economic data from the enterprises covered by the study that can give a full picture of efficiency against a selected set of criteria. In line with the arguments in chapter 5, however, one would expect that the economic success of an ‑enterprise would contribute positively to the effects of *de jure* participation unless the managerial value system is very much against it. Further, if employee participation is an integral part of the management strategy for the development or survival of the enterprise as a whole, we would expect mutual reinforcement. We find some support for this notion in the data on prevailing values and the degree of power equalization. In the Northern countries power-sharing, co-operation, and positive relations with supervisors are relatively highly valued. A managerial strategy for the enterprise should take this into consideration, and, according to the indices of power equalization in Chapter 7, the Northern countries (plus Yugoslavia) have a fairly equal distribution of power. In the Southern countries, where individual career opportunities are more highly valued, systems for participation that would equalize the collective influence of groups would receive less support and hence have less effect.

In some Northern countries and Yugoslavia, however, we also find that the systems for representative participation are quite elaborate and give worker representation at several levels (including the Board) and the general effects of participation are evaluated relatively positively. Altogether this could mean that we have merely registered that, in each group of countries, the systems for participation, the evaluation of their functioning, and the underlying culture (value system) are consistent rather than observing causal chains. The finding that an average of 70 per cent of the workers (with the exception of France, Italy, and Israel, where the figure is approximately 60 per cent) believe that indirect participation has the effect of making decisions more easily accepted, indicates that the participative system is having a positive effect on organizational efficiency. Realizing that union rights are recognized and security of employment fairly well-established, this makes sense. Management has to win employee support for its decisions. Using the participating bodies as a means towards this, is seen as an efficient measure by a majority in all countries. Thus, participaton will act as a part of the system for conflict resolution.

Disagreement between management and employees is more frequent where the system for participation is well-developed, and hence the power distance between organizational levels is relatively small. More conflicts can be expected as an outcome of democratization. This is not surprising nor necessarily ineffi-cient in economic terms. Disagreement can be seen as a constructive result of employee involvement. New arguments, new criteria for decision-making, and solutions to problems may become available.

So far, however, with the exception of Yugoslavia, participation has not developed beyond the provision of information, joint consultation, and minority representation in decision-making bodies. Still, employee representatives are being informed about coming decisions and can voice their opinion. If they are union leaders, they can—if they want to—also mobilize the employees against management. In most cases the system functions at this level, i.e. management knows that the employees may stop a decision unless their support or acceptance is secured. This explains why the most contentious issues in democratized organizations are related to hiring, firing, and the nomination of managers. Strategic issues like capital investment, the implementation of new products, and reorganization do not produce conflicts, or there may be genuine agreement over such issues at this stage of development. In the personnel matters mentioned employees can present alternatives. In the strategic issues this is much more problematic. Therefore industrial democracy has not yet challenged the central policy issues, but contributes to peaceful internal conflict resolution and social integration. This seems to be the case even when the arrangements for participation have been brought about through a revolution (Yugoslavia) rather than through the cautious, step-wise process of the other countries (IDE 1980, ch. 12).

Attitudes

Management frequently sees employee participation as a way of promoting the development of positive attitudes. Such attitudes in their turn, are often seen as instrumental for stability, productivity, and industrial peace. Our study certainly complicates this picture. There seem to be rather few relationships between participation and attitudes that are generally stable in all national samples, and within enterprises there is variation between departments and individuals.

Management wanting to promote the development of positive attitudes to the company may benefit from what seems to be the symbolic effect of institutionalized employee participation. Evaluation of, and interest in, the work of the representative body is related to its *de jure* authority. Thus, even if the bodies do not contribute to the equalization of power, they will affect employee's attitudes positively. The actual influence of groups as a whole (like workers), as perceived by experts in the company, however, is not related to satisfaction with the job or company.

At the individual level we find that the more a worker perceives himself to be involved in decision-making, the more positive is his evaluation of direct participation and the more satisfied he is, particularly with the company as a whole. In line with Pateman (1970) and Wall and Lischeron (1977), we may suggest that management can expect positive reactions even to small—or even just symbolic—increases in personal involvement. As demonstrated already, democratizing an authoritarian leadership style may be the simplest way to achieve this. However, the relationship between influence and satisfaction is more complex. Our findings may lend support to Emery and Thorsrud's theory (1969, 1976) that, if it goes beyond the symbolic level, participation and power-sharing may well increase dissatisfaction, as employees' aspirations rise, and earlier unknown constraints to the realization of their desires appear. The emergence of disagreement and conflict when power becomes more equally distributed points in the same direction.

There is little general agreement among employees in their preference for either direct or indirect participation, nor in their evaluation of or interest in such arrangements. Employees tend to emphasize what they have, i.e. ask for more direct involvement when they already have a fairly high level of discretion (e.g. as managers), and ask for representative participation if they are old, unskilled production workers with little autonomy in their jobs. This shaping of preferences according to experience explains some of the stability of industrial relations systems.

In the countries where power seems least unequally distributed (e.g. Yugoslavia and some Northern countries) there is a link between personal involvement in decision-making and evaluation of, and interest in, the functioning of representative bodies. In these countries the interest in representative participation is also higher for workers who desire an increase in direct involvement. This may be because the union or the self-management system in these countries acts as an integrator of persons, levels, and bodies.

SOME CRITICAL CONSIDERATIONS

The judgement of systems for participation will ultimately depend upon the value-position of the observer. We cannot go very far in any direction discussing whether our results confirm or falsify the many existing social and political theories and suggestions about the effects of participation. We can only deal with a limited number of these. A variety of ideological positions may be discussed, such as participation as an organizing principle of societies, the institutionalization of participation as a change agent, participation as a machiavellian manipulative device, participation as a system stabilizer or learning process, the differential functions of direct and indirect participation.

Yugoslavia is, in principle, a different case from the others because there a socialist revolution preceded the introduction of workers' self-management. The economic and political systems of the country are different from the capitalist, mixed-economy arrangements to be found in the other countries. Within these countries workers' participation has developed much more slowly, typically as a reformist process. As arrangements for participation within countries vary only a little, we do not know for certain what kind of difference the arrangements make. Would the level of satisfaction, involvement, and influence of the Dutch workers be lower if the works' council did not exist? The Scandinavian countries are clear examples of co-operation between management and unions on productivity matters, and it seems that this has been a central factor behind the development of welfare and material consumption in these countries. At the same time, these countries are internally rather homogeneous ethnically, socially, and politically. Peaceful conflict-resolution and co-operation would probably exist to a considerable extent without formal arrangements for employee participation.

Still, our data suggest that formal participation contributes to avoidance of open conflict between employer and employee. The arrangements create a process of harmonization of interest groups by providing mechanisms of conflict resolution.

The reforms have come rather slowly, step by step, and have not at any time during the last decades, threatened the stability of the enterprises. Rather, one can argue, with the support of some of our results, that the reforms have been successful (if at all significant) in providing stability, peaceful conflict-resolution, and productivity in industry. Satisfaction with the system for representation increases, the more elaborate the system is. The union argument that it is absence of participation that threatens stability not its presence, is well supported in our study.

The argument that worker participation is closely associated with manipulation should not be disregarded. The clear connection between the level of indirect participation (the involvement of representatives) and equality in the power distribution across hierarchical levels should, in principle, speak against manipulation. The finding, however, that a democratic leadership style creates job satisfaction and a feeling of individual involvement, can, by a critical reader, be interpreted as a sign of manipulation by management. This effect is not created by the formal participative arrangements but it does point to the possibility that workers may be satisfied with their own jobs and companies, feel quite highly involved in decision-making, and still as a group be quite powerless.

Mulder's (1977) argument that participation contributes to manipulation when there are large differences in expertise is indirectly supported in our study. We find, for example that there is little disagreement over long-range policy decisions like those about investments and new products, while disagreement is quite widespread in minor personnel decisions (selection, small regulations in payment etc.). Where policy decisions are concerned employees' representatives cannot easily provide alternatives to management's ideas and proposals. The general findings, however, that disagreement is more widespread when power is relatively equally distributed across levels, supports our view that we can see participation as a learning process. In the countries with the most elaborate systems, and hence fairly democratic power distribution, there seems to be less immediate acceptance of management's proposals at board level. Perhaps, then, the state of manipulation is temporary, and disappears once employees or their representatives have learned from participating in such decisions, and management has learnt to share their influence over internal decisions with them.

The many similarities between the Yugoslav sample and the samples from the other countries, however, point to what seems to be a more fundamental problem than those mentioned above. Our study clearly demonstrates that the hierarchical structure of the work organizations we are studying and the technical division of labour produce and reproduce the inequalities which arrangements for participation are aimed at reducing. It seems that such arrangements can contribute quite far to the equalization of power and influence, but do not automatically provide room for individual involvement, or learning on the job and thus the development of skills among the workers. These areas are largely left to management's discretion. It seems that a democratic leadership style can give a strong feeling of involvement without necessarily any influence or learning following. It could therefore be argued that formal participation can act as window-dressing for an authoritarian hierarchy and a traditional, suppressive kind of job design.

We have demonstrated that the development of a democratic leadership style seems important, but mainly affects individual involvement rather than the collective influence of workers. The structure of the organization, the technology, the tasks to be performed etc. are not affected, so that participation takes place mainly within a structure which is given or controlled by management prerogatives. The rules for participation have generally been oriented towards the formalization of employee rights and not to the limitation of managerial prerogatives. (Changes in Swedish and Norwegian laws challenging the managerial prerogatives occurred after this phase of the study was completed). Even if there were such rules, it is questionable whether employees would be able to use them immediately to their advantage. Also, to a large extent employees take the context of participation as given. Thus, formal participation may function mainly as a new legitimization of the status quo.

Differences in hierarchical level very much reflect differences in the scope and discretion of jobs. Increasing formal participation may be seen as an attempt to overcome the negative psychological, social, and political effects of increasing bureaucracy and de-skilling at lower levels. We have found that, in the large enterprises, workers are less involved in long-range decisions, and we also see that in plants with a high proportion of female employees, employee involvement in general is lower. At the same time, the influence of the specific bodies for participation seems to increase. Indirect influence in participating bodies thus may act as a compensation for little involvement in the job (assuming that large size and a high percentage of female employees indicate a high level of routine and monotony in the low-level jobs). This mechanism is also reflected in the fact that middle managers are more concerned to gain increased direct (rather than indirect) participation—showing opposite preferences to those of the workers. Among workers one can argue quite strongly that conditions for the development of a belief in one's own ability to participate directly are not very good— particularly if they are unskilled and continuously attend one particular piece of machinery. In addition, we expect blue-collar workers to be more collectively oriented and that as individuals they do not want to influence, or decide on, issues affecting the company as a whole or groups of employees. Within a managerial culture, individual decision-making, individual careers, and so forth are much more positively valued.

It follows that, in addition to extending the formal rules for indirect participation and democratizing the leadership style, measures such as job redesign, technological change, and the introduction of autonomous work groups might be applied to increase workers' chances for individual and group-level learning and decision-making, thus transcending the limitations set by the 'given' organizational structure. However, this requires a strategy beyond any exemplified in the enterprises in our sample and covering areas which today are sheltered by managerial prerogative.

Democratizing the leadership style within management mainly affects the individual's feeling of involvement positively, while changing the context as suggested above contributes to equalization of power across levels. Increasing the scope for representative participation has an effect both on involvement and the distribution of power, particularly in the area of medium-term decisions focussing on personnel matters. Our study shows that, at face value, extending the regulations for participation is a strategic measure, particularly if centred around personnel questions. However, it seems from action research (Susman and Evered 1978) that participation in other areas, covered by management prerogatives today, and usually taken care of by experts (technologists, system designers, engineers), may be even more central in the process towards democratization (Butera 1975, Elden 1979, Gardell 1977, Qvale 1976, Susman 1976).

So far, our study has been written in the spirit of optimism: Industrial democracy is developing rapidly in Europe and is changing the distribution of power and influence towards equality between the various groups of employees. It is, however, also possible to view the whole process in a pessimistic perspective. Industry is certainly developing rapidly—the companies grow bigger, new technologies for production, control, and design are being implemented, new professions and experts are increasing their dominance, the market and finance systems become rapidly more complex. Also the political authorities have problems in matching the growth in power and complexity in industry. We have shown that the systems for participation which are covered by this study, also act as a part of the managerial control system. Decisions are more easily accepted by employees. The participative bodies in themselves have an effect on employees' attitudes, irrespective of the effect of influence and involvement. The legitimacy of the establishment is increasing, possibly without any change in the distribution of power. Or the levels may become closer in terms of power, but the hierarchy still remains. As argued already, systems for participation, whether they are within or outside the management hierarchy, do not challenge this hierarchy, but might rather reinforce it.

In total, this could mean that increased participation is a defensive measure, a necessity for providing internal stability in a period of rapid restructuring. The process of increasing participation could be reducing possibilities for employees to influence the direction of this restructuring. We have shown that, quantitatively, there seems to be a movement towards power equalization across hierarchical levels. If the workers, in a parallel process, have systematically been deskilled and the expertise of management has been increasing, we are actually observing the kind of manipulation Mulder (1977) described. Our study was not designed to check this possible interpretation of our data. We have to warn that our definition of industrial democracy, participation, and our way of measuring the distribution of power point to conclusions which may be misleading. It is quite possible that what is really happening in the enterprises covered by the study is a process whereby the employees are being led towards something over which they have very little control. The formal arrangements for participation create a model for industrial democracy. If conditions for learning about alternative models are not present, then we would expect participation only to reinforce the bureaucratic organizational design which was at the root of the problem in the first place. In the enterprises covered by the study, only the presence of unions with links outside the enterprise was likely to create a counterweight to management dominance and expertise (see also IDE, 1980).

CONCLUSIONS

Industrial democracy seems empirically to derive its legitimacy mostly from the need to equalize the internal distribution of power and involvement in organizations. There is a clear connection between the degree to which there are formal provisions for employee representation within and outside the management hierarchy, and the level of power equalization. The strongest determinant of power inequality between groups of employees and also of differences in individual involvement is, however, the hierarchical structure of the work organization.

We have not tried to judge how far any enterprises in our samples are from any 'end stage' of industrial democracy—if such a stage may be defined at all. We have seen that the democratization process is slow, and there seems to be a long way to go before problems due to too much equality become larger than problems of currently existing inequality, between individuals and groups of employees, managers and owners. In this chapter we have mainly discussed strategies for minimizing the influence-gap between top management and the employee at lower levels. We have shown in our study that a higher level of employee participation contributes to a reduction in power inequality. The possible fear that reduced power inequality might lead to anarchy or a completely powerless top management does not find support in our study. Rather, we find that top management, through sharing power with employees over decisions related to daily work and personnel matters, should be more free to concentrate on long-range strategic issues.

Systems for employee representation can only partly compensate for the inequalities created by the technical division of labour and organizational hierarchy. Even when in principle employees have full control at the top policy-making level, this is in itself not sufficient to remove inequalities, nor is the arrangement automatically instrumental for the development of alternatives to the hierarchical organizational arrangement.

We have found that the introduction of systems for participation through representation create positive attitudes towards the participative system and desires for more indirect participation. On the other hand interest in becoming involved personally in decision-making related to the job, and in bodies for participation, is related to the level of discretion individuals already have in their jobs. Thus, the majority of employees in industrial organizations develop positive attitudes to the arrangements for participation (and also to the company and the job) and increased acceptance of the legitimacy of the decision-making individuals and bodies.

The model and concepts that are being conveyed to the employees through the introduction of systems for participation are very much that of active representatives and a passive and satisfied electorate. This model becomes self-confirming, particularly if special provisions are not made to provide resources to the representatives so that they can present alternatives to the ideas, criteria, and solutions of management. The types of arrangement for participation in the twelve countries covered by the study are in principle very similar, although there are fairly large variations in the scope and strength of the rules. The main difference between the arrangements that seems to account for differences in willingness to challenge management's prerogatives is related to union participation in the system. If independent unions are represented in the bodies for participation, the reduction in power inequality increases.

In spite of the seemingly elaborate systems for employee representation in several of the twelve countries, the effects on the distribution of power and level of individual involvement are mild, and generally we conclude that industrial democracy is still in an embryonic state. The growing trend in Europe of experimentation and the development of projects in industry aimed at changing the immediate job situation of employees to provide better opportunities for direct participation, is possibly attacking some of the basic problems shown in our study. It is possible that this approach will add new dimensions to the system for participation, both in terms of employee mobilization and direct involvement, and in terms of creating conditions for the development of alternatives to solutions suggested by management experts. There is a strong need for further research combining these aspects of industrial democracy. The example of Yugoslavia seems to show that total workers' control at the top decision-making level is *not* a sufficient condition for overcoming the inequalities created by a bureaucratic organizational structure and large differences in expertise (c.f., IDE, 1980, ch. 12).

We have found that, under otherwise equal conditions, a democratic enterprise (i.e. one with a relatively equal distribution of power and individual involvement) has the following characteristics:

i. an elaborate (several levels) and integrated (e.g. through the union) system of formal representation;

ii. rules for participation that prescribe employee involvement in decision-making over a wide range of issues and with strong powers;

iii. a democratic leadership style (i.e. the employees are being informed, consulted, and to some extent left to make their own decisions on matters related to the job by their superiors);

iv. a high level of unionization;

v. young, female supervisors;

Opportunities for individual involvement are better in smaller enterprises, while a relatively more egalitarian distribution of power is found in organizations that are larger, are functionally highly differentiated, and are relatively dependent upon customers and other external bodies.

There is weak connection between self-reported involvement by individuals and the influence of their group while both aspects are conditioned by the institutional arrangements for participation.

Workers' attitudes to participation, the job, and the company are fairly strongly influenced by the leadership style of managers. A democratic leadership style leads to positive attitudes and a feeling of involvement in one's job, while the effect on the distribution of power is small.

The external political environment and value system differ between groups of countries covered by our study. This is reflected in the different outcomes of the (in principle) similar formal systems for participation. The politization and unionization of white- and blue-collar employees, and the participation of union representatives in bodies for joint consultation and decision-making, are widespread in some countries and contribute towards power equalization in those countries. In other countries, the effects on attitudes and social stability are more strongly emphasized, and the bodies for participation are less connected to any political, external network. Such national, cultural differences appear to be particularly important when developing strategies for democratization.

Any strategy for democratization—whether it is management's, the unions's or a joint strategy—aiming at equalization of power has to include systematic development along several dimensions—rules for participation, the development of a democratic leadership style, the mobilization and extension of union membership, training, and information activities. Strategically, it seems that extending the formal regulations for participation, particularly in medium-range personnel matters creates involvement and rising aspirations leading to a self-reinforcing cycle. This has apparently so far been the standard sequence in the plants in our samples. The introduction of stronger rules has followed a bargaining process, and in most cases a piecemeal application has resulted. There is therefore good reason to claim that today there is a need to look in more detail, in practice and research, into the necessary conditions for new arrangements to function in the desired way. Lack of research and ideas in this area has been associated with a very strong concentration on formal rules—which, in most cases, have been created without direct participation from those supposed to benefit from them. We assume that once the basic rights of employees (security and the right to participate) have been legally established and guaranteed, the need emerges for a more democratic approach to the solutions of the problems associated with providing industrial democracy.

APPENDIX A

QUESTIONNAIRE AND PROCEDURES

A.1. List of decisions and exact wording for workers, foremen, and middle management.

A.2. Questionnaires.

A.3. Top management—interview guide.

A.4. Field handbook.

APPENDIX A.1

The following list contains the decisions with the exact wording for workers and foremen and middle management:

Involvement–workers		Involvement–foremen and middle management	
1	Improvements in work conditions of your work group (dust, noise, safety)	1	idem
2	Appointment of new department head	2	idem
3	Establishment of criteria and procedures for hiring and selection of new employees	3	idem
4	Whether you can follow a vocational training course (during) work hours)	4	**Whether your workers* can follow a vocational training course (during work hours)**
5	To be transferred to another job within the plant	5	Permanent transfer of workers to other jobs within the plant
6	Major capital investment, e.g. an additional production line, a new plant, etc.	6	idem
7	Whether the company should make a completely new product	7	idem
8	To establish who will be your immediate superior	8	idem
9	Changes in how much a certain grade (wage group) shall earn (beyond possible existing collective bargaining agreements)	9	idem
10	Replacement of your personal equipment or handtools (not trivial things like pencils etc.)	10	Replacement of personal equipment (handtools) of your workers (not trivial things like pencils etc.)
11	Change in the way one or more departments are organized	11	idem
12	Assignment of tasks you have to do	12	Assignment of tasks to your workers
13	Dismissal of one of your co-workers	13	Dismissal of one of your workers
14	Whether or not work study technique is to be used (e.g. stopwatch, time-and-motion studies)	14	idem
15	From when to when you can go on a holiday	15	idem
16	From when to when working hours are	16	idem

N.B.: If a respondent from level B or C has no subordinates, decisions 4, 5, 10, 12, and 13 are not applicable.
*Your workers always refer to level A people.

Additional explanations specifying the issues in relation to Influence and *De Jure* Participation were:

Decision 1.   Improvement of work conditions of work groups (emphasis on 'safety'. Improvement beyond minimum requirement of safety and health laws.).

Decision 2.   idem (appointment of a man of C-level being in charge of one or two supervisors. Internal promotion is not included).

Decision 3.   idem (emphasis on 'procedures'; e.g. whether to use tests, administrative procedures. Refers to employment of A-level people).

Decision 4.   Whether a worker can follow a vocational training course

Decision 5.   idem (*permanent* transfer to an equivalent job).

Decision 6.   idem

Decision 7.   idem (new product within the framework of the existing production of the firm. This item is not as far-reaching as item 6).

Decision 8.   To establish, who will be their immediate supervisor.

Decision 9.   idem (refers to negotiations on company level).

Decision 10. Replacement of personal equipment (handtools) of workers (not . . . . .).

Decision 11. idem (emphasis on 'more'—major restructuring within the company is meant).

Decision 12. Assignment of task to workers (Regular tasks, distribution of work).

Decision 13. Dismissal of one of the workers (Does not refer to disciplinary action but other reasons—'picking' one when it already had been decided that someone had to go).

Decision 14. idem (does not necessarily imply salaries).

Decision 15. From when to when they can go on a holiday (referring to holidays that can be chosen individually).

Decision 16. The general scheme of working times.

APPENDIX A.2

The following questionnaires were used:

Form 1.1 — P1F

Here are a number of questions about your background. It is understood that your information will be kept strictly confidential by the investigators. Please answer carefully.

1. What is your *main* JOB FUNCTION?
   Enter the appropriate number in the box provided.
   1) production (in manufacturing or service industry)
   2) administration, personnel, general non-specialized management
   3) technical, like: research and development, industrial engineering, quality control, operations research, work study, etc.
   4) sales, marketing, purchasing, stores, etc.
   5) finance, accounting

2. Give your JOB TITLE:
   To which of the four levels do you belong? Enter the appropriate number in the box provided.
   1) Top or senior management (within two levels of the chief executive)[*]
   2) Middle management
   3) Supervisor (usually first level)
   4) Shop floor

3. How many people are there in your department, section, or group (whichever is the smallest)?

4. How old are you?

5. Sex: Male (M)
        Female (F)

6. How long have you been with the company? (In years. If less than one year put 'Less'. Include mergers or change of name of company, etc.)

7. Level of EDUCATION completed (Enter appropriate number in box)
   1) Primary education
   2) Secondary education
   3) Higher education excluding university
   4) University degree or equivalent

(Please answer the following three questions by Yes = 1, No = 2)

8. Are you presently a member of a representative (participatory) body?

9. Were you ever a member of a representative (participatory) body? (In this company or previously).

10. Are you a member of a union or similar professional body?

[*]As not all firms will have a differentiated hierarchy according to these categories, take as top management those who are considered to be at the top of the firm.

11. Nationality (if not British)[1]

12. If not (British)[1] how many years have you worked in this country?

Form 1.2 CLIMS

Here are some statements about your job and the organization you are working in. Your opinion is asked on these statements. Please indicate your response by ticking your choice in the appropriate space.[2]

1. Everybody's job in this organization is clearly defined

yes, that is definitely true	that is often true	sometimes true sometimes not	that is often not true	no, that is definitely not true

2. In this organization, it's clear who has the authority to make a decision
3. The policies and structure of this organization are usually clearly explained to us
4. We usually get information from the top very easily
5. Most activities here are planned carefully
6. Work is checked to see if it is done properly and in time
7. There is a lot of wasted time here: few things have been planned right to the minute
8. Everyone in this organization knows exactly what his position and task is
9. Everyone in this organization knows the responsibilities task, and authority of other people
10. We all receive the information we need here
11. In general, I find the situation in this organization relaxed and easy going
12. In this company, management really looks after the workers
13. Management and workers in this organization usually don't get on well together

Form 1.3 PO2

Issue: (Add issues from Decision list PO1/PO2).
Improvement in work conditions of your work group (dust, noise, safety)
In this issue: Please tick here

1. I am not involved at all   □
   I am informed about the matter beforehand   □
   I can give my opinion   □
   My opinion is taken into account   □
   I 'take part with equal weight'   □
   I decide on my own   □

2. How would you like it to be?
   I am not interested at all   □
   I want to be informed about the matter beforehand   □

[1]If not (British, Norwegian, etc.) according to country in which survey is carried out.
[2]Abbreviated version. In the schedule administered, the choice categories appear after each question.

I want to be able to give my opinion beforehand   □
I want my opinion to be taken into account   □
I want to 'take part with equal weight'   □
I want to decide on my own   □
I don't know, have no opinion   □

3. Would you like the main representative body to have a say in this matter?

            Yes   □
            No   □
        Don't know   □

Decision list PO1/PO2

1. Improvements in work conditions of your work group (dust, noise, safety)

2. Appointment of a new department head

3. Establishment of criteria and procedures for hiring and selection of new employees

4. Whether your workers can follow a vocational training course (during work hours)
   *for workers:** Whether you can follow a vocational training course (during work hours)

5. Permanent transfer of workers to other jobs within the plant
   *for workers:** To be transferred to another job within the plant

6. Major capital investment, *e.g.* an additional production line, a new plant, etc.

7. Whether the company should make a completely new product

8. To establish who will be your immediate superior

9. Changes in how much a certain grade (wage group) shall earn (beyond possible existing collective bargaining agreements)

10. Replacement of personal equipment (hand tools) of your workers (not trivial things like pencils, etc.)
    for workers: Replacement of your personal equipment of handtools (not trivial things like pencils, etc.)

11. Change in the way one or more departments are organized

12. Assignment of tasks to workers
    for workers: Assignment of tasks you have to do

13. Dismissal of one of the workers
    for workers: Dismissal of one of your co-workers

14. Whether or not work study technique is to be used (e.g. stopwatch, time- and motion studies)

15. From when to when you can go on a holiday

16. From when to when working hours are.

---

*Whenever a separate formulation is used for workers it refers to group A

Form 1.4 – O – ROC

Industrial democracy and participation can have various consequences irrespective of whether one likes them or not. Therefore in this questionnaire we have listed some possible consequences and we want you to tick which of these consequences have been brought about by (your system of *representative participation*) in your firm.[1]

1. Do people through the work of the (main rep. body) know more about what is going on here?

   Definitely   May be   I don't   Definitely
   yes   yes   think so   not

2. Do people accept decisions easier because of the work of the (main rep. body)?

3. Has the quality of decisions increased because of the work of the (main rep. body)?

4. Are the interests of employees better represented because of the work of the (main rep. body)?

5. Do employees because of the work of the (main rep. body) have a greater say in what's going on in this firm?

*6. Has the (main rep. body) led to slow decision making?

*7. Has a better mutual understanding and trust developed between management and employees because of the work of the (main rep. body)?

*8. Do workers through the work of the (main rep. body) just seem to have a say in something but actually they don't?

*9. Has the work of the (main rep. body) brought about an equalization of power between employees and management?

Again we have listed the same possible consequences but this time we want you to tick which of these consequences have been brought about *by your direct and daily participation* in which is going on in the firm.[1]

1. Do people know more about what's going on here?

   Definitely   May be   I don't   Definitely
   yes   yes   think so   not

2. Do people accept decisions easier?

3. Has the quality of decisions increased because issues have been discussed widely?

4. Are interests of employees better represented?

5. Do employees have a greater say in what's going on here?

*6. Have the discussions led to too slow decision-making?

*7. Has there grown up a better mutual understanding and trust between employees and management?

*Optionals
[1] Abbreviated version. In the schedule administered, the choice categories appear after each question.

*7. Has there grown up a better mutual understanding and trust between emloyees and management?

*8. Do employees just seem to have a say in something but actually they don't?

*9. Has an equalization of power been brought about?

Form 1.5 – O – PART

With this form we would like to ask you about your experience with various forms of participation in this company.

Please indicate your response to each question by encircling the appropriate words corresponding most closely to your answer.

A. *Participation through the works' council (or the main representative bodies to be selected)*

1. How much do you usually hear about what goes on in the meetings of the Works' Council?

| Very much information | Much information | Some information | Little information | Very little information |

2. How interested are you personally in the work of the Works' Council?

| Very strong interest | Strong interest | Some interest | Little interest | Very little interest |

3. Do you think that, in this company, the Works' Council is given a real chance by management?

| Definitely yes | To a great extent | To some extent | To a little extent | Definitely no |

†4. If your colleagues ask you to become a candidate for the Works' Council in the elections would you be interested in accepting a candidacy?

| Definitely yes | Probably yes | Perhaps | Probably not | Definitely not |

5. Do you think that, in this company, the right people are available to represent the interests of the employees?

| Definitely no | To a little extent | To some extent | To a great extent | Definitely yes |

†6. How easily can you get in touch with your representatives in the Works' Council?

| Very easily | Quite easily | Rather easily | Quite difficult | Very difficult |

B. *Direct participation*

†7. How often does your superior/boss consult with you and your colleagues before he takes an important decision concerning your department?

| (Almost) always | Often | Sometimes | Rarely | (Almost) never |

*Optionals
†Not applicable for respondents from level D (top management) and occasionally not for level C (middle management).

*8. If changes in your own work occur, how often does your superior/boss give you the reason why?

| (Almost) always | Often | Sometimes | Rarely | (Almost) never |

*9. To what extent does your superior/boss give you the opportunity to decide on your own?

| Not at all | To a little extent | To some extent | To a great extent | To a very great extent |

*10. If you have an opinion different from your superior/boss, can you say so?

| (Almost) always | Often | Sometimes | Rarely | (Almost) never |

C. *Evaluation of participation*

*11. How satisfied are you with the functioning of direct participation in your department (*i.e.* your taking part in decisions of your superior/boss)?

| Very satisfied | Fairly satisfied | Neither satisfied nor dissatisfied | Somewhat dissatisfied | Very dissatisfied |

12. How satisfied are you with the functioning of the Works' Council?

| Very satisfied | Fairly satisfied | Neither satisfied nor dissatisfied | Somewhat dissatisfied | Very dissatisfied |

*13. Do you think *your* interests are represented by/in the Works Council?

| Yes very well | Yes somewhat | More or less | Not so well | Not at all |

14. If you have personal grievances (complaints) what can you do?
   □ I cannot do anything
   □ I ask for support from a superior
   □ I ask for support from a union representative
   □ I ask for support from my colleagues/work mates
   □ I go to court
   □ I shall leave the company

15. In general, how much do you think the following groups have to say about how things are decided?

	Nothing	Some influence	Moderate influence	Much influence	Very much influence
A					
B					
C					
D					
E					
F					
G					

*Not applicable for respondents from level C (middle managers) and D (top management).

A — Workers	E — Supervisory board
B — Foremen	F — Internal representative body
C — Middle managers	G — External groups
D — Top management	please specify

Optional questions

*16. Do you think you have some influence on decisions in this company through your representatives in the (Works' Council)?

Very often   Often   Sometimes   Rarely   Never

*17. How much influence do you think your representatives have upon what goes on in the company?

Very much   Much   Some   A little   Very little

18. Does the Works Council/the system of representatives offer you advantages, which you would otherwise not have?

Not at all   To a little extent   To some extent   To a great extent   To a very great extent

19. Do you think the (Works' Council) here is a suitable place to reconcile the interests of workers and of management?

Definitely yes   To a great extent   To some extent   To a little extent   Definitely no

20. Do you think the (Works' Council) here is a suitable place to enforce employee (worker) interests against management?

Definitely yes   To a great extent   To some extent   To a little extent   Definitely no

21. Do you think the (Works' Council) here is a suitable place for discussing problems, giving advice and making plans for the whole company?

Definitely yes   To a great extent   To some extent   To a little extent   Definitely no

22. In all, who benefits/loses the most from the establishment of the (Works' Council) here?

	Benefits			Loses	
	Very much	Some what	No impact	Some what	Very much
Management					
Unions					
Members of the Works Council					
Individual workers					

*23. If your legal or formal rights are offended, what do you do?

- ☐ I cannot do anything
- ☐ I ask for support from a superior
- ☐ I ask for support from a union representative
- ☐ I ask for support from my colleagues/work mates

*Not applicable for respondents from level C (middle managers) and D (top management).

☐ I go to court

☐ I shall leave the company

* 24. How is your contact with your representatives in the Works Council?

☐ No contact

☐ I am usually informed

☐ I can go to them and give my advice

☐ They often ask my opinion

*25. Do you think your representative has to take care of the interests of more groups than yours?

| Definitely yes | To a great extent | To some extent | To a little extent | Definitely no |

*26. Do you think your representative thinks too much like management?

| Definitely yes | To a great extent | To some extent | To a little extent | Definitely no |

*27. Do you think your representative is too overloaded with other functions to represent your interests effectively?

| Definitely yes | To a great extent | To some extent | To a little extent | Definitely no |

Form 1.6 − O − SAT

Here are some questions on how you evaluate your work situation at the present moment. Again, the answers are kept strictly confidential and are only accessible to the scientists. Please indicate your response by ticking your choice in the appropriate space.[1]

1. Are you doing the job you would really like to do?

Definitely yes	Yes	Don't know/Neither nor	No	Certainly not

2. Does your job give you much opportunity to talk with others?
3. Do you think that the general management of this company is satisfactory?
4. Are you informed regularly about the quality of your work?
5. Does your job give you the feeling of doing something worthwhile?
6. Do you find the working conditions here (time schedule, extra working hours, temperature, etc.) satisfactory?
7. Do you find your colleagues pleasant people?
8. Do you think you should earn more for the job you are doing?
9. Do you find your superior a capable person.
10. Do you think your skills are appropriate for your job?
11. Do you feel that others consider your job as a valuable one?
12. All things considered, are you satisfied presently with *your work*?
13. All things considered, are you satisfied presently with *this company*?

*Not applicable for respondents from level C (middle managers) and D (top management).

[1] Abbreviated version. In the schedule administered, the choice categories appear after each statement or question.

Form 1.7 – O – RON

Please rank order the following sentences according to what you feel is most important for you in your job. Mark below the *three most* important and the *three least important* items.

1. To have promotion opportunities
2. To have stability of employment
3. To have the opportunity to influence decisions about my own job
4. To be able to use my capacities in my work
5. To have a nice boss/superior
6. To have a good salary
7. To have effective representatives (*e.g.* in Works' Council)
8. To have a clean and safe work environment
9. To have good cooperation with my colleagues

Please fill in the
numbers of

☐   ☐   ☐

the three most
important items

Please fill in the
numbers of

☐   ☐   ☐

the three least
important items

Form 2.1 – PO1

Issue: (Add issues from Decision list PO1/PO2)[1]

Improvement in work conditions of your work group (dust, noise, safety)

1. How much influence do the different groups have over this decision?

	No influence	Little influence	Moderate influence	Much influence	Very much influence
A – Workers					
B – First line supervisors					
C – Middle management					
D – Top management					
E – Level above plant					
F – Internal repr. bodies					
G – External groups					

2. Is the decision usually reached through disagreement?
   (No = 1; Yes = 2; Don't know = 3)   ☐

3. In case of disagreement, who has the final say
   A   B   C   D   E   F   G

[1] See above Form 1.3.

Form 2.11 — PO1 Extension: Negative PO

*4. To what extent can the following groups oppose a change of salaries if this change goes against their interest?

Groups	Cannot oppose at all	Minimally oppose	To some extent	To large extent	Completely oppose
A					
B					
C					
D					
F					
E					
F					
G					

*5. To what extent can the following groups oppose a dismissal of co-workers if it goes against their interests?[1]

*6. To what extent can the following groups oppose a new product if it goes against their interests?[1]

Form 2.12 — PO1 Optional items

7. Is the decision-making in the Works Council subject to severe limitations or is there a wide range for what decision alternative it can choose?

No limitations	Small limitations	Some limitations	Extensive limitations	Virtually no choice

8. From whom or from what source do the limitations come?

- ☐ From superiors
- ☐ From experts, *e.g.* company staff departments
- ☐ From production technology
- ☐ From outside the company

9. Do you normally discuss issues like the previous ones with others, before they are discussed in the Works' Council?

- ☐ With shop stewards/union delegation
- ☐ With workers who may be affected
- ☐ With somebody from management

10. Do you think the present level of joint decision making reduces your possibilities for withholding your consent?

Definitely yes	To a great extent	To some extent	To a little extent	Definitely no

[1] Same answer categories as for question 4 — not reproduced.
*Optional items.

11. What is the most frequent way an issue is brought up for discussion in the Works' Council? (give rank 1–3)
   ☐ By initiative from management
   ☐ By initiative from representatives
   ☐ It is a regularly recurring issue (*e.g.* yearly)

12. Please rank order the decisions from Decision list PO1/PO2 according to what you feel is most important for the goals of each of the following levels.
   A. *For workers* (please select the *three* most important decisions)
   B. *First line supervision* (idem)
   C. *Middle management* (idem)
   D. *Top management* (idem)
   E. *Level above the plant* (please specify) (idem)
   F. *Representations in the plant* (idem)
   G. *External group* (idem)

Form 3.1 – CON (Contextual characteristics)[1]

The questionnaire will be administered to members of the top management or specialists assigned by management for that specific purpose. The questions cover five main categories:

1) Technology of firm under investigation

2) Organizational structure (*e.g.* professional differentiation, number of employees per level, functional specialization, and organizational formalization)

3) Personnel policy (*e.g.* payment system, work hour system)

4) Economic data (*e.g.* ownership, turnover, investment dependency on holding company)

5) Managerial philosophy.

Wherever possible the individual items were carefully chosen from established and standardized research instruments (*e.g.* from the Aston studies).

Form 3.2 – PS (Participation structure)

1. This questionnaire[2] is filled in for each establishment by the researcher. Experience from the pilot phase shows that it is helpful and mostly necessary to do this in consultation with
   a) a key informant from the establishment/company (*e.g.* union delegate, Works' Council member, top manager), because there may exist participative structures that are company specific such as management policies, bargaining contracts;
   b) an expert in company law/labour law.

2. Definition of participative structure:
   Formal (*i.e.* written down) *operative* (*i.e.* still 'living' and enforceable–*e.g.* by a labour court) regulations pertaining to the involvement of various groups in company decision making. 'Custom and practice' are *not covered* by this definition unless they are enforceable.

[1] This questionnaire, being very long, could not be reproduced here.
[2] The Answer Sheet for the PS form is not included here.

3. The groups (and their codes) are identical with the groups in PO1 and PO2:

A — Workers, white and blue collar, without supervisory functions

B — First line supervisors (last ones with supervisory functions)

C — Middle management: according to establishment usage: all hierarchical levels above B and below D

D — Top management: according to establishment usage all persons considered to belong to the top management of the establishment

E — Level above the establishment: supervisory body (SB), managerial bodies (*e.g.* conglomerate management (MB), shareholders or owners (OW)
Note: In this category it will be necessary to indicate specifically the groups that are involved.

F — Permanent representative bodies at the establishment level, no matter of what origin: works councils, workers councils, union representative bodies (RB)
Note: Again. Please specify which ones.

G — Bodies/institutions *outside of company* (not outside establishment!) banks, community councils, regional planning council etc. (BO)
Note: Again. Please specify which ones.

4. The measurement is done on the basis of the 16 decisions in the Decision list.[1] Two questions have to be answered for each decision, on an ordinal scale regarding the *base* and a Guttman-type scale regarding the *mode* of the involvement of groups.

5. Base question and categories (code): 'Do (in/for this company) formal written down) regulations exist which provide an opportunity for one or more of the groups A–G to participate in the making of the respective decision?' Indicate appropriate basis code number:

1) Constitution
2) National law
3) Regional law
4) National collective bargaining contract
5) Regional collective bargaining contract
6) Sectoral collective bargaining contract
7) Company (anything above plant) collective bargaining contract
8) Plan/establishment collective bargaining contract
9) Management policy (defined as written down regulations, otherwise see 10)
10) Other legal bases ("Richterrecht") *e.g.* regulations that are not written down, but are enforceable in court as custom and practice *e.g.* management prerogatives

Note: It may be that there exist several bases for a group's involvement that successively specify the parameters of a group's involvement. In such cases multiple nominations will have to be registered, *e.g.* 1/3/9.

6. Mode question and categories (code):
'What kind of participation is provided for different groups by the formal regulations?' Indicate appropriate code number:

1) No regulation
2) Information (unspecified) must be given to group
3) Information *ex ante* must be given to group
4) Consultation of group obligatory (*i.e.* group must always be consulted prior to the decisions taken)

[1] See above Form 1.3.

5) Joint decision-making with group (*i.e.* group has veto power, must give its approval: the decision outcome is a result of bargaining)

6) Group itself has the final say

Note: *a*) This is a Guttmann-type scale of the increasing degree to which a group must participate and can determine the decision outcome. Therefore, *only one code nomination* seems theoretically possible per decision (the higher codes presumably imply lower code modes). However, if we find that different *bases* provide for different *modes* we will make note of that by marking it as follows:

	Base	Mode
Decision 1:	2	2
	4	2
	9	4

b) All groups that have no formal basis for participation receive a *mode* code of 1 (= No information).

c) If a general law (*e.g.* commerce code) states that the directors have the top authority, this is coded 6 for all decisions, unless other rules/laws imply otherwise.

7. The PS-answer sheet has a separate column 'Notes on *base*'. Note down the exact reference of the bases, *e.g.* 'constitution §8 (2)', 'coll. barg. contr. January 12, 1966',

APPENDIX A.3

Strategy

(a) What critical events have given rise to the company's present position (open question).
(b) Would you discuss some of the strategic policies for the development of the company? (open question)
(c) Which function would you consider is of strategic importance to the company?

Managerial ideology

What is the self-concept of the top management? It seems important to obtain information regarding the top management's self-image about its

   i. role within the firm e.g. entrepreneur/manager/administrator/facilitator/ controller, etc.

   ii. role *vis-à-vis* personnel in general, e.g. leadership, direct participation of employees

  iii. attitude towards fringe benefits

  iv. attitude towards unions

   v. attitude towards employers' association

  vi. attitude towards local politics

 vii. attitude towards general economic situation

Administer the attached questionnaire to your top management informant(s).

To be asked from member of top management only:

We would like you to judge the performance of *your* organization relative to other organizations. Consider separately each of the following characteristics: profitability; efficiency; growth; morale; adaptability. For each characteristic, indicate your answer by putting a tick in one of the divisions of the scale.

6.1 very profitable   average   not very profitable

1	2	3	4	5	6	7

6.2 very efficient   average   not very efficient

1	2	3	4	5	6	7

6.3 high rate of growth   average   low rate of growth

1	2	3	4	5	6	7

6.4 high morale   average   low morale

1	2	3	4	5	6	7

6.5   very adaptable   not very
      (to market)   average   adaptable

1	2	3	4	5	6	7

6.6   very adaptable   not very
      (in technology)   average   adaptable

1	2	3	4	5	6	7

6.7   very adaptable   not very
      (in personnel policy)   average   adaptable

1	2	3	4	5	6	7

APPENDIX A.4

Approaching the firm

1. *Letter* to the management of a selected firm, containing
 i. aims of the study;
 ii. procedures;
iii. costs ('. . . we developed a new interview technique which reduces the amount of time to a minimum . . .');
 iv. mention our international and national sponsors;
 v. independents of either labour market party; and
 vi. a short, understandable (i.e. non-sociological), description of the project
2. 3–5 days later: telephone call, asking for the preliminary option to take part or not; give further information and ask strongly for an appointment, especially if your partner is hesitating.
If the contact has not already been blocked at stage 2:
3. Discuss the project with a competent representative of top management and, if possible from the beginning, a works' council representative. If not, the works' council should be informed and asked for his consent personally by the researcher. Have the following materials ready (in a sufficient number):
 i. description of your institute;
 ii. another short description of the project;
iii. a longer and more explanatory description of the project.
Give detailed information on:
 i. the advantages of this project for the firm as well as the further general development of this issue;
 ii. procedures (number of interviewees, selection criteria, interview methods, costs of time etc.);
iii. offer the feed-back of results.
If the firm (i.e. management *and* works' council!) makes a commitment to take part:

Organization of procedures

4. Get hold of a contact man (personnel manager?) responsible for the organization of the project within the firm; preferably a works' council member, too.
5. When sampling for the general survey:
 i. apply the sampling scheme described under 17 below;
 ii. make selection of PO–1 candidates dependent upon the situation, i.e. either before or after the general survey;
iii. ask for respondents for the specialist's questionnaires;
 iv. check firm specifics:
   a) labels for job functions (PIF, 1)
   b) labels for levels (PIF, 2b)
   c) number of members of representative bodies
   d) number of foreigners (PIF, 11)
   e) decision set for applicability.

6. Make sure the study is made known
 i. generally within the firm;
ii. specifically to selected respondents.
For this reason a (standard) 1-page letter should be ready; date, time, and place
of the interview should appear in a prominent place, signed by management *and*
works' council. If possible get a telephone directory to be able to call people if
necessary.
7. Check with your contact man room capacities and further facilities (black-
board, overhead projector, sufficient number of seats, ash trays, a place where
you can leave your materials).
8. Adapt questionnaires as far as possible; prepare a working copy of the set
of questionnaires and write up standard explanations ('. . . in this firm middle
management means. . .') for all possible or anticipated questions. Add to and
correct your notes each time you are in the field!

Specialist questionnaires

9. It is up to the individual strategy of the researcher when he will gather the
CON, PO1, PS, PO3 information etc.; has proved to be useful to do as much
of it as possible before the general survey starts, as it gives you information
and sensitiveness to react to people, answer questions, give explanations, etc.
during the interviews.
 i. prepare specialist questionnaires as in appendix 2–4—this format will give
you enough room for notes;
 ii. adapt the formulation of decisions, levels etc. according to firm terminology;
iii. arrange the decisions in PO1 and PS to types of decisions (according to the
agreed typology of decisions):
    a) work/social conditions—routine (dec. 1, 10, 12, 15, 16);
    b) work/social conditions—goals (dec. 9, 14);
    c) personnel decisions—routine (dec. 4, 5);
    d) personnel decisions—goals (dec. 2, 3, 8, 13);
    e) economic decisions—goals (dec. 11);
    f) economic decisions—policy (dec. 6, 7).
This order will provide for a more consistent discussion of the issues.

Interview procedures

10. Give a short introduction (5 minutes) containing:
 i. introduction of researchers, their institute; if necessary the financial sponsors and political independence);
 ii. subject of the study;
iii. confidential treatment of data;
 iv. project on our own initiative;
 v. internationality of the project;
 vi. short explanation on the structure of the questionnaires;
vii. selection procedure: random selection;
viii. feed-back at a later time.
11. Give standardized explanations according to your working copy.
12. Keep a notebook (diary) for records of the interview processes (time,
difficulties, special questions, refusals etc.); take care especially of:
 i. code numbers;

ii.   questions/decisions not presented;
iii. levels of PO1 respondents, numbers per level.

PO3 — procedures

13. A description of the PO3 — instrument and instructions are to be found in minutes of IDE-plenary meetings.
14. The procedures of the PO3 instrument must be left to the discretion of the researcher; what must be made sure in any case is, that your results can be brought in line with the agreed PO3 outline (if only in parts);
15. The minimum requirements are:
  i.   issues of conflict and respective objectives/saliencies;
  ii. participants (bargaining zones);
  iii. outcomes and relation of outcomes to objectives/saliencies.

Feed-back of results to firms

16. Selection and preparation of data for feed-back purposes are left to the individual researcher; what should be kept in mind:
  i.   equal presentation' to both management and works' council (or other representation of workers); if possible, get a larger auditorium than just the top manager and works' council secretary;
  ii. have a sufficient number of copies of graphs, tables etc. ready;
  iii. stimulate reaction to and discussion of your results;
  iv. prepare a feed-back report for your files.

17. Sampling scheme

Level	N_1	$\sqrt{N_1}$	$k\sqrt{N_1} = n_1$
1) workers			
2) first level supervisor			
3) middle management			
4) top management			
total		$\Sigma\sqrt{N_2}$	
$n_f = 0{,}05x + 35$			

N_1 = total number per level
n_f = firm sample
k = constant
n_1 = level sample $k = n_f/(\Sigma\sqrt{N_2})$
x = total number per firm

APPENDIX B

METRIC ASPECTS OF SCALES

App. Table 4.1*
a-coefficients for the three O-PART scales

Country		OPART–D	OPART–E	O–PART–I
Norway	a	.82	.50	.44
	N	538	441	537
Sweden	a	.86	.67	.61
	N	1370	1381	1361
Denmark	a	.78	.73	.53
	N	427	321	335
Finland	a	.84	.54	.65
	N	745	710	741
U.K.	a	.82	.68	.64
	N	452	435	430
Germany (West)	a	.81	.81	.70
	N	470	468	462
Holland	a	.74	.70	.44
	N	646	629	687
Belgium	a	.80	.69	.47
	N	456	416	428
France	a	.87	.62	.59
	N	610	603	634
Italy	a	.83	.71	.73
	N	370	385	392
Yugoslavia	a	.82	.67	.70
	N	504	503	499
Israel	a	.76	.68	.40
	N	313	308	314

*The tables in this appendix are numbered with a '4' since they refer to Chapter 4.

App. Table 4.2
a-coefficients for the two O–ROC scales

Country		OROC–D	O–ROC–I
Norway	a	.76	.84
	N	534	552
Sweden	a	.80	.77
	N	1366	1361
Denmark	a	.80	.78
	N	293	398
Finland	a	.79	.80
	N	726	721
U.K.	a	.85	.84
	N	690	576
Germany (West)	a	.83	.78
	N	527	518
Holland	a	.69	.80
	N	126	440
Belgium	a	.78	.76
	N	576	499
France	a	.84	.81
	N	585	636
Italy	a	.90	.90
	N	388	401
Yugoslavia	a	.81	.80
	N	536	535
Israel	a	.86	.82
	N	264	332

App. Table 4.3
a-coefficients for the three O–SAT scales

Country		O–SAT	O–SAT-W	O–SAT-C
Norway	a	.79	.64	.70
	N	540	582	573
Sweden	a	.84	.81	.73
	N	1367	!397	1395
Denmark	a	.70	.78	.72
	N	440	462	450
Finland	a	.81	.77	.70
	N	756	772	766
U.K.	a	.76	.74	.69
	N	684	689	694
Germany (West)	a	.76	.82	.62
	N	536	541	542
Holland	a	.82	.81	.65
	N	649	690	690
Belgium	a	.70	.81	.65
	N	560	578	575
France	a	.80	.71	.67
	N	535	599	594
Italy	a	.85	.80	.79
	N	384	400	397
Yugoslavia	a	.76	.64	.65
	N	522	534	535
Israel	a	.76	.74	.59
	N	330	340	340

App. Table 4.4
a-coefficients for the two CLIM-scales

Country		CLIM-S	CLIM-R
Norway	*a*	.78	.55
	N	533	571
Sweden	*a*	.81	.73
	N	645	1403
Denmark	*a*	.71	.75
	N	434	449
Finland	*a*	.80	.67
	N	766	781
U.K.	*a*	.85	.45
	N	681	695
Germany (West)	*a*	.83	.56
	N	525	540
Holland	*a*	.81	.60
	N	629	668
Belgium	*a*	.81	.51
	N	564	573
France	*a*	.83	.64
	N	556	624
Italy	*a*	.83	.59
	N	379	406
Yugoslavia	*a*	.82	.30
	N	519	526
Israel	*a*	.80	.63
	N	329	336

App. Table 4.5
Intercorrelation table O/D scales (N=7857)

	CLIM-S	CLIM-R	OROC-I	OROC-D	OPART-D	OPART-E	OPART-I	OSAT-W	OSAT-C
CLIM-R	.48	—							
OROC-I	.29	.21	—						
OROC-D	.26	.26	.52	—					
OPART-D	.30	.43	.22	.34	—				
OPART-E	.37	.32	.57	.40	.33	—			
OPART-I	.13	.13	.44	.36	.28	.48	—		
OSAT-W	.32	.34	.16	.22	.40	.24	.11	—	
OSAT-C	.49	.55	.23	.28	.48	.35	.10	.51	—

App. Table 4.6

Eigenvalues and percentages of explained variance

Factor	Eigenvalue	Percentage of variance	Cumulative percentage
1	3.67	40.8	40.8
2	1.52	16.9	57.7
3	.80	8.8	66.5
4	.67	7.5	74.0
5	.65	7.2	81.1
6	.49	5.4	86.6
7	.46	5.1	91.7
8	.39	4.3	96.0
9	.36	4.0	100.0

App. Table 4.7

Factor loadings on two factors after varimax rotation with Kaiser normalization. (General sample, N=7857)

Variables	Factors	
	I	II
CLIM–S	.57	.23
CLIM–R	.67	.16
OROC–I	.14	.76
OROC–D	.26	.57
OPART–D	.55	.27
OPART–E	.32	.67
OPART–I	.06	.61
OSAT–W	.57	.11
OSAT–C	.83	.12

App. Table 4.8
Factor loadings on two factors after varimax rotation with Kaiser normalization per country

	Norway		Sweden		Denmark		Finland		U.K.		Germany (West)		Holland		Belgium		France		Italy		Yugoslavia		Israel	
	I	II	I	II	I	II	I	II	I	II	I	II	I	II	I	II	I	II	I	II	I	II	I	II
	611		1438		470		791		701		546		740		591		665		418		544		342	
CLIM-S	.40	.38	.52	.25	.53	.22	.54	.23	.55	.04	.66	.01	.56	.36	.50	.30	.64	.16	.59	.27	.64	.22	.66	.08
CLIM-R	.65	.23	.71	.19	.61	.26	.68	.08	.57	.17	.68	.12	.53	.37	.52	.32	.64	.25	.64	.08	.56	.15	.74	.01
OROC-I	.16	.76	.13	.83	.14	.86	.08	.80	.25	.70	.21	.78	.26	.52	.17	.56	.14	.74	.16	.69	.14	.73	.05	.84
OROC-D	-.01	.57	.24	.75	.27	.51	.20	.71	.42	.45	.12	.52	.51	.32	.08	.24	.65	.18	.23	.22	.23	.73	.11	.66
O-PART-D	.53	.38	.59	.31	.54	.33	.61	.20	.55	.25	.40	.26	.72	.17	.46	.27	.71	.15	.58	.06	.49	.39	.47	.07
O-PART-E	.34	.64	.39	.60	.35	.59	.35	.53	.23	.74	.37	.61	.16	.91	.30	.66	.25	.73	.33	.58	.44	.65	.19	.78
O-PART-I	.06	.56	.17	.48	.14	.47	.08	.44	.11	.74	.04	.64	.21	.38	.14	.60	.11	.62	-.05	.60	.26	.62	-.19	.78
OSAT-W	.74	-.02	.57	.15	.63	.16	.48	.11	.56	.09	.57	.16	.45	.09	.63	.09	.62	.06	.53	.12	.30	.10	.64	-.01
OSAT-C	.83	.15	.85	.81	.80	.15	.84	.12	.83	.04	.72	.11	.66	.30	.82	.19	.75	.16	.71	.10	.60	.21	.89	.04

App. Table 4.9.
Number of respondents (general sample) per level (4 levels)

Countries	Workers (A)	Foremen (B)	Middle managers (C)	Top management (D)	Total	Level unknown	Total
Norway	372	140	86	12	610	1	611
Sweden	1034	233	120	43	1430	2	1432
Denmark	314	54	73	27	468	–	468
Finland	592	112	64	17	785	5	790
U.K.	361	195	114	31	701	–	701
Germany (West)	343	136	66	–	545	1	546
Netherlands	515	183	31	–	729	2	731
Belgium	378	128	64	16	586	2	588
France	418	151	83	6	658	5	663
Italy	336	61	17	–	414	3	417
Yugoslavia	315	68	118	31	532	11	543
Israel	223	72	17	29	341	1	342
Total	5201	1533	853	212	7799	33	7832

APPENDIX C

AGGREGATED AND DERIVED SCORES

APPENDIX C

AGGREGATED AND DERIVED SCORES

AGGREGATION AND WEIGHTING OF DECISIONS

As described in Chapter 4 sixteen decisions were selected for this study. The selection took place on theoretical, pragmatic, and empirical grounds. They have been classified in a 3 times 3 matrix with content (work and social conditions—personnel problems—economic aspects) and time (short-, medium-, and long-term) as dimensions.

From the empty cells in the matrix in Figure 4.1 it can be seen that the two dimensions are not independent of each other. Most of the work and social issues fall in the short- or medium-term category, and the long-term category is mainly restricted to economic issues.

Of course, in the analysis each decision has been used separately. In addition, however, it was felt necessary to combine a number of decisions, or to use the total set of decisions so as to give a more general insight into the structure of the major decision areas. Moreover, by clustering or adding the information over decisions the wealth of information is reduced to a manageable level; an important advantage, certainly for complex analyses.

Two questions had to be answered: (i) what is the most important *basis* for clustering of the decisions, (ii) what *weights* should be attributed to the different clusters in the total composite score.

i. Attempts have been made to utilize factor or cluster analysis procedures as a basis for grouping the decisions. Preliminary analyses in different countries and organizations showed, however, that the factors or clusters depended very much on the kind of organization, level of respondent, the country, and the type of question. In addition, factor analysis based on Influence (PO1) data produced quite different factors from those derived from an analysis of Involvement (PO2) data.

Second, an attempt was made to cluster the decisions on the basis of groups of decisions with similar importance or saliency. A prerequisite for this type of clustering was a reasonable similarity across countries. Five social scientists and organizational consultants were asked to act as expert judges in each country, and to rank the decisions in view of the importance for the survival of the company. In Table C.1. the results of this ranking exercise are presented (based on ranking in ten countries).

It is clear that, although general similarities do exist, the differences between countries are sometimes rather striking and that the rankings do not provide sufficient basis for a clustering of the decisions to be generally applicable. A specific country-clustering would be technically possible, but would lead to serious difficulties if cross-country comparisons were to be made.

On the basis of the foregoing considerations and some further analyses it was decided to take as the basis for clustering the *a priori* classification of the decisions into short-term, medium-term, and long-term. Decision 15 (Holidays) often produced little variance and was treated separately. Consequently, the following clusters have been used:

Table C.1
Average importance rank per decision per country[a]

Decision	Average rank	Norway	Sweden	Finland	U.K.	Germany (West)	Holland	Belgium	Italy	Yugoslavia	Israel
Working conditions	8	4.8[b]	8.4	7.2	7.2	6.6	8.6	7.8	11.5	11.4	7
New department head	6	11.2	7.6	7.2	10.6	8.2	5.0	7	4.5	7.6	7.8
Hiring procedures	4	5	3.8	6.8	7.3	4.2	6.2	5.7	6.5	3.4	5.8
Training courses	13	9.4	15	11	11.2	13.6	12.6	8.4	13.5	9.8	7
Transfers	10	12	10.2	11.8	7.2	9.4	12.6	8	8.5	11.2	7.8
Investment	1	1.6	1.6	1.2	3	2	1.6	1.5	1.75	2	3.8
New Product	2	2	3.8	2.4	1.6	1.8	1.4	1.5	1.75	1.8	5.4
Appointment own superior	9	10	7	7	10.8	10.8	6.8	9	7.5	4.2	11.2
Pay levels	7	5.6	12	6.2	6	6.2	8.4	9.5	6	9.4	8.4
Personal equipment	14	13.6	12.6	13.2	10.6	10.2	11.4	11	12.5	6.2	12
Reorganization	3	4.6	5.8	4.2	5.8	7	3	3.3	2.5	4.6	4
Task assignment	5	9.2	8	7.6	5.2	5.8	8.2	7.8	7.25	7	5.2
Dismissals	12	10.6	12.2	7.4	9.6	11.6	12.8	13	10	13	14.6
Work study	11	9.6	8.8	13.8	12.2	11.2	8.2	12.7	11.75	9.4	11.2
Holidays	16	12	14.8	16	15.8	15.6	16	15.5	15.25	15	15.4
Working hours	15	13.2	7.4	13.2	11.8	13.8	12.4	14	14.25	10.	10.6

[a] N = 5 per country

[b] 1 = highest importance

1. Holidays (decision 15*),
2. Short-term decisions (1, 4, 5, 10, 12, 16),
3. Medium-term decisions (2, 3, 8, 9, 11, 13, 14),
4. Long-term decisions (6, 7).

ii. The second problem, the weighting for the calculation of the total score (over all decisions), solved itself. Importance was chosen as the most appropriate viewpoint for the attribution of weight scores. Since, however, the perception of importance within management did not have to run parallel to that of the workers two separate indices of importance were selected:

a) The sequence of decision clusters described above, weighted with the scores 1, 2, 3, and 4 respectively.

b) Weights based on the average scores for Desired Involvement (PO2–b) for workers as an operationalization of 'significance'.

In actual practice, however, the weighted and unweighted scores showed intercorrelations high in the 90's as well as highly similar patterns of interrelationship with other variables. Any weighting procedure, therefore, seemed redundant and has been omitted in the actual analyses.

VARIOUS DE JURE PARTICIPATION SCORES (PS-SCORES)

In this section we present a general description of the various scores based on or derived from the original data in the basic *De Jure* Participation data matrix presented in Figure 4.3. The matrix indicates the PS scores for the sixteen decisions for all six groups A through F. The matrix could be expanded with three rows for the three clusters (2, 3, 4) and a row for the total set of decisions (to), and a column for the sum of the PS Mode scores over groups A, B, C, D, and E (TO).

Consequently, there are basically five types of PD scores (see examples in Fig. C.1.):

i. Workers' (A) *De Jure* Participation in work condition decisions (1)–PS1 (A). Scores for the other fifteen decisions, and other six groups can be similarly classified.

ii. Workers' (A) *De Jure* Participation in short-term decisions—PScl.2(A). Scores for the other two clusters, and other six groups can be similarly classified.

iii. Workers' (A) total *De Jure* Participation—PSto(A). Scores for the other six groups can be similarly classified.

iv. *De Jure* Participation in short-term decisions in the whole organization—TOPScl.2. Scores for the other two clusters can be similarly classified.

v. Total *De Jure* Participation in the whole organization—TOPSto.

In addition these basic scores can be used to generate score patterns, through which insight can be gained into the distribution of *De Jure* Participation scores over the different levels, and into the relative strength of the participation structures, Not only can a graphical presentation of the PS Mode scores over groups A to G serve as basis for interpretations (see for example chapter 6, where several of these graphs at a national level are reproduced), but also a number of specific measures can be derived from the basic data indicated in Figure C.1.

The following kinds of measures can be listed in this connection:†

i. Variance (VAR) in total *De Jure* Participation between hierarchical groups: VARPSto. This measure is simply the standard deviation of PSto scores over groups A to E.

---

*This 'cluster' of course will not result in a new score.
†For a full and more detailed description of the list of derived scores, see Appendix D.

Decisions	Workers (A)	Foremen (B)	Middle managers (C)	Top management (D)	Level above plant (E)	Representative bodies (F)	External groups (G)	A+B+C+ +D+E Total
1	PS1(A)							
2								
3								
.								
.								
.								
cluster 2	PScl.2(A)							TOPScl2
cluster 3								
cluster 4								
Total set	PStot(A)							TOPSto

Figure C.1. Expanded basic *De Jure* Participation (PS) data matrix

ii. Differences in *De Jure* Participation scores between various groups. This can be established for various pairs of groups and for the three clusters of decisions (cl. 2, 3, 4) or the total set of decisions (to). The difference in total *De Jure* Participation between top management and workers (PSto(D–A)) is calculated by: PSto(D)–PSto(A)

iii. Inequality in *De Jure* Participation for various groups. This can be established for the three clusters (cl. 2, 3, 4) and for the total set of decisions (to). Inequality for a certain group is measured by calculating the mean difference in PS score between that group and the other hierarchical groups in the organization. The inequality in total *De Jure* Participation for workers (EQPSto(A)) is calculated according to the formula:

$1/3 \Sigma$ [PSto(A)–PSto(x)].

where x is B, C, and D. The inequality score indicates the under- or over-privileged position that a particular group has with respect to *De Jure* Participation as compared with the other levels in the organization.

VARIOUS INFLUENCE SCORES (PO1)[*]

In this section a description of the various influence (PO1) scores will be presented similar to the *De Jure* Participation (PS) scores in the previous section. Except for the five-point scale and the averaging of the ratings over key persons in order to generate the Influence scores in the matrix presented in Figure 4.4, the further expansion and derivation of the PO1 scores is similar to the procedure with PS scores. Figure C.1 can, therefore, also be used to illustrate the various derived Influence scores if one reads PO1 instead of PS. As with *De Jure* Participation (PS), there are basically five types of Influence (PO1) scores (again a specific group and decision have been used as prototype):

  i. Workers' (A) Influence in work condition decisions (1)–PO1.1(A). Scores for the other fifteen decisions, and other six groups can be similarly classified.

  ii. Workers' (A) Influence in short-term decisions–PO1cl.2(A). Scores for the other two clusters, and other six groups can be similarly classified.

  iii. Workers' (A) total (to) Influence–PO1to(A). Scores for the six other groups can be similarly classified.

  iv. Influence in short-term decisions in the whole organization TOPO1cl.2. Scores for the other two clusters can be similarly classified.

  v. Total Influence in the whole organization–TOPO1to.

Here also the PO1 scores can be averaged over organizations per country so as to obtain PO1 scores at a national level.

  As with the PS scores a curve, comparing the PO1 scores over the different levels, can be constructed, and can serve as basis for interpretation. Also a number of specific measures has been derived from the basic data described in the previous paragraph (see Appendix D). For example:

  i. Variance (VAR) in total Influence between hierarchical groups: VARPO1to, i.e. the standard deviation of PO1 scores over the groups A to E.

  ii. Differences in Influence scores between various groups established for various pairs of groups, and for the three clusters of decisions (cl. 2, 3, 4) or the total decision set (to). The difference in total Influence between top management and workers (PO1to(D–A)) is calculated by: PO1to(D)–PO1to(A).

  iii. Inequality in Influence for various groups calculated for the three clusters

---

[*]The description has been restricted to PO1a scores, in this section described as PO1 scores.

(cl. 2, 3, 4) and total decision set (to). The inequality in total Influence for workers (EQPO1to(A)) is calculated according to the formula:

$1/3 \Sigma [PO1to(A)-PO1to(x)]$,

where x is B, C, and D.

VARIOUS INVOLVEMENT SCORES (PO2)

As has been made clear before, the Involvement questionnaire was administered to the general sample respondents. Therefore, PO2 scores are primarily individual scores.

Involvement (PO2a)

At the individual level for each decision the Involvement score (PO2a score: six-point scale) is given, and for the three clusters of decisions the average score can be computed (acronyms for decision 1 and cluster 2: PO2a1 and PO2acl.2 respectively). For the sum-score over all decisions (PO2ato) it was decided that no weighting procedure should be followed, since no useful indicators for such weights were available.

If the Involvement scores are aggregated over individuals per level, the resulting mean scores can be used at a group and an organizational level and can then be compared with the Participation (PS) and Influence (PO) scores. The basic matrix for these organizational data is shown in Figure C.2. At this level we have mean scores on the PO2a scale for groups A, B, C, D, and F with respect to:

i. all sixteen decisions (for decision 1 and group A: PO2a1(A), meaning 'workers' Involvement in working conditions decisions')

ii. the three clusters 2, 3, and 4 (for cluster 2 and group A: PO2acl2(A), meaning 'workers' Involvement in short-term decisions')

iii. The total set of decisions (for group A: PO2ato(A), meaning 'workers total Involvement').

A final derived PO2a score is the sum of the PO2ato scores over three levels A, B, and C (TOPO2ato). This score indicates the total involvement in the organization.

Desired Involvement (PO2b)

What has been said above for PO2a scores applies for PO2b scores. A totally comparable set of individual scores for the sixteen decisions, three cluster scores, and the total set score is available. The only difference is that one should read 'Desired Involvement' instead of 'Involvement'.

At the aggregated level we also have similar derived scores for the various groups with respect to the sixteen decisions separately, the three clusters of decisions, and the total set. A score TOPO2bto (total Desired Involvement in the organization) did not seem to make much sense and has not been used in the analysis.

Differences between Actual Involvement (PO2a) and Desired Involvement (PO2b)

It is very appealing to construct and use a derived score based on differences between PO2b (Desired Involvement) and PO2a (Actual Involvement.) Such a

Decisions	Workers (A)	Foremen (B)	Middle managers (C)	Top management (D)	Level above plant (E)	Representative bodies (F)
1						
2						in each cell score 1–6,
3						indicating average score
.						on PO2a scale.
.						
16						

Figure C.2 Data matrix for Involvement (PO2a) data at organizational level score would have theoretical significance as an index of 'aspirations', 'satisfaction with involvement', 'relative deprivation', etc. From the methodological point of view, however, the use of the 'discrepancy score' raises quite a number of difficulties (see for instance Cronbach and Furby 1970, Wall and Payne 1973, Hoekman 1970, Wanous and Lawler 1972). Among these are the following:

i. The more the variance in the two measures differ the more the variance in difference scores will be determined by the variable with the largest variance. It was expected that in most cases Desired Influence would have a smaller variance (desired scores are mostly higher than actual, thus varying within a smaller range) than Actual Influence, and that the actual score variance would therefore be the stronger determinant of the discrepancy variance.

In a study on part of the sample (N firms = 71, N respondents = 3959), however, this expected difference in variance was not found. Both variables showed sufficient and about equal variance; the standard deviation for PO2a varied over decisions from 1.04 to 2.93 and for PO2b from 1.40 to 2.30. Variances of PO2ato and PO2bto were .71 and .74 respectively.

ii. Next, the sign problem might arise. If a desired score is lower than the actual score the deficiency score is negative. Questions have to be answered such as: has the sign to be disregarded? have negative scores to be treated as zero? have negative scores to be treated as a separate category? In this particular case the magnitude of the problem was small, since desired scores were mostly higher than actual scores.

iii. The reliability of difference scores is dependent on:

a) reliability of both component scores;

b) correlations between component scores, according to the formula (for variables with equal variance):

$$r_D = \frac{r_{x_1} + r_{x_2 x_2} - 2r_{x_1 x_2}}{2(1 - r_{x_1 x_2})}$$

where $r_{x_1 x_1}$ and $r_{x_2 x_2}$ are reliabilities, and $r_{x_1 x_2}$ = inter-correlation (Drenth 1975: 225). Without special effort it was very difficult to obtain reliability estimates of PO2a and PO2b measures for single decisions. The inter-correlations between the two measures, however, was quite high: for the total set .57. This means that the reliability of the difference scores will be quite low.

ii. There is another problem caused by the restriction of range of the desired Involvement score, and it being almost always higher than the Actual Involvement score. The higher the 'actual' score, the more restricted the range for the 'desired' score will be. As a consequence a negative relationship will be found between deficiency scores and 'actual' scores, and also by definition a negative correlation between deficiency scores and all other variables that are positively related with 'actual' scores (e.g. level of participation, experience with participation, and the like).

Of course, one can use discrepancy scores by partialling out the 'Actual' score, but it is questionable whether this purified discrepancy score will contain any information beyond that which is based on 'Desired' scores *per se*. In fact, this was supported by a comparison between PO2b scores and these purified discrepancy scores for all the decision scores. Almost all correlations with other variables such as group size, age, sex, tenure, educational level, membership of a representative body, and membership of a union, showed either exactly or almost similar patterns. In other words, the discrepancy scores corrected for

PO2a scores, measure more or less the same as PO2b scores.

On the basis of these methodological and metrical considerations, and in view of the empirical findings, no further analyses with difference scores were carried out in this study. In the analysis of relationships between PO2b and other variables PO2a has always been partialled out.

We should emphasize that not all of these arguments pertain to all difference scores. In fact, in this study a great many differences (e.g. PO1(D) minus PO1(A), PO2a(D) minus PO2a(A)) are interpreted. It should be pointed out that some of the artefacts and spurious relationships mentioned above result from the use of differences in scores obtained from the same individuals ('should' minus 'is now' in satisfaction research, PO2b minus PO2a in this study). This is not the case with differences in PO2a scores for levels D and A, and to a lesser degree with PO1 scores, since these are *average* ratings by key respondents.

APPENDIX D

TERMS, SCORES, AND VARIABLES IN THE IDE STUDY

D.1. Glossary of terms, definitions, and measurement.
D.2. Labels for decisions and clusters.
D.3. Over-view of variables and scores at different levels of aggregation.

APPENDIX D.1

GLOSSARY OF TERMS, DEFINITIONS, AND MEASUREMENT

PS1(A)
Description: *De Jure* Participation regarding decision 1.
Measurement: Score of group A on PS scale
Name: **Workers' De Jure Participation in working conditions decisions**[*]
  idem decision 2 . . . 16.
  idem group B, C, D, E, F, G.

PScl.2(A)
Description: *De Jure* Participation regarding decisions cluster 2.
Measurement: Mean PS score of decisions in cluster 2 for group A.
Name: **Workers' De Jure Participation in short-term decisions.**
  idem cluster 3, 4   idem group B, C, D, E, F, G.

PSto(A)
Description: *De Jure* Participation regarding total set of decisions.
Measurement: Unweighted PS sum score over sixteen decisions for group A.
Name: **Workers' total De Jure Participation.**
  idem group B, C, D, E, F, G.

TOPScl.2
Description: Total amount of *De Jure* Participation over all groups in the organization regarding decision cluster 2.
Measurement: Sum of mean PS cluster scores for cluster 2 over groups A, B, C, D, and E.
Name: **De Jure Participation in short-term decisions in the whole organization.**
  idem cluster 3, 4.

TOPSto
Description: Total amount of *De Jure* Participation over all groups in the organization regarding the total set of decisions.
Measurement: Sum of unweighted PS sum scores over groups A, B, C, D, and E.
Name: **Total De Jure Participation in whole organization.**

VARPSto
Description: Variance in *De Jure* Participation regarding total set of decisions over all groups in the organization.
Measurement: Variance for unweighted PS sum scores (sixteen decisions) over groups A, B, C, D, and E.
Name: **Variance of De Jure Participation between hierarchical groups.**

PScl.2(E-A)
Description: Difference in *De Jure* Participation between supervisory Board and workers regarding cluster 2.
Measurement: Difference in mean scores for cluster 2 between groups E and A.

[*]For labels for decisions and clusters, see Appendix C.

Name: **Differences between Board and Workers in De Jure Participation in short-term decisions.**
     idem cluster 3, 4.

PScl.2(D-A)
Description: Difference in *De Jure* Participation between top management and workers regarding cluster 2 decisions.
Measurement: Difference in mean scores for cluster 2 between groups D and A.
Name: **Top Management Worker difference in De Jure Participation in short-term decisions.**
     idem cluster 3, 4.

PSto(E-A)
Description: Difference in *De Jure* Participation between supervisory Board and workers regarding the total set of decisions.
Measurement: Difference in unweighted PS sum scores over sixteen decisions between groups E and A.
Name: **Differences between Board and Workers in total De Jure Participation**

EQPScl.2(A)
Description: Difference in *De Jure* Participation for cluster 2 decisions between workers and other groups in the organization.
Measurement: Mean difference in mean PS cluster score (cluster 2) between group A and groups B, C, D. Score is negative in case $A < 1/3(B+C+D)$.
                Formula: $1/3 \Sigma [PScl.2(A)-PScl.2(x)]$
                       $x = B, C, D.$
Name: **Inequality of De Jure Participation in short-term decisions for workers.**
     idem cluster 3, 4.

EQPSto(A)
Description: Difference in *De Jure* Participation for the total set of decisions between workers and other groups in the organization.
Measurement: Mean difference in unweighted PS sum score between group A and groups B, C, D.
Name: **Inequality of total De Jure Participation for workers.**

EQPScl.2(F)
Description: Difference in *De Jure* Participation for cluster 2 decisions between representative body and other groups in the organization.
Measurement: Mean difference in mean PS cluster score (cluster 2) between group F and groups B, C, D.
Name: **Inequality of De Jure Participation in short-term decisions for representative body.**

EQPSto(F)
Description: Difference in *De Jure* Participation for the total set of decisions between representative body and other groups in the organization.
Measurement: Mean difference in unweighted sum PS score between group F and groups B, C, D.
Name: **Inequality of total De Jure Participation for representative body.**

PO1.1(A)
Description: Influence regarding decision 1.

Measurement: Mean rating of PO1 for decision 1 for group A.
Name: **Workers Influence in work condition decisions.**
   (idem decision 2 16
   idem group B, C, D, E, F, G)

PO1cl.2(A)
Description: Influence regarding decision cluster 2.
Measurement: Average mean rating of PO1 for decisions in cluster 2 for group A.
Name: **Workers' Influence in short-term decisions.**
   idem cluster 3,4
   idem group B, C, D, E, F, G.

PO1to(A)
Description: Influence regarding total set of decisions.
Measurement: Unweighted sum of mean ratings of PO1 for total set of sixteen decisions for group A.
Name: **Workers' total Influence.**
   idem group B, C, D, E, F, G.

TOPO1cl.2
Description: Total amount of Influence over all groups in the organization regarding the total set of decisions.
Measurement: Sum of mean PO1 cluster scores for cluster 2 over groups A, B, C, D, and E.
Name: **Influence in short-term decisions in the whole organization.**
   idem cluster 3, 4.

TOPO1to
Description: Total amount of Influence over all groups in the organization regarding the total set of decisions.
Measurement: Sum of unweighted PO1 sum scores over groups
Name: **Total Influence in the whole organization.**

VARPO1to
Description: Variance in Influence regarding total set of decisions over all groups in the organization.
Measurement: Variance for unweighted PO1 sum scores (sixteen decisions) over groups A, B, C, D, and E.
Name: **Variance of Influence between hierarchical groups.**

PO1cl.2(E-A)
Description: Difference in Influence between supervisory Board and workers regarding cluster 2.
Measurement: Difference in average PO1 scores for cluster 2 between group E and A.
Name: **Differences between Board and Workers in Influence in short-term decisions.**
   idem cluster 3, 4.

PO1cl.2(D-A)
Description: Difference in Influence between top management and workers regarding cluster 2 decisions.
Measurement: Difference in average PO1 scores for cluster 2 between group D and A.

Name: **Top Management/Worker difference in Influence in short-term decisions.**
idem cluster 3, 4.

PO1to(E-A)
Description: Difference in Influence between supervisory Board and workers regarding the total set of decisions.
Measurement: Difference in unweighted PO1 sum scores over sixteen decisions between groups E and A.
Name: **Differences between Board and Workers in total Influence.**

PO1to(D-A)
Description: Difference in Influence between top management and workers regarding the total set of decisions.
Measurement: Difference in unweighted PO1 sum scores over sixteen decisions between groups D and A.
Name: **Top Management/Worker difference in total Influence.**

EQPO1cl.2(A)
Description: Difference in Influence for cluster 2 decisions between workers and other groups in the organization.
Measurement: Mean difference in mean PO1 score for cluster 2 between group A and groups B, C, and D.
Formula: $1/3 \ \Sigma [PO1cl.2(A)-PO1cl.2(x)]$
$x = B, C, D.$
Name: **Inequality of Influence in short-term decisions for workers.**
idem cluster 3, 4.

EQPO1cl.2(F)
Description: Difference in Influence for cluster 2 decisions between representative body and other groups in the organization.
Measurement: Mean difference in mean PO1 score for cluster 2 between group F and groups B, C, and D.
Name: **Inequality of Influence in short-term decisions for representative body.**
idem cluster 3, 4.

EQPO1to(A)
Description: Differences in Influence for the total set of decisions between workers and other groups in the organization.
Measurement: Mean difference in unweighted PO1 sum score over sixteen decisions between group A and groups B, C, D.
Name: **Inequality of total Influence for workers.**

EQPO1to(F)
Description: Differences in Influence for the total set of decisions between the representative body and other groups in the organization.
Measurement: Mean difference in unweighted PO1 sum score (over sixteen decisions) between group F and groups B, C, D.
Name: **Inequality of total Influence for representative body.**

PO1b-CONFL.(1)
Description: Level of conflict attached to decision 1.
Measurement: Mean percentage of key figures that have indicated yes on PO1b question for decision 1.

Name: **Level of conflict attached to working conditions decisions.**
   idem decisions 2 16
   cluster 2, 3, 4, to set

PO2a1
Description: Involvement regarding decision 1.
Measurement: Score on PO2a scale for decision 1.
Name: **Involvement in working conditions decisions.**
   idem decision 2 16

PO2a1(A)
Description: Involvement of workers regarding decision 1.
Measurement: Mean score on PO2a scale for group A.
Name: **Workers' Involvement in working conditions decisions.**
   idem decisions 2 16
   idem groups B, C, D, F.

PO2acl.2
Description: Involvement regarding decision cluster 2.
Measurement: Mean cluster score on PO2a scale.
Name: **Involvement in short-term decisions.**
   idem cluster 3, 4.

PO2acl.2(A)
Description: Involvement of workers regarding decision cluster 2.
Measurement: Average of mean cluster scores on PO2a scale.
Name: **Workers' Involvement in short-term decisions.**
   idem cluster 3, 4.
   idem group B, C, D, F.

PO2ato(A)
Description: Involvement of workers regarding the total set of decisions.
Measurement: Unweighted sum of PO2a scores for the sixteen decisions averaged
               for group A.
Name: **Workers total Involvement.**
   idem group B, C, D, F.

TOPO2ato
Description: Total amount of Involvement regarding total set of decisions in
               the organization.
Measurement: Sum of unweighted PO2a sum scores (sixteen decisions) over
               groups A, B, and C.
Name: **The total Involvement in the organization.**

PO2b1
Description: Desired Involvement regarding decision 1.
Measurement: Score on PO2b scale.
Name: **Desired Involvement in working conditions decisions.**
   idem decisions 2 16

PO2b1(A)
Description: Desired Involvement of workers regarding decision 1.
Measurement: Mean score in PO2b scale for group A.
Name: **Workers' Desired Involvement in working conditions decisions.**
   idem decision 2 16
   idem groups B, E, D, F.

PO2bcl.2
Description: Desired Involvement regarding decision cluster 2.
Measurement: Mean cluster score on PO2b scale.
Name: **Desired Involvement in short-term decisions.**
    idem cluster 3, 4.

PO2bcl.2(A)
Description: Desired Involvement of workers regarding decision cluster 2.
Measurement: Average of mean cluster score on PO2b scale for group A.
Name: **Workers' Desired Involvement in short-term decisions.**
    idem cluster 3, 4.
    idem group B, C, D, F.

PO2bto(A)
Description: Desired Involvement of workers regarding the total set of deci-
                sions.
Measurement: Unweighted sum of PO2b score for sixteen decisions averaged
                for group A.
Name: **Workers total Desired Involvement.**
    idem group B, C, D, F.

PO2c1
Description: Desired Influence for representative body regarding decision 1.
Measurement: Answer on PO2c scale.
Name: **Desired Influence for representative body regarding working
                conditions decisions.**
    idem decision 2 . . . . . 16.

PO2c1(A)
Description: Desired Influence for representative body regarding decision 1,
                as expressed by workers.
Measurement: Percentage 'yes' on PO2c scale for decision 1 computed for
                group A.
Name: **Desired Influence for representative body regarding working
                conditions decisions as expressed by workers.**
    idem decision 2 16
    idem group B, C, D, F.

PO2ccl.2(A)
Description: Desired Influence for representative body regarding decision
                cluster 2, as expressed by workers.
Measurement: Mean percentage 'yes' on PO2c scale for decision cluster 2, com-
                puted for group A.
Name: **Desired Influence for representative body regarding short-term
                decision as expressed by workers.**
    idem cluster 3, 4.
    idem group B, C, D, F.

PO2cto(A)
Description: Desired Influence for representative body regarding the total set
                of decisions as expressed by workers.
Measurement: Mean percentage 'yes' on PO2c scale for total set of decisions,
                computed for group A.

Name: **Total desired Influence for representative body as expressed by workers.**

   idem group B, C, D, F.

OPART-D
Name: **Rating of Direct Participation**
Measurement: Mean score of items 7–11 on O–PART scale, times 10.

OPART-E
Name: **Evaluation of the Representative Body.**
Measurement: Mean score of items 3, 5, 12, 13 on O–PART scale, times 10.

OPART-I
Name: **Interest in the Representative Body.**
Measurement: Mean score of items 1, 2, 4, 6 on OPART scale, times 10.

OPART-15
Name: **Control graph.**
Measurement: Pattern of 4 scores indicating average ratings for groups A, B, C, and D on OPART–15 question.

OROC-R
Name: **Rating of Consequences of the Representative Body.**
Measurement: Mean score of items 1–5 on OROC–R scale, times 10.

OROC-D
Name: **Rating of Consequences of Direct Participation.**
Measurement: Mean score of items on OROC–D scale, times 10.

OSAT-W
Name: **Satisfaction with Work.**
Measurement: Mean score of items 1, 5, 10, 12 on OSAT scale, times 10.

OSAT-C
Name: **Satisfaction with Company.**
Measurement: Mean score of items 3, 6, 9, 13 on SAT scale, times 10.

OSAT
Name: **General Satisfaction.**
Measurement: Mean score of items 1–10, on SAT scale, times 10.

CLIM-S
Name: **Clarity of Communication and Structure of the Organization.**
Measurement: Mean score of items 1–10 in CLIM scale, times 10.

CLIM-R
Name: **Quality of Management–Employee Relations.**
Measurement: Mean score of items 11–13 on CLIM scale, times 10.

ORON (3)
Name: **Rank Order of Need for Direct Participation.**
Measurement: Score 0, 1, or 2 for need 3 in O–RON scale (i.e. belonging to 'least', 'medium' or 'most important' category).

ORON (7)
Name: **Rank Order of Need for Good Representation.**
Measurement: Score 0, 1, or 2 for need 7 in O–RON scale (i.e. belonging to 'least', 'medium' or 'most important' category).

APPENDIX D.2

LABELS FOR DECISIONS AND CLUSTERS

1. Working conditions decisions (Working conditions)
2. Appointing new department head (New department head)
3. Deciding hiring rules (Hiring procedures)
4. Granting permission to an employee to follow a training course (Training course)
5. Transfer an employee to another job (Transfers)
6. Major investment decisions (Investment)
7. New product decisions (New product)
8. Appointment immediate superior (Appointment own superior)
9. Readjusting pay level for a certain group (Pay levels)
10. Deciding about replacement of personal equipment (Personal equipment).
11. Reorganization decisions (Reorganization)
12. Assigning tasks to an employee (Task assignment)
13. Dismissals (Dismissals)
14. Deciding to carry out a work study (Work study)
15. Settle holiday dates (Holidays)
16. Fixing working hours (Working hours)

Cluster no.
   2. short-term decisions
   3. medium-term decisions
   4. long-term decisions

OVER-VIEW OF ALL VARIABLES AND SCORES AT DIFFERENT LEVELS OF AGGREGATION

Levels of aggregation

Variables	Group A–G per organization			Organization			Country		
	Individual	Mean of individual scores — Global scores	Frequencies	Global	Mean of level means	Frequencies	Overall mean	Mean per level	Frequencies
PS 1–16		✓						✓	
PScl 2–4		✓						✓	
PSto		✓						✓	
TOPScl 2–4				✓			✓		
TOPSto				✓			✓		
VARPSto				✓			✓		
PScl 2–4(E–A)				✓			✓		
PScl 2–4(D–A)				✓			✓		
PSto (E–A)				✓			✓		
PSto (D–A)				✓			✓		
EQPScl 2–4 (A,F)				✓			✓		
EQPSto (A,F)				✓			✓		
PO1 1–16		✓						✓	
PO1 2–4		✓						✓	
PO1to		✓						✓	
TOPO1 cl 2–4				✓			✓		
TOPO1 to				✓			✓		
VARPO1 to				✓			✓		

Appendix D3 (cont.)

Variables	Mean of individual scores		Frequencies	Mean of level means		Mean per level	
	Individual	Global		Global	Frequencies	Overall mean	Frequencies
PO1cl 2–4(E–A)				✓		✓	
PO1cl 2–4(D–A)				✓		✓	
PO1to(E–A)				✓		✓	
PO1to(D–A)				✓		✓	
EQPO1cl 2–4(A,F)				✓		✓	
EQPO1to (A,F)				✓		✓	
PO1b CONFL 1–16				✓		✓	
PO1b CONFL to				✓		✓	
PO1c frequencies		✓					
PO2c 1–16	✓	✓		✓		✓	✓
PO2c cl.1–4	✓	✓		✓		✓	✓
PO2c to	✓	✓		✓		✓	✓
PO2a 1–16	✓	✓		✓		✓	✓
PO2acl 2–4	✓	✓		✓		✓	✓
PO2a to	✓	✓		✓		✓	✓
TOPO2a to	✓	✓		✓		✓	✓
PO2b 1–16	✓	✓		✓		✓	✓
PO2bcl 1–14	✓	✓		✓		✓	✓
PO2b to	✓	✓		✓		✓	✓
OPART-D	✓	✓		✓		✓	✓
OPART-E	✓	✓		✓		✓	✓
OPART-I	✓	✓		✓		✓	✓
OPART-15	✓	✓		✓		✓	✓
OROC-R	✓	✓		✓		✓	✓

OROC-D

ORON-3
ORON-5
OSAT
OSAT-W

OSAT-C
CLIM-S
CLIM-R

PIF
COMP CON
CON CON

APPENDIX E

'SOCIAL CONTRACT' OF THE IDE INTERNATIONAL RESEARCH GROUP

OBJECTIVE

The purpose of the 'social contract' is to ensure a continuing harmonious and productive relationship between members of a large multi-national research team over a number of years. This relationship can only be sustained if equitable acknowledgement to individuals in the group, research organizations, funding bodies, etc. are made, and if other conditions described in this document are fulfilled. Scientists in different countries, and even in different disciplines within the same country are likely to have a variety of expectations and professional practices. It would therefore seem advisable to blend these expectations and practices into an acceptable code of conduct, that is to say, an agreed social contract.

INTRODUCTION

Most problems seem to come up in relation to acknowledgements and publication rights. Basic to these is the question of ownership. The international research study on Industrial Democracy is fairly unique in having been devised *jointly* by a group of some sixteen social scientists coming from twelve different countries. The theoretical framework, hypotheses, field methodology, and research instruments have been worked out by varying sub-groups or individuals within the team or by most of them together. Some have contributed more than others. Moreover, some of the work has been self-generated while in other cases it was borrowed from established theory, method, and instrumentation.

Furthermore, some institutions, principally the International Institute of Management, Fritz Thyssen Foundation, and the Ford Foundation, have played important roles in translating the motives of the research into reality. Finally in each country there are institutions and/or individuals which play key roles in financing or launching the research. In these circumstances, the task of giving fair acknowledgement is clearly complex. Lack of acknowledgement is usually due to thoughtlessness rather than malevolence. Hence it seems desirable (i) to adopt some common and agreed formulation of words; (ii) to have some means of getting a check on one's interpretation of the appropriate procedure if there is even the slightest doubt. Experience suggests that interpersonal relationships can be very seriously affected by errors or omissions. The problems become more serious as the research produces data and gets close to publication.

AGREEMENTS

Acknowledgements

i. Acknowledgements must be given according to the work done. Work means scientific work (e.g. theory, methodology, data analysis, writing, more than administration and routine field work).
ii. Research institutions as well as individual scientists should be mentioned.

iii. Financial inputs must be acknowledged separately. If one country helps another financially, this too should be mentioned.

iv. Acknowledgements should be prominently displayed. Usually this means the first page of an article or text.

v. In a study lasting several years some scientists may not stay with us to the end (though naturally we want to avoid this). The people are nevertheless entitled to the appropriate acknowledgements (see (vi) (xvi) (xvii)).

vi. The social contract is designed mainly for the principal researchers. Nevertheless in certain circumstances, some students or research assistants may come to play important roles. Depending on the contribution acknowledgement should be given in the text or in a footnote.

Ownership

vii. The international data are owned collectively by the International Research Group. The data generated in each country belong primarily to that country and to no other. However, each country has a solemn obligation to pool its data with everybody else for the total analysis. Each country has responsibility for its own data but see (xii) (xiv) (xviii).

viii. The interpretation of the data for any country is primarily the duty and prerogative of the principal researcher(s) in that country. The international comparison however is the primary responsibility of the international group, which appoints a drafting committee for preparatory work.

ix. In the unlikely event of a conflict of interpretation between a national group (relating to its own data) and the International Research Group, the national teams' views must be allowed to appear in the report, article, book, etc. (this could be handled like a minority report in a Commission's Report).

x. No member of a team and no national group can publish any material belonging to:

a) the International Research Group (any general statement about the research theory, hypotheses, methods or findings etc. resulting from the collective effort of the IRG)

b) any other individual or group in the IRG

without prior agreement.

xi. Publications (theses, articles) using data belonging to the International Research Group or a national team can appear only after publication of the original studies and with proper acknowledgement.

xii. Each member of the International Research Group has access to the international and/or national data, but only after the official international/national publications have appeared.

xiii. No person or team should give promises or undertakings to sponsors which conflict with the social contract.

Timing

xiv. Timing is important in providing the necessary data, interpretation, etc. for the final analysis. Any team or individual considerably out of step with the rest, holds up everybody, risks reputations, and courts serious trouble with funding bodies. A negative acknowledgement or a request for withdrawal may be a consequence.

xv. No national team has the right to report on, or to publish results from, the international study.

xvi. No national team has the right to report on, or to publish results from, any other national study prior to the actual publication of the national study, unless both partners agree to produce a joint publication.

xvii. A clearing house function collecting information on all publications, planned or in process, should be performed by the International Institute of Management. Each country has the obligation to keep the International Institute of Management informed about such plans or publications.

Quality of data

xviii. The quality of data from each country is obviously the concern of every-body in a comparative study. If any country cannot produce standard data by the agreed standards, this must be freely admitted. A consequence of such a problem may be negative acknowledgement (however polite) or omission. Agreed standards include the possibility of 'equivalent' data (but of high quality) where identical data are not available or would not make sense.

Authorship

xix. The final report will be authorized jointly by the IDE International Research Group, which other things being equal, will be the group as listed in Appendix A in the article 'Industrial Democracy in Europe' (IDE 1976). In addition, due acknowledgements will be made to any important input (e.g. drafting commit-tee, analysis committee).

xx. In other reports, articles, papers etc. presenting parts of the international study the following guidelines should be accepted as standards: if the 'input' of different people to an article, etc. is equal, names will appear alphabetically. Alternatively, the person who takes on primary responsibility for drafting a script and/or interpreting data for an article etc. will be senior author (his name will appear first). It is suggested that 'work' rather than general 'seniority' is the major criterion for senior authorship rights.

xxi. Where a national team has several scientists, the same general principles from this social contract should operate intra-nationally.

xxii. Each country has a responsibility for searching the available literature, both of its own country and generally. The national literature should be used as a starting point for the national data analysis. Useful references should be shared in the international group.

Royalties

xxiii. The International Research Group decides at a later stage the destination of the eventual royalties from publications.

Arbitration

xxiv. In case of lack of agreement on any aspects of the social contract a per-manent three-man arbitration team will solve potential conflicts. If the conflict cannot be solved the arbitration team brings the case to the International Research Group. Action will be suspended until the IRG takes a decision.

APPENDIX F

ADDITIONAL DATA TABLES

App. Table 5.1
Inter-correlation matrix of CON variables

	CO1	CO2	CO3	CO4	CO5	CO6	CO7	CO8	CO9	CO10	CO11	CO12	CO13	CO14	CO15	CO16	CO17	CO18	CO19
CO1	–																		
CO2	-05	--																	
CO3	25	-05	–																
CO4	30	-31	30	–															
CO5	01	-12	03	41	–														
CO6	14	22	19	21	04	–													
CO7	-01	15	02	-17	02	20	–												
CO8	12	15	-03	-15	16	26	18	–											
CO9	21	25	-05	-14	-09	25	10	27	–										
CO10	01	23	07	-00	-05	16	-04	03	35	–									
CO11	11	02	16	11	17	12	-09	00	31	09	–								
CO12	11	14	-13	-15	-11	07	-18	04	34	14	16	–							
CO13	-06	-08	16	27	21	08	05	09	-22	02	00	-12	–						
CO14	08	-01	03	-14	-26	-09	-06	-07	-02	-04	-09	06	-04	–					
CO15	-31	15	-28	-66	-17	-29	06	02	04	05	-15	15	-18	25	–				
CO16	19	-06	12	01	-03	03	02	00	-00	-20	04	09	-10	04	-02	–			
CO17	17	04	00	15	17	10	-01	05	02	-08	13	11	-06	-10	-18	04	–		
CO18	08	-10	04	15	19	13	03	17	18	26	14	03	18	-24	-14	09	04	–	
CO19	18	26	14	-02	-14	33	06	08	68	32	37	31	-23	15	03	-05	12	05	–
V146	06	08	-12	11	-17	12	04	-03	23	25	-12	-05	01	-10	-04	-13	18	05	16
V147	16	01	-02	26	-18	01	-20	-26	00	18	-20	-01	06	11	-05	04	14	-05	11
V150	14	-03	03	31	06	-05	-28	-12	05	15	-10	-01	12	-05	-02	18	16	08	02
V246	03	-07	-17	04	-07	-03	22	04	11	-10	-03	-06	-00	-02	03	01	22	03	-04
V247	13	-03	-11	06	-28	-06	-12	-04	-05	-05	-13	07	01	28	-03	05	09	-04	-06
V250	08	05	-09	-01	-16	-04	-13	-04	-05	-00	-03	07	-05	01	00	08	17	01	-02
V346	-04	-11	-11	11	05	-08	-04	04	09	-01	-12	-20	09	-12	-03	-11	20	28	06
V347	20	-17	04	19	03	-01	-14	-16	-08	00	06	-01	02	01	-14	08	15	07	02
V350	15	-15	08	24	-01	-01	-11	-11	-11	-14	-01	01	-11	-05	-15	13	12	-07	-01
22A	-06	15	-08	00	-01	00	-06	08	-00	01	-05	-03	-03	-21	-06	-06	-20	-11	02
22B	-29	-20	-06	-29	-28	-06	13	-06	07	-05	09	11	-17	23	32	06	-15	-19	12
C405	-37	07	-26	-30	-02	-10	07	-02	-05	12	-11	-09	-10	-26	25	-05	-10	13	-27
C406	-33	05	-07	-22	08	02	05	16	-15	-14	-36	-13	-01	-09	15	-04	-13	-24	-29
C407	31	-08	-26	-26	-18	-10	04	14	12	00	-23	22	16	11	20	-00	07	-05	01
C410	56	-07	21.	17	04	04	05	04	10	-03	13	-19	-12	-08	-25	38	17	19	04
C411	42	04	07	-06	-04	-12	-07	11	27	03	-22	-13	-14	-19	-04	-04	-09	07	-02
C414	-25	11	-05	17	28	-15	-00	-07	-12	11	-25	-21	06	-19	04	-05	12	09	-04
C416	-38	04	-08	-43	-31	-12	16	03	-01	-12	-13	-03	-02	15	35	00	-14	-16	02

CO1	Formal Independence of Enterprise	CO11	Formalization
CO2	Market Domination of Enterprise	CO12	Span of Top Management
CO3	Political Instability	CO13	Intensity of Control
CO4	Sector	CO14	Stability of Work-force
CO5	Skill	CO15	Male Domination
CO6	Automatization	CO16	Mobilization
CO7	Technological Interdependence	CO17	Evaluation of Success
CO8	Product Complexity	CO18	Growth of Enterprise
CO9	Functional Differentiation	CO19	Log size
CO10	Vertical Span	V146	Climate-Structure (workers)

	V146	V147	V150	V246	V247	V250	V346	V347	V350	22A	22B	C405	C406	C407	C410	C411	C414	C416
CO1																		
CO2																		
CO3																		
CO4																		
CO5																		
CO6																		
CO7																		
CO8																		
CO9																		
CO10																		
CO11																		
CO12																		
CO13																		
CO14																		
CO15																		
CO16																		
CO17																		
CO18																		
CO19																		
V146	—																	
V147	55	—																
V150	35	64	—															
V246	60	29	15	—														
V247	34	61	36	49	—													
V250	01	28	30	14	48	—												
V346	37	22	18	40	11	11	—											
V347	14	49	32	21	45	50	30	—										
V350	10	35	28	10	33	47	27	55	—									
22A	−20	−15	−09	−26	−15	07	−14	−17	09	—								
22B	04	−11	−23	04	02	−33	−10	−18	−34	−04	—							
C405	03	−21	−13	03	−26	−10	−11	−26	−34	03	07	—						
C406	−14	−33	−09	−19	−20	−25	−16	−37	−17	25	−06	19	—					
C407	06	−09	−11	14	08	−01	−13	01	−00	−08	13	09	07	—				
C410	01	00	09	02	03	−02	07	05	−13	02	−07	04	−10	02	—			
C411	03	−09	−00	−10	−07	13	−06	−20	04	25	−35	17	13	11	29	—		
C414	01	−03	08	−02	−03	07	19	−05	01	04	−07	−03	08	−01	15	04	—	
C416	−01	−06	−13	09	14	06	−11	−20	−18	06	37	13	−04	09	−02	02	−03	—

V147	Climate-Relations (workers)	C405	Year of Foundation
V150	Direct participation (workers)	C406	Directors Founders
V246	Climate-Structure (foremen)	C407	No Financial Dependence
V247	Climate-Relations (foremen)	C410	Public Accountability
V250	Direct participation (foremen)	C411	Principal Unit
V346	Climate-Structure (middle managers)	C414	Order Product Mainly
V347	Climate-Relations (middle managers)	C416	Dominating Customer
V350	Direct participation (middle managers)		
CON22A	Quitting Rate		
CON22B	Absenteeism		

App. Table 7.1
Analysis of variance with multiple classification: Country, Sector, and Size as independent variables and Conflict as dependent variable[a]

Dependent variable—conflict over:	Independent variables			Interactions			Multiple R^2
	Country	Sector	Size	C×Se	C×Si	Se×Si	
Short-term decisions	.58	.16	.13	.37	.48	.37	.39
Medium-term decisions	.55	.04	.39	.88	.78	.82	.48
Long-term decisions	.45	.14	.07	.77	.68	.87	.22
All decisions	.61	.14	.17	.43	.49	.55	.43

[a]Values in first three columns are adjusted beta coefficients, values in the next three columns are significance of F values, and in the last column are multiple R^2.

App. Table 7.2
Desired Influence for representative bodies by country

Level	Belgium	Denmark	Finland	France	Germany (West)	U.K.	Italy	Israel	Holland	Norway	Sweden	Yugoslavia
Workers (A)	79[a]	45	66	65	75	60	78	76	66	67	74	79
Foremen (B)	62	50	50	53	65	43	66	58	56	48	71	79
Middle managers (C)	47	49	30	49	55	35	56	41	56	47	73	78
Total ∓	71	54	60	60	70	51	75	69	63	59	73	79

[a]Percentage of yes answers of respondents to the question: would you like the main representative body to have a say in this matter?

App. Table 7.3
Analysis of variance with multiple classification: Country, Size, and Sector are independent variables, and Actual Involvement the dependent variable[a]

Dependent variable—Actual Involvement for:	Independent variables			Interactions			Multiple R^2
	Country	Sector	Size	C×Se	C×Si	Sex Si	
Workers (A)	.83	.12	.10	.02	.00	.24	.72
Foremen (B)	.63	.28	.12	.05	.01	.26	.50
Middle managers (C)	.57	.10	.13	.64	.69	.50	.35
Representative bodies (F)	.62	.13	.10	.36	.12	.81	.41
All levels	.73	.12	.10	.57	.34	.72	.63
All decisions	.67	.11	.10	.18	.21	.19	.46
Short-term decisions	.69	.08	.14	.42	.32	.31	.49
Medium-term decisions	.66	.20	.09	.14	.21	.16	.48
Long-term decisions	.75	.18	.24	.01	.01	.01	.65
Difference C–A	.59	.10	.11	.10	.21	.06	.35
Difference between workers and other groups	.57	.35	.15	.02	.01	.07	.49

[a]Values in first three columns are adjusted beta coefficients, values in the next three columns are significance of F values, and in the last column are multiple R^2.

App. Table 7.4
Inter-correlations between Actual Involvement over decisions and Education

Correlation Actual Involvement and Education	Working conditions	New department head	Hiring procedures	Training courses	Transfers	Investment	New product	Appointment own superior	Pay levels	Personal equipment	Reorganization	Task assignment	Dismissals	Work study	Holidays	Working hours
Workers' Involvement×Workers' Education										-.17	.14	-15			.16	
Workers' Involvement×Education of foremen and middle management															.21	
Foremen's Involvement×Workers' Education	-.13		-.20	-.20	-.20	-.18			-.15	-.32		-.19	-.21	-.19		
Foremen's Involvement×Education of foremen and middle management															.22	
Middle managers' Involvement×Workers' Education				-.17	-.18	-.14			-.14	-.29		-.14				
Middle managers' Involvement×Education of foremen and middle management							.14				.14					

	All decisions	STa	MT	LT
Inequality of Involvement between foremen and workers×Workers' Education	.21	.27	.16	.17

aST = short-term decisions, MT = medium-term decisions, LT = long-term decisions.

App. Table 7.5
Inter-correlations between workers' Actual Involvement and workers' Education for metal industry and banks[a]

Country	Metal Industry				Banks			
	ST[b]	MT	LT	Σ	ST	MT	LT	Σ
Belgium	.09	.23	.34	.43	.23	.24	.44	.33
Denmark	.01	.06	.05	.01	.08	.02	.11	.04
Finland	.001	.28	.28	.005	.001	.02	.008	.001
France	.05	.35	.20	.20	.44	.48	.40	.35
Germany (West)	.01	.02	.15	.32	.13	.19	.21	.29
U.K.	.25	.005	.41	.09	.002	.11	.31	.08
Israel	.41	.29	.34	.42	–	–	–	–
Italy	.21	.12	.42	.23	.46	.18	.10	.42
Holland	.06	.18	.02	.37	.46	.19	.30	.44
Norway	.11	.05	.02	.04	.12	.40	.37	.26
Sweden	.001	.16	.42	.001	.001	.001	.001	.001
Yugoslavia	.008	.008	.05	.006	.29	.08	.49	.21

[a]$p \leqslant 0.5$ if $r = 0.15$

[b]ST = short-term decisions, MT = medium-term decisions, LT = long-term decisions, Σ = all decisions.

App. Table 7.6
Multiple regressions: Actual Involvement of workers in some decisions regressed on a number of independent variables[a]

Predictors	Actual Involvement of Workers				
	Working conditions	Transfers	Personal equipment	Task assignment	Holidays
Sector		.28		.35	.38
Skill		−.17		−.17	
Automatization					
Functional differentiation					
Vertical span		.29			
Mobilization		.29			−.21
De Jure Participation:					
Workers, ST	.40				
Workers, MT	.20				−.32
Foremen, ST					
Top management, MT	−.32	−.18		−.22	−.21
Level above plant, LT	−.30				−.15
Representative bodies, ST	−.30				
Representative bodies, MT					.52
Representative bodies, LT	−.30				
Rating of Direct Participation (OPART)	.38	.28	.45	.48	
Influence:					
Workers	.16				
Top management					
Representative bodies					

		.20	−.20		−.23
Climate–Structure bodies (CLIM–S)					
Climate–Relations (CLIM–R)					
Multiple R	.777	.715	.582	.668	.680
Adjusted R^2	.53	.42	.21	.34	.46
F	8.3	5.7	2.8	4.4	4.7
p	.000	.000	.000	.000	.000

[a]Df = 20, 110

App. Table 7.7
Zero order correlations between Influence and Involvement controlling for correspondent De Jure Participation scores (same levels, clusters)[a]

	Actual Involvement															
	Levels				Workers			Foremen			Middle managers			Representative bodies		
Influence	A	B	C	F	STᵇ	MT	LT	ST	MT	LT	ST	MT	LT	ST	MT	LT
Workers (A)	.45 .37*															
Foremen (B)		.53 .54*														
Middle managers (C)			.22 .22*													
Representative bodies (F)				.23 .09*												
Workers: ST					.30 .28*											
Workers: MT						.62 .49*										
Workers: LT							.68 .61*									
Foremen: ST								.48 .48*								
Foremen: MT									.52 .52*							

Foremen: LT	.58	.57*
Middle managers: ST	.16	.16*
Middle managers: MT	.18	.18*
Middle managers: LT	.42	.39*
Representative bodies ST	.01	−.04*
Representative bodies MT	.34	.14*
Representative bodies: LT	.48	.47*

[a] $p \leq .05$ if $r > .15$. Values with* are controlling for correspondent *De Jure* Participation (PS) variable

[b] ST = short-term decisions, MT = medium-term decisions, LT = long-term decisions.

App. Table 7.8
Zero order correlations between Influence and De Jure Participation controlling for correspondent Involvement scores[a]

	De Jure Participation		Workers			Foremen			Middle managers		
Influence	Workers	Foremen	ST[b]	MT	LT	ST	MT	LT	ST	MT	LT
Workers (A)	.43 .34*										
Foremen (B)		-.01 -.13*									
Workers: ST			.17 .14*								
Workers: MT				.54 .38*							
Workers: LT					.45 .25*						
Foremen: ST						-.12 -.19*					
Foremen: MT							.09 .10*				
Foremen: LT								.13 .003*			
Middle managers: ST									.08 .06*		

| Middle managers: MT | .15 | .20* |
| Middle managers: LT | .17 | .06* |

[a]p ≤ .05 if r > .15. Values with* are controlling for correspondent Involvement (PO2a) variable.

[b]ST = short-term decisions, MT = medium-term decisions, LT = long-term decisions.

App. Table 7.9
Correlations between De Jure Participation (PS) and Influence (PO1a– upper figure) and Involvement (PO2a– lower figure) for levels and clusters[a]

| | De Jure Participation | | | | | | | | | | | | | | | |
| | Levels | | | | Workers | | | Foremen | | | Middle managers | | | Representative bodies | | |
PO1a PO2a	A	B	C	F	ST	MT	LT	ST	MT	LT	ST	MT	LT	ST	MT	LT
Workers (A)	.43 .32															
Foremen (B)		−.01 .16														
Middle managers (C)			.17 .00													
Representative bodies (F)				.65 .24												
Workers: ST					.17 .10											
Workers: MT						.54 .45										
Workers: LT							.45 .41									
Foremen: ST								−.12 .06								
Foremen: MT									.09 .15							

Foremen LT	.13	.24
Middle managers ST	.08	−.04
Middle managers MT	.15	.01
Middle managers LT	.17	.27
Representative bodies: ST	.50	.11
Representative bodies: MT	.70	.35
Representative bodies: LT	.30	.11

[a]$p \leqslant .05$ if $r > .15$

BIBLIOGRAPHY

Abell, P. (ed.) (1975), *Organizations as Bargaining and Influence Systems.* London: Heinemann.
—— (1976), 'Integrative and Disintegrative Social Structures in Decision-Making Groups, in Collins, L. (ed.), *The Use of Models in Social Sciences.* London: Tavistock.
—— (1977), 'The Many Faces of Power and Liberty: Revealed Preference, Autonomy, and Teleological Explanation' in *Sociology,* 11.
—— (1979), 'Hierarchy and Democratic Authority' in Burns, T.; Rus, V. (eds.), *Work and Power.* London: Sage.
Agersnap, F. and **Junge-Jensen, F.** (1973), 'Rapport om Samarbejdsforsøg i jernindustrien' in *Handelshøjskolen,* Copenhagen.
Agurén S., Hansson, R. and **Karlsson, K. G.** (1976), *The Volvo Kalmar Plant: The Impact of New Design on Work Organization.* Stockholm: Rationalization Council, SAF–L.
Aiken, M. and **Hage, J.** (1966), 'Organizational Alienation: a Comparative Analysis' in *American Sociological Review,* 31.
Ajiferuke, M. and **Boddewyn, J.** (1970), 'Socio-economic Indicators in Comparative Management' in *Administrative Science Quarterly,* 15.
Almond, G. A. and **Verba, S.** (1963), *The Civic Culture: Political Attitudes and Democracy in Five Nations,* Princeton: Princeton University Press.
Alutto, J. and **Belasco, J.** (1972), 'A Typology for Participation in Organizational Decision-Making' in *Administrative Science Quarterly,* 22.
Andrews, F. M., Morgan, J. N., Sonquist, J. A. and **Klem, L.** (1973), *Multiple Classification Analysis: a Report on a Computer Programme for Multiple Regression Using Categorical Predictors.* (2nd ed.). Ann Arbor: The Institute for Social Research, The University of Michigan.
Ansoff, I. H. (1965), *Corporate Strategy.* New York: McGraw-Hill.
Argyle, M., Gardner, G. and **Cioffi, F.** (1958), 'Supervisory Methods Related to Productivity, Absenteeism, and Labour Turnover' in *Human Relations,* 11.
Arzensz, V. (1977), Alienation and Self-management'. Paper for Second International Conference on Participation, Workers' Control, and Self-management. Paris.

Bachrach, P. and **Baratz, M.** (1972), 'Two Faces of Power' in *American Political Science Review,* 56.
—— (1970), *Power and Poverty: Theory and Practice.* London: Oxford University Press.
Bass, B. and **Eldridge, L.** (1973), 'Accelerated Managers' Objectives in Twelve Countries' in *Industrial Relations,* 12.
Batstone, E. and **Davies, P. L.** (1976), *Industrial Democracy: European Experience.* London: HMSO.
Baumgartner, T., Burns, T., Buckley, W. and **Schuster, P.** (1976), 'Meta-power and the Structuring of Social Hierarchies' in Burns, T. and Buckley, W., *Power and Control.* London: Sage.
Bavelas, A. (1955), 'Communication Patterns in Task-oriented groups' in Lazarsfeld, P., Rosenberg, M., *Language of Social Research.* Glencoe, Illinois: Free Press.

Bell, C. and Newby, H. (eds.) (1977), *Doing Sociological Research*. London: Allen and Unwin.

Beyme, K. von (1976), *Gewerkschaften und Arbeitsbeziehungen in kapitalistischen Ländern*. München: Piper Verlag.

Bilitza, K. (1978), 'Organisationpsychologische Aspekte der Forschung' in *Gruppendynamik*, 9.

Black, D. (1976), *The Behavior of Law*. London: Academic Press.

Blalock, H. M. (1961), *Causal Inference in Non-experimental Research*. Chapel Hill: University of North Carolina Press.

Blankenburg, E., 'Über die Unwirksamkeit von Gesetzen' in *Archiv für Rechts- und Sozialphilosophie*, 63.

Blau, P. (1964), *Exchange and Power in Social Life*. New York: Wiley.

–– and Schoenherr, R. (1971), *The Structure of Organizations*. New York: Basic Books.

Blauner, R. (1964), *Alienation and Freedom: The Factory Worker and his Industry*. Chicago: University of Chicago Press.

Blumberg, P. (1968), *Industrial Democracy: the Sociology of Participation*. London: Constable.

Bolweg, J. F. (1976), *Job Design and Industrial Democracy*. Leiden: Nijhoff.

Borucka-Arctowa, M. (1977), 'Innovation through Law in the System of Social Planning' in *SSIP-Bulletin*, 46.

Boston Consulting Group (1968), *Perspectives on Corporate Strategy*. Boston, Mass.

Brannen, P., Batstone, E., Fatchett, D. and White, P. (1976), *The Worker Directors: A Sociology of Participation*. London: Hutchinson.

Braverman, H. (1974), *Labor and Monopoly Capital: the Degradation of Work in the Twentieth Century*. New York and London: Monthly Review Press.

Brislin, R. W., Lonner, W. J. and Thorndike, R. M. (1973), *Cross Cultural Research Methods*. New York: Wiley.

Burns, T. (1967), 'The Comparative Study of Organizations' in Vroom, V. (ed.), *Methods of Organizational Research*. University of Pittsburgh Press.

–– and Stalker, G. M. (1961), *The Management of Innovation*. London: Tavistock.

Business International S.A. (1974), *Industrial Democracy in Europe–the Challenge and Management Responses*. Geneva: Business International S.A.

Butera, F. (1975), 'Environmental Factors in Job and Organization Design: the Case of Olivetti' in Davis, L. E. and Cherns, A. (eds.), *The Quality of Working Life*. Vol. II. London: Macmillan.

Buzzel, R. D., Gale, B. T. and Sultan, R. G. M. (1975), 'Market Share–a Key to Profitability' in *Harvard Business Review*, 53.

Carnap, R. (1939), 'Foundations of Logic and Mathematics' in *International Encyclopaedia of Unified Science*, 1.

Cartwright, D. (1959), *Studies of Social Power*. Ann Arbor: University of Michigan Press.

Castri, F. Di, (1978) 'Planning International Inter-disciplinary Research' in *Science and Public Policy*, 5.

Centers, R. and Bugental, D. E. (1966), 'Intrinsic and Extrinsic Job Motivations Among Different Segments of the Working Population' in *Journal of Applied Psychology*, 50.

Chandler Jr., A. D. (1962), *The History of the Industrial Enterprise*. Massachusetts: M.I.T. Press.

Chauvey, D. (1970), *Autogestion*. Paris: Seuil.

Child, J. (1972), 'Organizational Structure, Environment, and Performance: the Role of Strategic Choice' in *Sociology*, 6.

—— (1980), 'Culture, Contingency and Capitalism in the Cross-national Study of Organizations' in Staw, B. and Cummings, L. (eds.), *Research in Organizational Behaviour*. Vol. III. Greenwich, Con.: J. A. I. Press.

—— and **Kieser, A.** (1979), 'Organization and Managerial Roles in British and West German Companies: an Examination of the Culture-free Thesis' in Lammers, C. J. and Hickson, D. J. (eds.), *Organizations Alike and Unlike*. London: Routledge and Kegan Paul.

Chinoy, E. (1955), *Automobile Workers and the American Dream*. New York: Doubleday.

Claessens, D. (1962), 'Forschungsteam und Persönlichkeitstruktur' in *Kölner Zeitschrift für Soziologie und Sozialpsychologie*, 14.

Clark, T. (1968), *Community Structure and Decision-making: Comparative Analysis*. San Francisco: Chandler.

Clegg, H. (1976a), *The System of Industrial Relations in Great Britain*. Oxford: Basil Blackwell.

—— (1976b), 'Trade Unions as an Opposition which can never Become a Government' in McCarthy, W. E. J. (ed.), *Trade Unions*. Harmondsworth: Penguin Press.

Coch, L. and **French, J. R. P.** (1948), 'Overcoming Resistance to Change' *Human Relations*, 1.

Coetsier, P. (1966), *Organismen voor Medezeggenschap in de Onderneming*. Antwerpen: Standaard.

Comstock, D. and **Scott, W.** (1977), 'Technology and the Structure of Sub-units: Distinguishing of Individual and Work-group Effects' in *Administrative Science Quarterly*, 21.

Conway, J. A. (1976), 'Test of Linearity Between Teachers' Participation in Decision-making' in *Administrative Science Quarterly*, 21.

Cook, T. D. and **Campbell, D. T.** (1976), 'The Design Conduct of Quasi-experiments and True Experiments in Field Settings' in Dunnette, M. D., *Handbook of Industrial and Organizational Psychology*. Chicago: Rand McNally.

Coser, L. (1956), *The Functions of Social Conflict*. London: Routledge and Kegan Paul.

Cox, R. and **Jacobson, H.** (1974), *The Anatomy of Influence*. New Haven: Yale University Press.

Cronbach, L. J. (1970), *Essentials of Psychological Testing*. New York: Harper.

—— and **Furby, L.** (1970), 'How Should We Measure "Change"—or Should We?' in *Psychological Bulletin*, 74.

Crozier, M. (1964), *The Bureaucratic Phenomenon*. London: Tavistock.

—— (1971), *The World of the Office Worker*. Chicago: Chicago University Press.

—— and **Thoenig, J.** (1976), 'The Regulation of Complex Organizational Systems' in *Administrative Science Quarterly*, 21.

Dachler, H. P. and **Wilpert, B.** (1978), 'Conceptual Dimensions and Boundaries of Participation in Organizations: a Critical Evaluation' in *Administrative Science Quarterly*, 23.

Dahl, R. (1957) 'The Concept of Power' in *Behavioral Science*, 2.

—— (1970), *After the Revolution: Authority in a Good Society*. New Haven: Yale University Press.

Dahrendorf, R. (1965), *Das Mitbestimmungsproblem in der deutschen Sozial-forschung, Eine Kritik.* München: Piper.
Dalton, M. (1959), *Men Who Manage: Fusions of Feeling and Theory in Adminis-tration.* New York: Wiley.
D.I.O. (1979), 'Participative Decision-making in Organizations: a Three-country Comparative Study' in *Industrial Relations*, 18.
Derber, M. (1970), *The American Idea of Industrial Democracy: 1876–1965.* Urbana: University of Illinois Press.
Docherty, P. H. G. et al. (1977), *How to Succeed with Systems Development.* Stockholm: Economic Research Institute, Research Paper 6085.
Dongen, H. J. Van (1970), 'Over Gebieden van Medezeggenschap' in *Mens en Onderneming*, 24.
Dore, R. (1973), *British Factory–Japanese Factory.* London: Allen and Unwin.
Drenth, P. J. D. (1973), 'The Works' Council in the Netherlands: an Experiment in Participation' in Pusić, E. (ed.), *Participation and Self-management*, Vol. 4. Zagreb: Institute for Social Research.
—— (1975), *Inleiding in de Testtheorie.* Deventer: Kluwer.
—— and **Van der Flier, H.** (1976), 'Cultural Differences and Comparability of Test Scores' in *International Review of Applied Psychology*, 25.
Dubin, R. (1958), *The World of Work.* Englewood Cliffs, N. J.: Prentice Hall.
—— (1961), *Who Governs? Democracy and Power in an American City.* New Haven: Yale University Press.
Dunlop, J. T. (1958), *Industrial Relations System.* Southern Illinois University Press.
Dupuy, F. and **Martin, D.** (1977), *Jeux et Enjeux de la Participation.* Paris: CRESST.
Durkheim, E. (1974), *Division of Labor in Society.* (2nd ed.). Glencoe, Ill.: Free Press.

Edelstein, J. D.; Warner, H. (1975), *Comparative Union Democracy.* London: Allen and Unwin.
Ehrmann, H. (1976), *Comparative Legal Cultures.* Englewood Cliffs, N. J.: Prentice Hall.
Eisenstadt, S. N. (1965), 'Transformation of Social, Political and Structural Orders in Modernization' in *American Sociological Review*, 30.
Elden, J. M. (ed.). (1979), *Working on the Quality of Working Life.* Leiden: Nijhoff.
Emerson, R. (1962), 'Power Dependence Relations' in *American Sociological Review*, 27.
Emery, F. E. (ed.) (1969), *Systems Thinking.* Harmondsworth: Penguin Press.
—— and **Thorsrud, E.** (1969), *Form and Content in Industrial Democracy.* London: Tavistock.
—— and —— (1976), *Democracy at Work.* Leiden: Nijhoff.
—— and **Trist, E.** (1960), 'Socio-technical Systems' in Churchman, C. W. and Verhulst, M. (eds.), *Management Science: Models and Techniques.* New York: Pergamon.
—— and **Trist, E.** (1965), 'The Causal Texture of Organizational Environments' in *Human Relations*, 18.
Enbom, M. (1969), *Yrutysdemokratia ja Eturistitiita Järjestäytyneem Työn-tekijän Tajunnassa.* University of Tampere: Institute of Sociology Research Report.

Engelstad, P. H. and **Qvale, T. U.** (1977), *Insynn og Innflytelse i Styre og Bedriftsforsamling.* Oslo: Tiden.

England, G. W. (1975), *The Manager and his Values: an International Perspective from the U.S.A., Japan, Korea, India, and Australia.* Cambridge, Mass.: Ballinger.

Evan, W. M. (1965), 'Toward a Sociological Almanac of Legal Systems' in *International Social Science Journal,* 17.

—— (1968), 'A Data Archive of Legal Systems: A Cross-national Analysis of Sample Data' in *Archives Européens de Sociologie,* 9.

—— (1976), *Organization Theory: Structures, Systems, and Environments.* New York: Wiley.

—— (1977), 'Hierarchy, Alienation, Commitment, and Organizational Effectiveness' in *Human Relations,* 30.

—— (1978), 'Systems Theory and the Sociology of Law'. Paper at the Ninth World Congress of Sociology, Uppsala (Sweden).

Farah, B. and **Jennings, M. K.** (1977), 'Continuities in Comparative Research Strategies: the Mannheim Data Confrontation Seminar' in *Social Science Information,* 16.

Farris, G. F. (1975), 'Chickens, Eggs, and Productivity in Organizations' in *Organizational Dynamics,* 3.

Faxén, K-O. (1978), *Quality of Working Life—Disembodied Technical Progress: Does Employee Participation in Decision-making Contribute to Change and Growth?* Stockholm: Swedish Employers' Confederation.

Feeley, M. M. (1976), 'The Concept of Laws in Social Science' in *Law and Society Review,* 4.

Fisch, R. (1977), 'Psychology of Science' in Spiegel-Rösing, I. and De Solla Price, D. (eds.), *Science, Technology, and Society—a Cross-disciplinary Perspective.* London: Sage.

FitzRoy, F. R. and **Hiller, J. R.** (1978), 'Efficiency and Motivation in Productive Organizations'. Berlin: International Institute of Management Discussion Paper.

Flanders, A. (1976), 'What are Trade Unions for?' in McCarthy, W. E. J. (ed.), *Trade Unions.* Harmondsworth: Penguin Press.

Fourcade, J-M. and **Wilpert, B.** (1975), *Group Dynamics and Management Problems of an International Inter-disciplinary Research Team.* Berlin: International Institute of Management Report IV/76—1.

Fox, A. (1974), *Beyond Contract: Work, Power and Trust Relations.* London: Faber.

—— (1974) *Man Mismanagement.* London: Hutchinson.

French, J. R. P. (1956), 'A Formal Theory of Social Power' in *Psychological Review,* 63.

—— and **Raven, B.** (1959), 'The Bases of Social Power' in Cartwright, D. (ed.), *Studies of Social Power.* Ann Arbor: University of Michigan Press.

French, W. L. (1978), *The Personnel Management Process.* Boston: Houghton Mifflin.

Gallie, D. (1978), *In Search of the New Working Class: Automation and Social Integration within the Capitalist Enterprise.* Cambridge University Press.

Gardell, B. (1971), *Produktionsteknik och Arbetslädje.* Stockholm: PA-Council.

—— (1976), *Arbetsinnehäll och Livskvalitet.* Lund: Prisma.

—— (1977), 'Autonomy and Participation at Work' in *Human Relations*, 30.

Garson, G. D. (1977), 'Paradoxes of Worker Participation' in Garson, G. D. (ed.), *Worker Self-management in Industry*. New York: Praeger.

Gasparini, G. (1977), 'Organizational Power, Strategy and Social Classes' in Warner, M. (ed.), *Organizational Choice and Constraint*. London: Saxon House.

Gerth, H. H. and Mills, C. W. (1958), *From Max Weber: Essays in Sociology*. New York: Oxford University Press.

Gerwin, D. (1977), *Inter-dependencies between Structure and Technology*. Milwaukee: University of Wisconsin-Milwaukee Press.

Glaser, W. A. (1977), 'The Process of Cross-national Survey Research' in Szalai, A. and Petrella, R. (eds.), in collaboration with Rokkan, S. and Scheuch, E., *Cross-national Comparative Survey Research*. Oxford: Pergamon Press.

Gorz, A. (1973), *Critique de la Division du Travail*. Paris: Seuil.

Granick, D. (1962), *The European Executive*. London: Wheaton.

Gundelach, P. and Tetzschner, H. (1976), 'Measurement of Influence in Organizations—Critique of the Control-graph Method' in *Acta Sociologica*, 19.

Gustavsen, B. (1973), 'Environmental Requirements and the Democratization of Industrial Relations' in Pusić, E. (ed.), *Participation and Self-management*. Vol. 4. Zagreb: Institute for Social Research.

Haire, M., Ghiselli, E. and Porter, L. W. (1966), *Managerial Thinking: an International Study*. London: Wiley.

Haraszti, M. (1977), *A Worker in a Workers' State: Piece Rates in Hungary*. Harmondsworth: Penguin Press.

Harbison, J. and Myers, C. A. (1959), *Management in the International World: an International Analysis*. New York: McGraw Hill.

Harsanyi, J. G. (1962), 'Measurement of Social Power, Opportunity Costs and the Theory of Two Person Bargaining Games' in *Behavioral Science*, 7.

Heller, F. A. (1971), *Managerial Decision Making*. London: Tavistock.

—— (1976), 'Decision Process: an Analysis of Power-sharing at Senior Organizational Levels' in Dubin, R. (ed.), *Handbook of Work Organizations and Society*. Chicago: Rand McNally.

——, Mays, R. and Wilpert, B. (1976), 'The Use of Contingency Models in a Multi-national Study of Managerial Behaviour'. London: Tavistock Institute of Human Relations (mimeo).

—— and Rose, J. S. (1973), 'Participation and Decision-making Re-examined' in Pusić, E. (ed.), *Participation and Self-management*. Vol. 4. Zagreb: Institute for Social Research.

—— and Wilpert, B. (1977), 'Limits to Participative Leadership: Task, Structure and Skill as Contingencies—a German/British Comparison' in *European Journal of Social Psychology*, 7.

—— and Wilpert, B. (1979), 'Managerial Decision-making: an International Comparison' in England, G. W., Negandhi, A. R. and Wilpert, B. (eds.), *Organizational Functioning in a Cross Cultural Perspective*. Kent, Ohio: Kent State University Press.

—— and Wilpert, B. (Forthcoming 1980), *Competence and Power in Managerial Decision Making*. New York: Wiley.

Herbst, P. G. (1976), *Alternatives to Hierarchies*. Leiden: Nijhoff.

Herzberg, F., Mausner, B., Peterson, R. and Capwell, D. (1957), *Job Attitudes: Research and Opinion*. Pittsburgh: Psychological Service of Pittsburgh.

Hickson, D. (1971), 'A Strategic Contingencies Theory of Intra-Organizational

Power' in *Administrative Science Quarterly*, 2.

——, **Pugh, D. S.** and **Pheysey, D. C.** (1969), 'Operations Technology and Organization Structure: an Empirical Reappraisal' in *Administrative Science Quarterly*, 14.

Hirsch, E. (1971), 'Rechtssoziologie heute' in *Studien und Materialien zur Rechtssoziologie*, 11.

Hoekman, K. (1970), 'Satisfactie-meting: Overweging en Modellen' in Drenth, P. J. D., Willems, P. J. and Wolff, Ch. J. de (eds.), *Bedrijfspsychologie Onderzoek en Evaluatie*. Deventer: Kluwer.

Hofstede, G. (1976a), *Measuring Hierarchical Power Distance in Thirty-seven Countries*. Brussels: European Institute for Advanced Studies in Management (Working Paper 76-32).

—— (1976b), *Occupational Determinants of Stress and Satisfaction*. Brussels: European Institute for Advanced Studies in Management (Working Paper 76-39).

—— (1977a), *Humanization of Work: the Role of Values in a Third Industrial Revolution*. Brussels: European Institute for Advanced Studies in Management (Working Paper 77-16).

—— (1977b), *Cultural Determinants of the Exercise of Power in a Hierarchy*. Brussels: European Institute for Advanced Studies in Management (Working Paper 77-8).

—— and **Krannenburg, R. Y.** (1974), 'Work Goals of Migrant Workers' in *Human Relations*, 27.

Hondrich, K. O. (1970), *Mitbestimmung in Europa—ein Diskussionsbeitrag*. Köln: Europa Union Verlag.

Hulin, C. L. and **Blood, M. R.** (1968), 'Job Enlargement; Individual Differences in Workers' Responses' in *Psychological Bulletin*, 69.

IDE-International Research Group (1976), 'Industrial Democracy in Europe (IDE)—an International Comparative Study' in *Social Science Information*, 15.

—— (Forthcoming 1980), *European Industrial Relations*. Oxford University Press.

Jacob, B. M. and **Jacob, P. E.** (1979), 'Humanized Productivity under Advanced Industrial Technology'. Honolulu: Research Corporation of the University of Hawaii (draft).

—— and **Ahn, C.** (1978), 'Impetus for Worker Participation'. Paper at the Ninth World Congress of Sociology, Uppsala (Sweden).

—— and —— (1979), 'Neither Capitalism nor Socialism Creates the Activist Auto Worker. What Does?' in *The Wharton Magazine*, The Wharton School, University of Pennsylvania.

Janowitz, M. (1975), 'Sociological Theory and Social Control' in *American Journal of Sociology*, 84.

Jenkins, C. (1978), 'Industrial Democracy in the U.K.—a Union View' in *Proceedings of the International Conference on Industrial Democracy*. Adelaide: GCH Australia Ltd.

Jenkins, D. (1973), *Job Power*. New York: Doubleday.

Joerges, B. (1977), 'Wissenschaftliche Kreativität—Emprische und Wissenschaftspraktische Hinweise' in *Zeitschrift für Allg. Wissenschaftstheorie*, 8.

Kaase, M. and **Miller, W. E.** (Undated), 'Report on a Conference on Cross-national Research in the Social Sciences. ZUMA, Mannheim (mimeo).

Kadishin, C. (1968), 'Power, Influence and Social Circles: a New Methodology for Studying Opinion Makers' in *American Sociological Review*, 33.

Kahn, R. L. (1974), 'The Work Module: a Proposal for the Humanization of Work' in O'Toole, J., *Work and the Quality of Life*. Massachusetts Institute of Technology.

Kahn, R. L., Wolfe, D. M., Quinn, R. P., Snoek, J. D. and Rosenthal, R. A. (1964), *Organizational Stress: Studies in Role Conflict and Ambiguity*. New York: Wiley.

Kaiser, H. P. (1958), 'The Varimax Criterion for Analytic Rotation in Factor Analysis' in *Psychometrica*, 23.

Katz, D. and Kahn, R. L. (1966), *The Social Psychology of Organizations*. New York: Wiley.

Katzell, R. A., Barrett, R. S. and Parker, T. C. (1961), 'Job Satisfaction, Job Performance and Situational Characteristics' in *Journal of Applied Psychology*, 45.

Kendall, W. (1973), 'Industrial Democracy in Western Europe' in *Free Labour World* (IFCTU), July–August.

Kerr, C. and Siegel, A. (1954), *The Inter-industry Propensity to Strike–an International Comparison*. Berkeley: University of California Press.

King, C. D. and Van de Vall, M. (1978), *Models of Industrial Democracy*. New York: Mouton.

Kommission der Europäischen Gemeinschaft (1975), *Mitbestimmung der Arbeitnehmer und Struktur der Gesellschaften in der Europäischen Gemeinschaft*. KOM (75) 570 endg. Luxemburg.

König, R. (1971), 'Das Recht im Zusammenhang der sozialen Normensysteme' in *Kölner Zeitschrift für Soziologie und Sozialpsychologie*, 11.

Koopman, P. L. and Werkman, B. (1973), 'Het Verhoudingsmodel bij de Meting van Werksatisfactie' in Drenth, P. J. D., Willems, P. J. and Wolff, C. J. de, *Arbeids en Organisatiepsychologie*. Deventer: Kluwer.

Korman, A. K. (1971), *Industrial and Organizational Psychology*. Englewood Cliffs, N. J.: Prentice-Hall.

Kornhauser, A. (1965), *Mental Health of the Industrial Worker*. New York: Wiley.

Laaksonen, O. (1972), *Yrityskuva ja Työpaikan Valinta*. Tapiola: Weilin & Göös.

Lammers, C. J. (ed.) (1965), *Medezeggenschap en Overleg in het Bedrijf*. Utrecht: Spectrum.

—— (1967), 'Power and Participation in Decision-making in Formal Organizations' in *American Journal of Sociology*, 73.

—— (1973), 'Self-management and Participation: Two Concepts of Democratization in Organizations' in Pusić, E. (ed.), *Participation and Self-management*, Vol. 4. Zagreb: Institute for Social Research.

—— (1977), *The Sociological Significance of Organizational Sociology*. Leyden: University of Leyden, Institute for Sociology.

—— and Hickson, D. J. (eds.) (1979), *Organizations Alike and Unlike*. London: Routledge and Kegan Paul.

Lansberger, H. A. (ed.) (1970), *Comparative Perspectives on Formal Organizations*. Boston: Little, Brown and Co.

Lanzardo, L. (1977), 'I Consigli di Gestione nella Strategia della Collaborazione' in *Fondazione Giangiacomo Feltrinelli: Annali*, 16.

Lawrence, P. R. and Lorsch, J. W. (1967), *Organization and Environment*.

Boston: Harvard University Press.

Lecher, W. and Sieling-Wendeling, U. (1977), 'Neue Entwicklungen in der Europäischen Mitbestimmungsdiskussion', (I) and (II) in *Das Mitbestimmungsgespräch*, 11 (I) and 12 (II).

Lewin, K. (1951), *Field Theory in Social Science*. New York: Harper.

Likert, R. (1961), *New Patterns of Management*. New York: McGraw-Hill.

—— (1967), *The Human Organization, its Management and Value*. New York: McGraw-Hill, 1967.

Litwin, G. H. and Stringer, A. (1968), *Motivation and Organizational Climate*. Boston: Harvard Business School publication.

Locke, E. A. and Whiting, R. J. (1974), 'Sources in Satisfaction and Dissatisfaction Among Solid Waste Management Employees' in *Journal of Applied Psychology*, 59.

Lord, R. (1977), 'Functional Leadership and Behavior: Measurement and Relation to Social Power and Leadership Perceptions' in *Administrative Science Quarterly*, 22.

Lukes, S. (1974), *Power: a Radical View*. London: Macmillan.

Mabry, J. H., Cartwright, A., Pearson, J., Silver, G. and Vukmanovic, C. (1966), 'The History of an International Collaborative Study of Medical Care Utilization' in *Social Science Information*, 5.

Macbeath, I. (1978), 'Industrial Democracy—the Background' in *Professional Administration*, October.

Macdonald, D. F. (1976), *The State and the Unions*. 2nd ed. London: Macmillan.

March, J. (1955), 'An Introduction to the Theory of Influence'. in *American Political Science Review*, 49.

—— (1966), 'The Power of Power' in Easton, D. (ed.), *Varieties of Political Theory*. Englewood Cliffs, N.J.: Prentice Hall.

—— and Simon, H. A. (1958), *Organizations*, New York: Wiley.

Maurice, M. et al. (1977), *Production de la Hierarchie dans l'Enterprise Recherche d'un effet Societal*. Centre National de la Recherche Scientifique Laboratoire d'Économie et de Sociologie du Travail, Aix-en-Provence.

——, Sorge, A. and Warner, M. (1980), 'Societal Differences in Organizing Manufacturing Units' in *Organizational Studies*, 1. .

Mazzolini, R. (1978), 'The Influence of European Workers over Corporate Strategy' in *Sloan Management Review*, 43.

Merritt, R. (1975), 'Theory and Method in Comparative International Research' in Merritt, R., Brzezinski, S. (eds.), *Comparative International Studies*. Urbana-Champaign: University of Illinois, Centre for International Comparative Studies.

Metcalfe, J. L. (1975), *Organizational Strategies and Inter-organizational Networks: a Development of the Organizational-Set*. London: London Graduate School of Business Studies.

Miles, R. (1965), 'Human Relations or Human Resources?' in *Harvard Business Review*, 43.

Millar, J. A. (1978), 'Contingency Theory, Values and Change' in *Human Relations*, 31.

Miller, D. C. and Form, W. H. (1951), *Industrial Sociology*. New York,: Harper Row.

Mohr, L. (1971), 'Organizational Technology and Organizational Structures' in *Administrative Science Quarterly*, 17.

Možina, S. (1971), *Interes Samoupravljalcev za Oldločanie*. Ljubljana: RCEF.
Mulder, M. (1971), 'Power Equalization through Participation?' *Adminsitrative Science Quarterly*, 16.
Mulder, M. (1977), *The Daily Power Game*. Leiden: Nijhoff.;
—— and Wilke, H. (1970), 'Participation and Power Equalization' in *Organizational Behaviour and Human Performance*, 5.

Nagel, J. M. (1975), *The Descriptive Analysis of Power*. London: Yale University Press.
Nagel, S. (1970), 'Overview of Law and Social Change' in *American Behavioral Scientist*, 13.
Nagels, K. and Sorge, A. (1977), *Industrielle Demokratie in Europa. Mitbestimmung und Kontrolle in der Europäischen Aktiengesellschaft*. Frankfurt, New York: Campus.
Naschold, F. (1969), *Organisation und Demokratie*. Stuttgart: Kohnhammer Verlag.
Näslund, B. and Sellstedt, B. (1977), *Ökad Iöntagarmakt: Bakgrund, Utveckling och Ekonomiska Konsekvenser*. Stockholm: SNS.
Negandi, A. R. and Prasad, S. B. (1971), *Comparative Management*. New York: Appleton Century-Crofts.
Nicholson, N., Wall, T. D. and Lischeron, J. (1977), 'The Predictability of Absence and Propensity to Leave for Employee's Job Satisfaction and Attitudes towards Influence in Decision-making' in *Human Relations*, 30.

Obradović, J., 'Participation and Work Attitudes in Yugoslavia' in *Industrial Relations*, 9.
Olson, M. (1970), *Power*. London: Macmillan.
Ouchi, W., 'The Relationship between Organizational Structure and Organizational Control' in *Administrative Science Quarterly*, 22.

Parsons, T. (1963), 'On the Concept of Power' in *Procedures of the American Philosophical Society*, 107.
—— (1966), *The Social System*. Glencoe, Ill.: Free Press.
Pateman, C. (1970), *Participation and Democratic Theory*. Cambridge University Press.
Payne, R. L. and Pheysey, D. C. (1971), 'G. C. Stern's Organizational Climate Index' in *Organizational Behaviour and Human Performance*, 6.
——, Pheysey, D. and Pugh, D. S. (1971), 'Organization Structure, Organization Climate and Group Structure: an Exploratory Study of their Relationship in Two British Manufacturing Companies' in *Administrative Science Quarterly*, 16.
Pennings, J. M. (1975), 'The Relevance of the Structure-Contingency Model for Organizational Effectiveness' in *Administrative Science Quarterly*, 20.
Perrow, C. (1965), 'Hospitals: Technology, Structure and Goals' in March, J. G. (ed.), *Handbook of Organizations*. Chicago: Rand McNally.
—— (1970), 'Departmental Power and Perspective in Industrial Firms' in Meyer, M. and Zald, J., *Power in Organizations*. Vanderbild University Press.
—— (1972), *Complex Organizations: A Critical Essay*. Glenview, Ill.: Scott Foresman.
Pfeffer, J. and Salancik, G. R. (1978), *The External Control of Organizations: a Resource Dependence Perspective*. New York: Harper Row.

——, **Salancik, G.** and **Leblebici, H.** (1976), 'The Effects of Uncertainty on the Use of Influence in Organizational Decision-making' in *Administrative Science Quarterly*, 21.

Pheysey, D. C., Payne, R. L. and **Pugh, D. S.** (1971), 'Influence of Structure at Organizational and Group Levels' in *Administrative Science Quarterly*, 16.

Phillips, D. (1973), *Abandoning Methods*. San Francisco: Jossey Bass.

Pipkorn, J. (1972–I) (1973–II) 'Zur Entwicklung des Europäischen Gesellschafts- und Unternehmensrechts' in *Zeitschrift für das ges. Handelsrecht und Wirtschaftsrecht*, 136 (Part I) and 137 (Part II).

—— (1977), 'Zur Entwicklung des Europäischen Gesellschafts- und Unternehmensrechts' in *Zeitschrift für das ges. Handelsrecht und Wirtschaftsrecht*, 141.

—— (1978), 'Die Bedeutung der Rechtsvergleichung für die Harmonisierung sozialrechtlicher Normen in den Europäischen Gemeinschaften' in Zacher, H. F. (Hrsg.), *Sozialrechtsvergleich im Bezugsrahmen Internationalen und Supranationalen Rechts*. Berlin: Duncker and Humblot.

Porter, L. W. and **Lawler, E. E.** (1965), 'Properties of Organization Structure in Relation to Job Attitudes and Job Behaviour' in *Psychological Bulletin*, 64.

Prior, J. (1978), 'Industrial Democracy—the Conservative Approach' in *Professional Administration*, September.

Przeworski, A. and **Teune, H.** (1970), *The Logic of Comparative Social Enquiry*. New York: Wiley.

Pugh, D. S. and **Hickson, D. J.** (1976), *Organizational Structure in its Context*. London: Saxon House, Lexington Books.

——, **Hickson, D. J., Hinings, C. R.** and **Turner, C.** (1968), 'Dimensions of Organizational Structure' in *Administrative Science Quarterly*, 13.

——, ——, ——, and —— (1969), 'The Context of Organizational Structures' in *Administrative Science Quarterly*, 14.

Pusić, E. (ed.) (1972 and 1973), *Participation and Self-management*. Vols. 1 and 2, and Vols. 3–6. Zagreb: Institute for Social Research.

Qvale, T. U. (1970), 'The Industrial Democracy Project in Norway' Paper presented at the Second World Congress of the International Industrial Relations Association, Geneva, September.

—— (1976), 'A Norwegian Strategy for the Democratization of Industry' in *Human Relations*, 29.

Rhenman, E. (1973), *Organization Theory for Long-range Planning*. London: Wiley.

Rice, A. K. (1963), *The Enterprise and its Environment*. London: Tavistock.

Richardson, J., Gray, L. and **Maylow, B.** (1968), 'Influence Attempts and Effective Power' in *Sociometry*, 3.

Roberts, K. (1967), *International Research Related to Organizational Behavior: an Annotated Bibliography*. Stanford: Graduate School of Business, Stanford University.

—— (1970), 'On Looking at an Elephant: an Evaluation of Crosscultural Research related to Organizations' in *Psychological Bulletin*, 74.

Robinson, W. S. (1950), 'Ecological Correlations and the Behavior of Individuals' in *American Sociological Review*, 15.

Rokkan, S. (ed.) (1968), *Comparative Research across Cultures and Nations*. The Hague: Monton.

—— (1969), 'Cross-cultural, Cross-societal and Cross-national Research' in Rokkan, S. (ed.), *Main Trends of Research in the Social and Human Sciences, Part I: Social Sciences.* New York: Uni. Pub. Inc.

Rosenstein, E. (1973), 'Problematic Issues in the Israeli Worker Participation System'. Paper at the International Conference on the Role of Co-operative and Public Economies in Democratic Societies, Tel Aviv, May 1973.

Rubenowitz, S. (1977), *The Impact of Members' Participation in Swedish Industrial Organizations.* Gothenburg: University of Gothenburg, Department of Applied Psychology.

Ruedi, A. and **Lawrence, P.** (1970), 'Organizations in Two Cultures' in Lorsch, J. W. and Lawrence, P. (eds.), *Studies in Organizational Design.* Homewood, Ill.: Irwin and Dorsey.

Rus, V. (1972), 'The Limits of Organized Participation' in Pusić, E. (ed.) *Participation and Self management*, Vol. 2, Zagreb: Institute for Social Research.

—— (1977a), *Liberation of Work: its Conditions and Restrictions: Yugoslav Experience.* Ljubljana: Fakulteta za Sociologijo.

—— (1977b), 'The External and Internal Influences Affecting Industrial Enterprises' in Karpik, L. (ed.), *Organizations and Environment.* London: Sage.

—— (1979a), 'Positive and Negative Power' in *Organization Studies*, 1.

—— (1979b), 'Limited Effects of Workers' Participation and Political Counter Power' in Burns, T., Karlsson, and Rus, V. (eds.), Work and Power. London: Sage.

——, **Odar, M., Heller, F** and **Brown, A.** (1978), *Participative Decision-making Under Conditions of Uncertainty.* Berlin: International Institute of Management.

——, ——, ——, ——, **Drenth, P., Koopman, P., Wierdsma, A., Bus, F.,** and **Kruyswyk, A.** 'Participative Decision-making Under Conditions of Uncertainty' Paper for the Second International Conference on Participation, Workers' Control and Self-management. Paris, September, 1977.

Saleh, S. D. and **Otis, F. J.** (1964), 'Age and Level of Job Satisfaction' in *Personnel Psychology*, 17.

Schenk, E. K. (1966), 'Cross-national Comparisons Using Aggregate Data: Some Substantive and Methodological Problems' in Merritt, R., Rokkan, S. (eds.), *Comparing Nations: the Use of Quantitative Data in Cross-national Research.* New Haven: Yale University Press.

Schoeffler, S., Buzzel, D. and **Heany, D. F.** (1974), 'Impact of Strategic Planning on Profit Performance', *Harvard Business Review*, 52.

Schweitzer, T. (1975), 'Data Quality and Data Quality Control in Cross-cultural Studies' Paper at IIM Conference on Problems of Cross-cultural Comparative Research, 28–30 November 1975.

Seashore, S. E. and **Yuchtman, E.** (1967), 'A System Resource Approach to Organizational Effectiveness' in *American Sociological Review*, 32.

——, and —— (1968), 'Factorial Analysis of Organization Performance' in *Administrative Science Quarterly*, 12.

Selznick, P. (1952), *The Organizational Weapon.* New York: McGraw-Hill.

—— (1957), *Leadership in Administration.* Evanston, Ill.: Row Peterson.

Sexton, W. P. and **Yu-Chi-Chang** (1976/77), 'Value Orientation as a Mediator of Job Structure, Satisfaction and Productivity: an Empirical Investigation and Contingency Model' in *Organization and Administrative Sciences*, 7.

Sheppard, H. L. and **Herrick, N. Q.** (1972), *Where have All the Robots Gone?*

Worker Dissatisfaction in the 70s. New York: The Free Press.

Simon, H. A. (1953), 'Notes on the Observation and Measurement of Political Power' in *Journal of Politics*, 15.

–– (1969), 'Rational Choice and the Structure of the Environment' in Emery, F. E. (ed.), *Systems Thinking*. Harmondsworth: Penguin Press.

Smart, C. and Vertinsky, I. (1977), 'Designs for Crisis Decision Units' in *Administrative Science Quarterly*, 22.

Steiner, G. A. (1970), 'Strategic Factors in Business Success' in *Tijdschrift voor Efficient Directiebeleid*, (40) 434–41.

Stinchcombe, A. L. (1965), 'Social Structure and Organizations' in March, J. G. (ed.), *Handbook of Organizations*. Chicago: Rand McNally.

Stokes, B. (1978), *Worker Participation*. Washington D.C.: Worldwatch Institute (Worldwatch Paper 25).

Streeck, W. (1978), *Staatliche Ordnungspolitik und Industrielle Beziehungen: Der Britische Industrial Relations Act von 1971*. Berlin: International Institute of Management (paper 78–3).

Stymne, B. (1970), *Values and Processes: a Systems Study of Effectiveness in Three Organizations*. Lund: Studentlitterature.

–– (1977), *To Organize for Participation*. Stockholm: The Economic Research Institute (Research Paper 6091).

Sumner, W. (1940), *Folkways*. Boston: Ginn.

Susman, G. I. (1976), *Autonomy at Work: A Socio-technical Analysis of Participative Management*. New York: Praeger.

––, Evered, R. D. (1978), 'An Assessment of the Scientific Merits of Action Research' in *Administrative Science Quarterly*, 23.

Szalai, A. and Scheuch, E. (1972), 'The Organizational History of the Multinational Comparative Time-budget Research Project' in Szalai et al., *The Use of Time*. The Hague, Paris: Mouton.

Tannenbaum, A. (1961), 'Control and Effectiveness in a Voluntary Organization' in *American Journal of Sociology*, 67.

–– (1968), *Control in Organizations*. New York: McGraw-Hill.

––, Kavčič, B., Rosner, M., Vianello, M. and Wieser, G. (1974), *Hierarchy in Organizations*. San Francisco: Jossey Bass.

–– and Rozgonyi, T. (eds.) (Forthcoming), *Authority and Reward in Organizations*. Oxford: Pergamon Press.

Tagiuri, R. and Litwin, G. (eds.) (1968), *Organizational Climate*. Boston: Harvard University, Graduate School of Business.

Taylor, J. C. (1972), 'Some Effects of Technology in Organizational Change' in Davis, L. E., and Taylor, J. C. (eds.), *Design of Jobs*, Harmondsworth: Penguin Press.

Thompson, J.D. (1967), *Organizations in Action*. New York: McGraw-Hill.

Thorsrud, E. and Emery, F. E. (1969), *Mot en ny Bedriftsorganisasjon: Eksperimenter i Industrielle Demokrati*. Oslo: Johan Grundt Tanum Forlag (Fra Samarbeidsprosjektet LO/NAF).

Tinbergen, J. (1971), *Dali se Samoupravljanje Priblizava Optimalnom Uredjenju* Vol. 12. Beograd: Gledista.

Triandis, H. (1972), *The Analysis of Subjective Culture*. New York: Wiley.

Trist, E. L. and Bamforth, K. W. (1951), 'Some Social and Psychological Consequences of the Long-wall Method of Coal-getting' in *Human Relations*, 4.

––, Higgin, C., Murray, H. and Pollock, A. (1963), *Organizational Choice*. London: Tavistock.

Turner, A. N. and Lawrence, P. R. (1959), *Industrial Jobs and the Worker*. Boston: Harvard University Graduate School of Business Administrative.

Vanek, J. (1970), *The General Theory of Labor-managed Economies*. Ithaca: Cornell University Press.
Vervinckt, P. (1975), 'Studie van de relatie Tussen Structurele Kenmarken van de Organisatie en de Attitude van de Leider. University of Ghent: doctoral dissertation.
Vroom, V. H. (1964), *Work and Motivation*. New York: Wiley.;
— — and Yetton, P. (1973), *Leadership and Decision-making*. Pittsburgh: University of Pittsburgh Press.

Walker, C. and Guest, R. (1952), *Man on the Assembly Line*. Cambridge, Mass: Harvard University Press.
Wall, T. D. and Lischeron, J. A. (1977), *Worker Participation: a Critique of the Literature and Some Fresh Evidence*. London: McGraw-Hill.
— — and Payne, R. (1973), 'Are Deficiency Scores Deficient?' in *Journal of Applied Psychology*, 58.
Wanous, J. P. and Lawler, E. E. (1972), 'Measurement and Meaning of Job Satisfaction' in *Journal of Applied Psychology*, 56.
Ward, B. (1958), 'The Firm in Illyria: Market Syndicalism' in *American Economic Review*, 48.
Warner, M. (1972), 'Bureaucracy, Participation and Self-government in Organizations: Observations on the Possibility of Comparative Measurement' in Pusić, E. (ed.), *Participation and Self-management*. Vol. 2. Zagreb: Institute for Social Research.
Weber, M. (1947), *The Theory of Social and Economic Organization*. New York: Oxford University Press.
Weekes, B., Mellish, M., Dickens, L., and Lloyd, J. (1975), *Industrial Relations and the Limits of Law*. Oxford: Basil Blackwell.
Weston, J. F. (1961), 'The Management of Corporate Capital: a Review Article' in *Journal of Business*, 34.
Williamson, O. E. (1975), *Markets and Hierarchies: Analysis and Anti-trust Implications*. New York: The Free Press.
Wilpert, B. (1976), 'Die Harmonisierung nationaler Mitbestimmungsmodelle in Europa' in Schriften des Vereins für Socialpolitik, Neue Folge Band 88: *Die Bedeutung Gesellschaftlicher Veränderungen für die Willensbildung in Unternehmen*. Berlin: Duncker und Humblot.
— — (1977), 'Europa und die Mitbestimmung' in *Wirtschaft und Gesellschaft*, 3.
— — and Freidank, G. (1977), 'Formal Norms in Industrial Democracy. Paper for the Second International Sociological Conference on Participation, Workers' Control and Self-management, Paris.
— — and Heller, F. A. (1973), 'Power-sharing at Senior Management Levels' in *Omega*, 1.
Wold, H. (1977), 'Ways and Means of Multi-disciplinary Studies'. Paper at the Sixth International Conference on the Unity of Sciences, San Francisco.
Woodward, J. (1958), *Management and Technology*. London: HMSO.
— — (1965), *Industrial Organization: Theory and Practice*. London: Oxford University Press.
Wright Mills, C. (1956), *The Power Élite*. London: Oxford University Press.

Zaleznik, A., Ondrack, J. and Silver, A. (1970), 'Social Class, Occupation and Mental Illness' in Mclean, A. (ed.), *Mental Health and Work Organizations.* Chicago: Rand McNally.

Zupanov, J. (1973), *Soudlućivanje Radnika i Socialna moč u Industriji*, Kranj: Organizacija i Kadrovi No. 5.

IDE-PUBLICATIONS 1975-1980

1. *Collective publications of the IDE-Team*

Collectively were published or are in print as the product of IDE-research:

Industrial Democracy in Europe: An international comparative study, in: *Social Science Information* 1976, (15), pp. 177-203.

Participation: Formal Rules, Influence and Involvement, in: *Industrial Relations*, Vol. 18 (3), 1979, pp. 273-294.

Die Messung von Mitbestimmungsnormen–Darstellung eines international vergleichenden Forschungsansatzes, in: Blankenburg, Erhards;, Lenk, Klaus (eds.): *Jahrbuch der Rechtssoziologie und Rechtstheorie*, Opladen: Westdeutscher Verlag 1979.

Industrial Democracy in Europe: Oxford University Press 1980.

Industrial Relations in Europe: Oxford University Press 1980.

2. *Individual or group publications*

Individual team members or subgroups of the IDE-team published various books or articles directly or indirectly based on the IDE-research:

Andriessen, J. H. T. H.: Meer Zeggenschap voor de Nieuwe Ondernemingsrad? *Intermediair* 1976 (12).

Andriessen, J. H. T. H.: The Dutch Industrial Relations System. *Industrial Relations Journal*, 1976, (2) pp. 49-59.

Heller, Frank; Wilders, Malcolm; Abell, Peter; Warner, Malcolm: *What do the British want from Participation and Industrial Democracy?* London: Anglo-German Foundation for the Study of Industrial Society, 1979.

Laaksonen, Oiva; Kauhanen, Juhani; Kivisaari, Sirkku; Vanhala, Sinikka: *Päätöksentekoon Osaliistuminen, Arvot Ja Tyytyväisyys Yrityksissä.* Helsinki: Helsingin Kauppakorkeakoulun Julkaisuja 1979.

Martin, Dominique; Dupuy, François: Les Jeux et Enjeux de la Participation. Sceaux: CRESST, 1977.

Martin, Dominique, Participation et Pouvoir dans l'enterprise, Sceaux, CRESST, 1980.

Sandberg, Thomas; Björklund, Lars; Molin, Roger: *Företags Democrati i sex Verkstadsföretag.* Lund: Studentlitteratur 1979.

Wilpert, Bernhard: Research on Industrial Democracy: The German Case. *Industrial Relations Journal* 1975, (6) pp. 53-64.

Wilpert, Bernhard: Meshing Internationality with Interdisciplinarity in: Barth, Richard (ed.), *Interdisciplinary Research*, Vancouver 1980.

3. *Presentations at meetings*

Various IDE-team members were given the opportunity to present papers directly or indirectly related to the IDE-research (either on behalf of the collective team or under their own data) at national or international scientific conferences. A minimum of *30* presentations were made in a five year perod. Among the most important must be counted:

— Munich 1976: Conference on Leadership (Drenth/Wilpert)

— Milan 1976: EGOS-Conference on comparative research design (Freidank/ Pusič)

— Aachen 1976: Verein für Socialpolitik (Wilpert)

— Paris 1977: Second international conference on participation, workers' control and selfmanagement (Freidank/Wilpert; Andriessen; Rus;

— MIT 1978: MIT-conference on industrial democracy in Europe (Pusič/ Warner/Wilpert)

— Munich 1978: International Congress of Applied Psychology (Drenth/ Heller/Wilpert; Rayley/Wilpert)

— Uppsala 1978: International Sociological Association (Rus; Andriessen/ Lammers)

— Stanford 1979: IDE-Seminar (Heller/Wilpert)

— Nordwejk 1979: EGOS-Seminar on industrial relations (Abell/Warner)

— New York 1979: Symposium on IDE, American Psychological Association Annual Convention (Drenth/Heller/Wilpert)

SUBJECT INDEX

INDEX OF NAMES